I0729593

OREGON

BARBARA TRICARICO

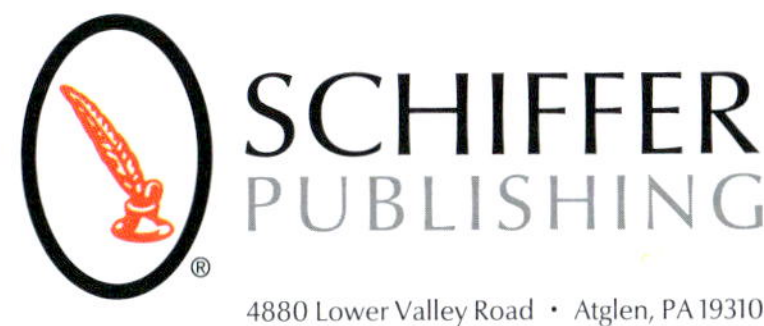

SCHIFFER PUBLISHING

4880 Lower Valley Road • Atglen, PA 19310

CONTENTS

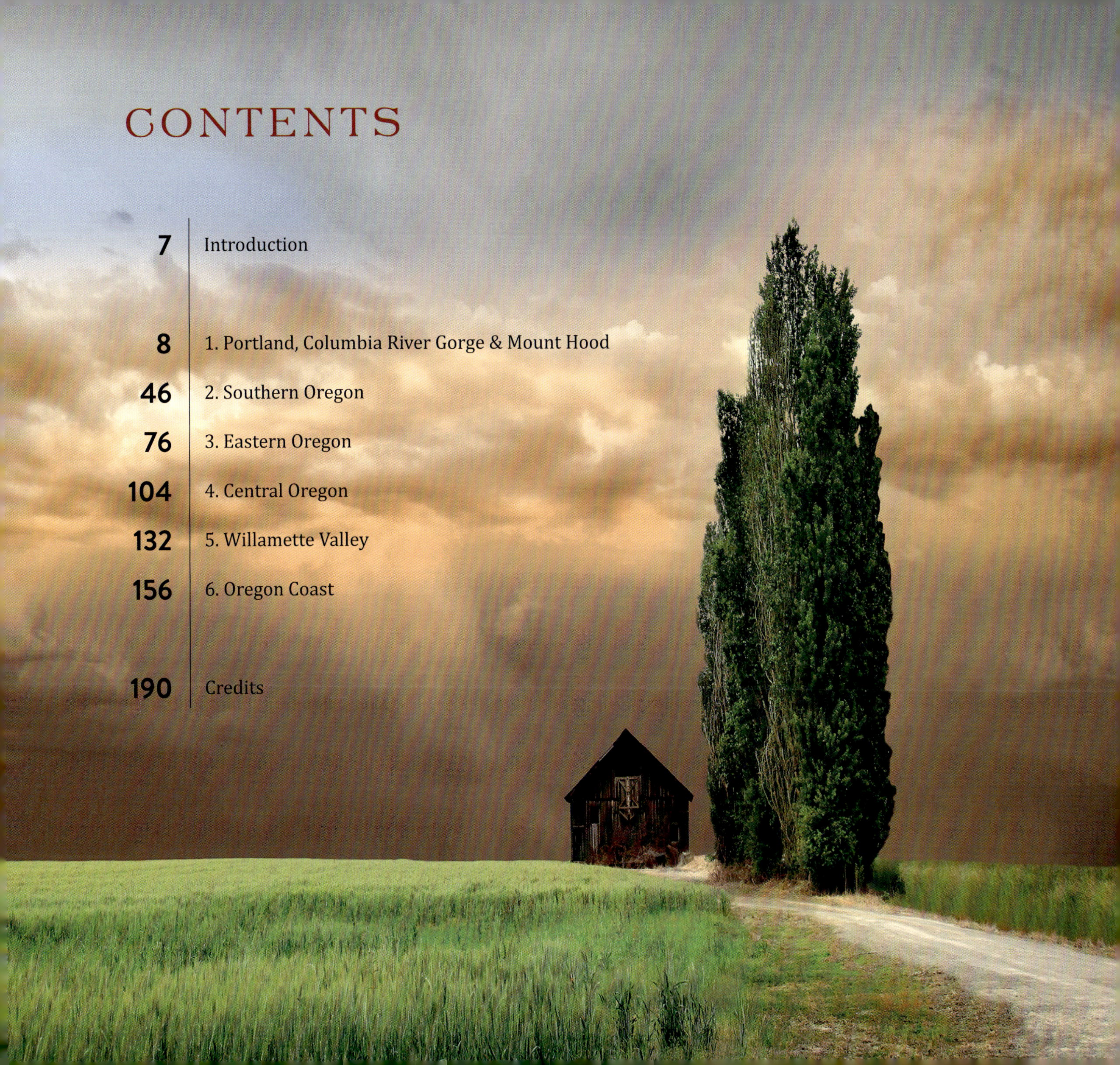

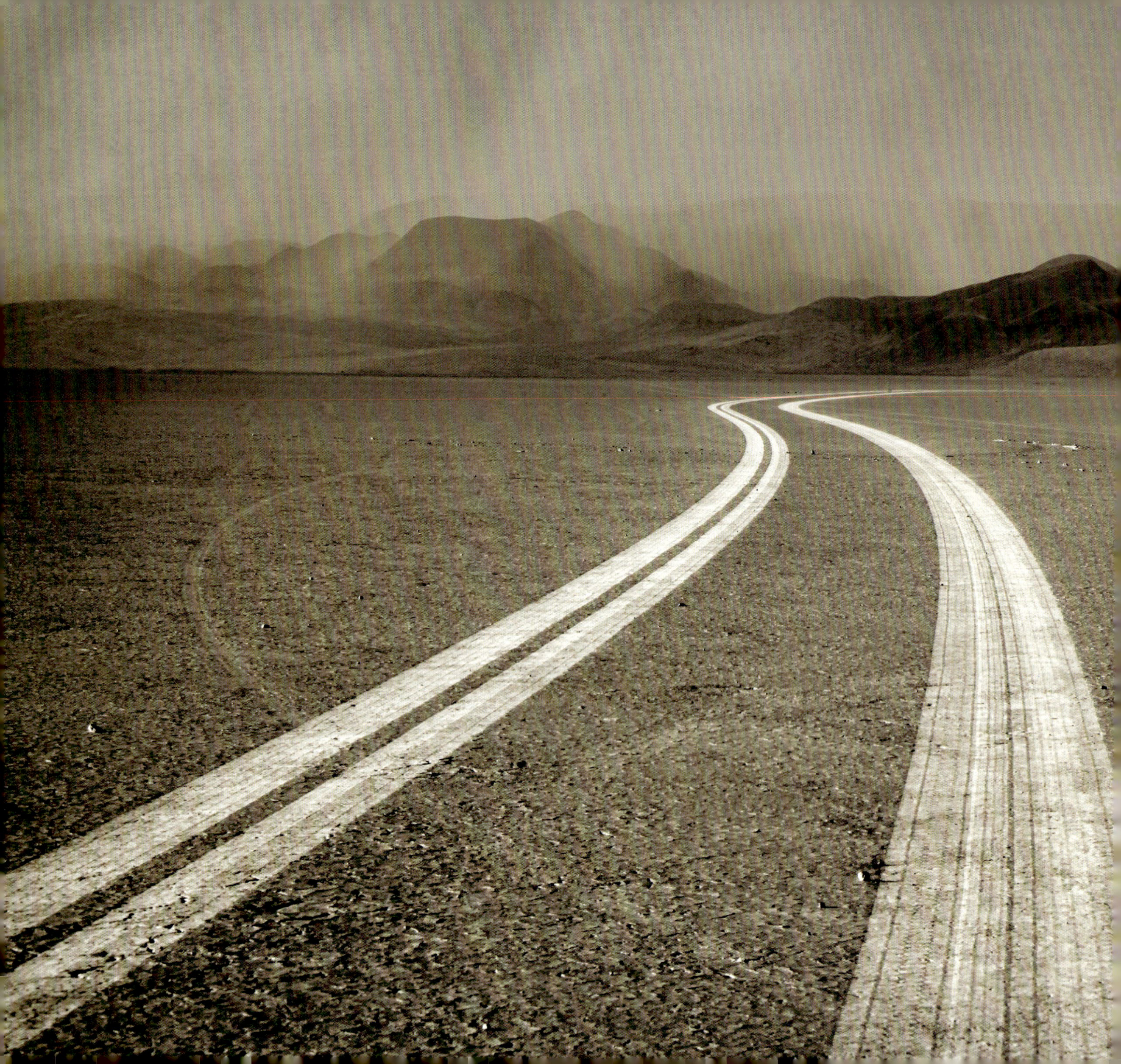

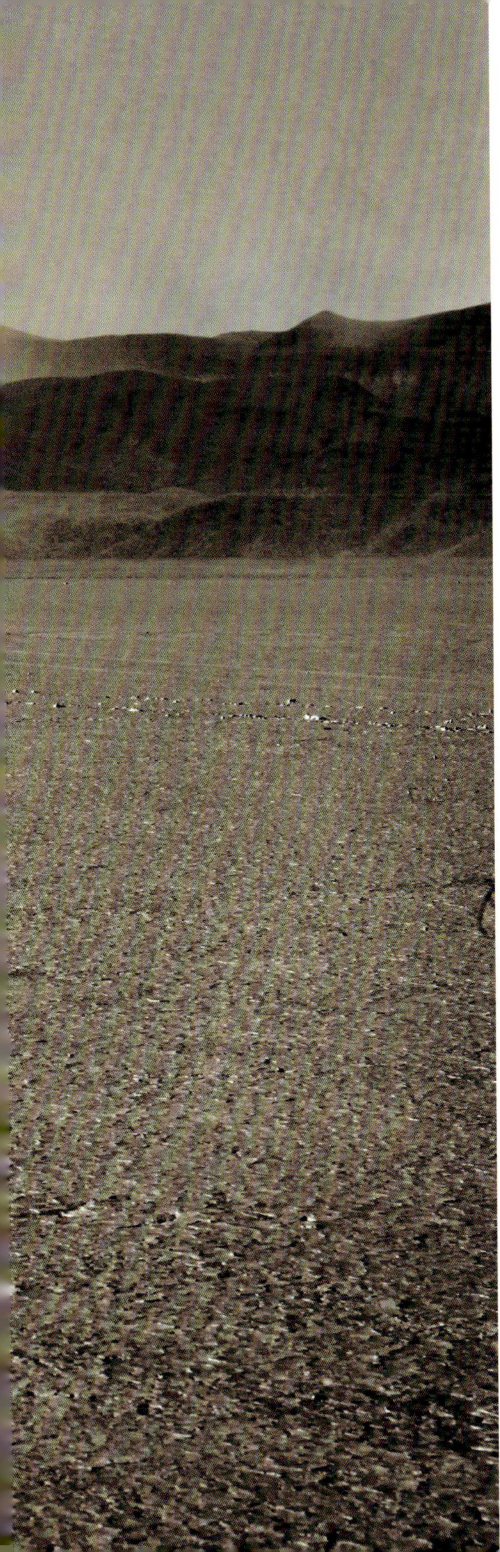

DEDICATION

This book is dedicated to the 50 talented photographers whose images grace these pages. Special love goes to my family: my husband Bill, our sons Jim and Vinny, their wives Taylor and Kathryn, and our treasured grandchildren Gemma, Oscar, and Benny. I am especially grateful to Cornelius Matteo for his friendship, talent, and unwavering support; to Neal R. Thompson, John Kirk, Nicki Stroo, and Charles Hillestad for their eye for detail; to David Vanderlip, my guiding light; and to my sounding board—my early morning walking friends: Audrey Thompson, Nicki Stroo, Diane Demerritt, Pat Franks, Donna Ritchie, Laurie Todd, and the late, but oh, so missed, Suzanne Duncan.

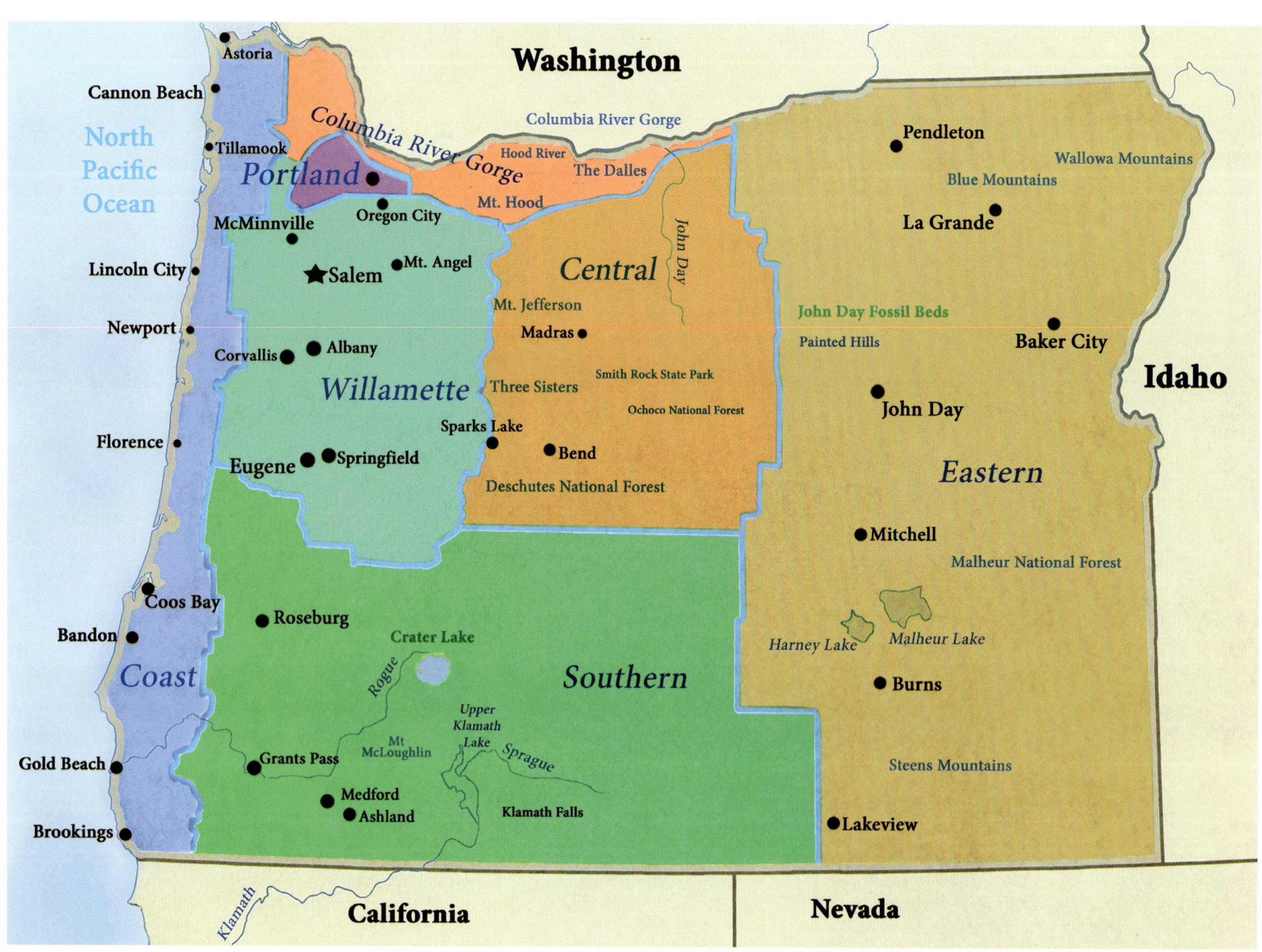

Map of Oregon. *Created by Cornelius Matteo.*

INTRODUCTION

"She Flies with Her Own Wings"

is a fitting motto for Oregon. The phrase conjures not only the fierce independence of Oregon's historic past, it also brings to mind soaring eagles, the wild and scenic Rogue River emptying into the rugged Pacific Ocean, shimmering salmon, whitewater rafts, trees as far as the eye can see, and a vast blue caldera called Crater Lake, one of the most spectacular wonders of the natural world.

Oregon possesses the best of the West. Sandwiched between California and Washington, it has something for everyone, especially when it comes to outdoor activities. There is an endless abundance of state parks, campgrounds, hiking trails, and water activities. Crater Lake, the deepest lake in the US, is the state's only national park. The Portland metropolitan area, its largest city, has over two million inhabitants. It is ranked the third-best bicycle city in the nation, while Oregon ranks among the top bicycle-friendly states.

Oregon is made up of seven regions, all with distinct climates, terrain, cultural attractions, and jaw-dropping beauty—and all comprising one big outdoor playground. Its microclimates keep meteorologists on their toes. You'll find arid deserts, a rocky coastline, hot springs, fertile farmland, wildflower carpets, vineyards, and Jurassic Park-sized redwood trees. The Pacific Northwest is rainy, eastern Oregon is dry, and Southern Oregon has moderate weather.

The state is proud of its Native American heritage, with familiar names such as Umpqua, Siskiyou, Clackamas, Takelma, Coquille, Klamath, Galice, Chetco, Coos, Applegate, Modoc, Tillamook, Walla Walla, Shasta, Yachats, and Umatilla.

Lewis and Clark forged their way to Oregon in 1805. They ended their journey at Fort Clatsop, near the city of Astoria on the Columbia River. Today that rugged beauty they first saw is still evident. While the name "Oregon" is said to come from the Spanish word *oregano*, based on the wild sage in eastern Oregon, today the state's best-known plant is the grapevine. There are more than 725 wineries across the state, and it ranks fourth among states for wine production. Microbreweries offer some of the finest craft beers and ales in the country.

While Oregonians are known for being ecofriendly and nature lovers, culture abounds. Both Bend and Ashland host yearly independent film festivals. The Oregon Shakespeare Festival (OSF) in Ashland opened in 1935 and has produced countless performances (not all Shakespearean). The vibrant cities of Portland, Eugene, McMinnville, Medford (and even the small town of Talent) host theater, dance, opera, music, and more.

The Pacific Crest Trail runs right through the state, starting in Mexico and ending in Canada. Oregon is also the home of extreme sports—world-class kite sailing and windsurfing on the Columbia River, fly fishing on the Rogue River, and even an annual naked bike ride in Portland to protest dependence on fossil fuel.

Travel Oregon has named seven "Wonders of Oregon": Crater Lake, Columbia River Gorge, Mount Hood, the Painted Hills, the Oregon Coast, Smith Rock, and the Wallowas. How many have *you* seen? Whether it's your first or fifth visit (or you are lucky enough to live here), once you start to explore Oregon, you'll never stop!

PORTLAND, COLUMBIA RIVER GORGE & MOUNT HOOD

When people decide to visit Oregon, they usually think of Portland first. With 632,309 residents, it contains almost two-thirds of Oregon's total population. The territory became widely known thanks to Lewis and Clark's journey in 1805.

Portland is known for its culture and ecological awareness. Bicycles dot the landscape. Good restaurants, coffee houses, and microbreweries are abundant. In fact, Portland is known as one of the top beer towns in the US.

While Portland has a reputation for being damp (receiving more rain than the average American city), the good news is that there are approximately 144 sunny days each year. Beautiful summers make up for the long winters. Known as the Rose City, it contains the 410-acre Washington Park, with its countless nature trails, beautiful Japanese Garden, and Oregon Zoo. The International Rose Testing Garden often has more than 10,000 rose bushes on display.

The Oregon Museum of Science and Industry educates young and old. The historic Arlene Schnitzer Concert Hall on Broadway (affectionately called "the Schnitz"), with its iconic "Portland" sign, seats 2,776. The expansive Oregon Convention Center has twin spires that are a prominent part of the Portland skyline. The convention center houses the world's largest Foucault pendulum. The Portland Art Museum is the oldest art museum in the Pacific Northwest and has a collection of more than 42,000 objects. Powell Books is the largest independent bookstore in the world and takes up an entire city block.

Just outside this bustling city is the remarkable Columbia River Gorge. The Gorge is regarded as one of the top-ten drives in America. You'll want to start at the Portland Women's Forum State Scenic Viewpoint. It yields a postcard view of the Columbia River, with the distinctive (and visit-worthy) Vista House in the foreground. Along the drive are dozens of picturesque waterfalls, including everyone's favorite, the mighty Multnomah Falls. The powerful Bonneville Dam and the Bonneville Fish Hatchery are both interesting and educational. Hood River is known as the Windsurfing Capital of the World. In spring, wildflowers are quite a sight along the river.

The Columbia and Willamette Rivers have fourteen bridges zigzagging across them. The most recent to cross the Willamette is Tilikum Crossing (Bridge of the People). The first bridge of its kind in the US, it carries only bicyclists, pedestrians, MAX trains, buses, and streetcars, but no cars.

Framing almost any viewpoint within a hundred miles is majestic Mount Hood, the state's highest volcano. It is the second-most-climbed mountain in the world and boasts eleven glaciers. The 11,250-foot mountain is especially beautiful viewed from the edge of the historic Pittock Mansion or while riding the Oregon Health & Science University Hospital aerial tramway. Mount Hood was first documented in 1792 and was noted by Lewis and Clark in 1805. It is the only ski area in North America open all year long. The historic Timberline Lodge was built and furnished by local artisans during the Great Depression and is now a National Historic Landmark.

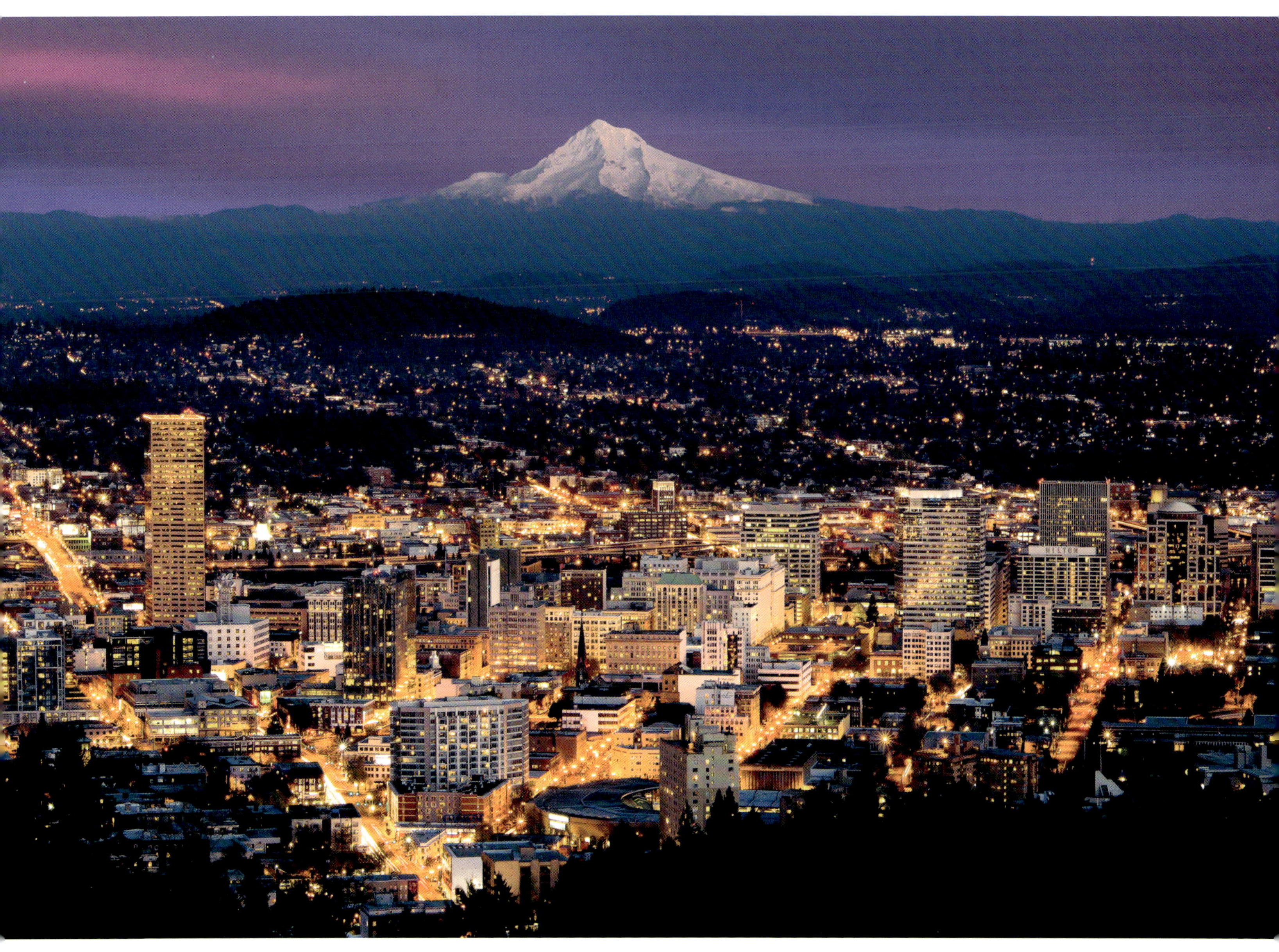

View of Mount Hood and downtown Portland from Pittock Mansion. *Photo by Clem Paslack.*

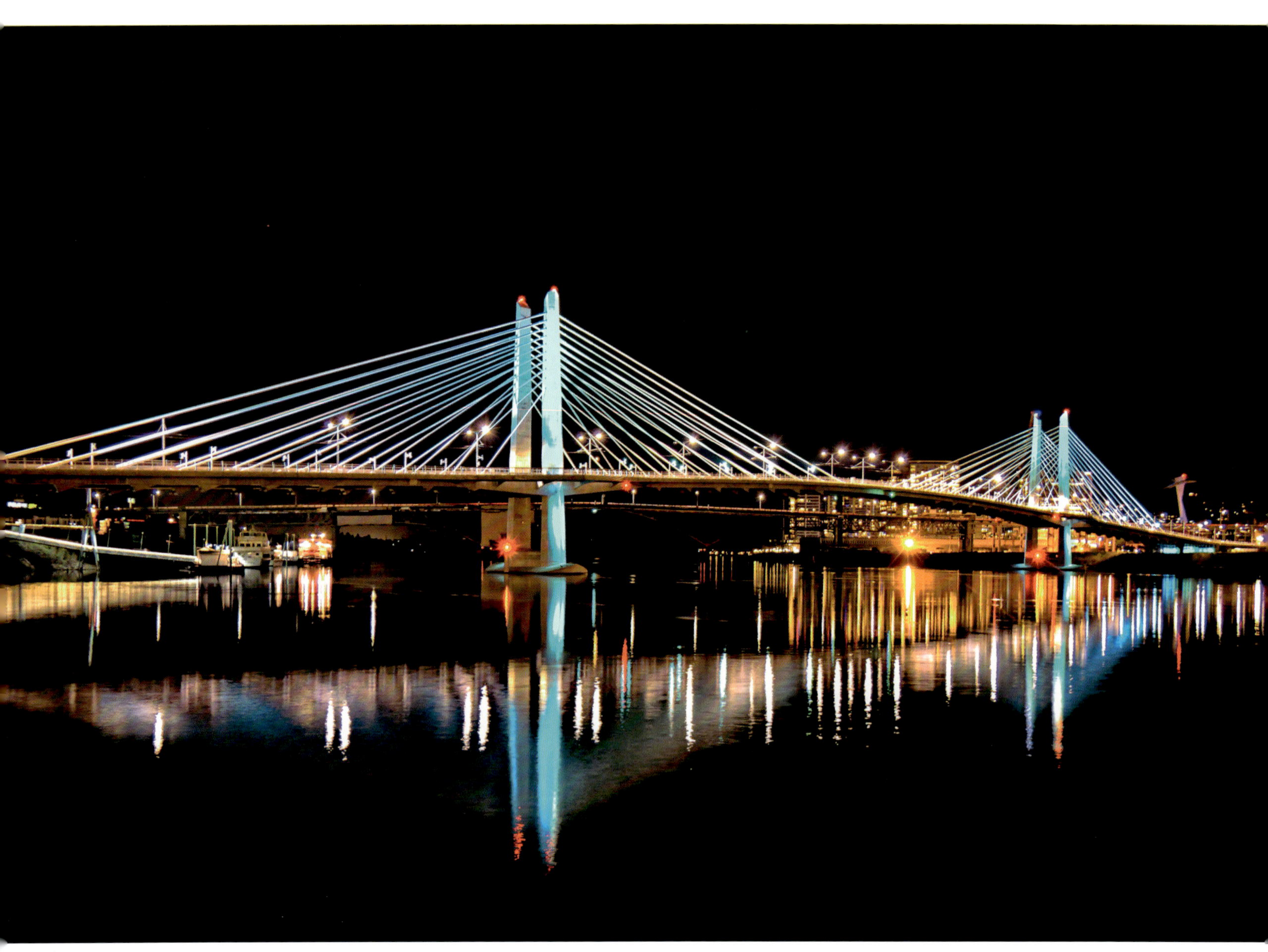

The Tilikum Crossing Bridge is called Bridge of the People. It is the largest car-free water crossing in the United States and opened in 2015. *Photo by Barbara Tricarico.*

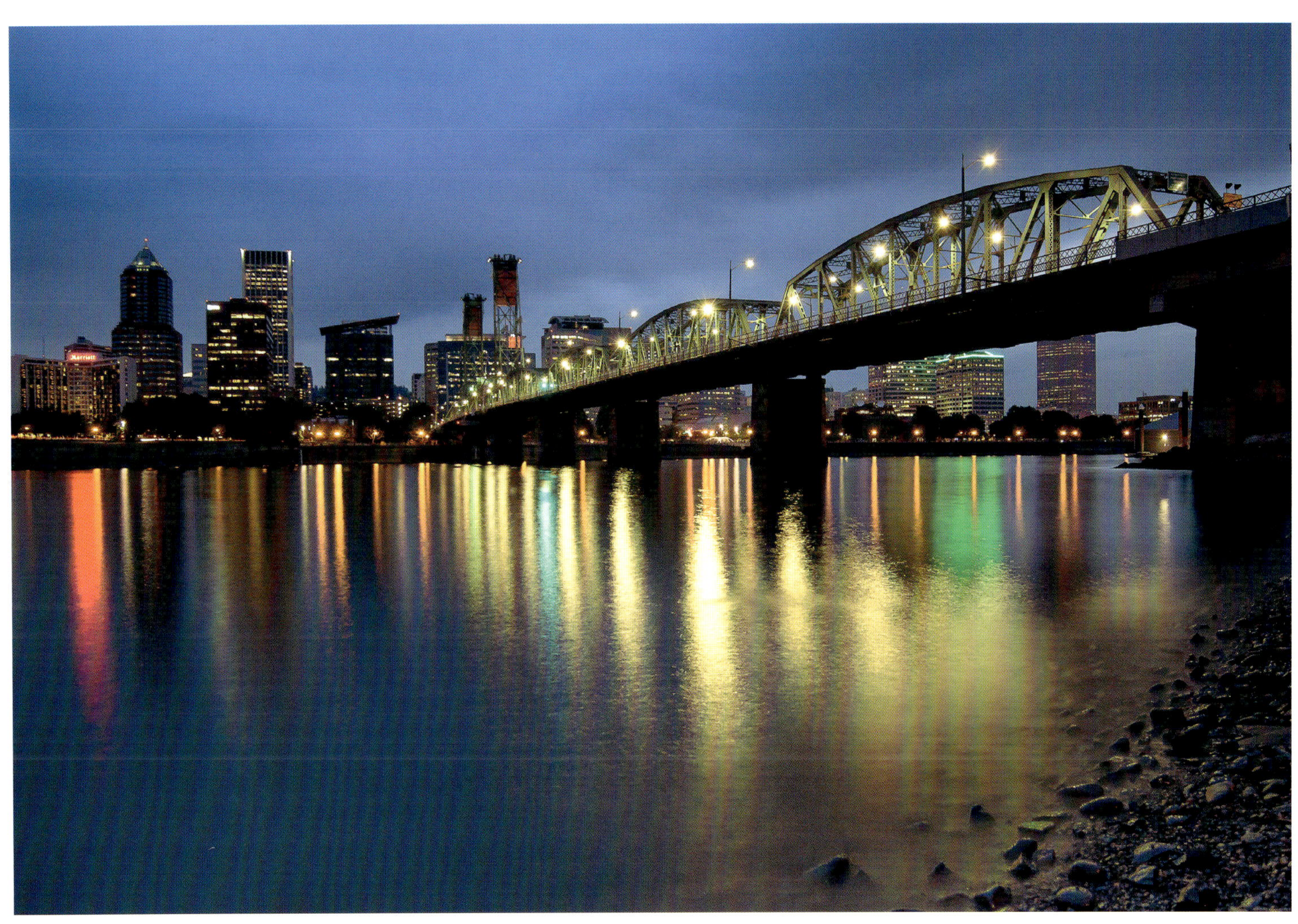

Hawthorne Bridge at the blue hour. *Photo by Clem Paslack.*

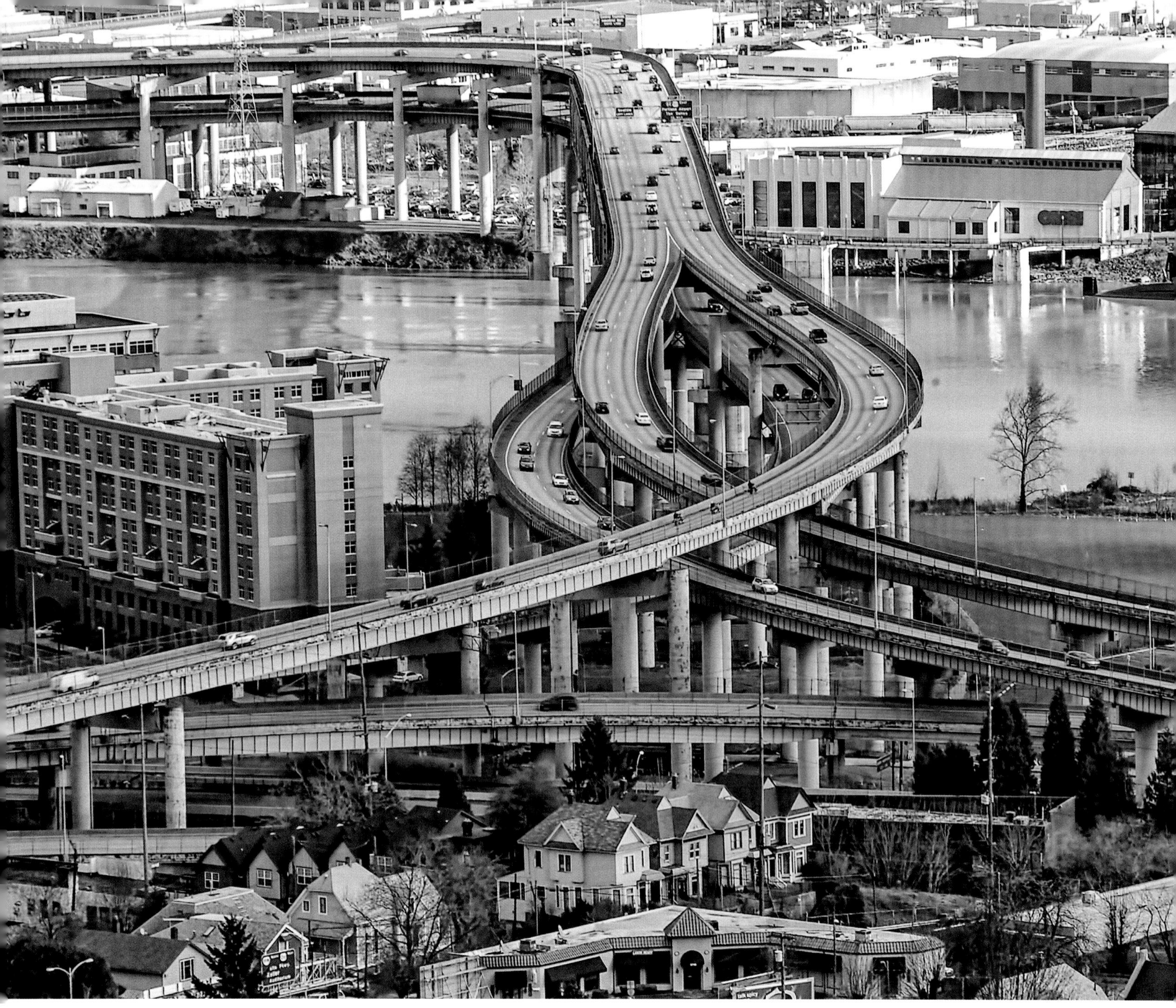

 Marquam Bridge and Willamette River from Portland Aerial Tram. *Photo by Barbara Tricarico.*

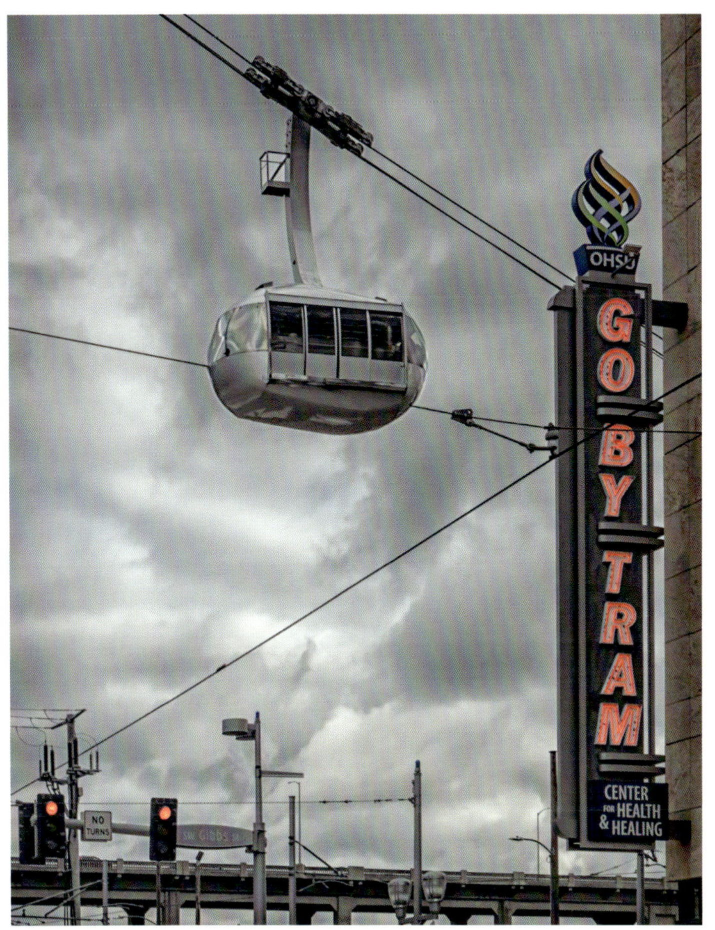

Portland Aerial Tram leaving the South Waterfront district for Oregon Health and Science University (OHSU). *Photo by Barbara Tricarico.*

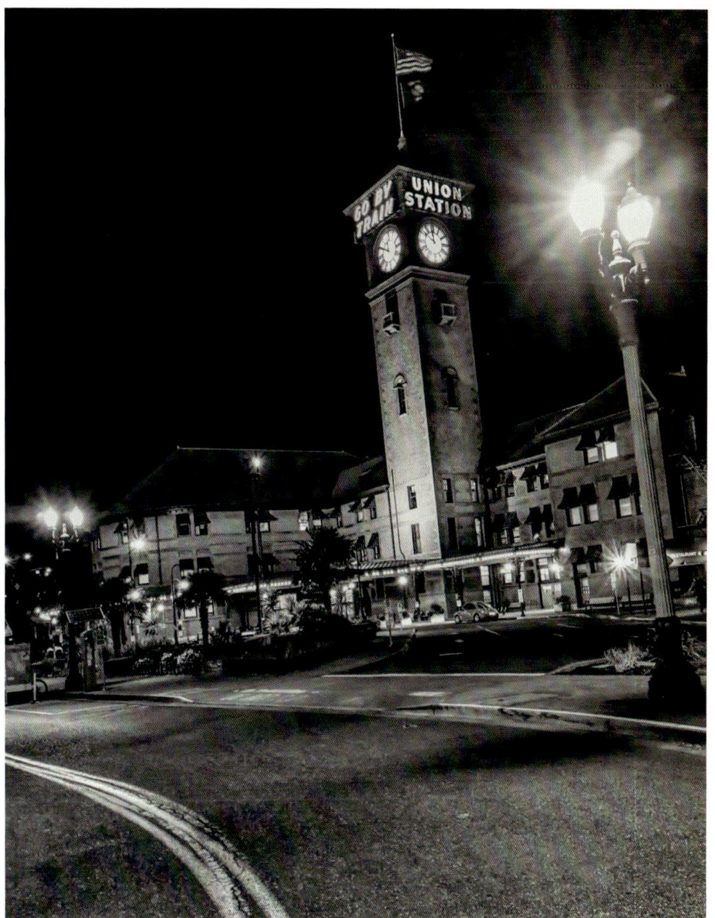

Union Station. *Photo by Cornelius Matteo.*

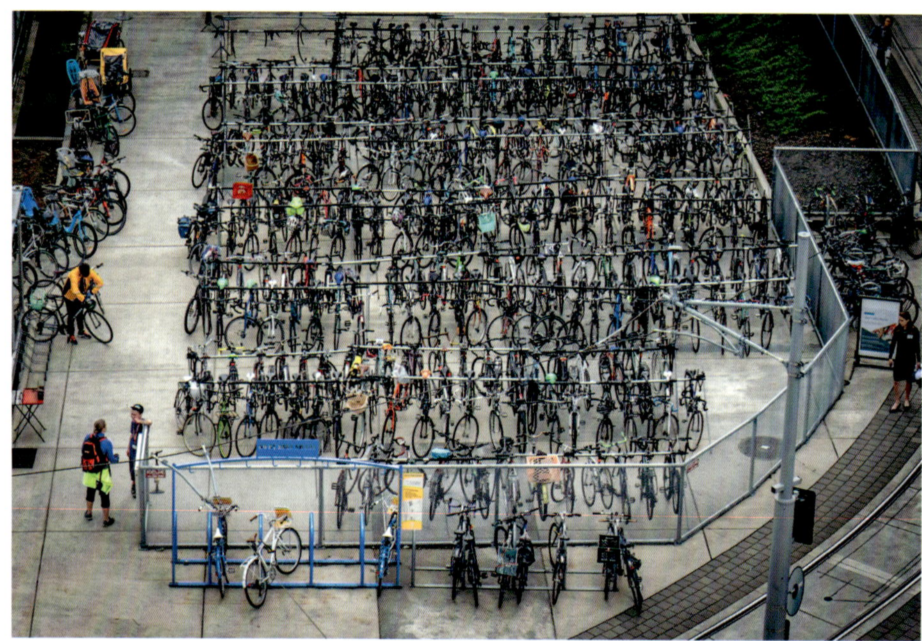

"Go by Bike" lot under the Portland Aerial Tram.
It is the largest bike valet in North America.
Photo by Barbara Tricarico.

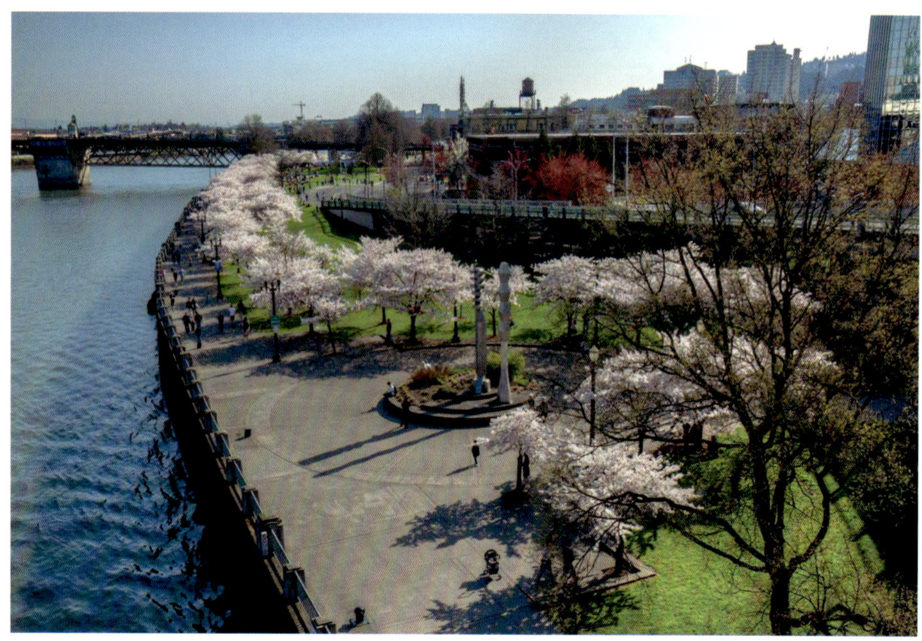

Portland waterfront and cherry blossoms at
Tom McCall Park. *Photo by Sue Newman.*

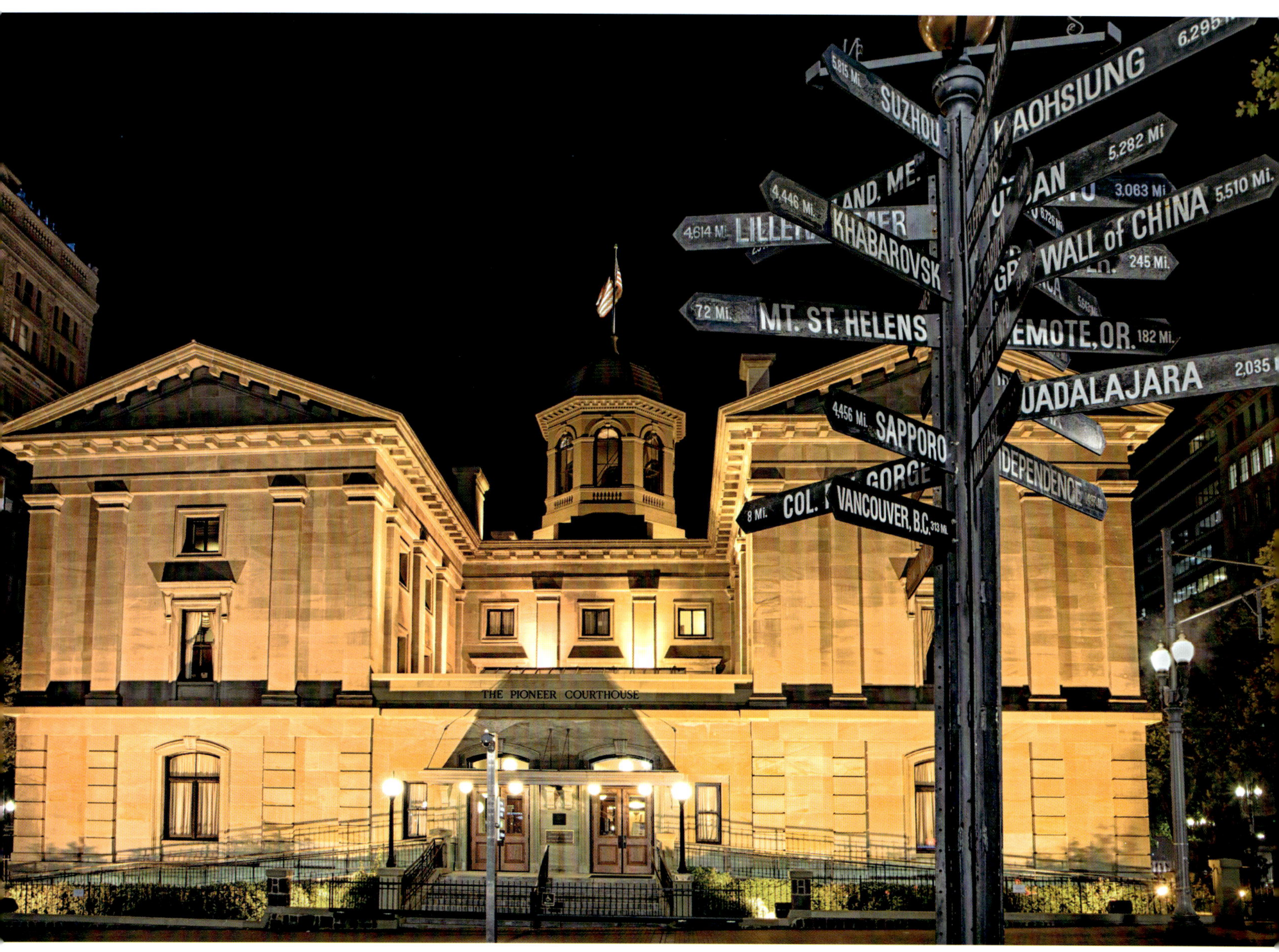

Pioneer Courthouse, built in 1869, and milepost sign. *Photo by Barbara Tricarico.*

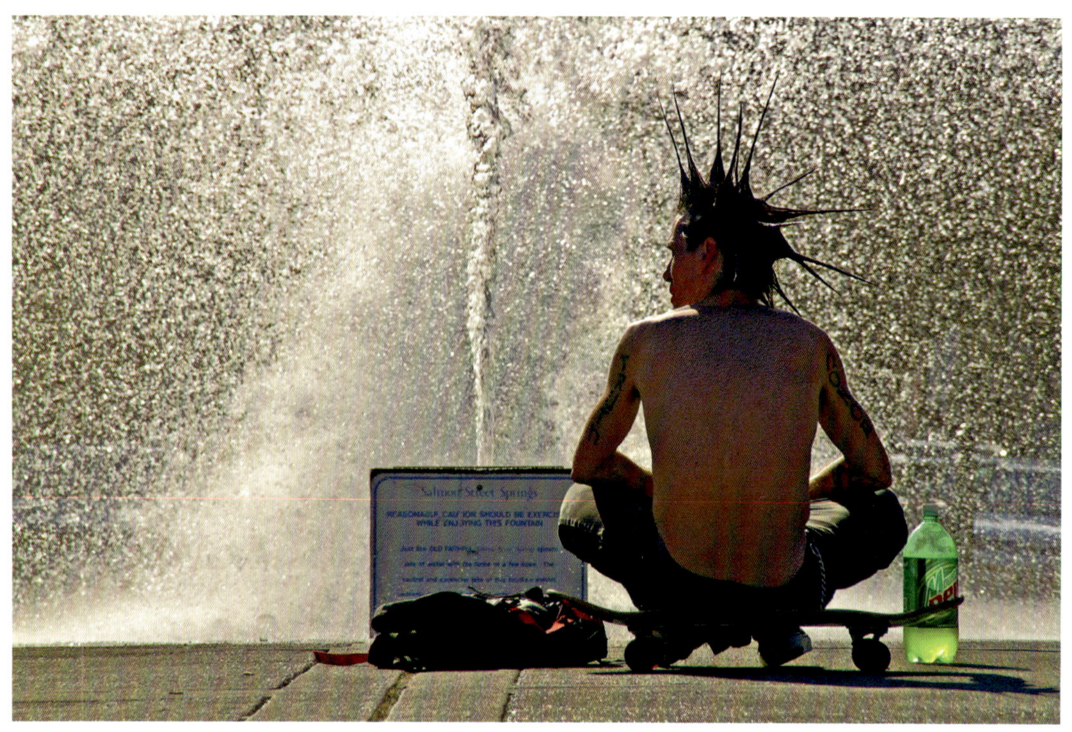

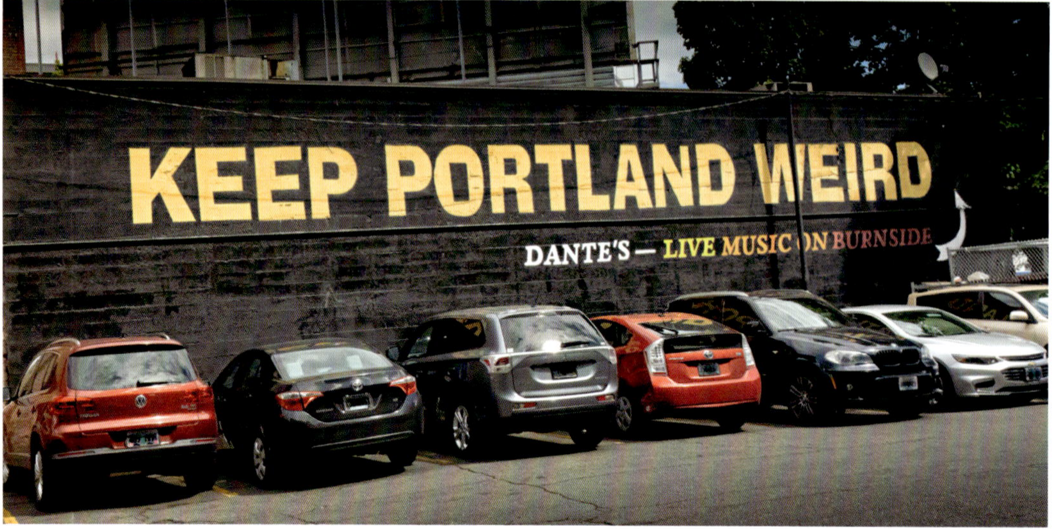

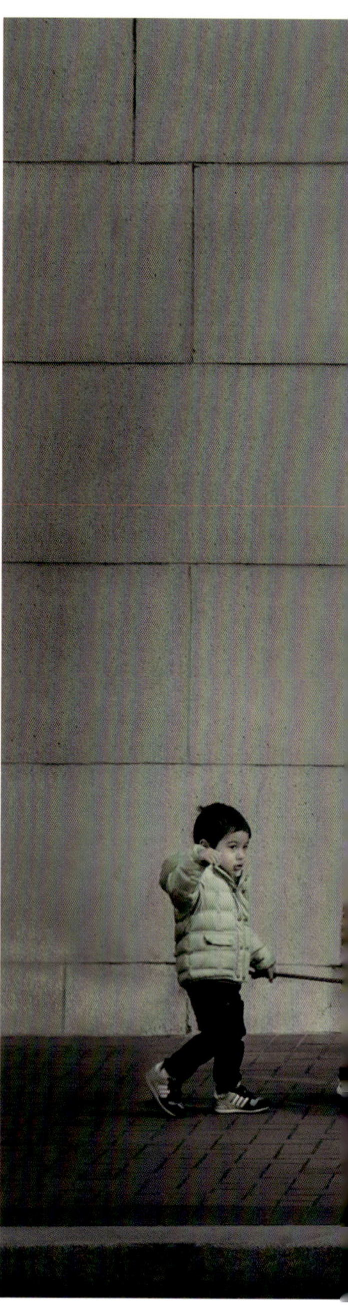

 (Top) Portland punk. *Photo by Jay Newman.* • (Bottom) Iconic "Keep Portland Weird" sign. *Photo by Barbara Tricarico.*

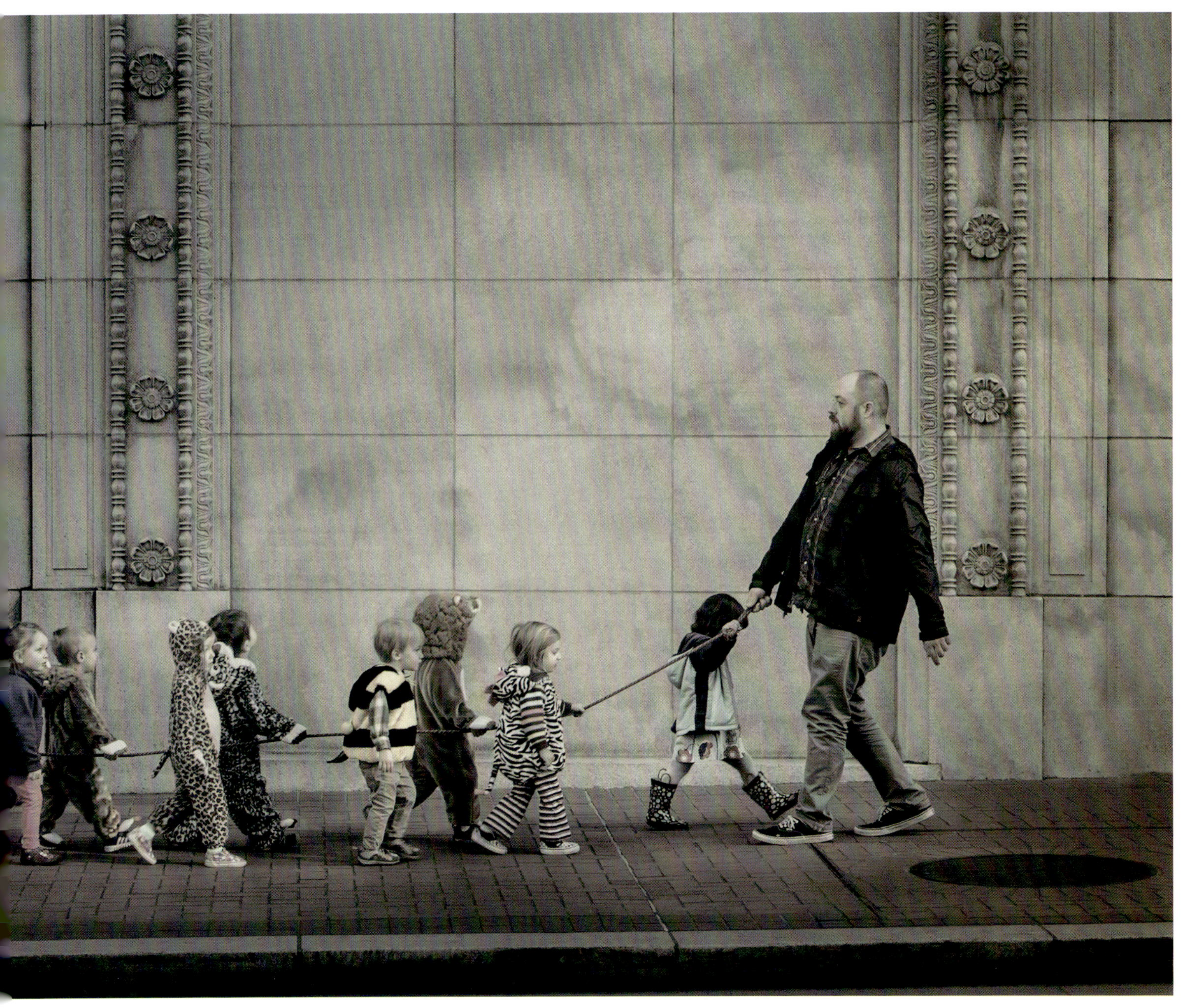

Portland street scene. *Photo by Geri H. Mathewson.*

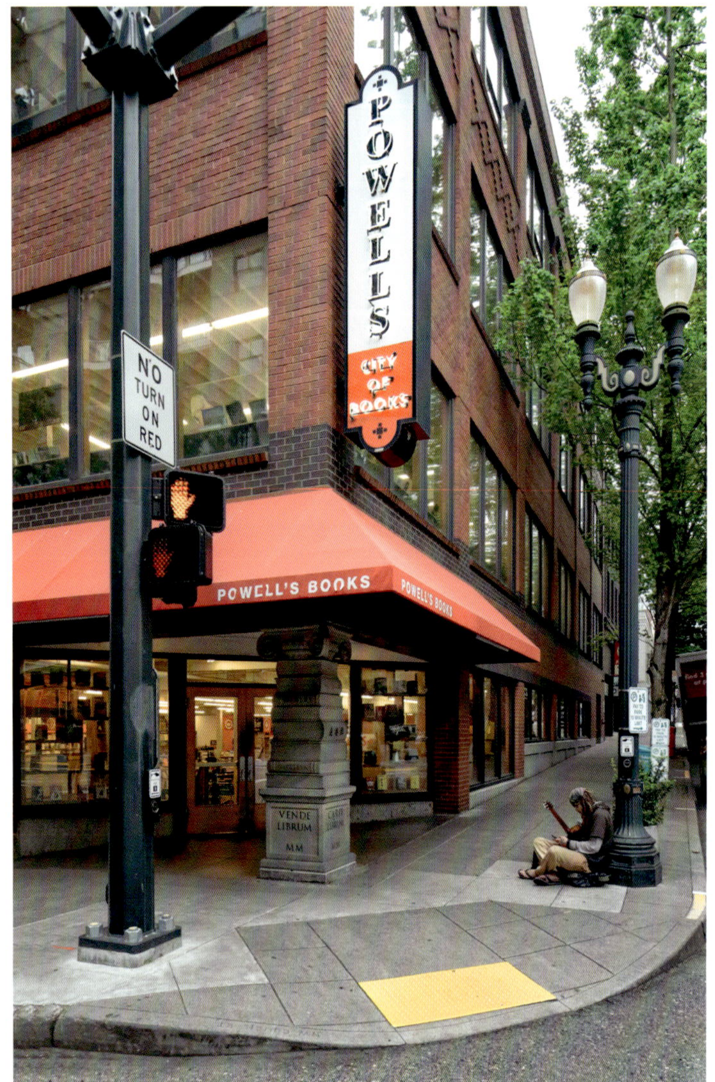

Powell's Books, the world's largest independent bookstore.
Photo by Barbara Tricarico.

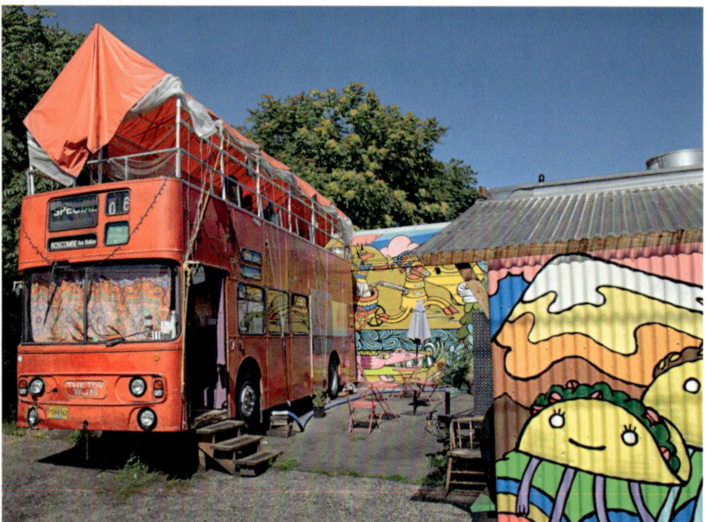

The double-decker *Tōv* Coffee bus in Portland. *Photo by Barbara Tricarico.*

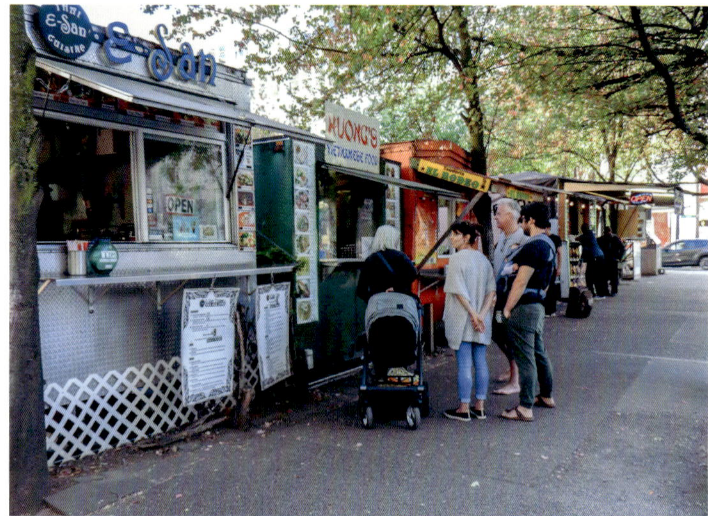

Portland has more than 500 food carts grouped in pods
throughout the city. *Photo by Charles Hillestad.*

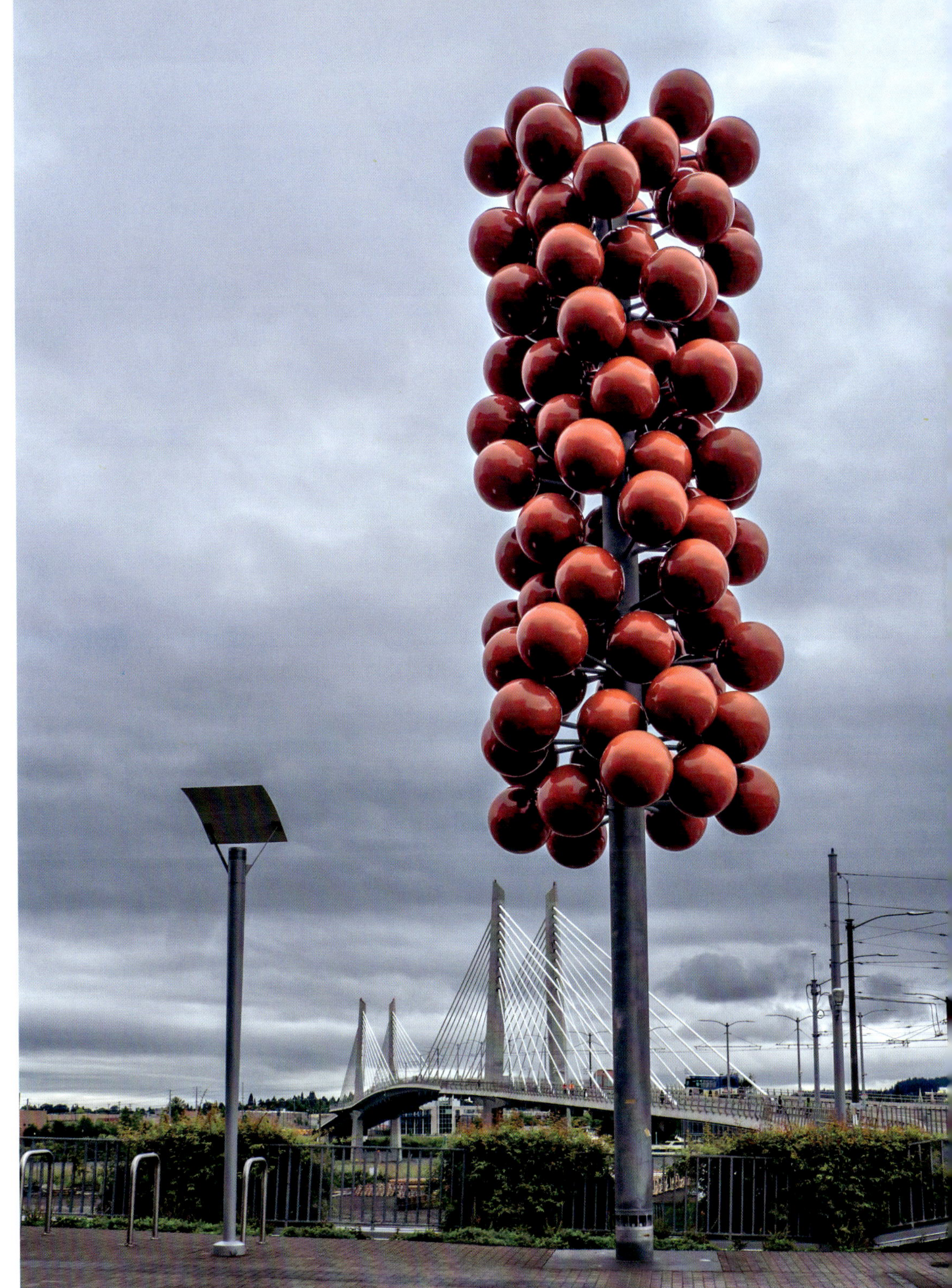

Aril sculpture by Christian Moeller at Collaborative Life Sciences Building (CLSB) at the South Waterfront near the foot of the Tilikum Bridge. *Photo by Barbara Tricarico.*

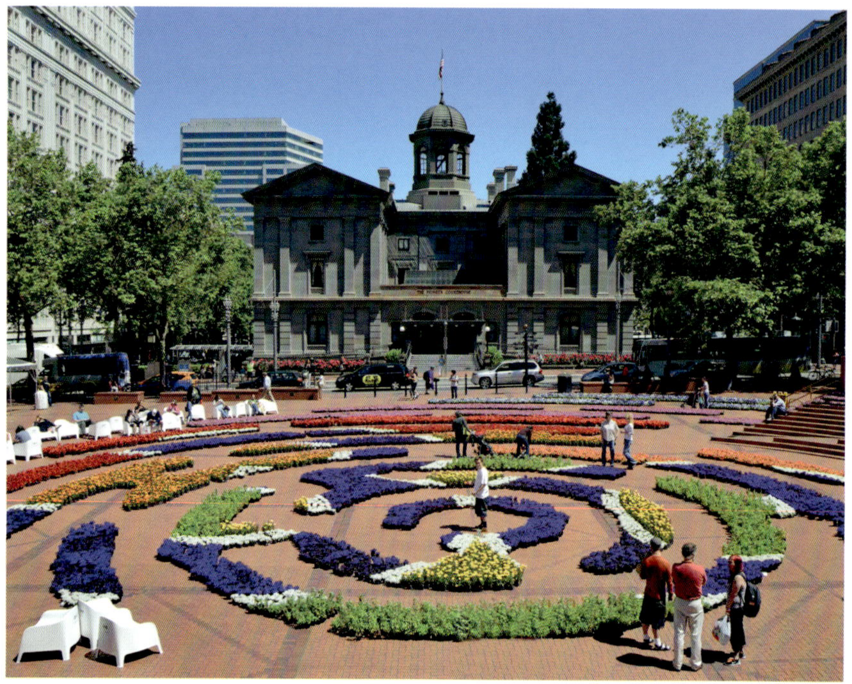

Pioneer Square, often called Portland's Living Room, and Pioneer Courthouse. *Photo by Tysen Mueller.*

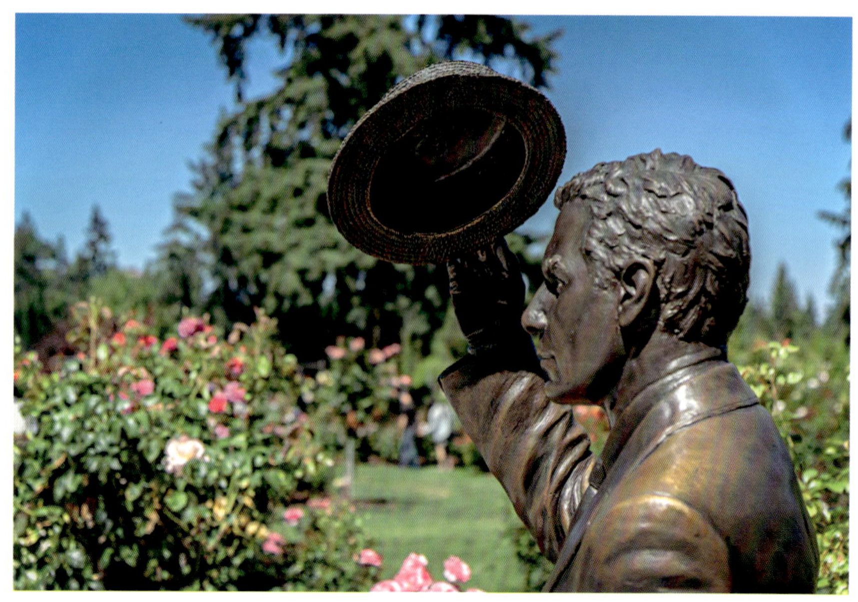

Royal Rosarian is a 2011 bronze sculpture by Bill Bane in the International Rose Test Garden, Washington Park. *Photo by Barbara Tricarico.*

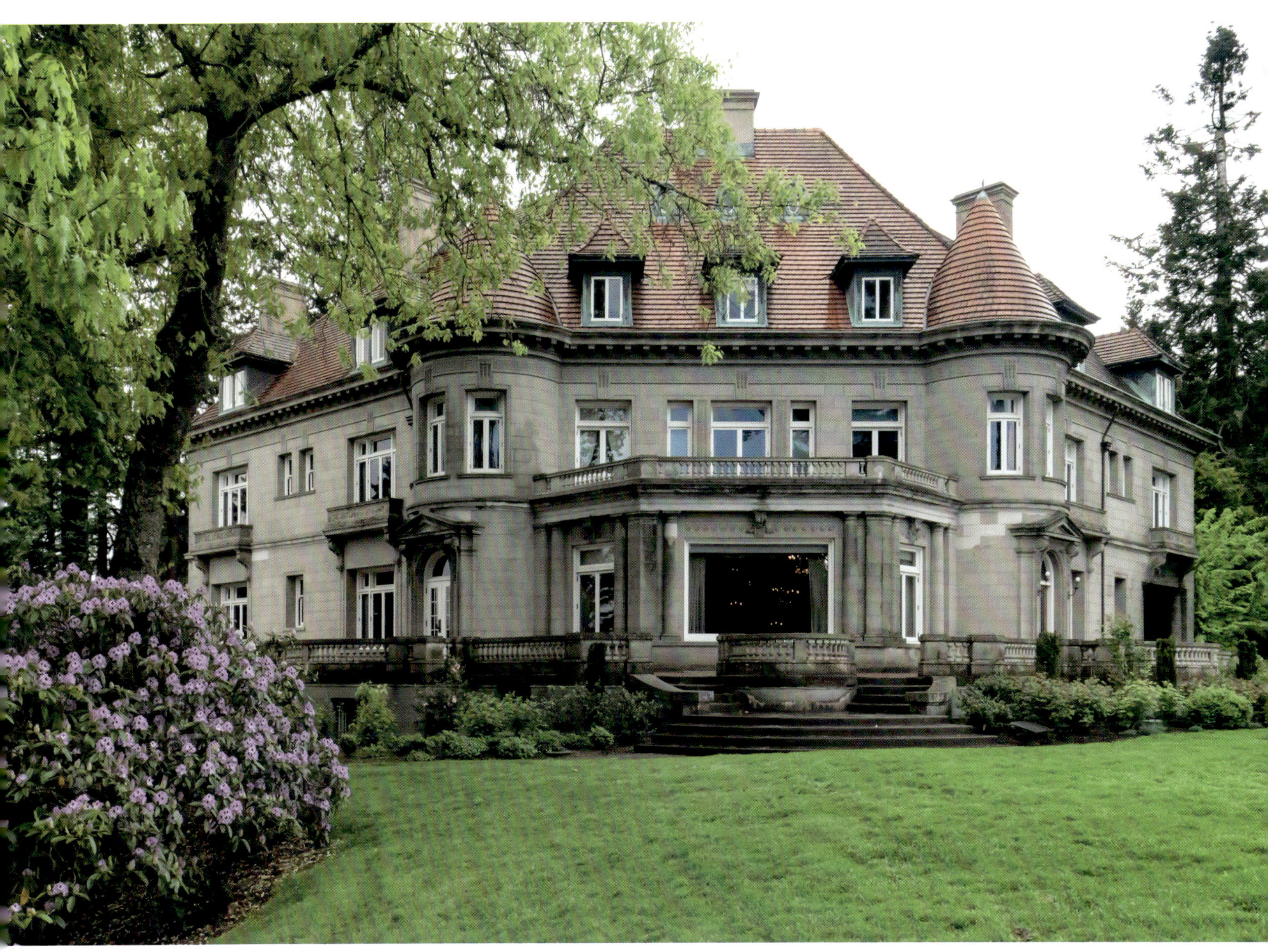

Pittock Mansion, built in 1914 by *Oregonian* publisher Henry Pittock, and his wife, Georgiana. Both had traveled on the Oregon Trail from the East in 1853 and 1854, respectively. *Photo by Barbara Tricarico.*

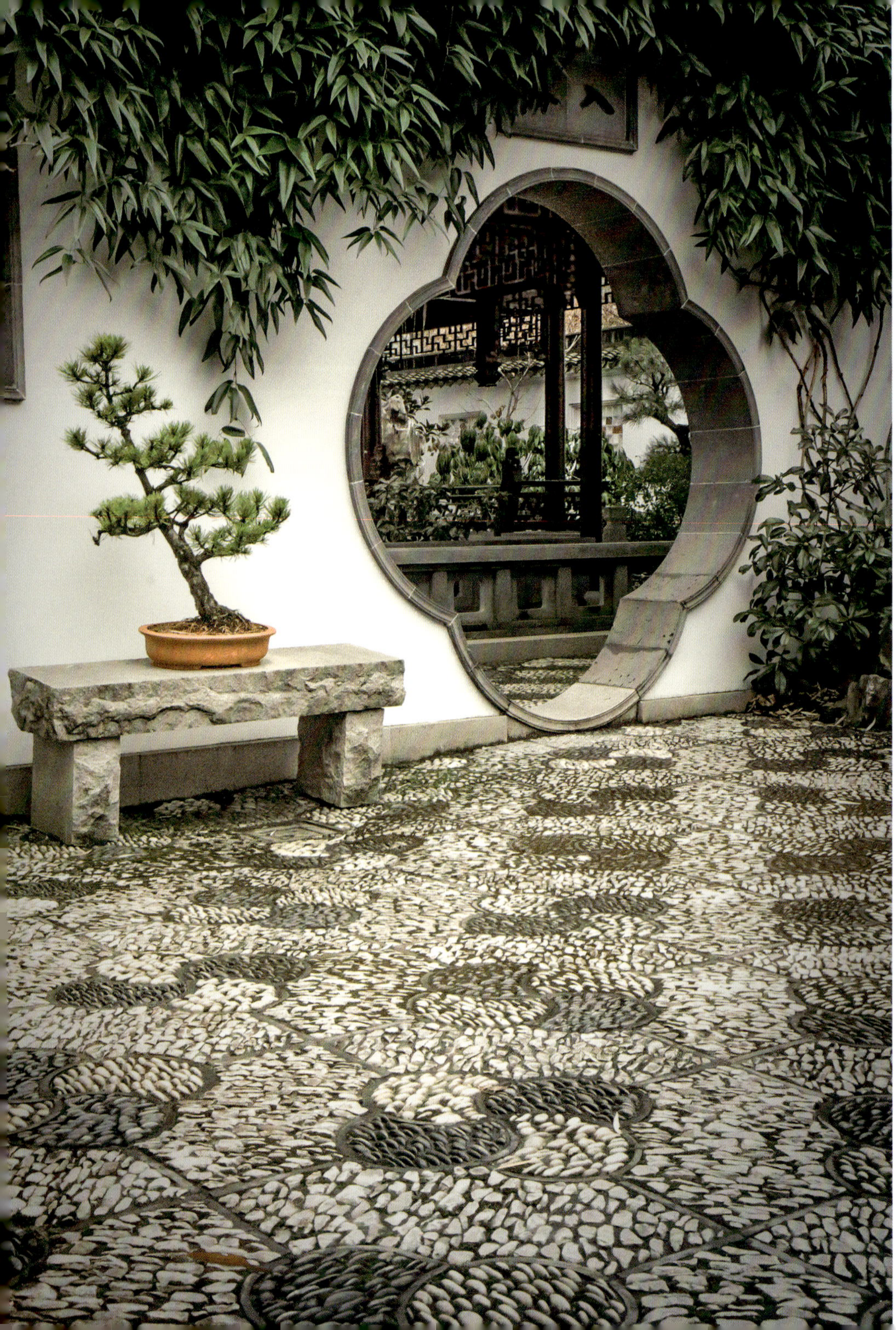

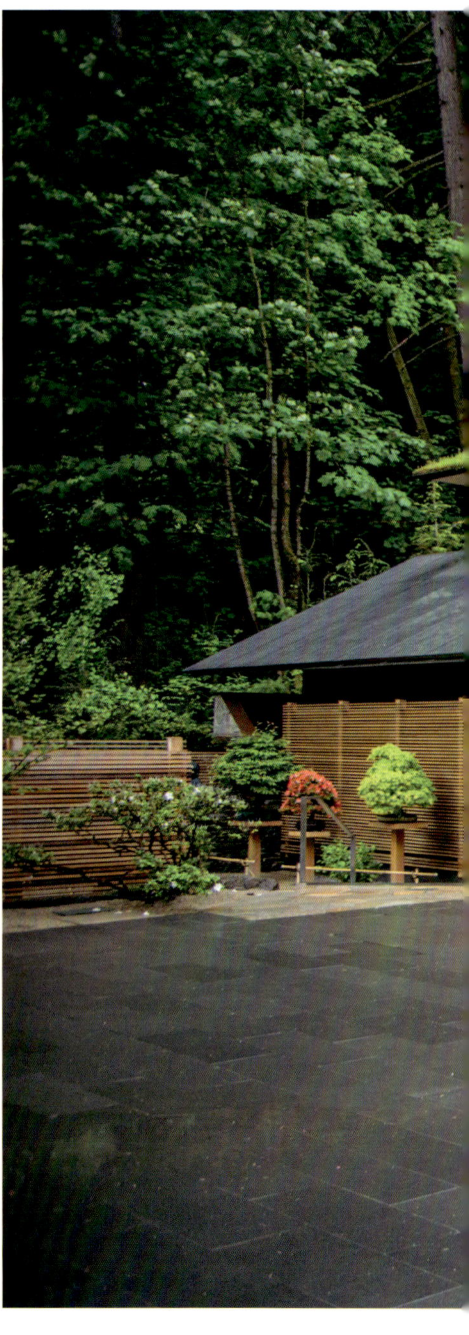

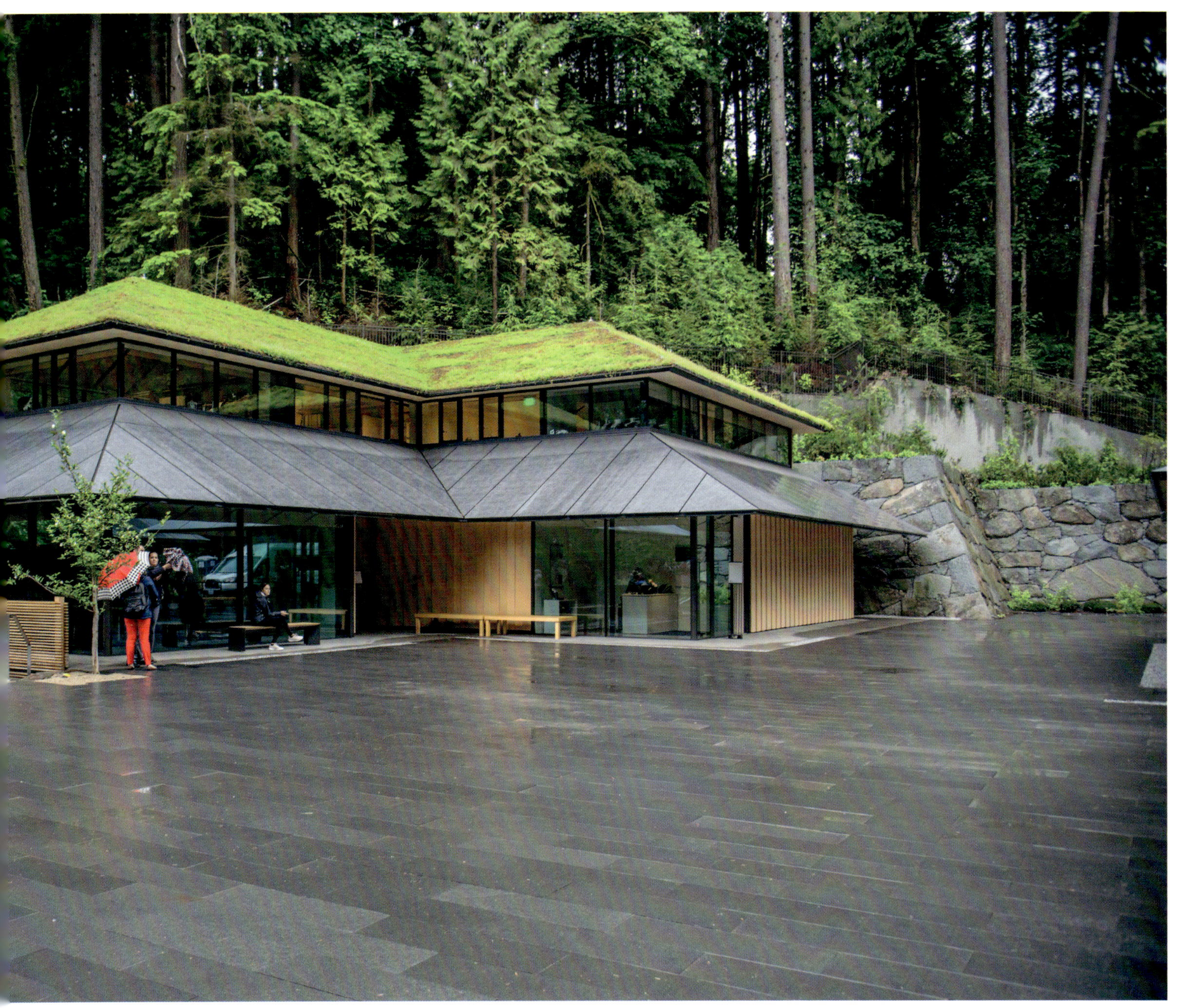

(Opposite) Lan Su Chinese Garden is a walled Chinese garden in Old Town Chinatown. *Photo by Kate Geary.*
(Above) Portland Japanese Garden. *Photo by George F. Peterson.*

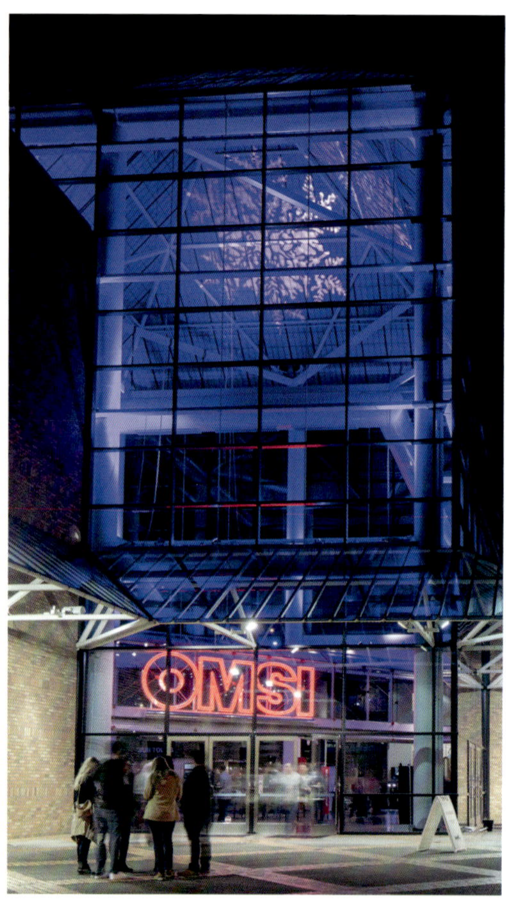

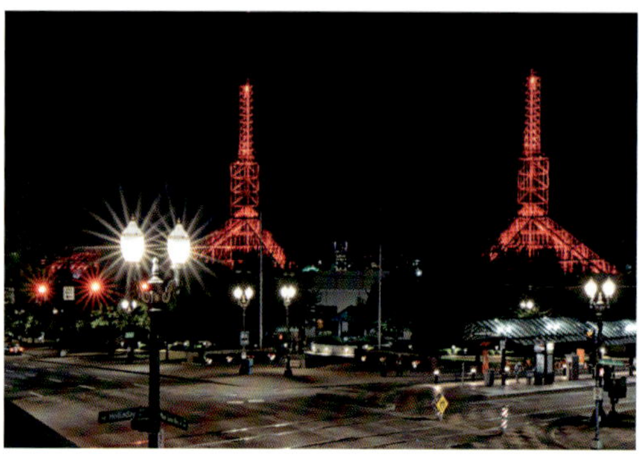

 (Top left) Oregon Museum of Science and Industry (OMSI). *Photo by Barbara Tricarico.* • (Bottom left) Oregon Convention Center. The twin glass spires admit light into the interior, which houses the world's largest Foucault pendulum. *Photo by Barbara Tricarico.*

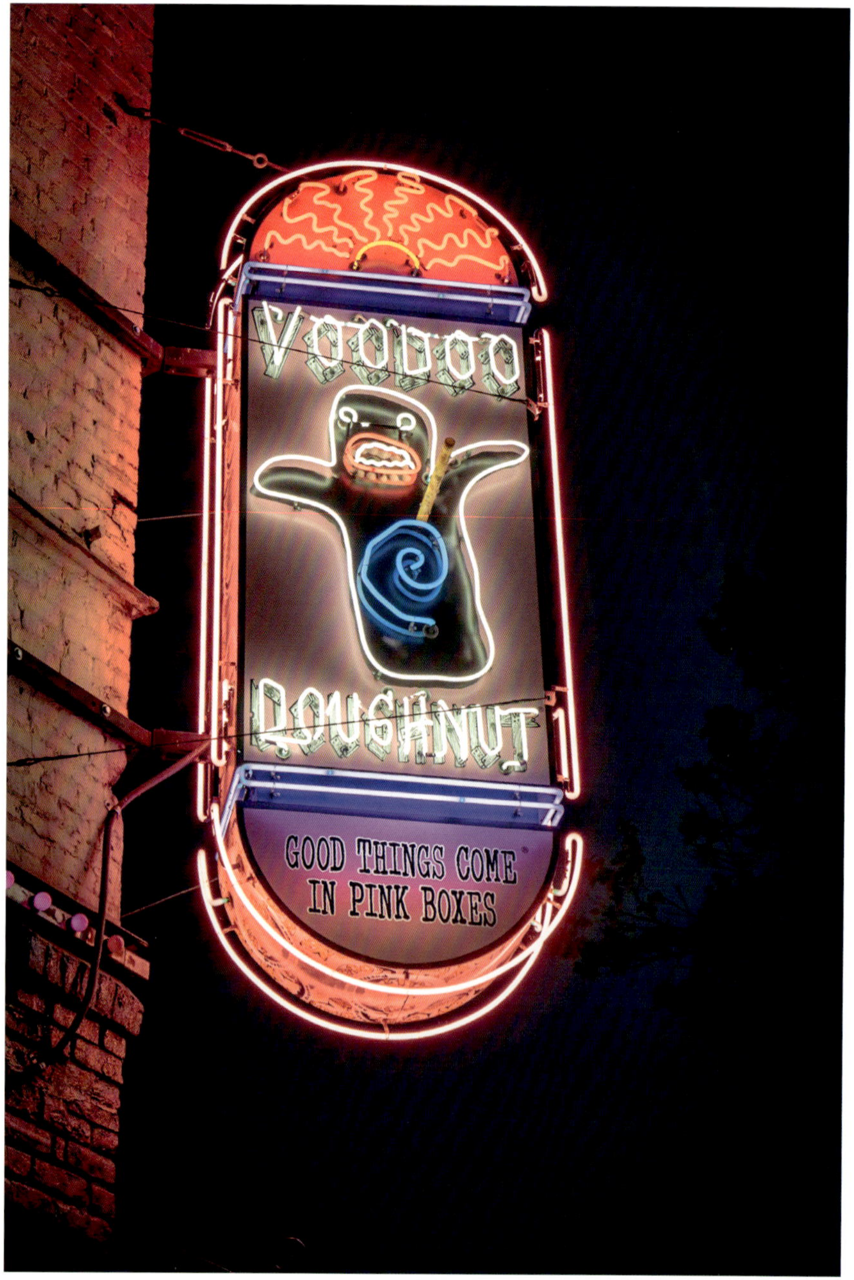

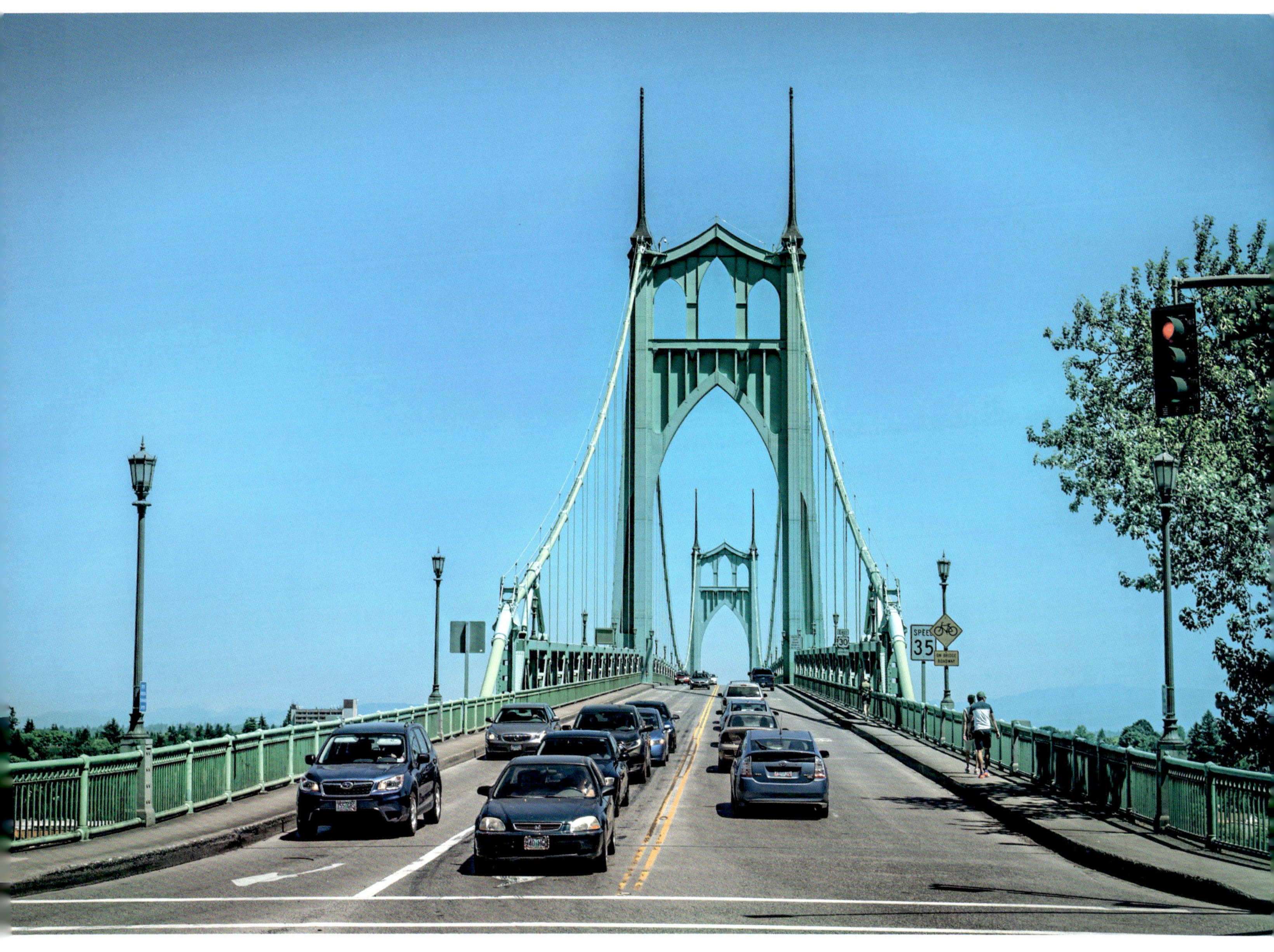

(Opposite right) Voodoo Doughnut. The original location, just south of the Burnside Bridge, opened in 2003. *Photo by Barbara Tricarico.*
(Above) St. Johns Bridge, which opened in 1931, spans the Willamette River from Cathedral Park to Northwest Portland. *Photo by Barbara Tricarico.*

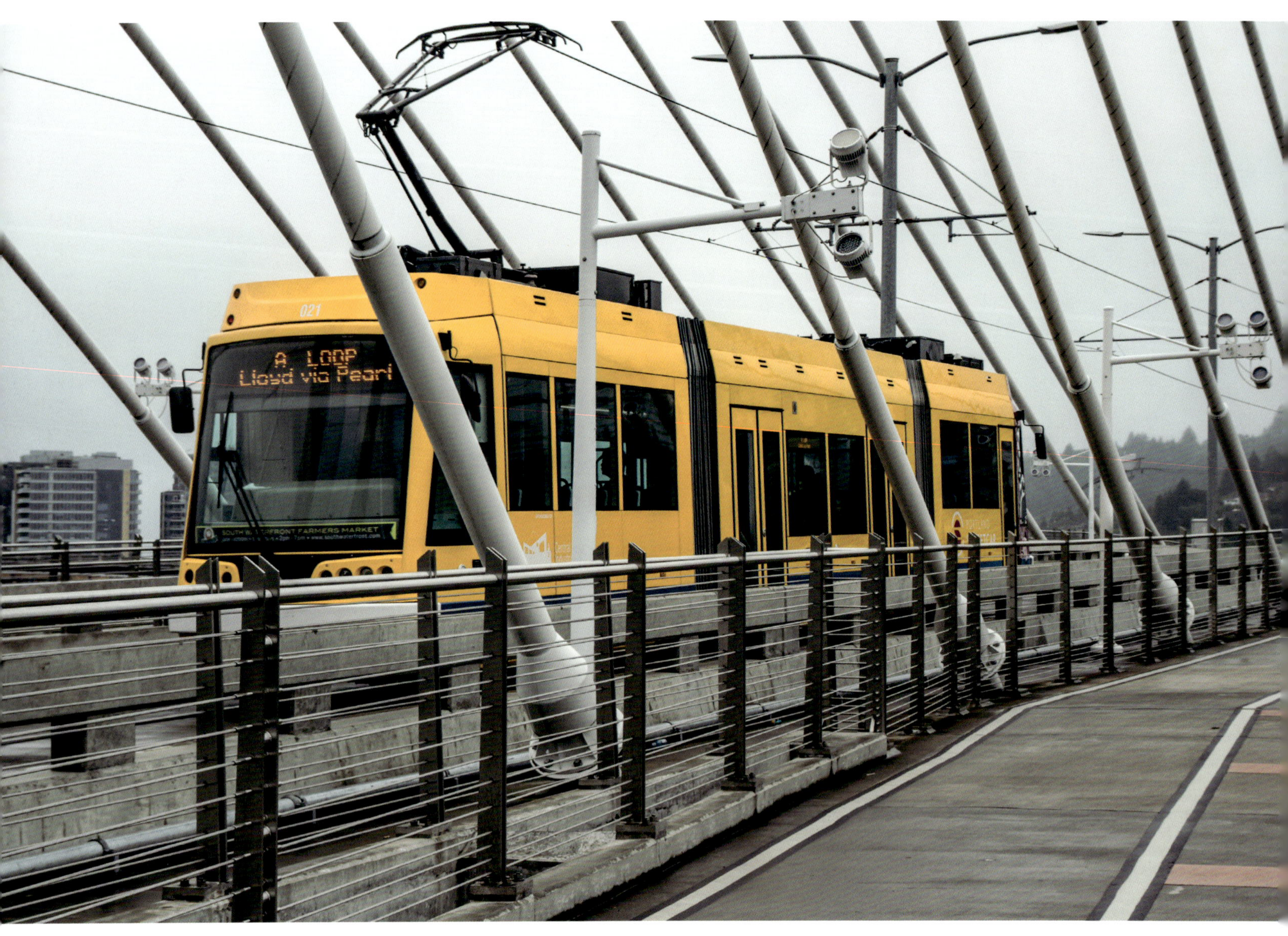

Street car on Tilikum Crossing Bridge. *Photo by George F. Peterson.*

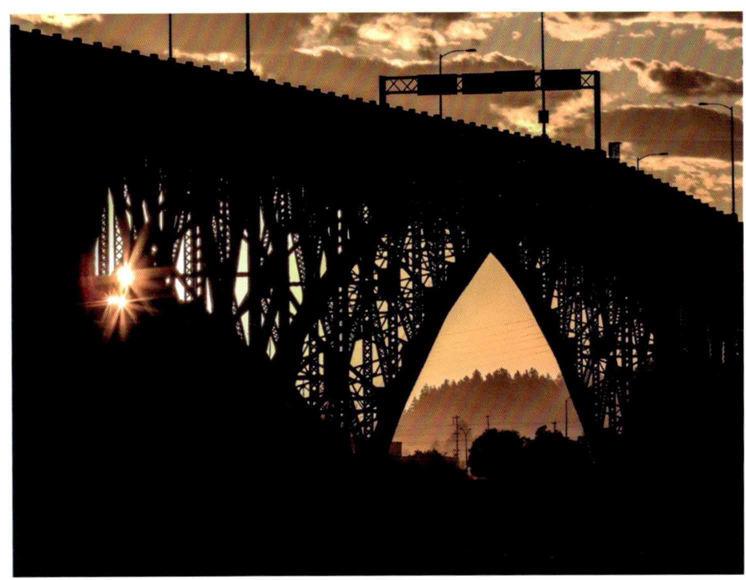

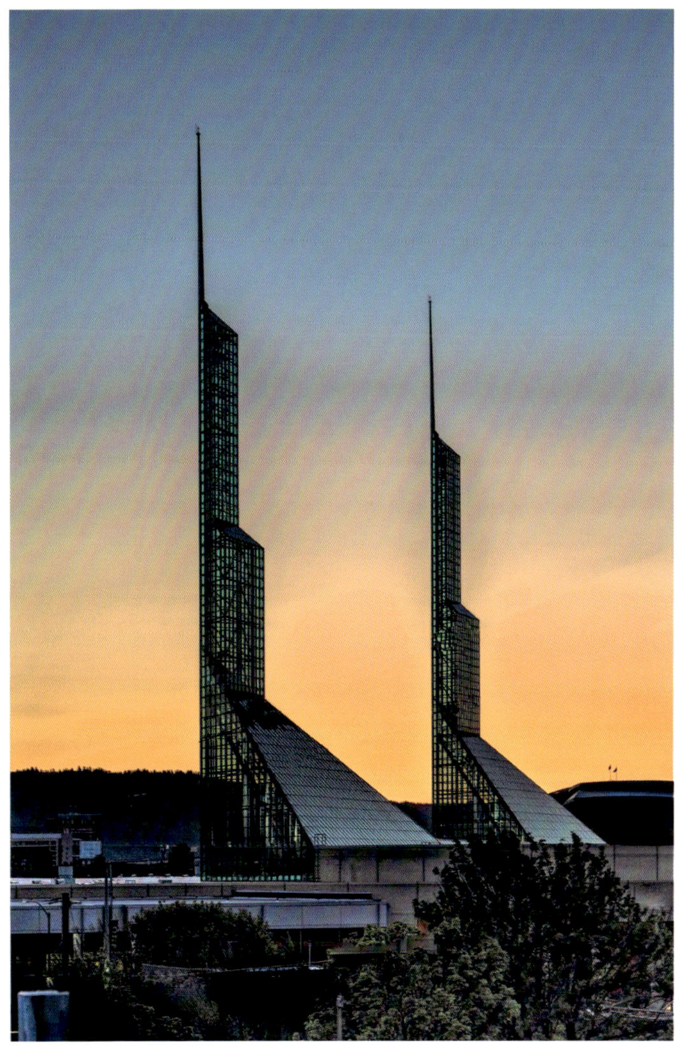

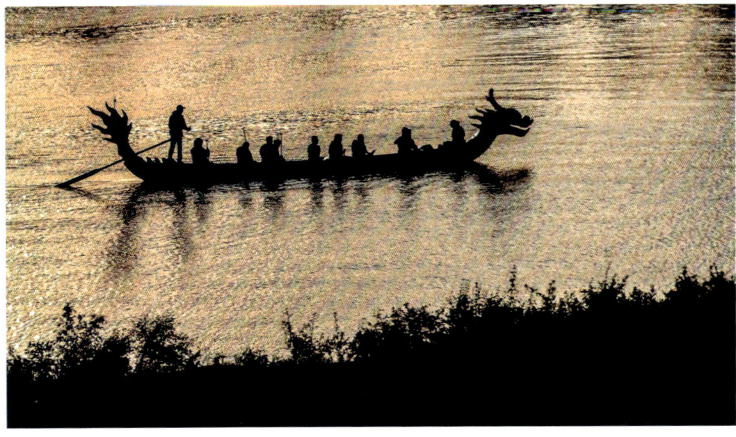

Ross Island Bridge. *Photo by Charles Hillestad.*

Twin spires, Oregon Convention Center at sunset. *Photo by Barbara Tricarico.*

Dragon boat on the Willamette River. *Photo by Charles Hillestad.*

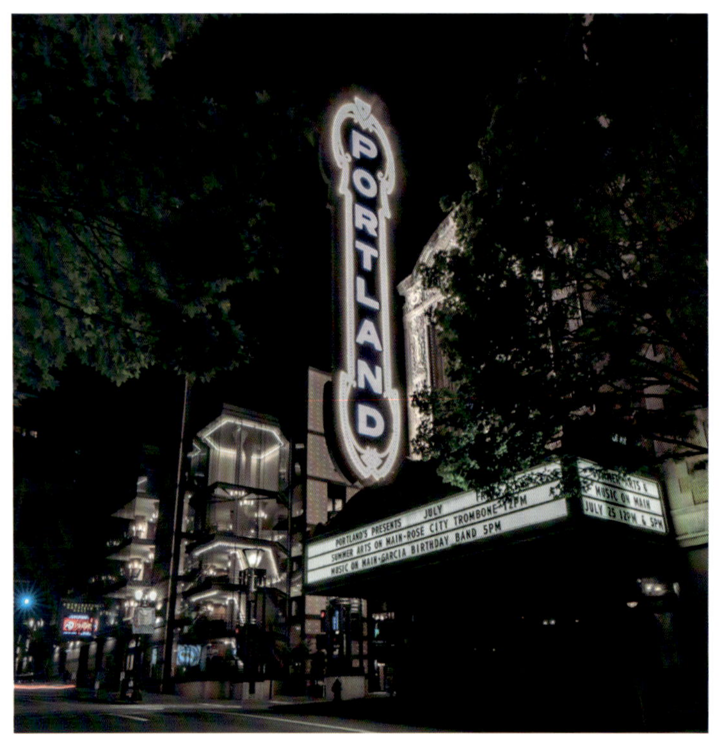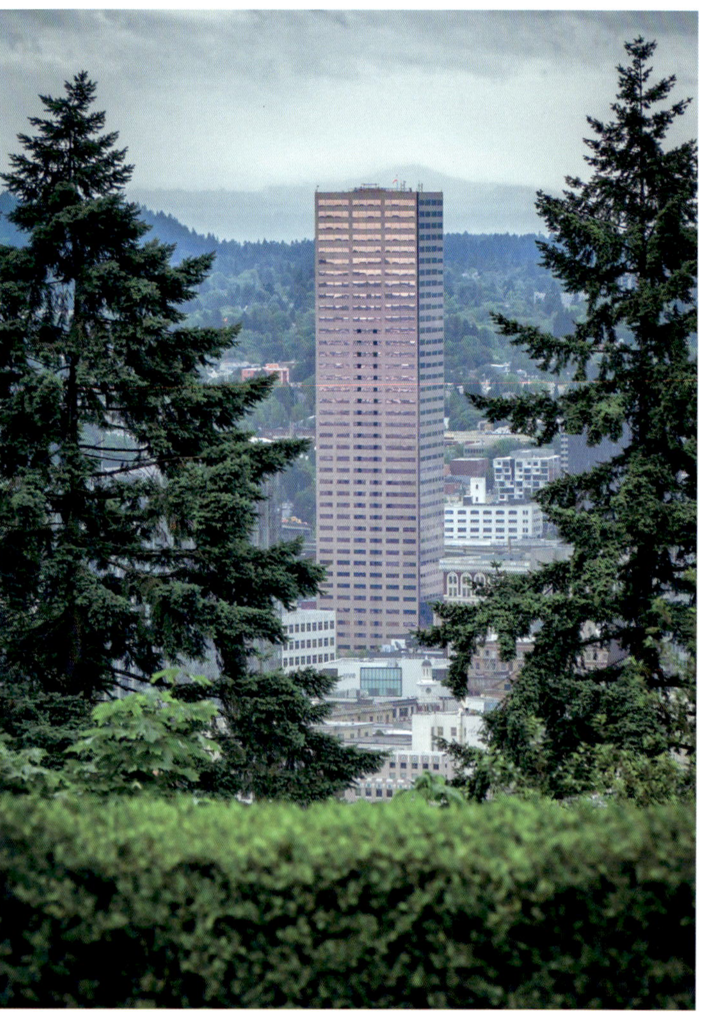

Historic "Portland" sign at Arlene Schnitzer Concert Hall.
Photo by Barbara Tricarico.

"Big Pink" (US Bancorp Tower) from the Portland Japanese Garden.
Photo by Barbara Tricarico.

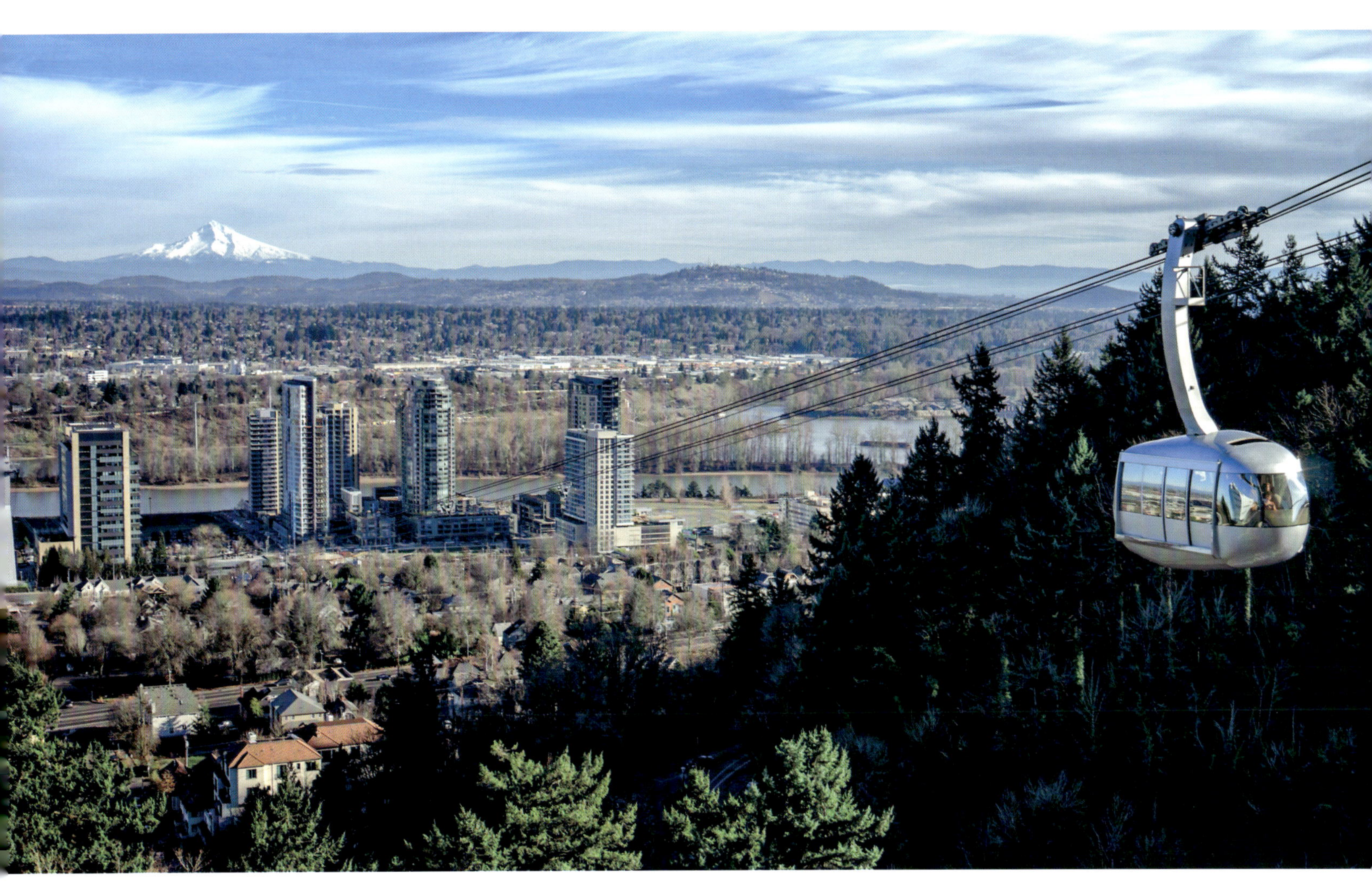

Portland Aerial Tram, with Mount Hood in background. *Photo by Barbara Tricarico.*

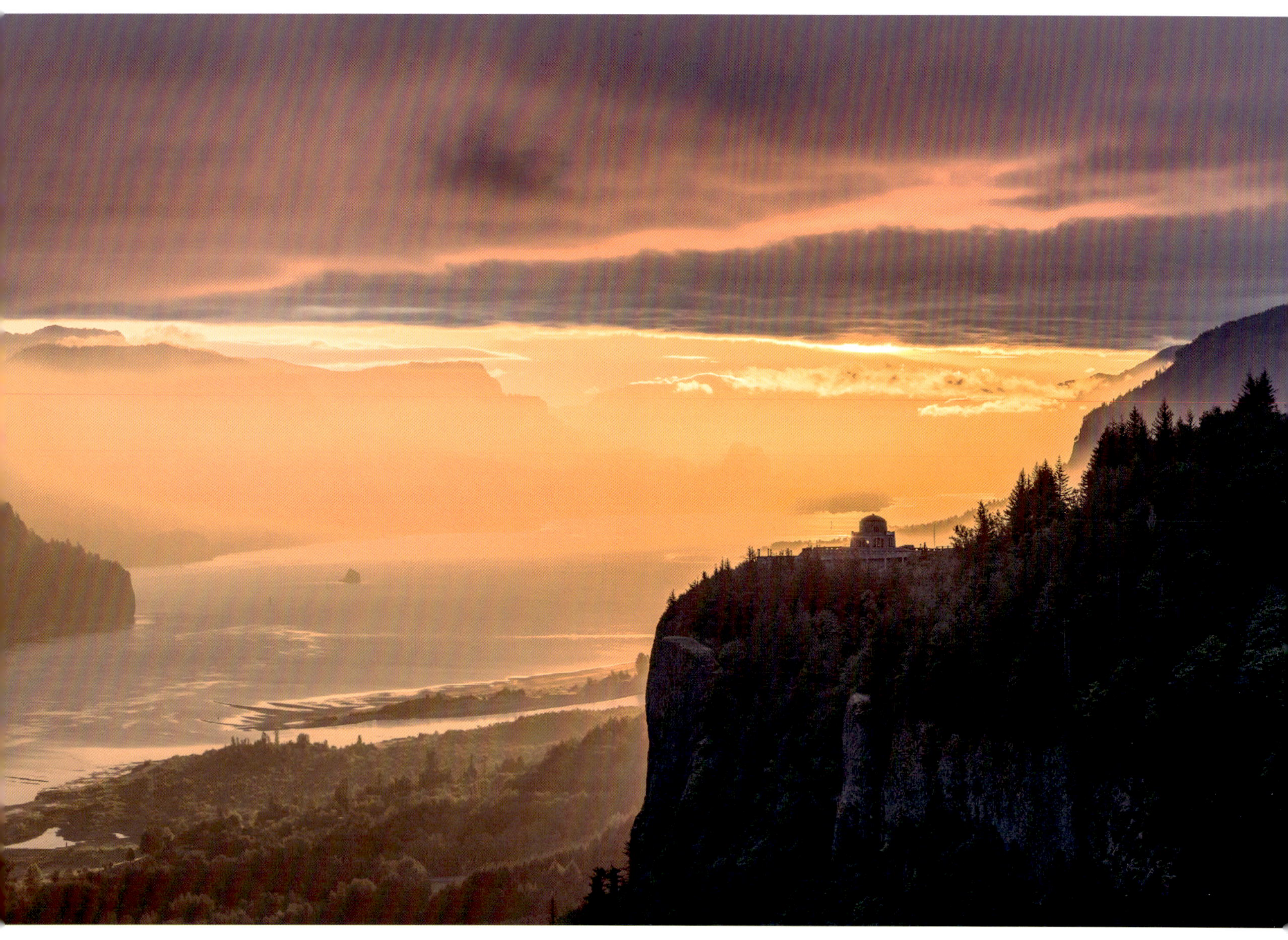

Columbia River Gorge sunrise. Vista House in foreground. *Photo by Vldn Taylor.*

(Opposite top) Bridge of the Gods. Originally named by Native Americans for a natural dam, this steel toll bridge over the Columbia River was built in 1926. *Photo by Barbara Tricarico.*

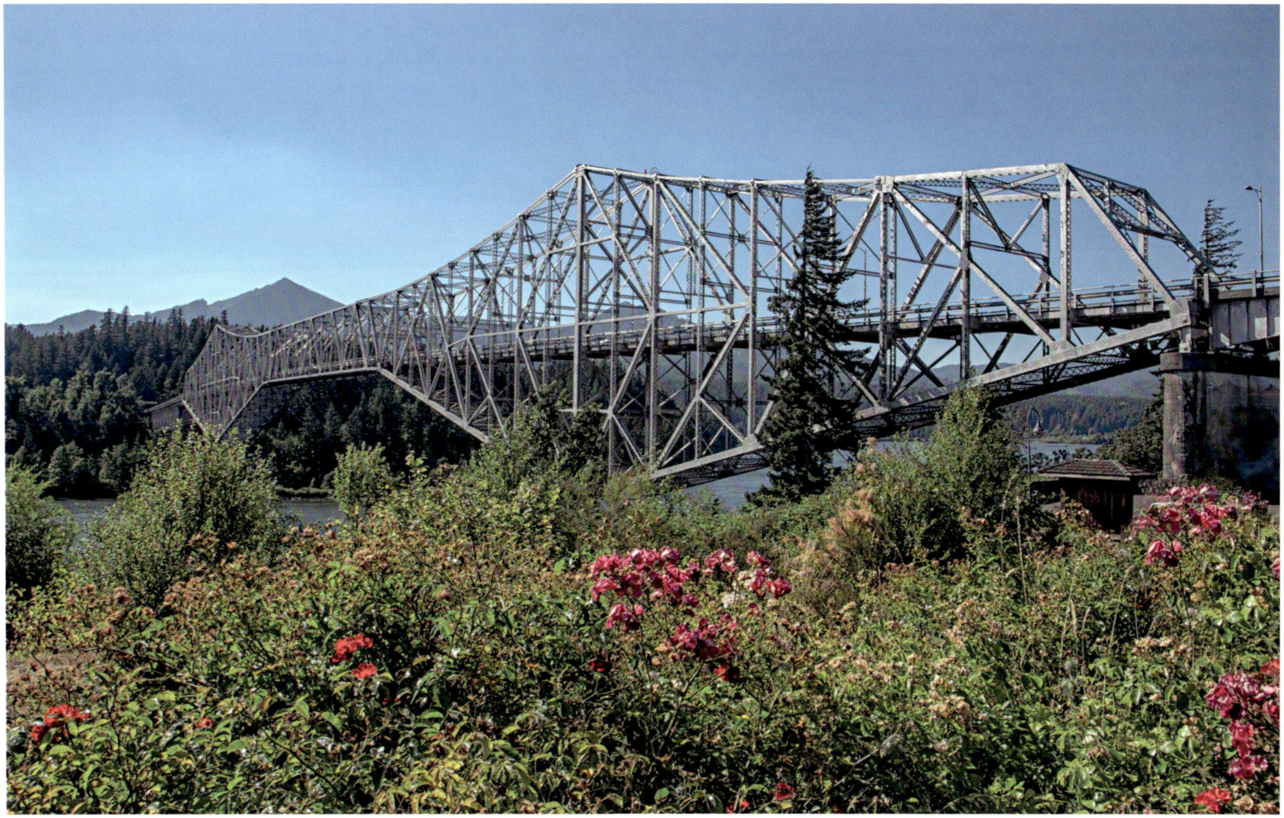

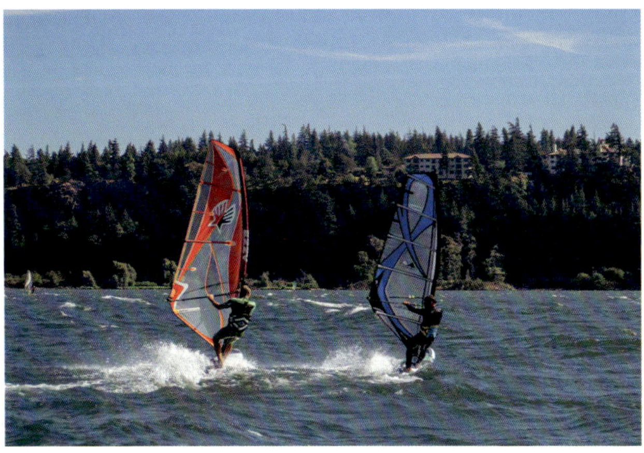

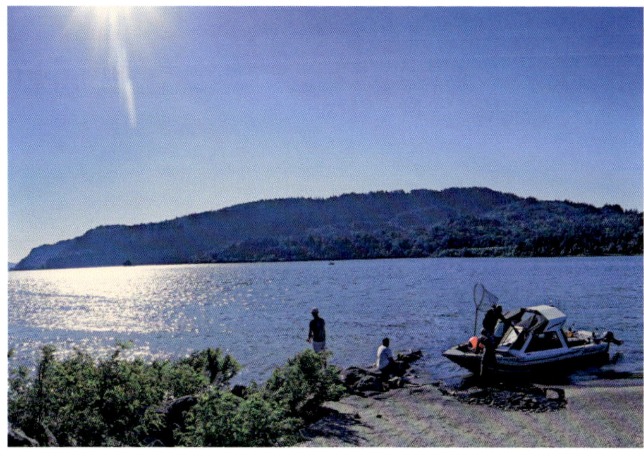

(Bottom left) Windsurfing on the Columbia River Gorge. *Photo by Vldn Taylor.* • (Bottom right) Fishing on the Columbia River. *Photo by Cornelius Matteo.*

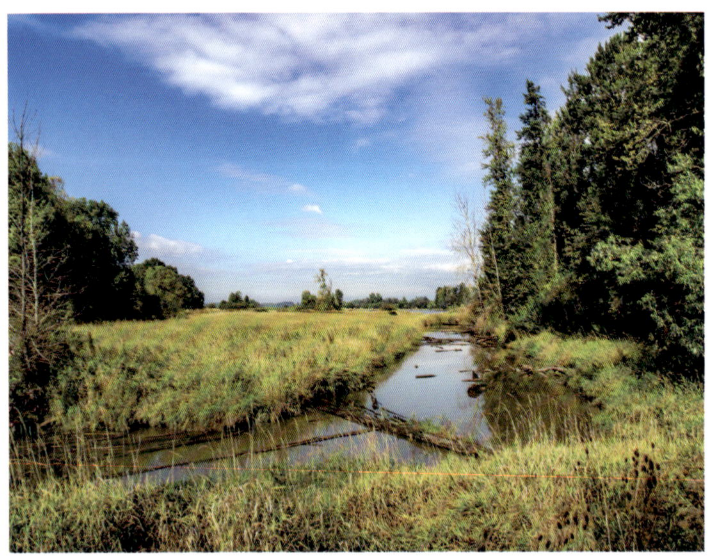

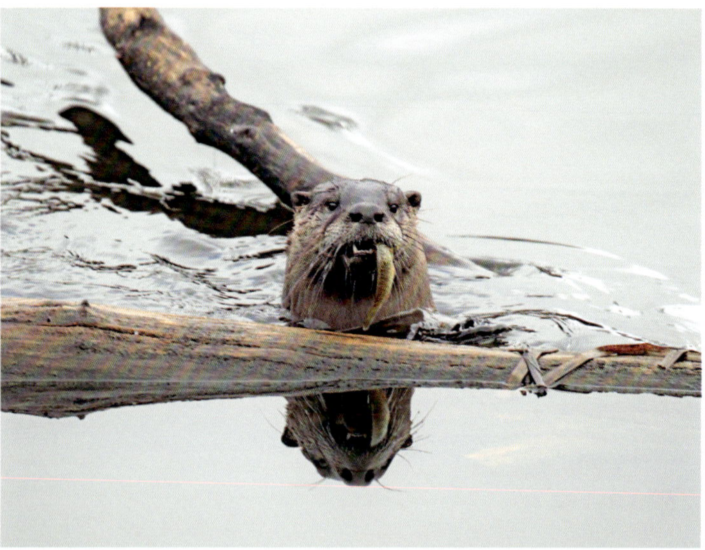

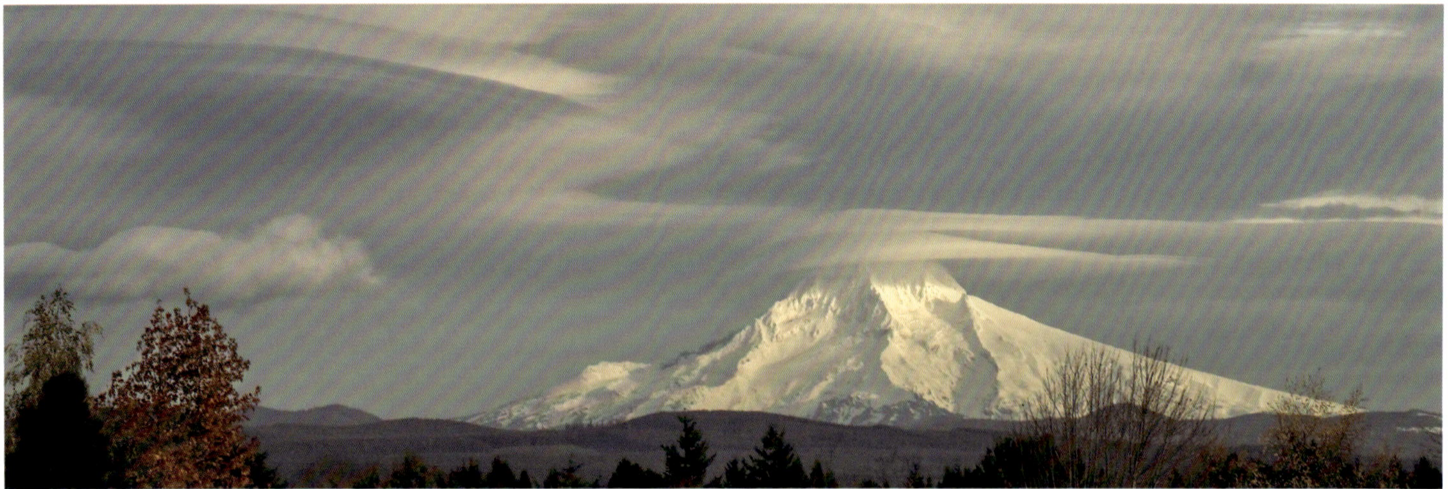

(Top left) Sauvie Island, a wildlife refuge surrounded by abundant farmland, is just outside Portland. It is the largest island along the Columbia River. *Photo by Nick Viani.*

(Top right) River otter. *Photo by Dan Elster.*

(Bottom) Lenticular clouds over Mount Hood. *Photo by Jay Newman.*

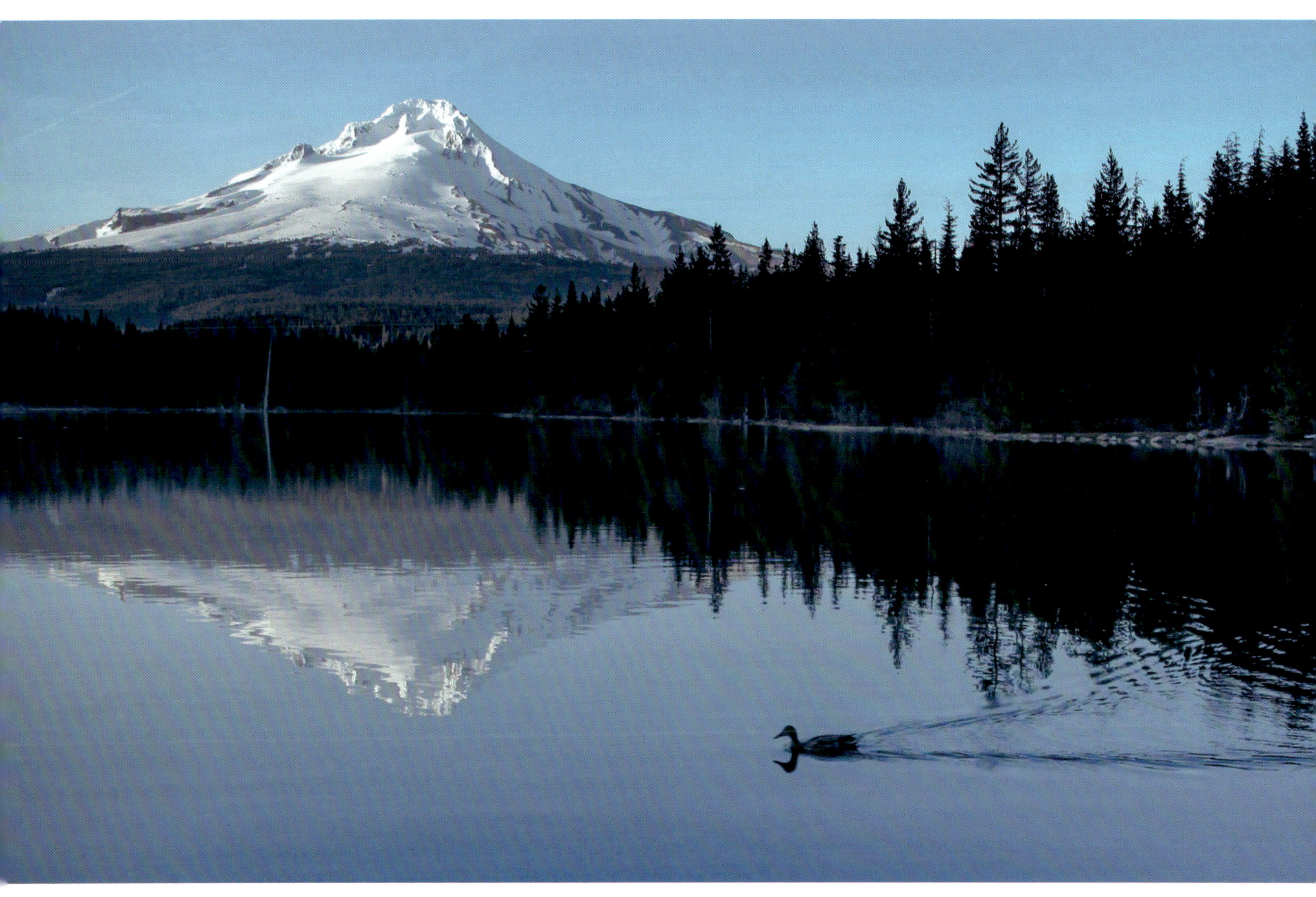

Trillium Lake and Mount Hood. *Photo by John Kirk.*

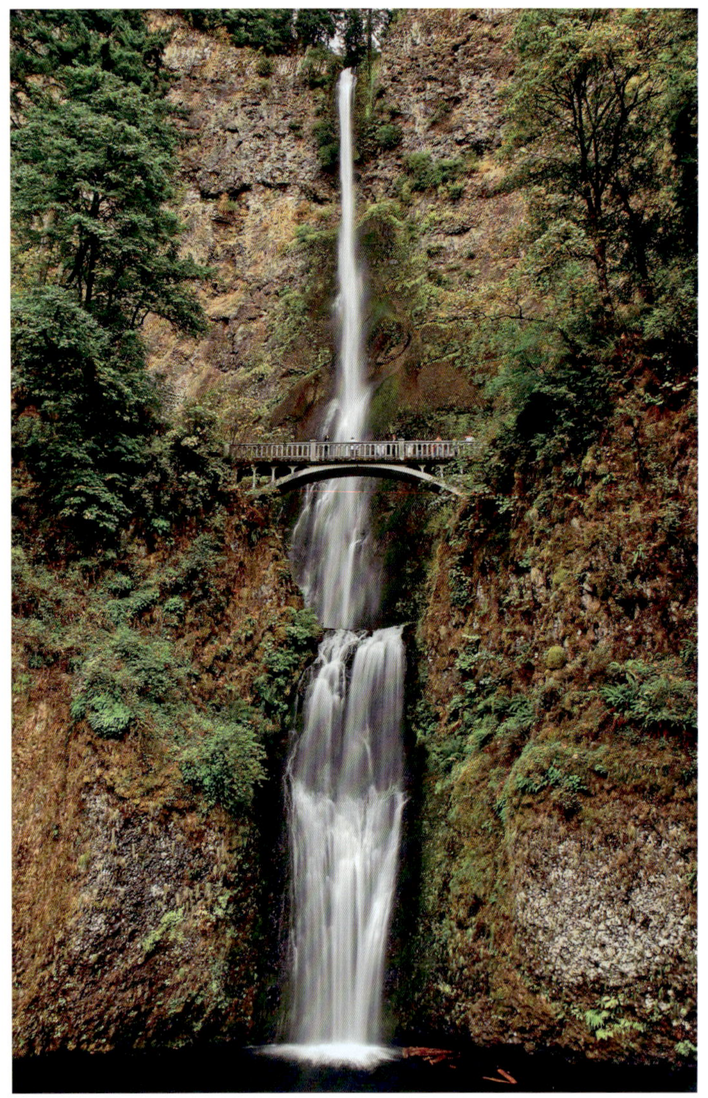

Multnomah Falls is the tallest waterfall in Oregon at 620 feet. *Photo by Jay Newman.*

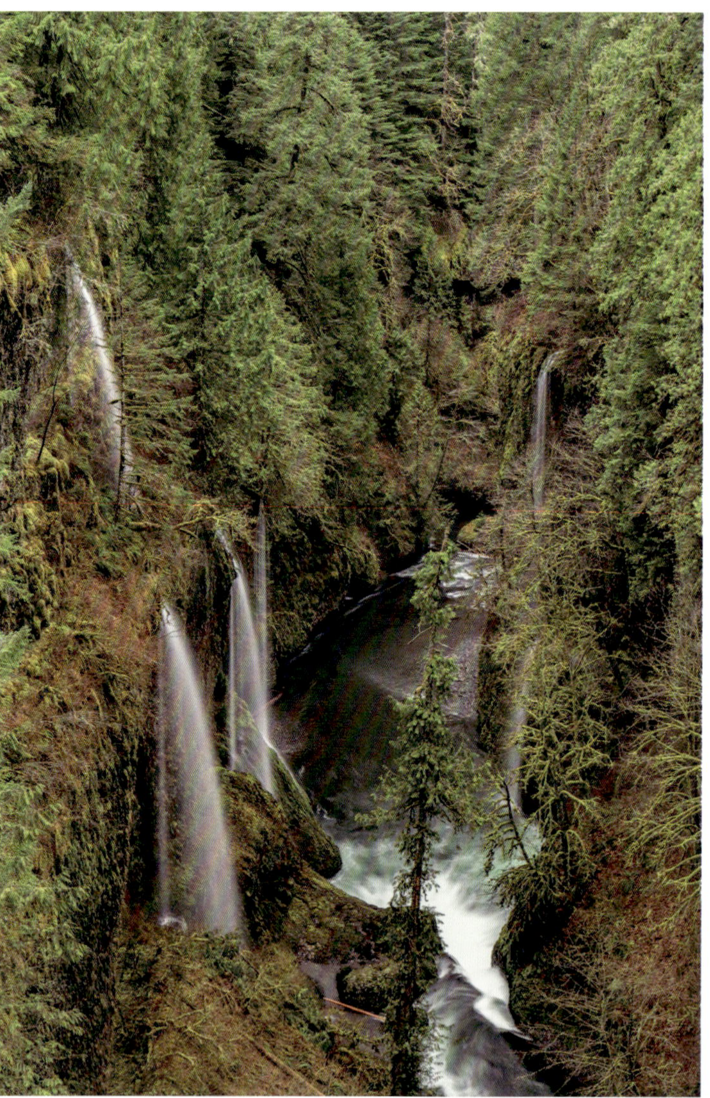

Weeping Walls, Eagle Creek Trail, Columbia River Gorge. *Photo by Vldn Taylor.*

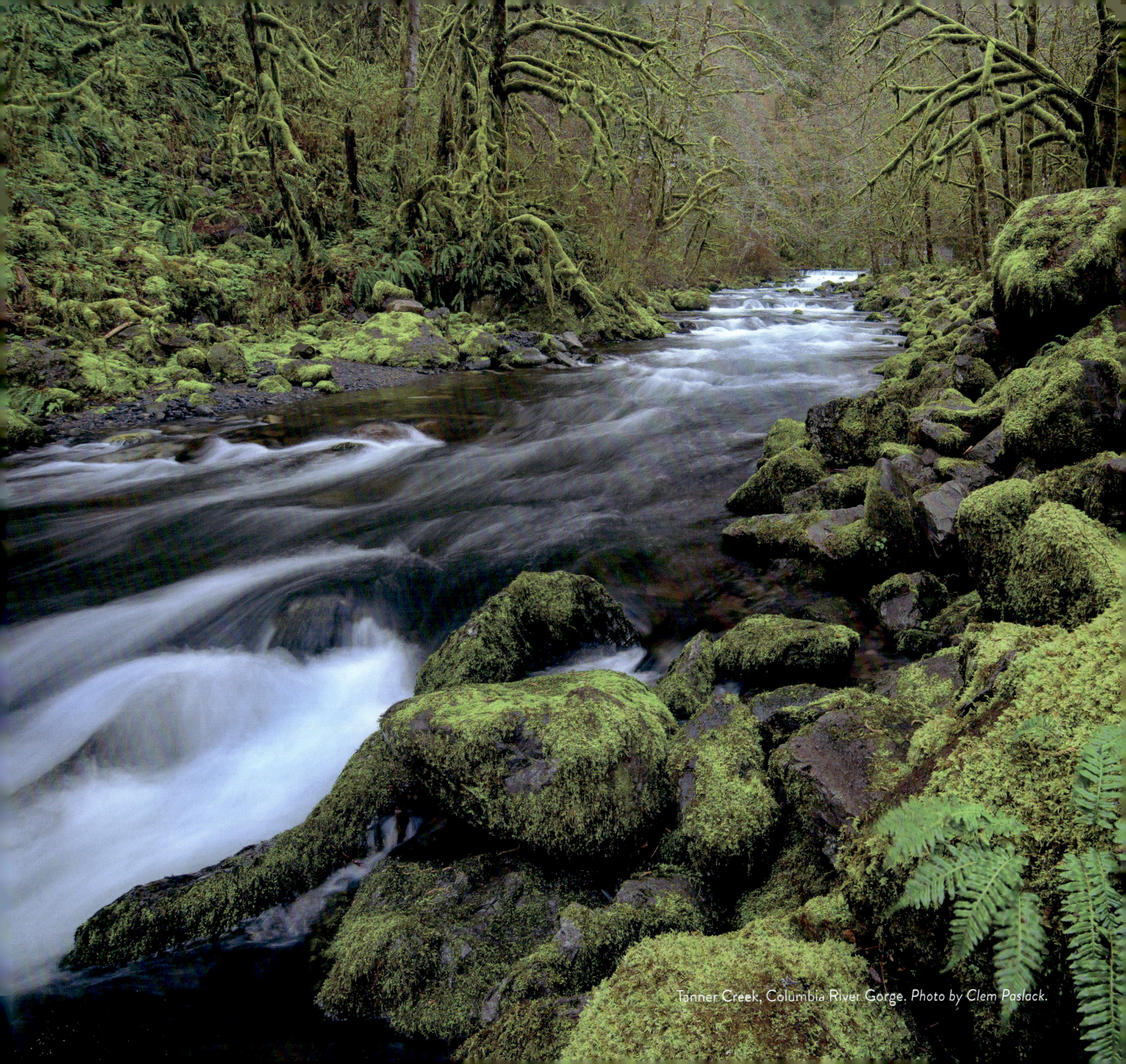

Tanner Creek, Columbia River Gorge. Photo by Clem Paslack.

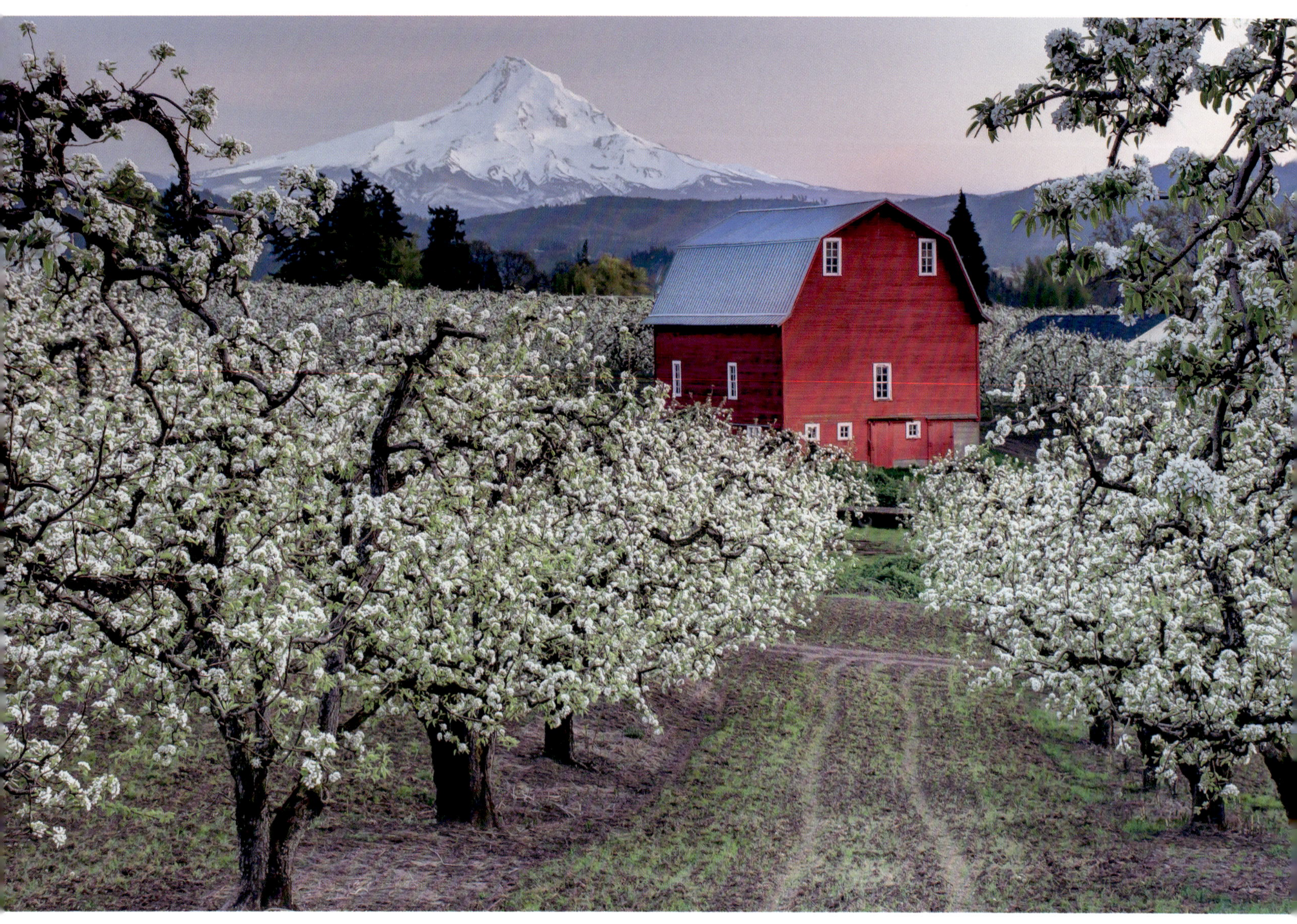

 Orchard blossoms near Hood River. *Photo by Clem Paslack.*

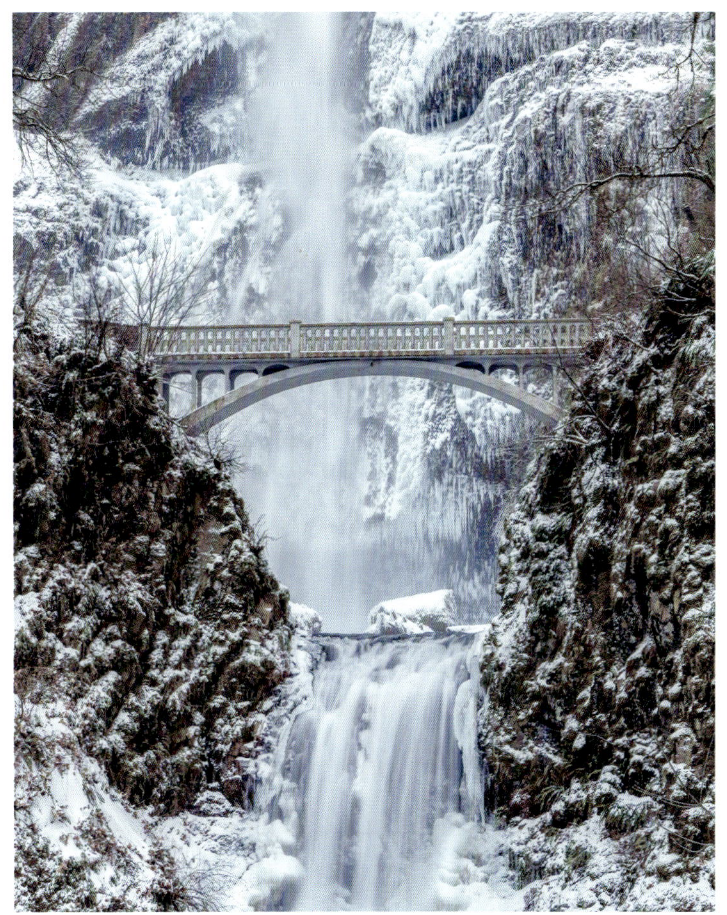

Multnomah Falls is the most visited recreation site in the Northwest, year-round. *Photo by Vldn Taylor.*

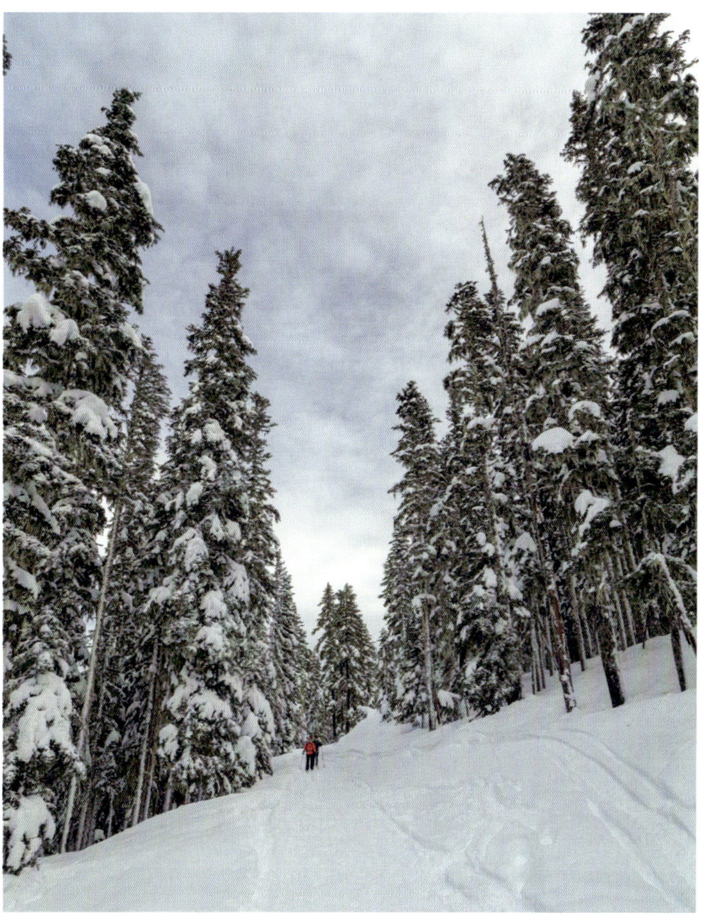

Skiing at Mount Hood. *Photo by Vldn Taylor.*

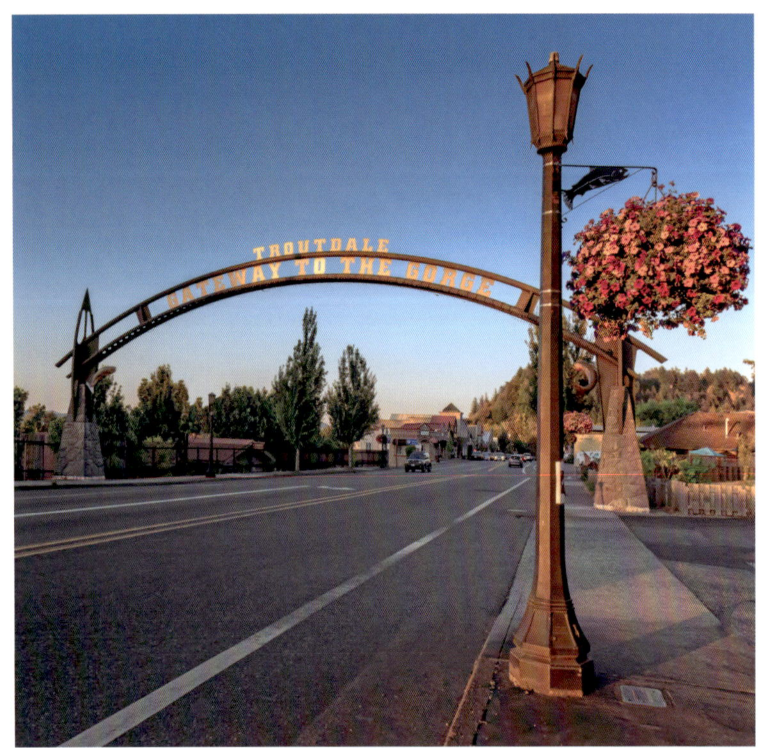

Troutdale, "Gateway to the Gorge." The sculpture by Rip Caswell was installed in 2010 to commemorate the 100th birthday of Troutdale. *Photo by Barbara Tricarico.*

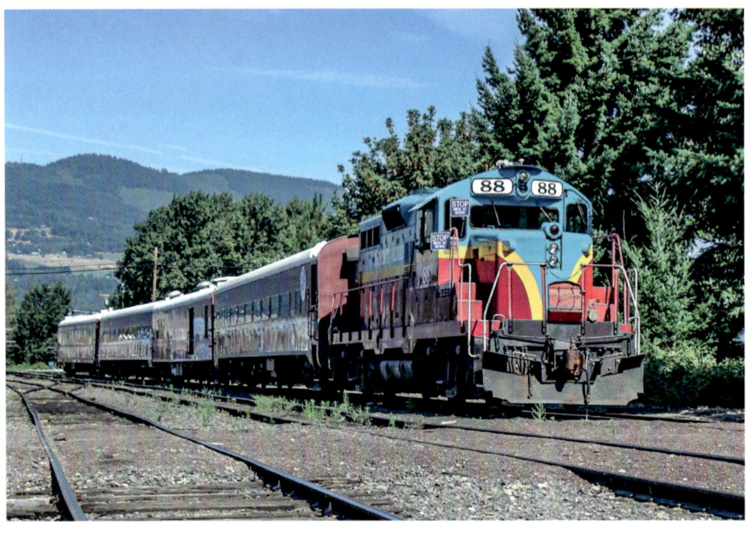

The Mount Hood Railroad is a tourist railroad operating between Hood River and Parkdale. It began operating in 1906. *Photo by George F. Peterson.*

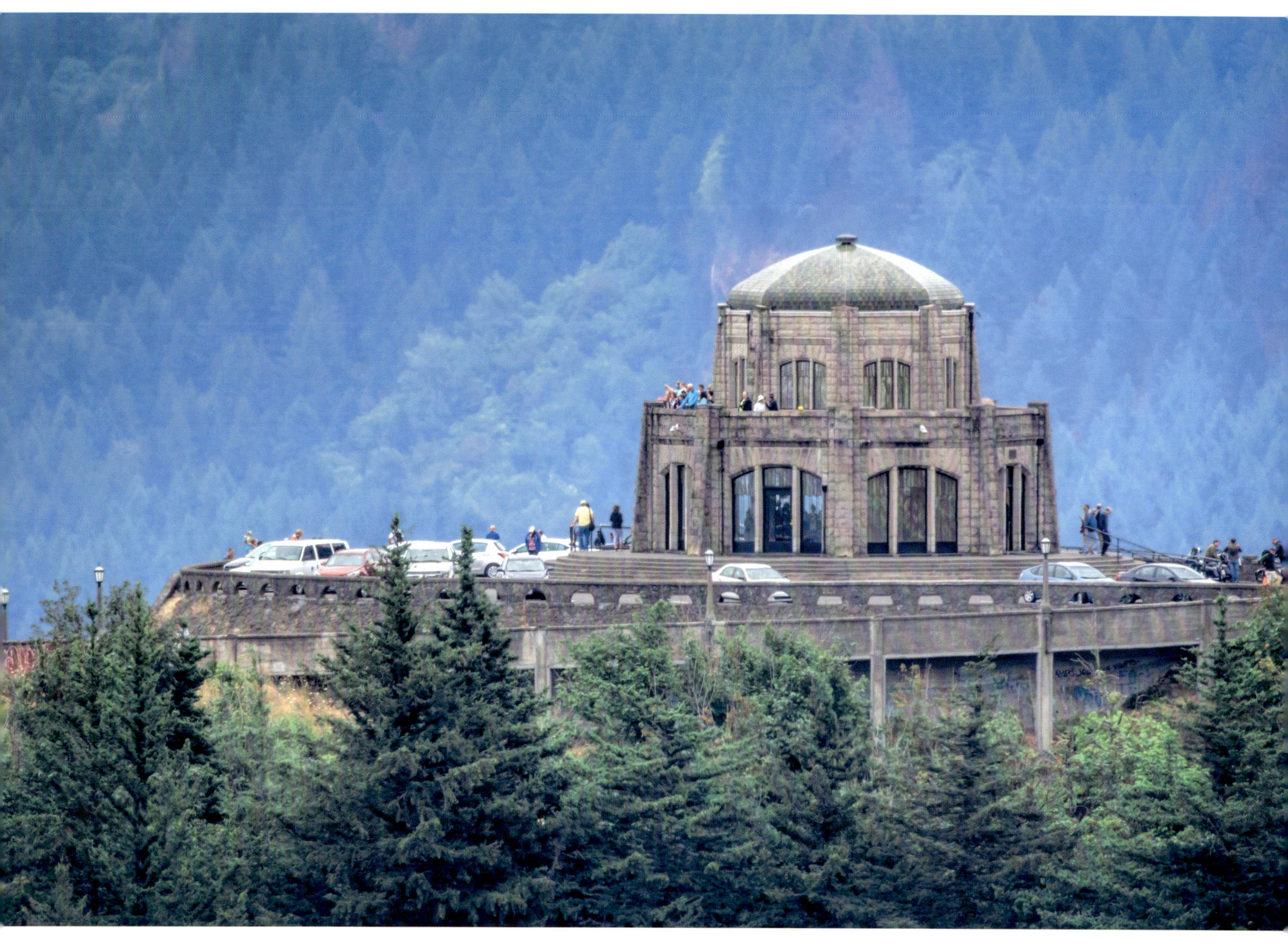

Vista House juts out prominently along the Historic Columbia River Highway about 733 feet above the Columbia River. It was completed in 1918. *Photo by Barbara Tricarico.*

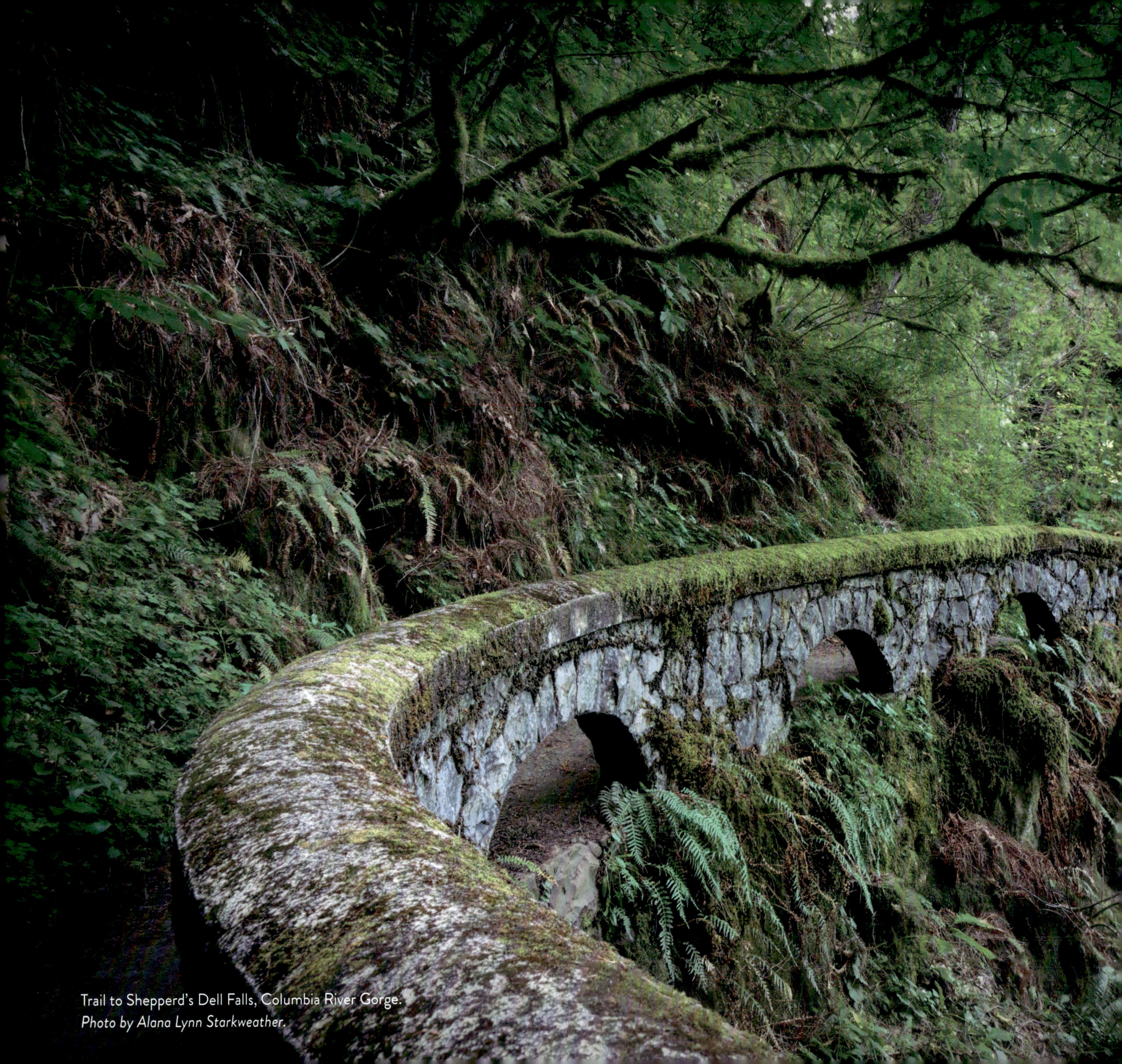

Trail to Shepperd's Dell Falls, Columbia River Gorge.
Photo by Alana Lynn Starkweather.

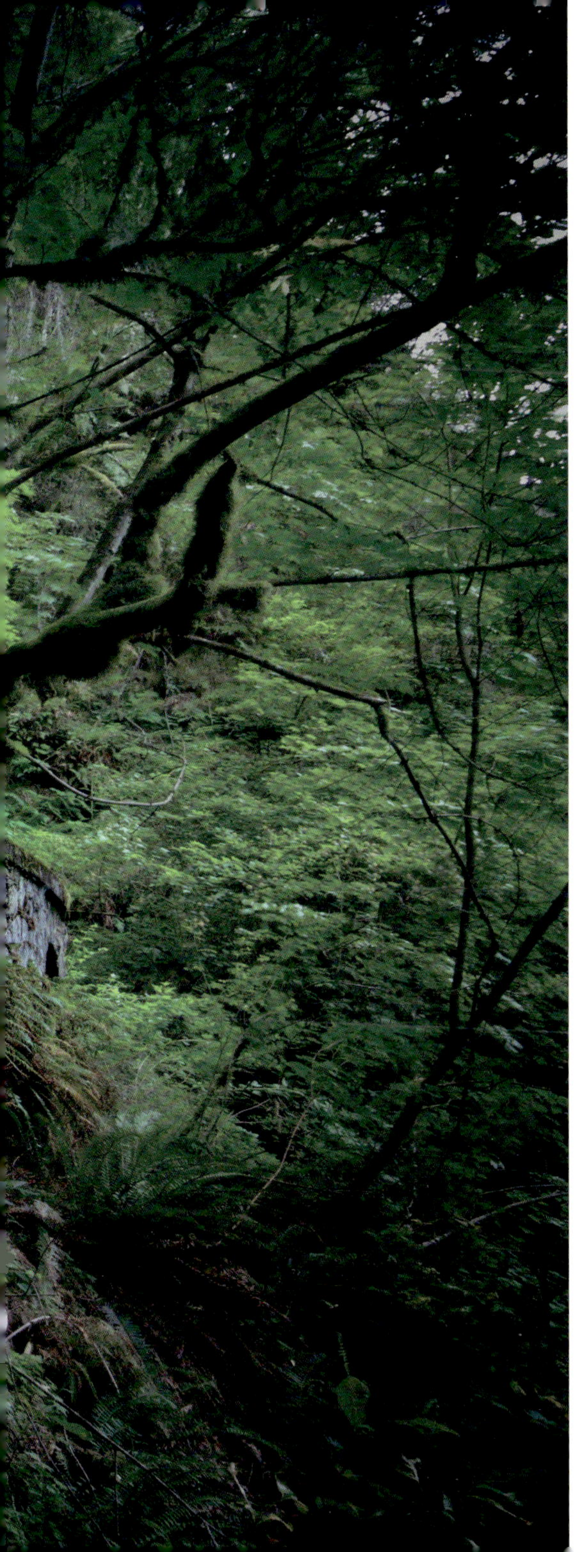

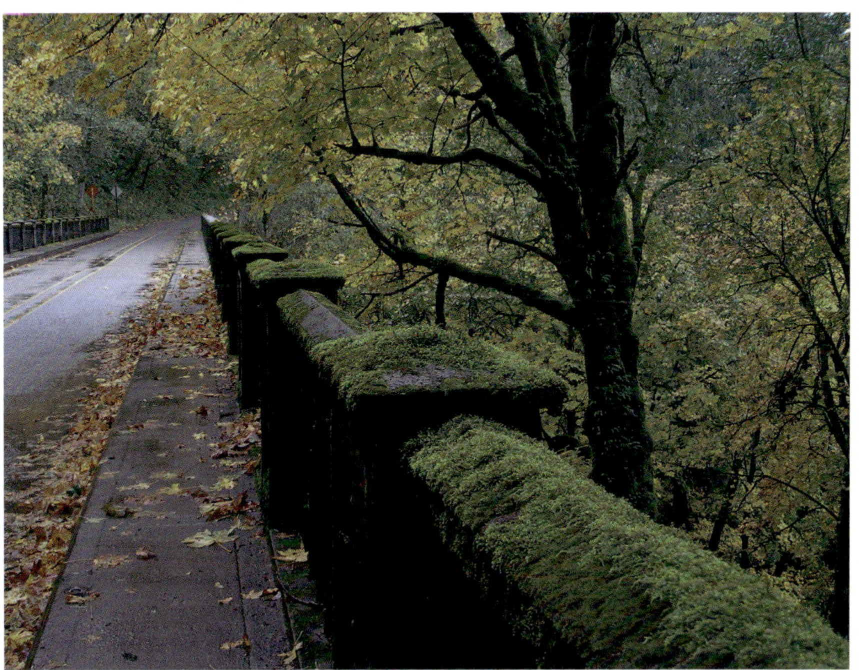

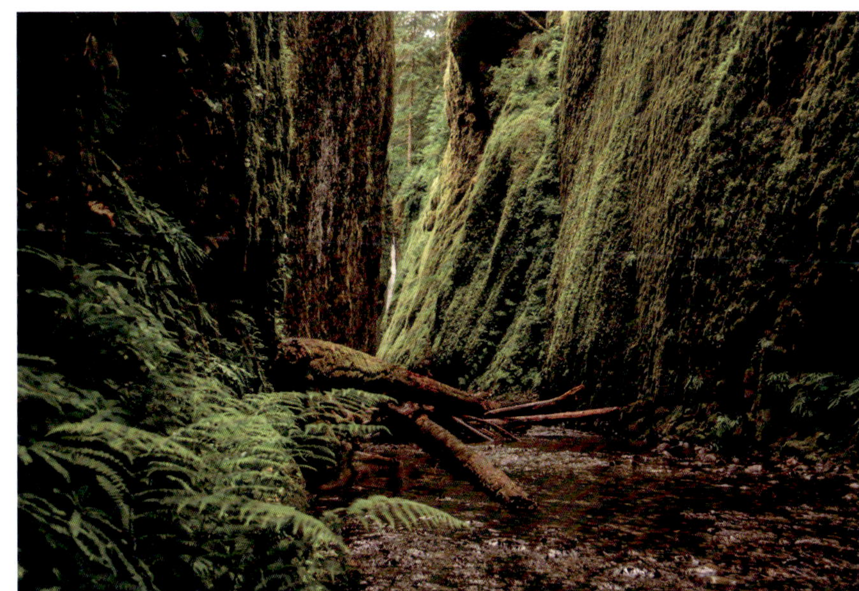

(Top) Multnomah Falls roadway. *Photo by Bob Palermini.*
(Bottom) Oneonta Gorge. *Photo by Hans Stroo.*
41

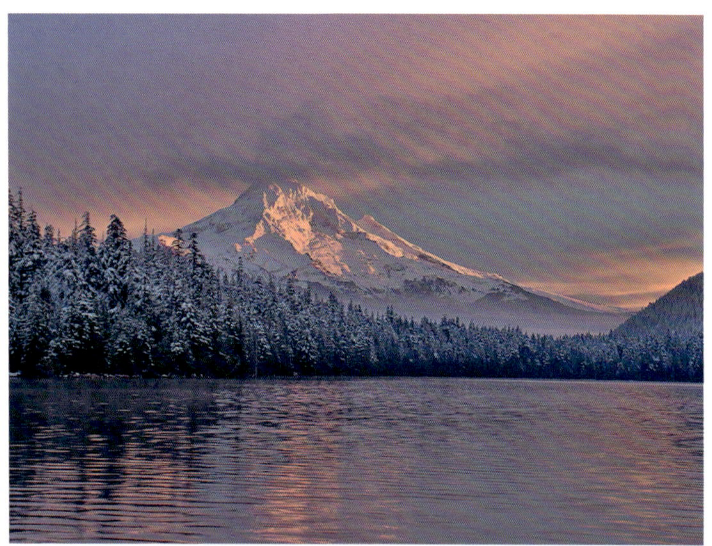

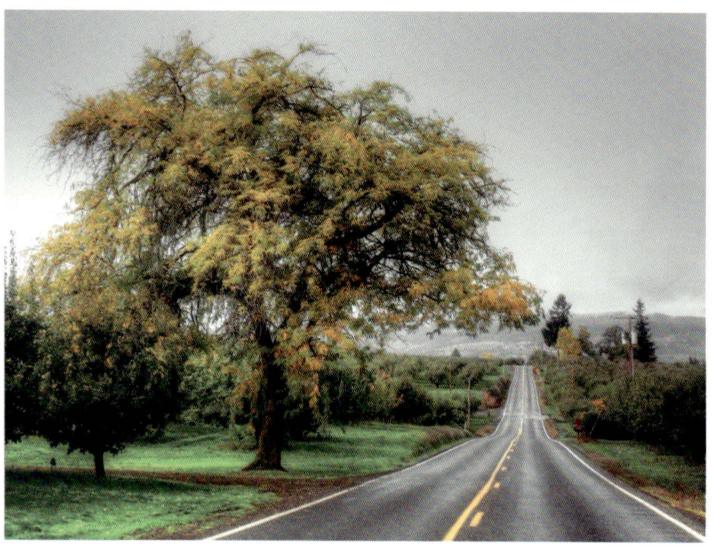

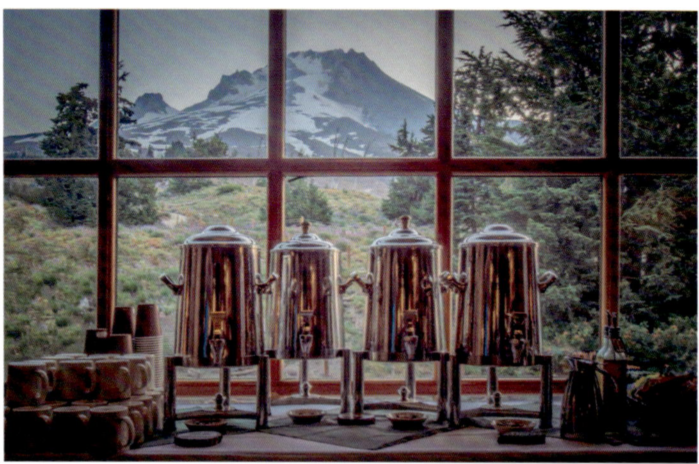

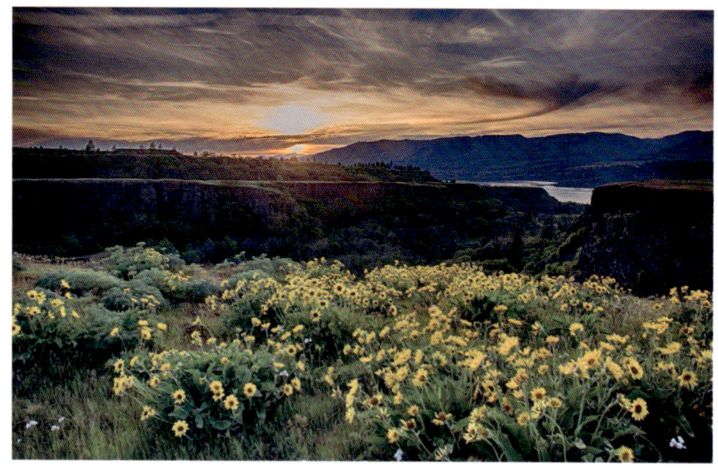

Mount Hood, called Wy'east by the Multnomah tribe.
Photo by Clem Paslack.

Hood River Drive. *Photo by John Kirk.*

View of Mount Hood from interior of Timberline Lodge.
Photo by Randy Bryan.

Wildflowers at Rowena Crest, Columbia River Gorge.
Photo by Terry Tuttle.

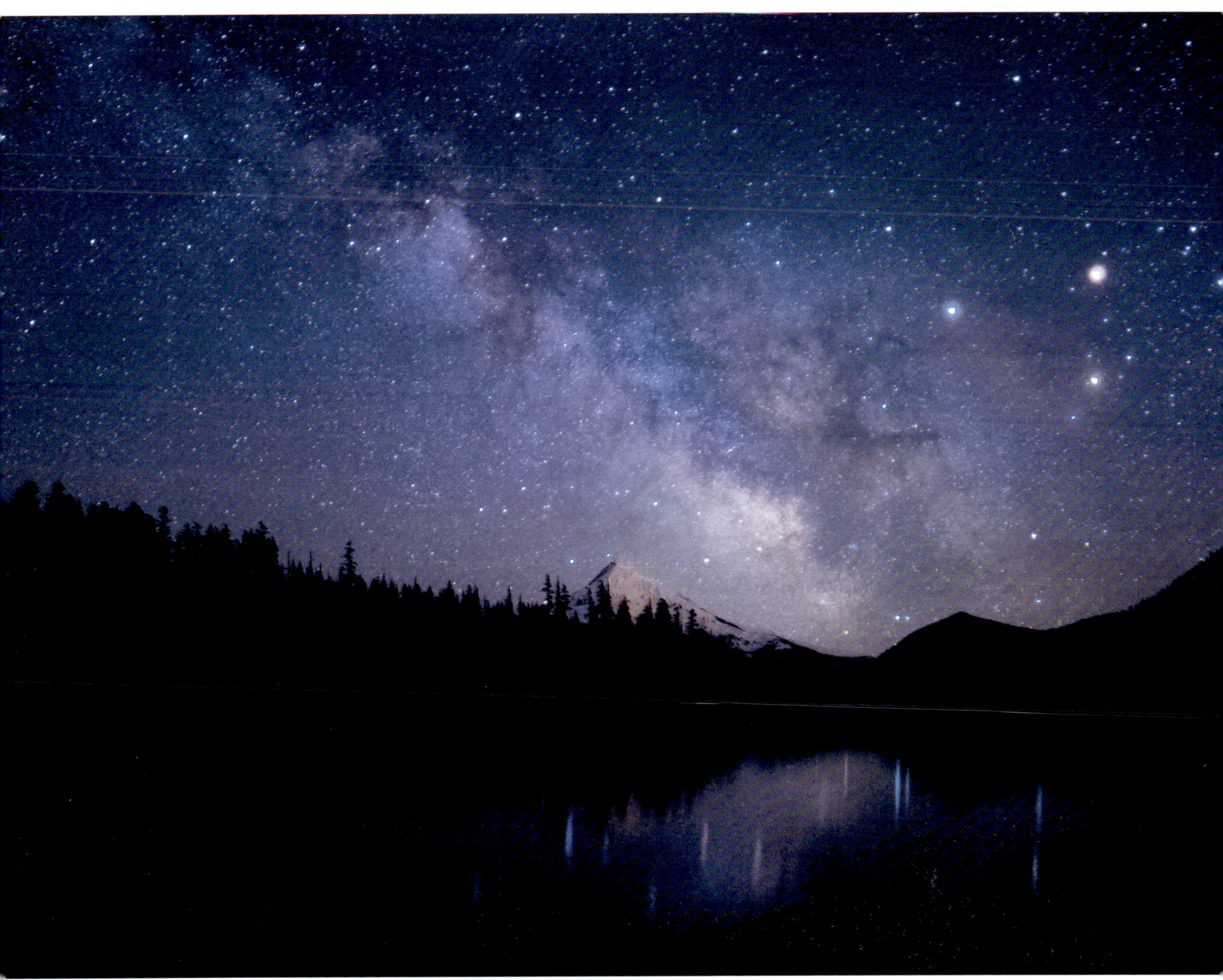

Milky Way over Mount Hood and Lost Lake. *Photo by Clem Paslack.*   43

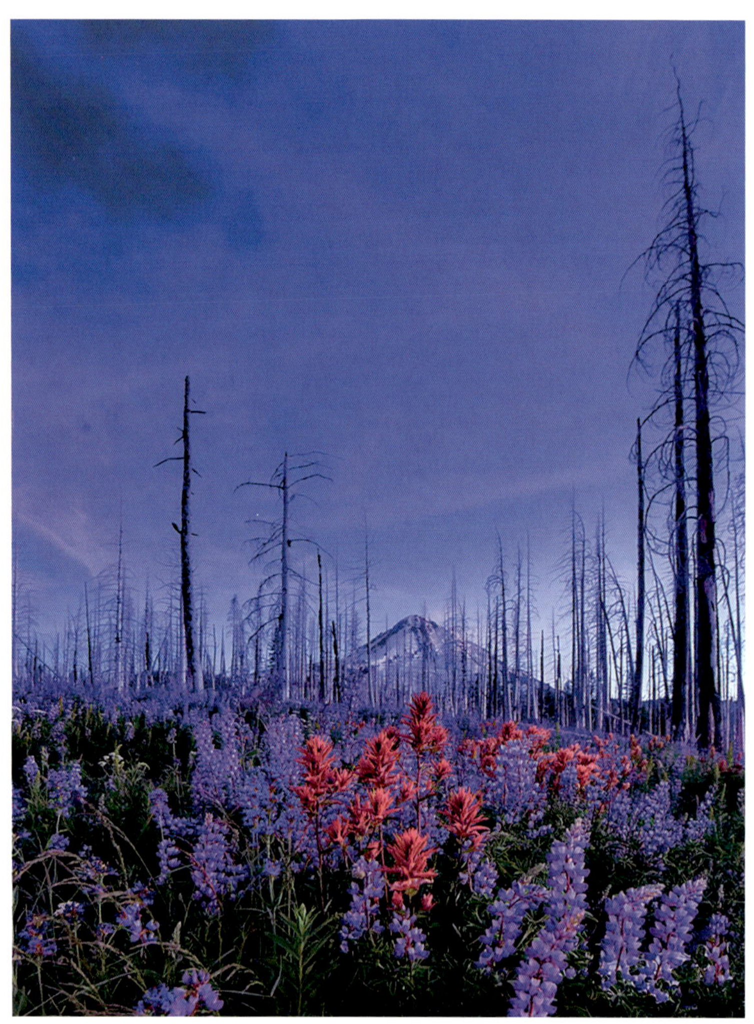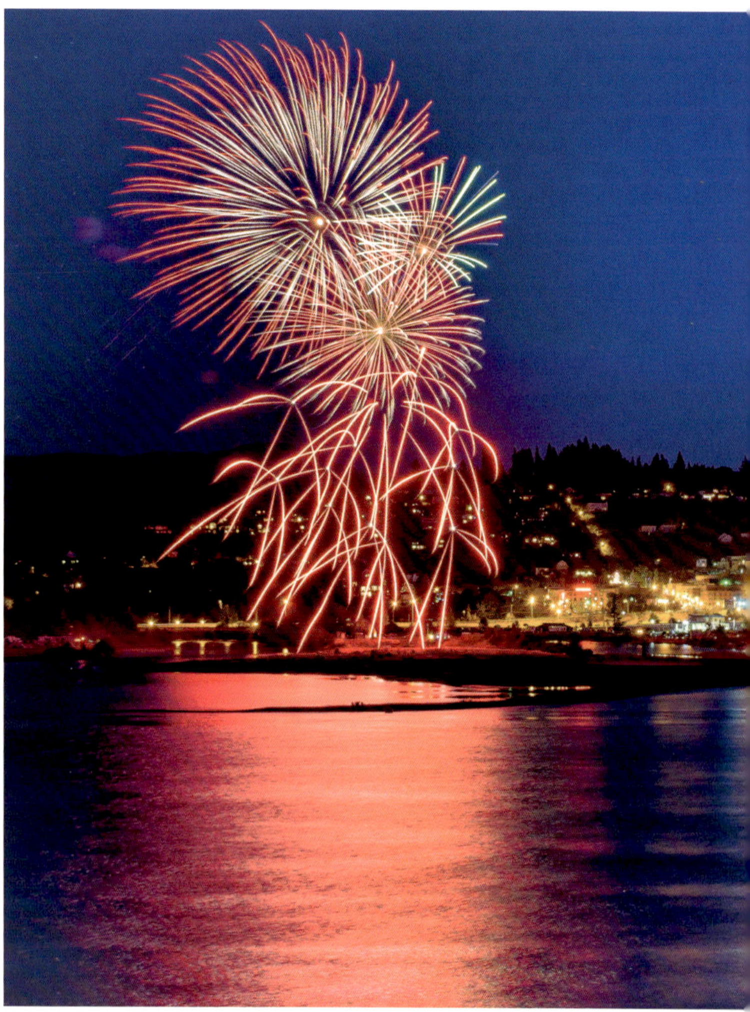

  Mount Hood National Forest rebirth. *Photo by Clem Paslack.* • July 4th fireworks at Hood River. *Photo by Clem Paslack.*

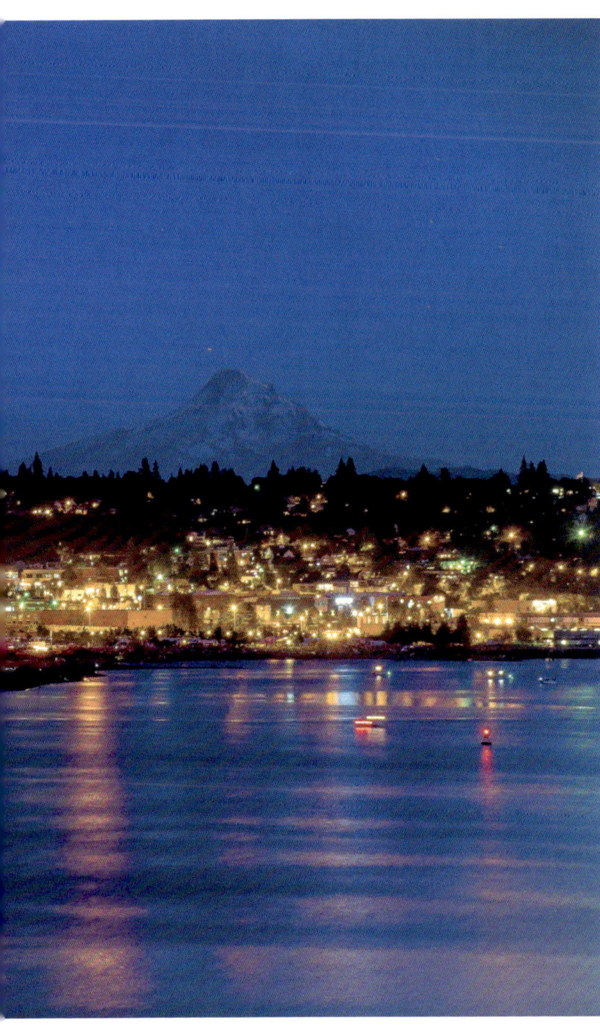

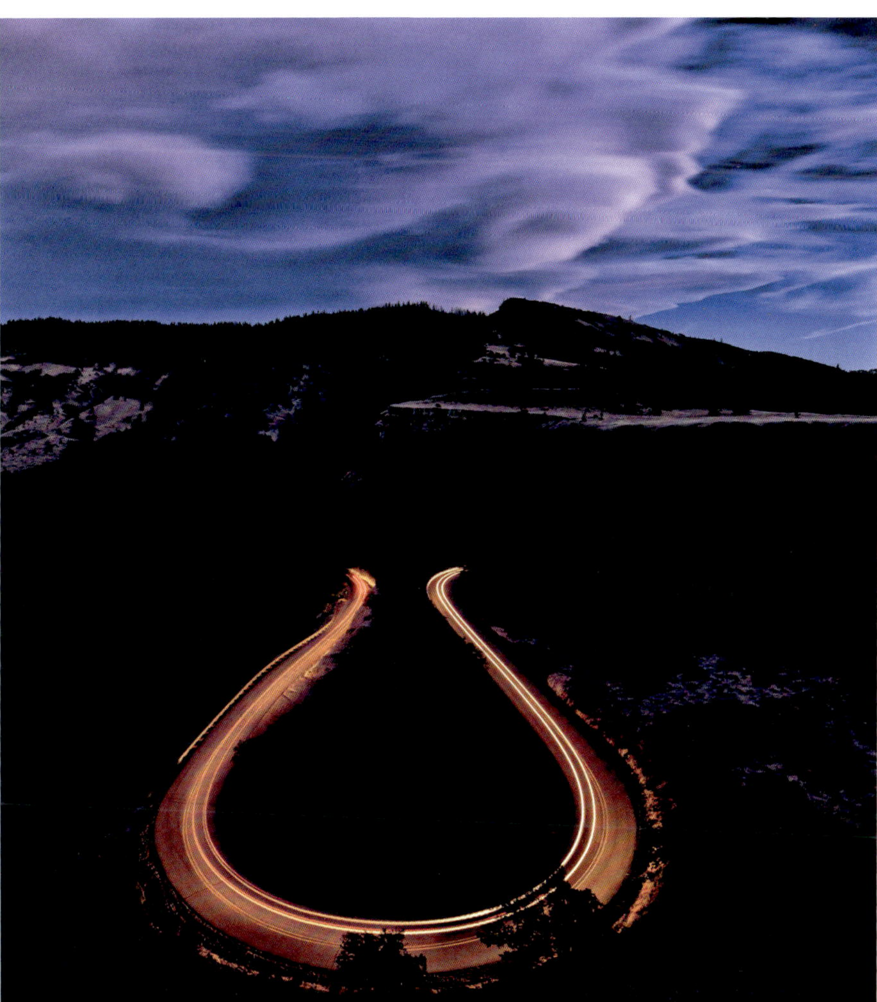

Rowena Crest viewpoint, Columbia River Gorge. *Photo by Clem Paslack.* 45

SOUTHERN OREGON

Southern Oregon is surrounded by postcard-perfect natural beauty. The Rogue, Umpqua, Illinois, and Christmas Valleys dip beneath the Cascade and Siskiyou mountain ranges, providing miles of hiking trails, lakes, streams, and scenery.

This part of the state has four mild but distinct seasons. Known for its summer Mediterranean weather, Grants Pass's motto is "It's the Climate." The Rogue River, which flows 215 miles from Crater Lake to the Pacific Ocean at Gold Beach, was one of the original eight rivers designated "Wild and Scenic" in 1968. Locals and visitors enjoy whitewater rafting, fishing, camping, hiking, and plentiful nature and wildlife. Lake of the Woods, Hyatt Lake, Howard Prairie Lake, and Emigrant Lake also draw outdoorsy types. The vibrant blue-green Illinois River provides a variety of water activities, as does nearby Lake Selmac. Venturing into the Umpqua River Valley (not far from Crater Lake), visitors can relax at beautiful Diamond Lake and explore countless waterfalls.

Crater Lake is the best-known treasure in Southern Oregon. Follow Rim Drive by car; hike to Watchman Peak for out-of-this-world views of the bluest lake you'll ever see; relax at Crater Lake Lodge; swim, fish, or take a boat ride to Wizard Island; explore the nearby Pinnacles; or snowshoe in winter.

There are many artsy towns, such as Ashland, Grants Pass, and Jacksonville (not to mention a plethora of picturesque wineries and tasting rooms). Good restaurants, unique shops, art, music, and culture abound. Ashland has been voted one of America's "best small towns" many times over. Halfway between Portland and San Francisco, it is home to the Oregon Shakespeare Festival, which draws patrons from all over the world. Other landmarks include Lithia Park (the "jewel" of Ashland), Southern Oregon University, and Mount Ashland Ski Resort. Jacksonville, another small-town gem in Southern Oregon, is a former gold-rush town and home to the annual Britt Music & Arts Festival. At the mouth of the lush Applegate Valley, there are countless wineries to visit. Cave Junction's motto is "Gateway to the Oregon Caves," with more than 4,554 acres to explore.

While large parts of the 2,650-mile Pacific Crest Trail are considered rugged (and a challenge to many hikers), some of the sections that pass through Oregon are gentle and peaceful. Hikers can enjoy a day trip or even a week's adventure through old-growth forests. Nature lovers enjoy exploring Table Rocks, Mount Ashland, or Mount McLaughlin during wildflower season.

Birdwatchers and photographers will delight in seeing an abundance of owls, bald eagles, and countless species of birds and waterfowl as they migrate near Klamath Falls each year at the Lower Klamath National Wildlife Refuge.

The distinctive Pilot Rock, part of the Cascade-Siskiyou National Monument, can be seen for miles in each direction and is known for its scenic vistas and hiking paths. The monument is one of the world's top-ten ecosystems.

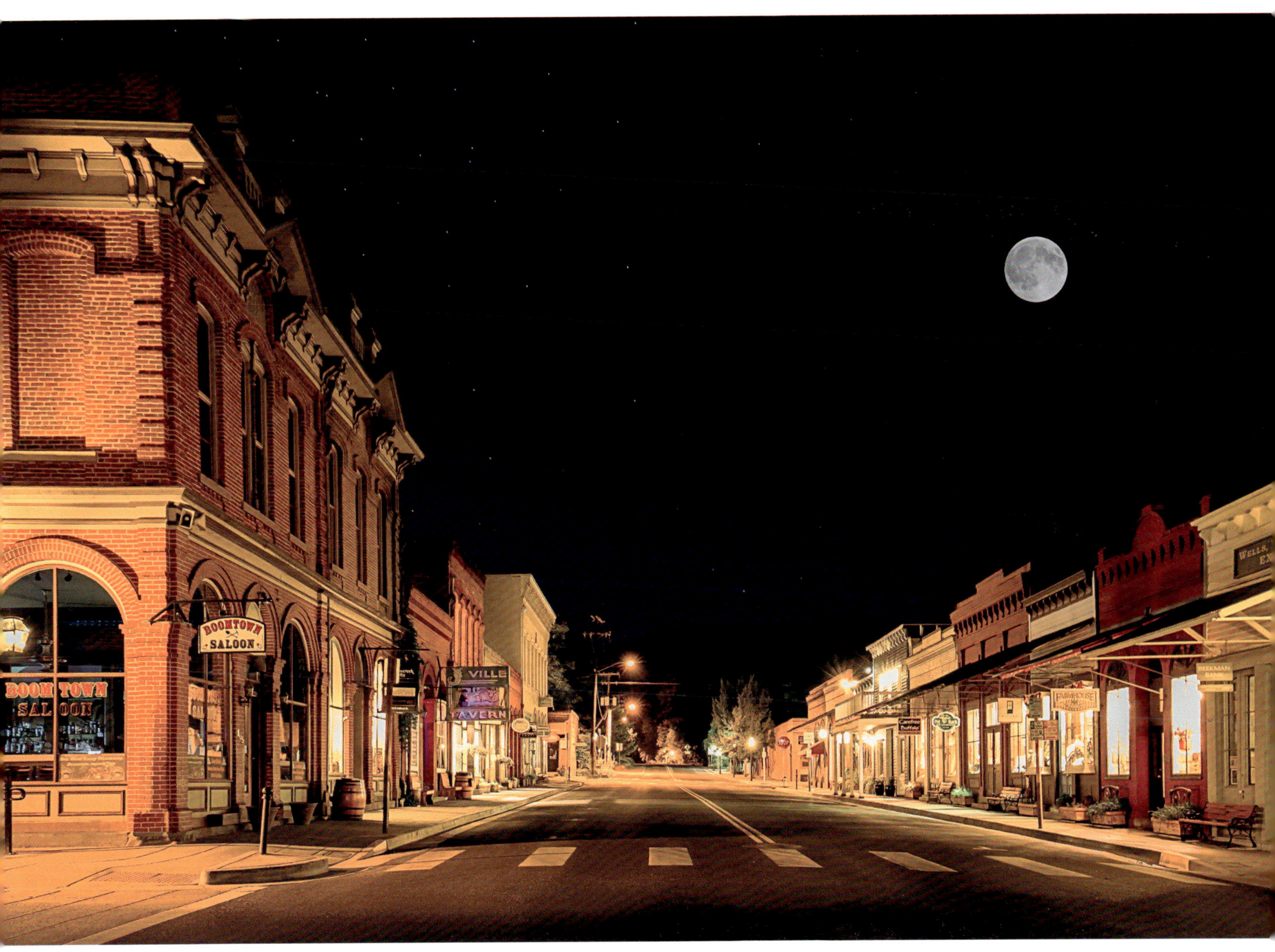

Historic Jacksonville's city center. *Photo by Gary Hill.*

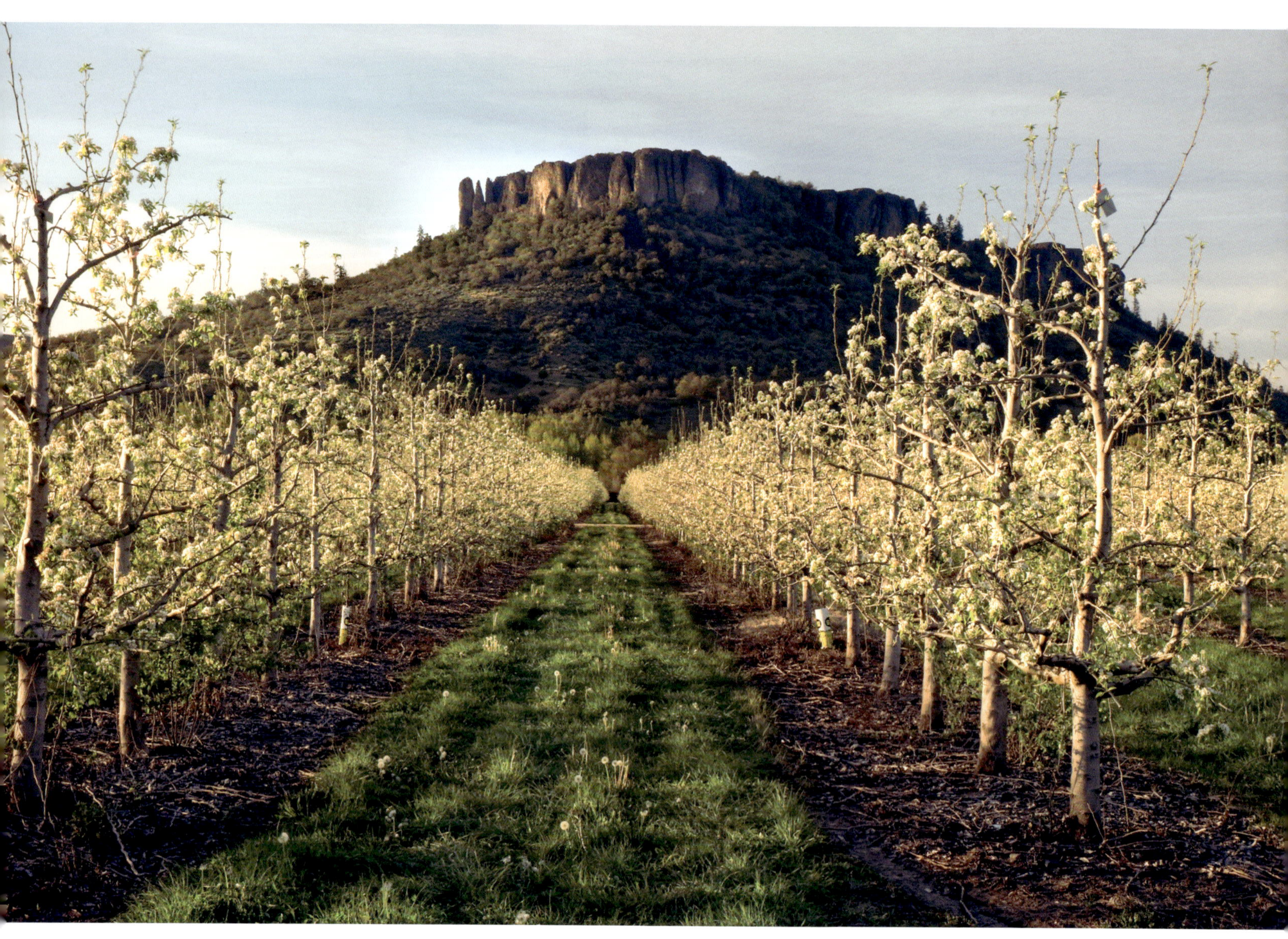

   Lower Table Rock and orchards, Central Point. *Photo by Jay Newman.*

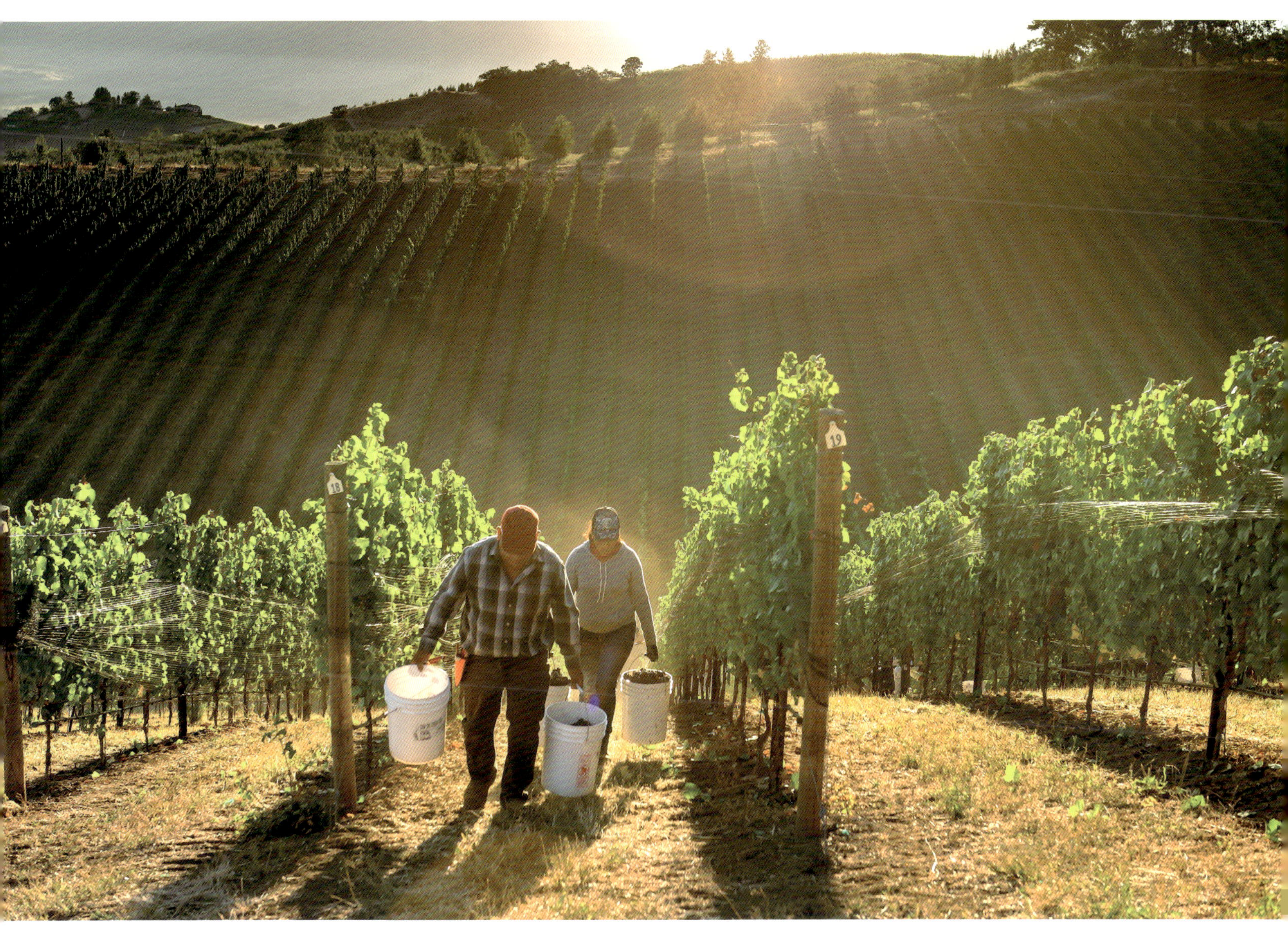

Pinot noir harvest, Jacksonville. *Photo by Jim Craven.*   49

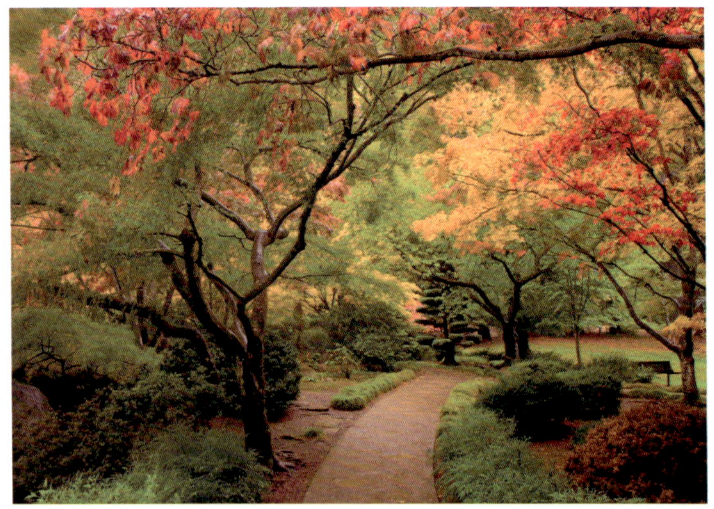 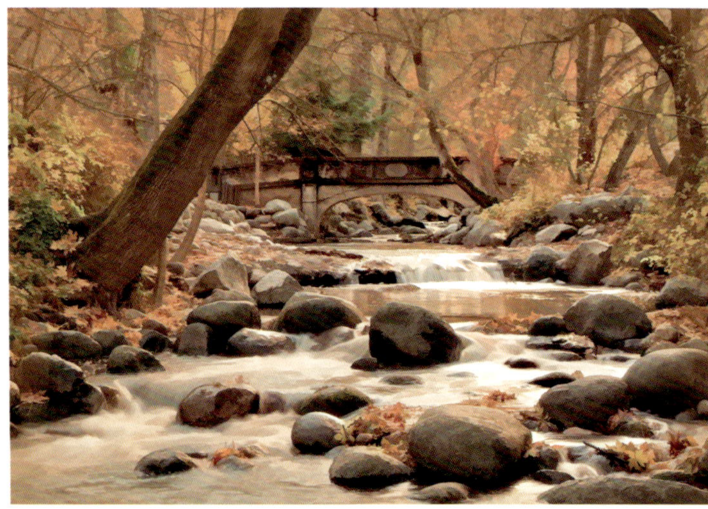

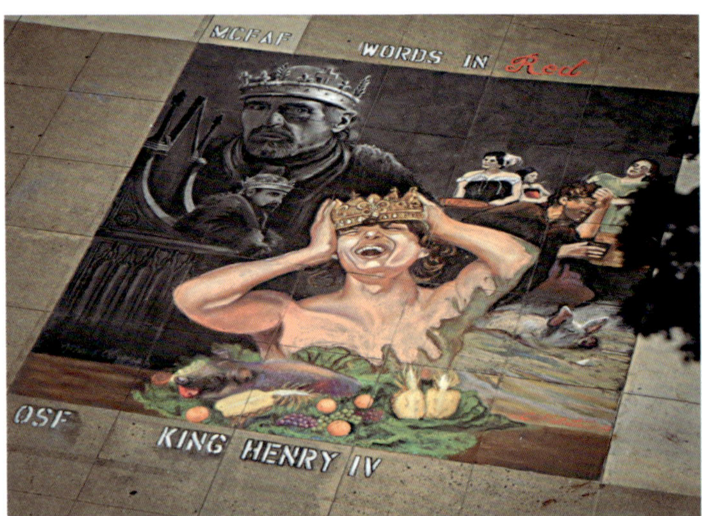

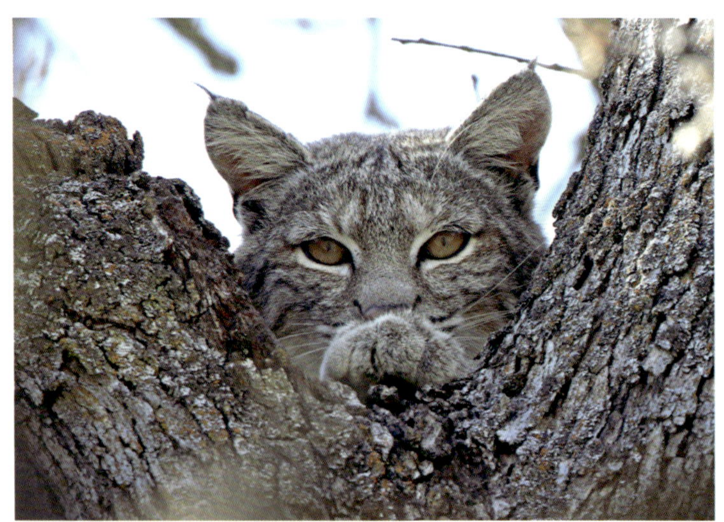

Lithia Park's Japanese Garden, Ashland. *Photo by Clem Paslack.*

Ashland Creek in Lithia Park, Ashland. *Photo by Vivian McAleavey.*

King Henry IV chalk painting in front of Oregon Shakespeare Festival's Black Swan Theatre, by artist Cathy Gallatin. *Photo by Graham Lewis.*

Bobcat. *Photo by Dan Elster.*

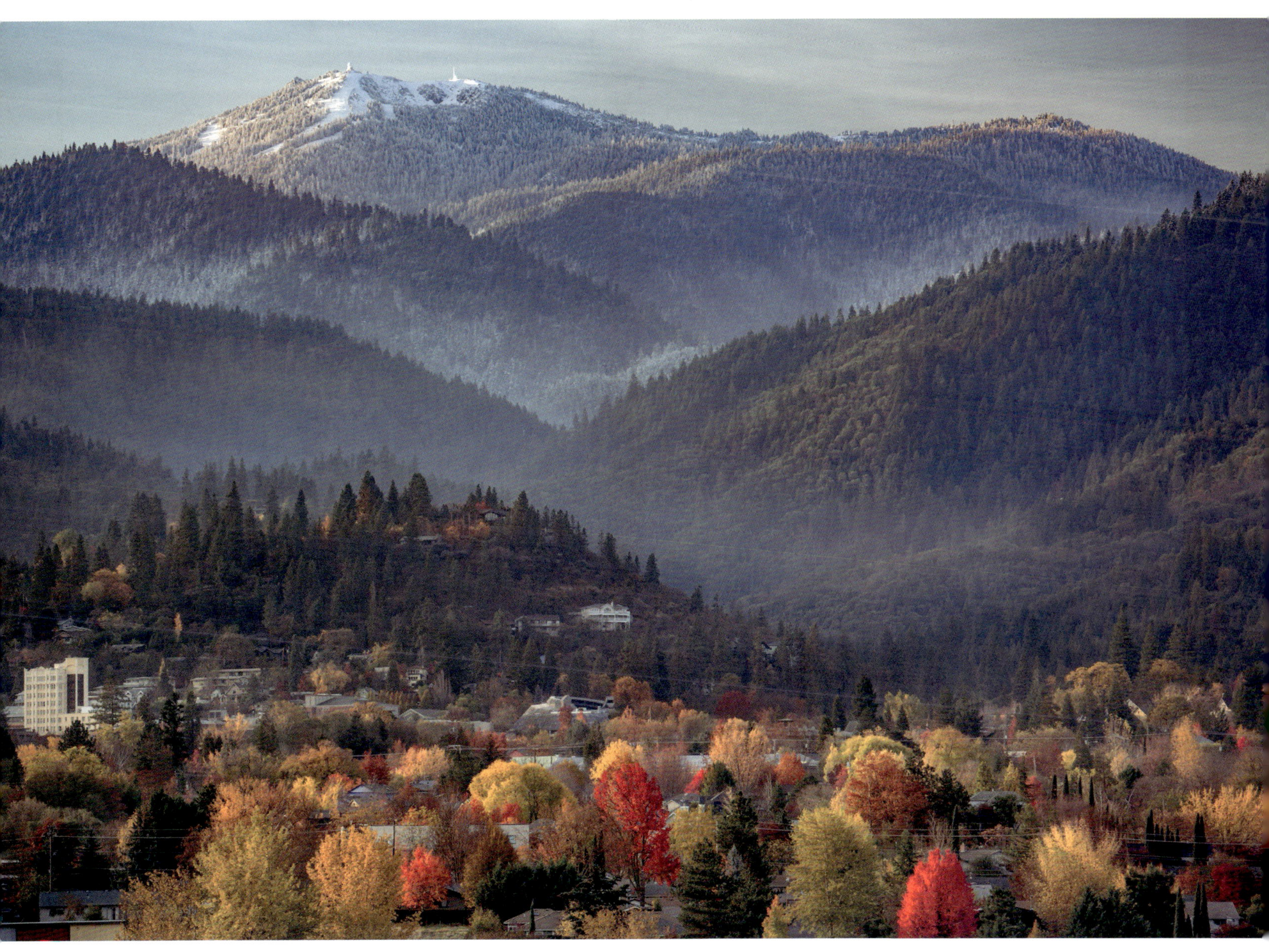

Ashland in the fall, with Mount Ashland in the background. *Photo by Sean Bagshaw.*   51

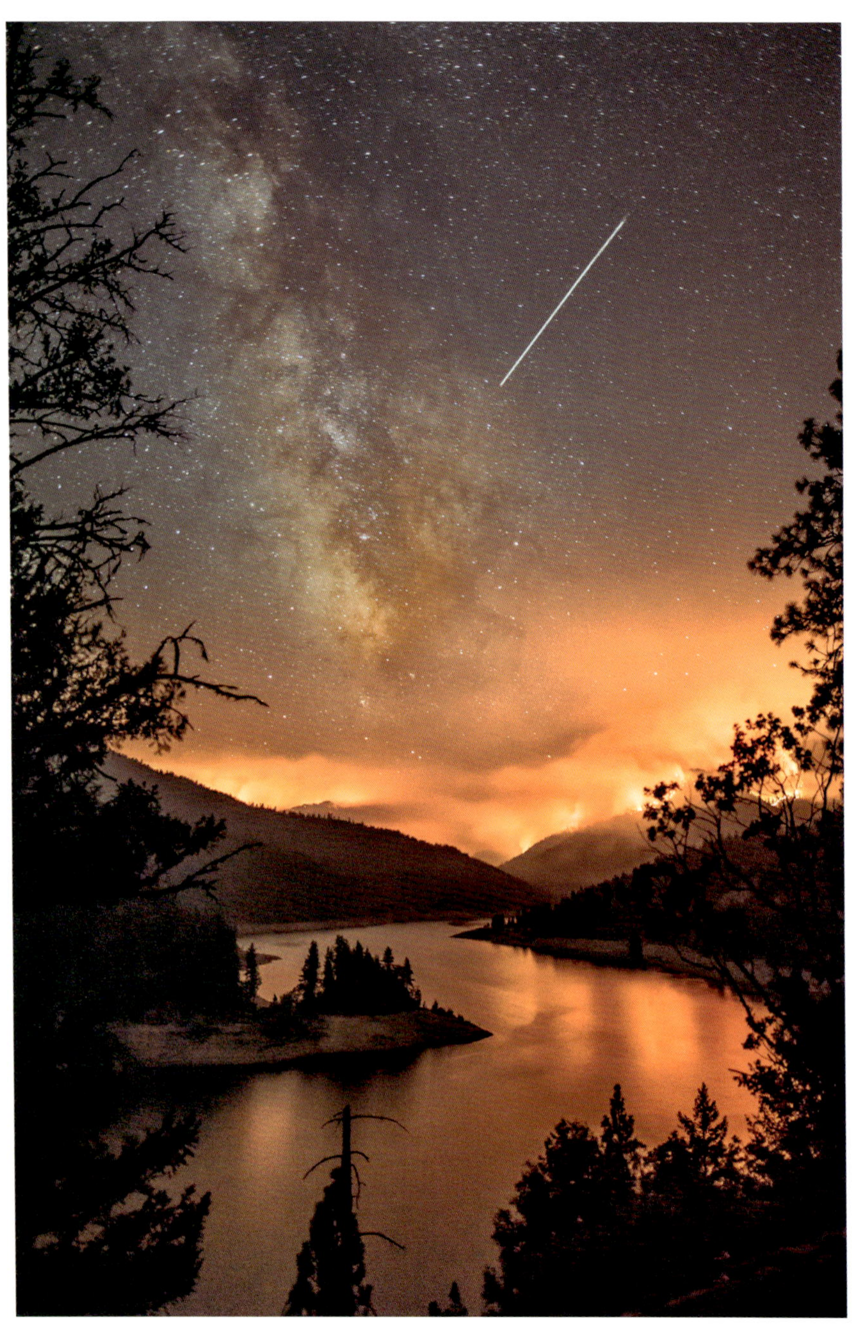

 Milky Way and fire at Applegate Lake. *Photo by Rudy Dierks.*

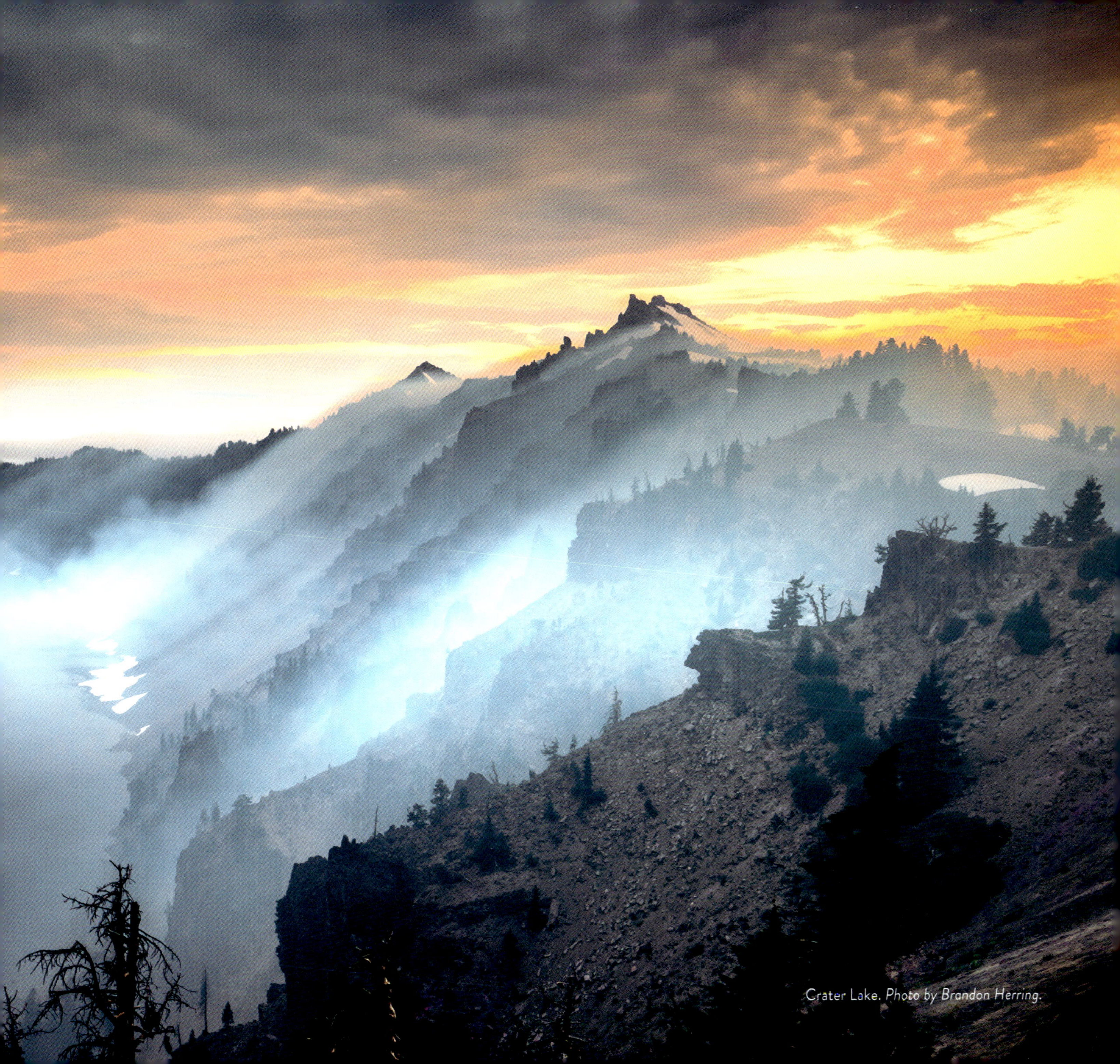

Crater Lake. Photo by Brandon Herring.

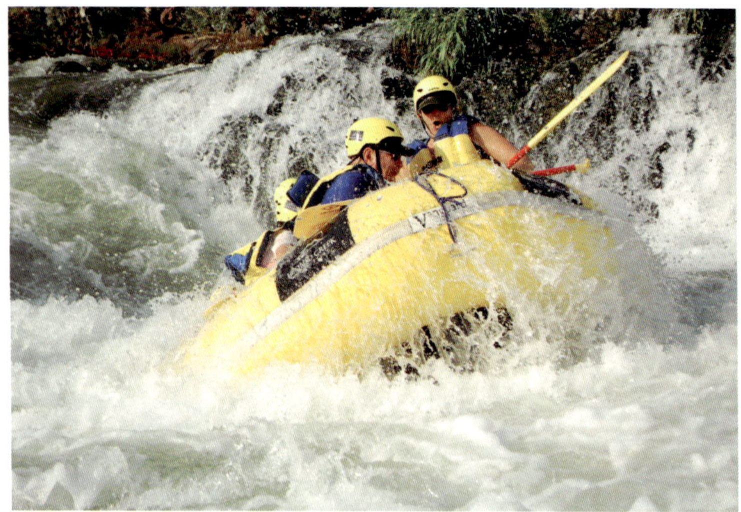

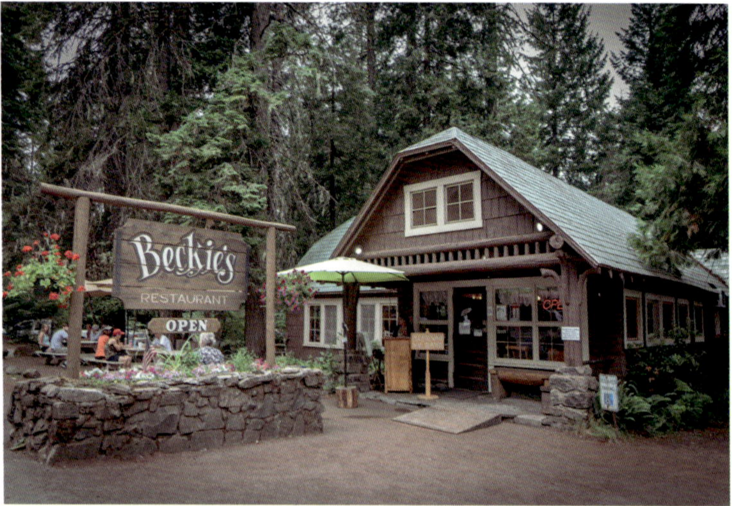

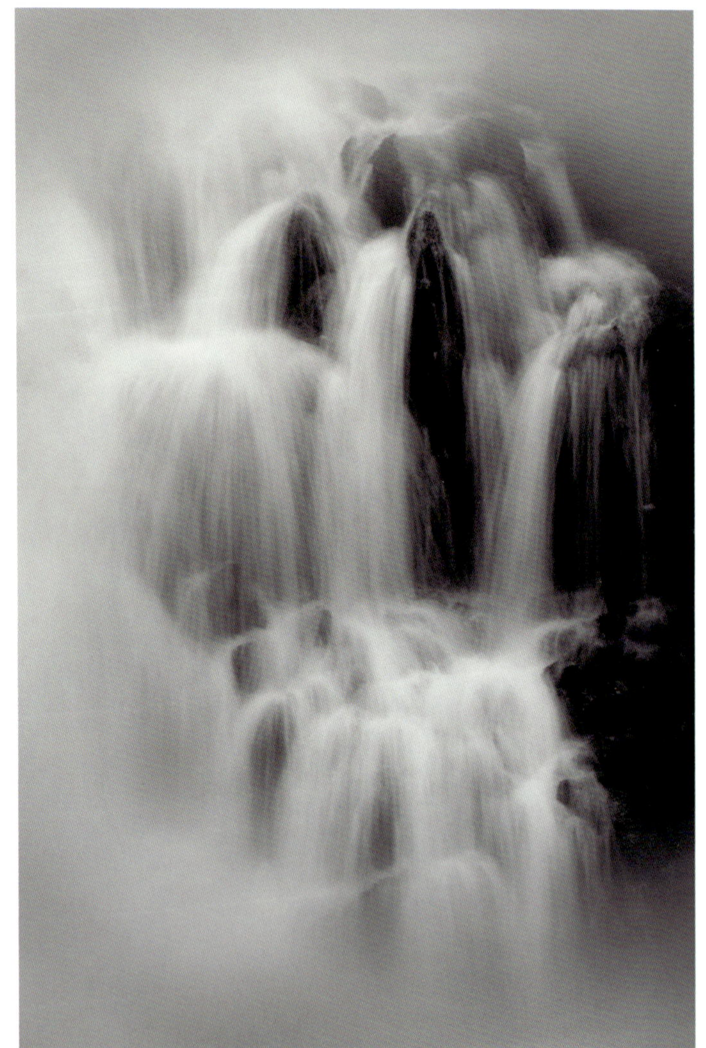

Rafting on Powerhouse Rapids through Ti'lomikh Falls, on the Rogue River. *Photo by Will Volpert, Indigo Creek Outfitters.*

Pearsony Falls, Prospect. *Photo by Julie Bonney.*

Beckie's Restaurant, built in 1926, Union Creek. *Photo by Barbara Tricarico.*

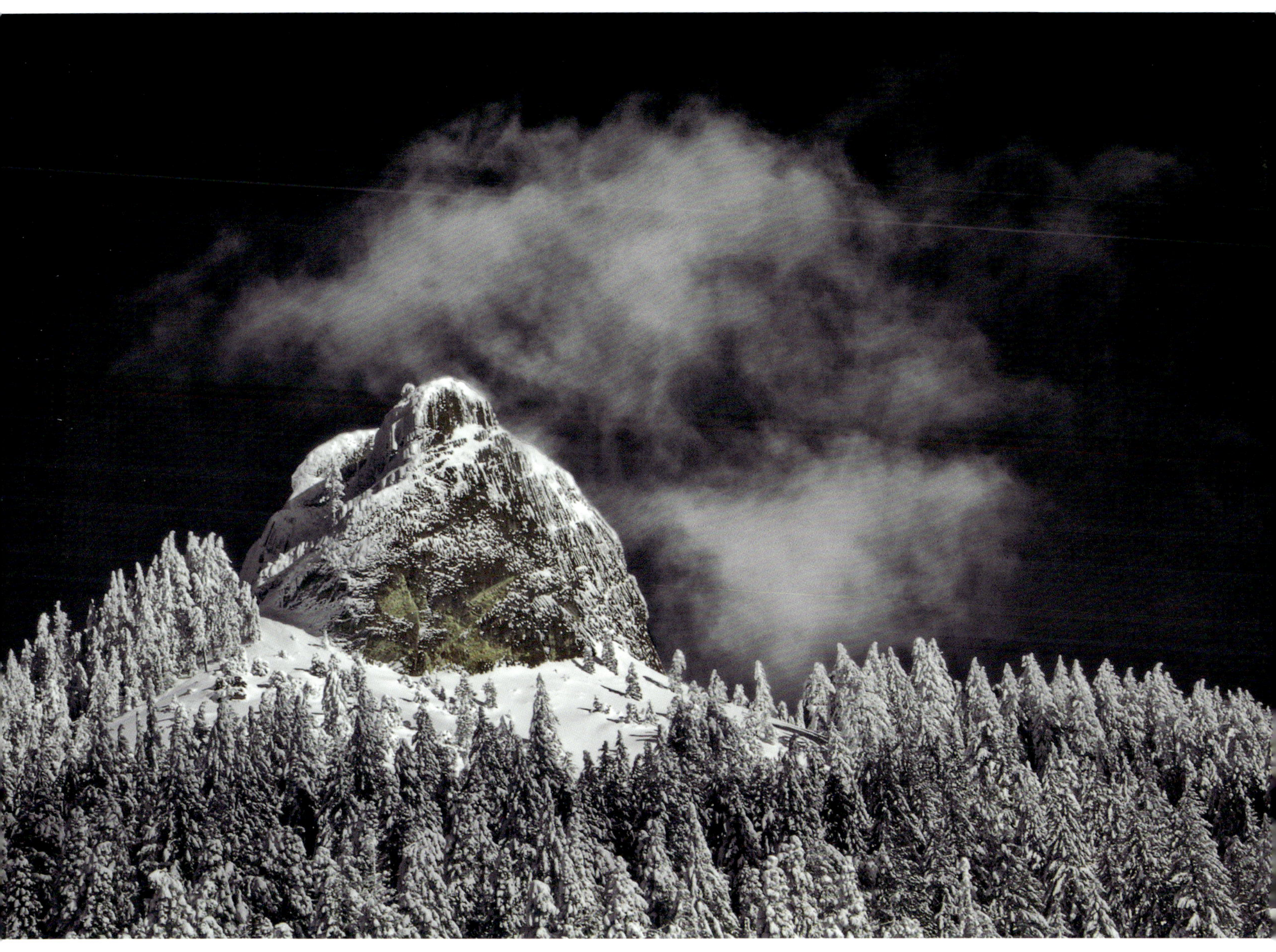

Pilot Rock in the Cascade-Siskiyou National Monument. *Photo by Matt Witt.*

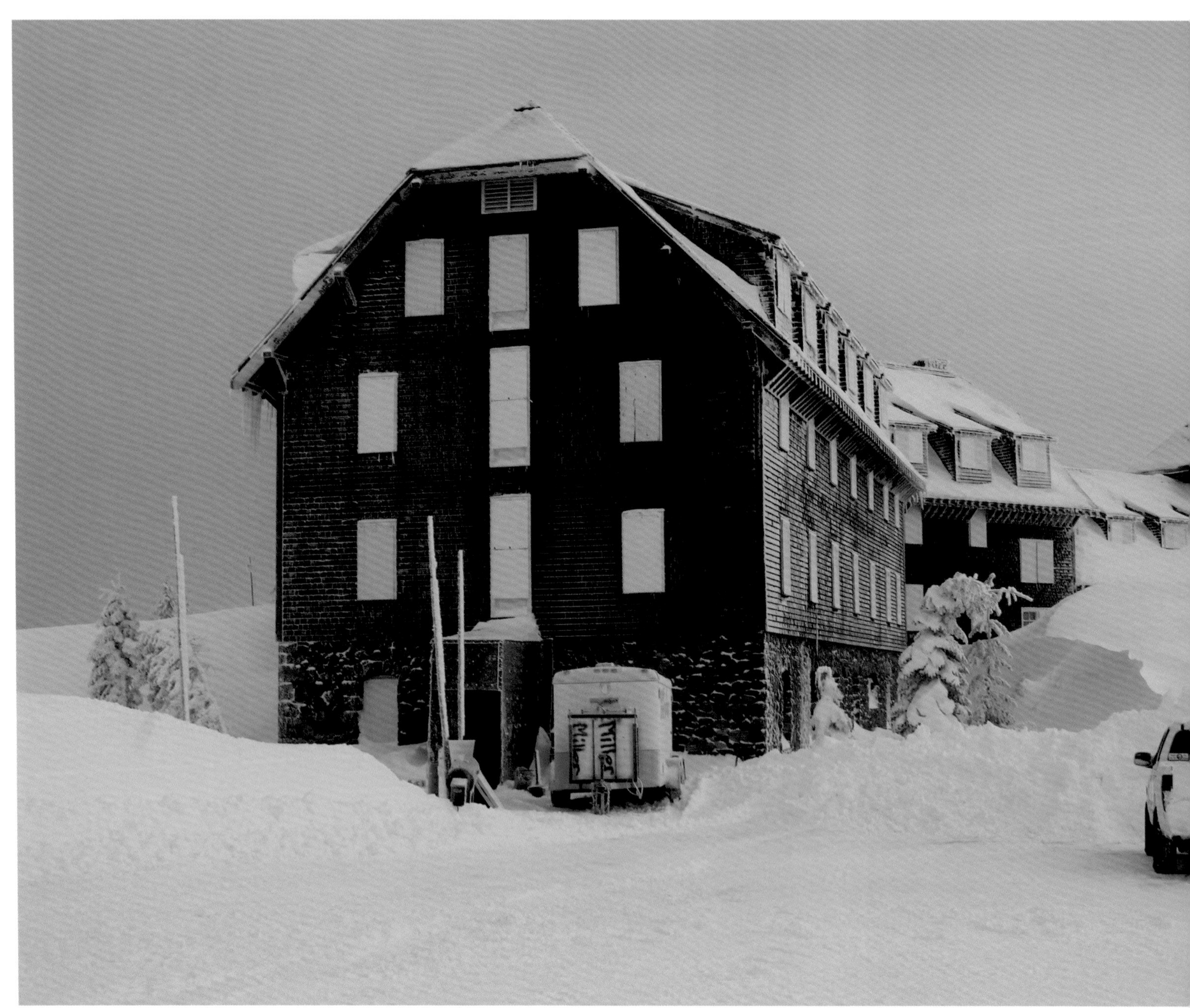

 Crater Lake Lodge. *Photo by John Kirk.*

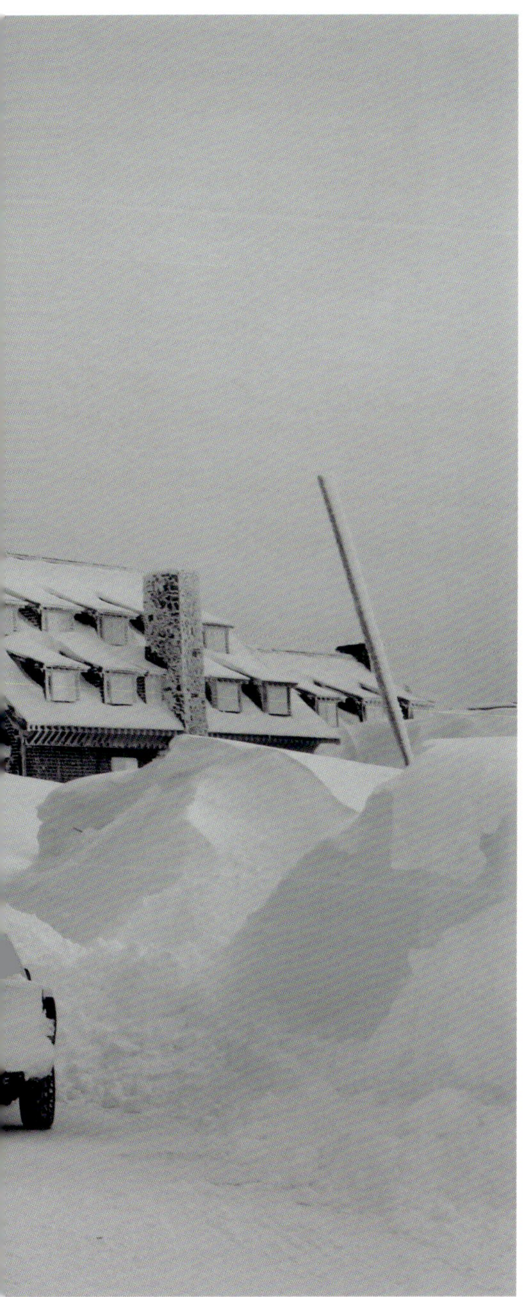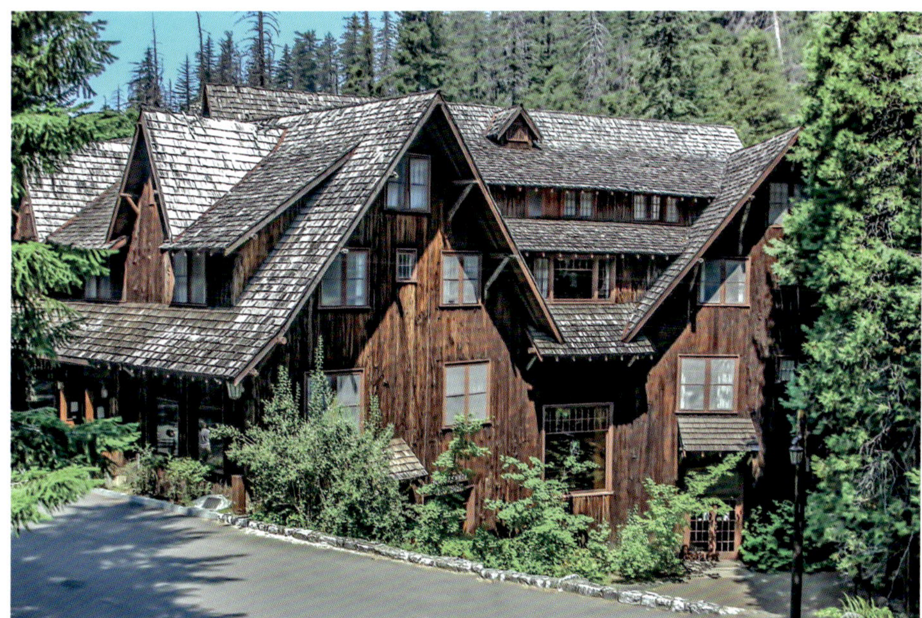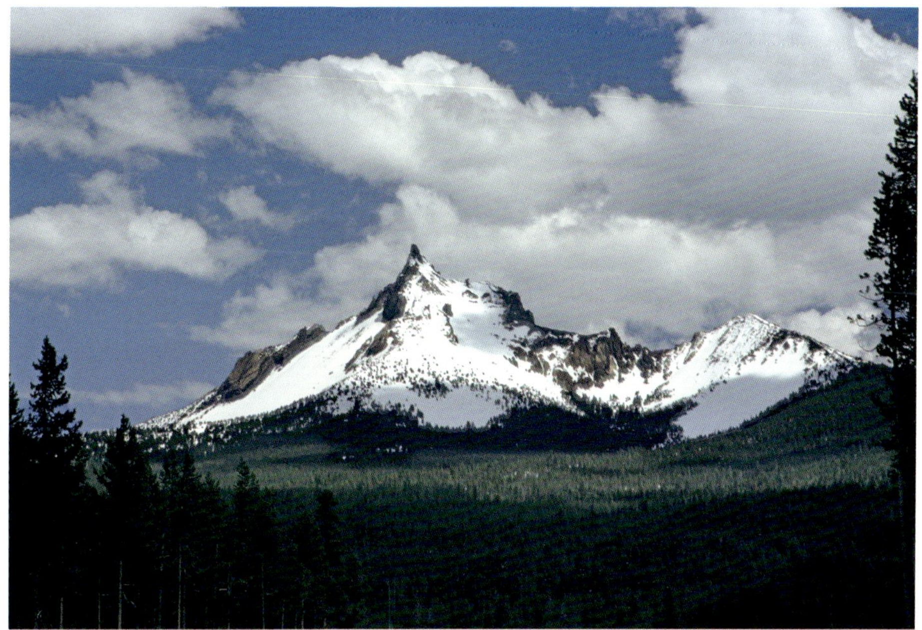

(Top) Oregon Caves Chateau, Cave Junction, built in 1934. *Photo by George F. Peterson.* • (Bottom) Mount Thielsen. *Photo by Nomeca Hartwell.*

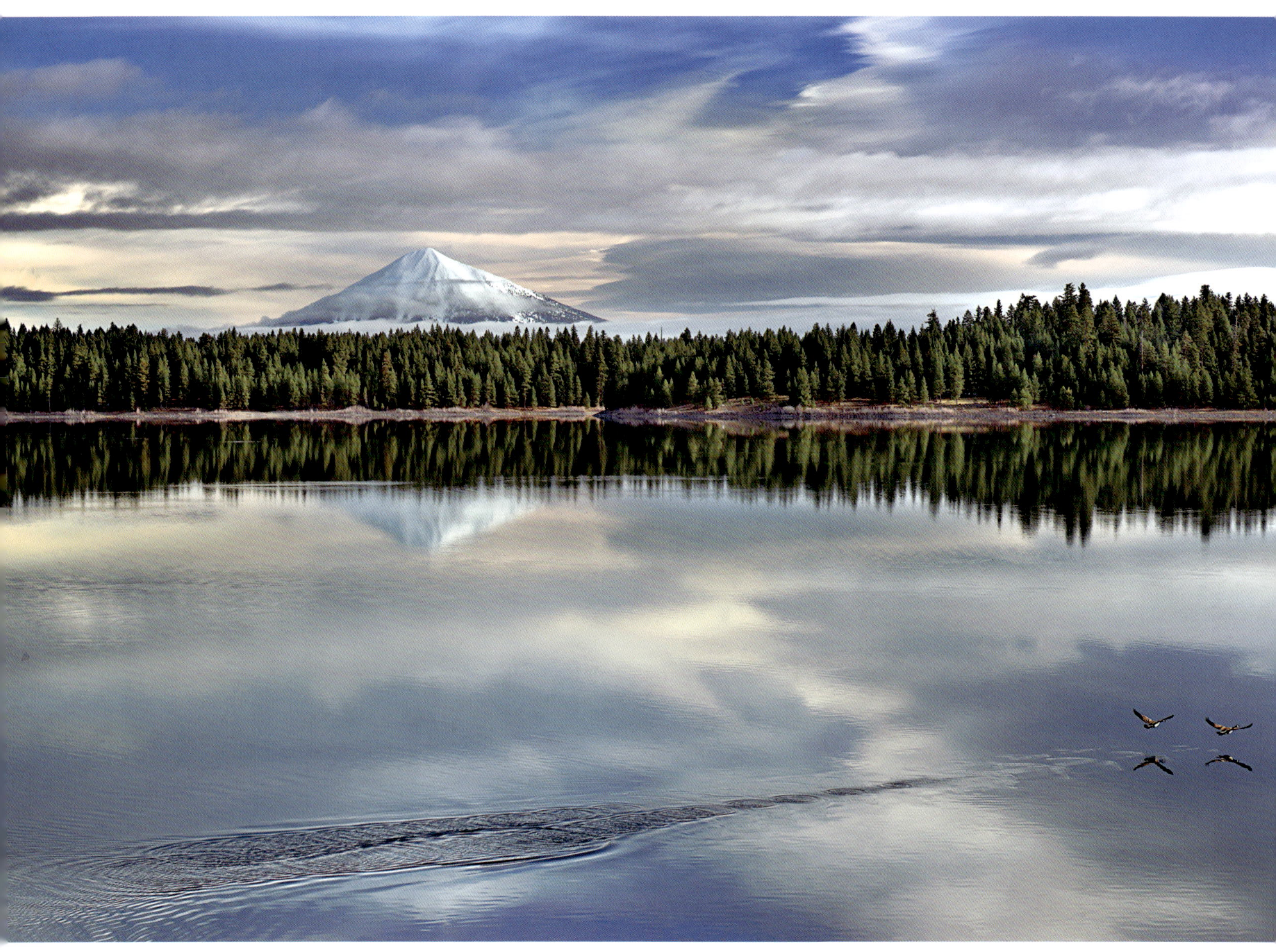

Howard Prairie Lake and Mount McLaughlin. *Photo by Jim Craven.*

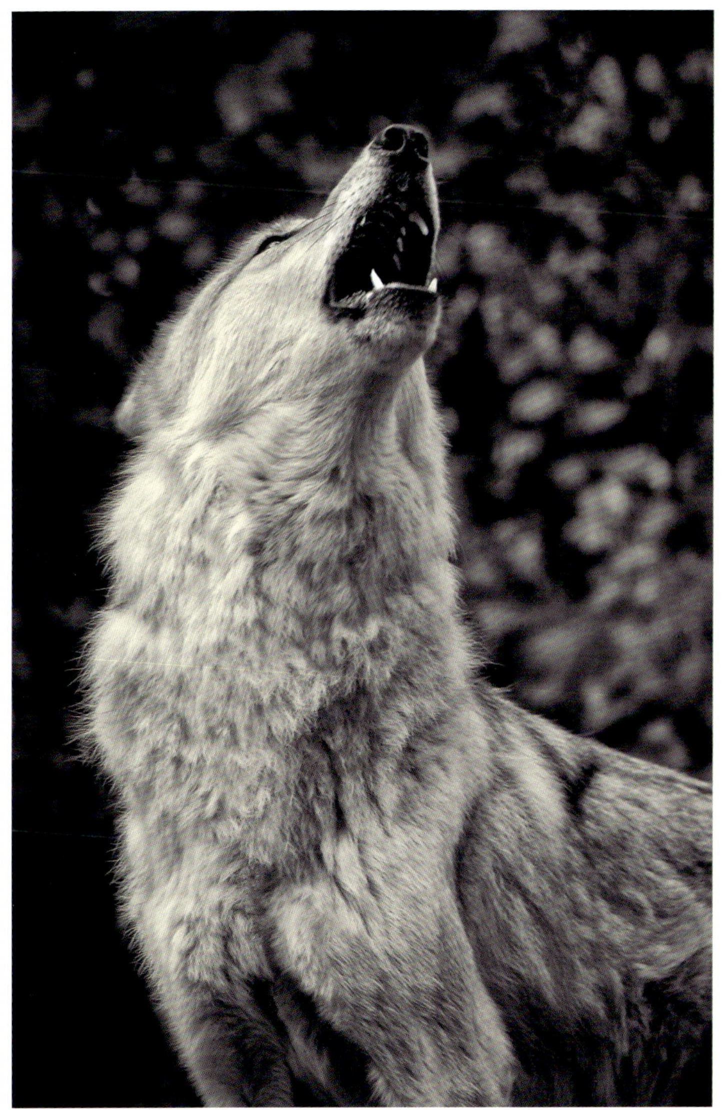

Howling wolf at Wildlife Images Rehabilitation and Education Center. *Photo by Judy Benson LaNier.*

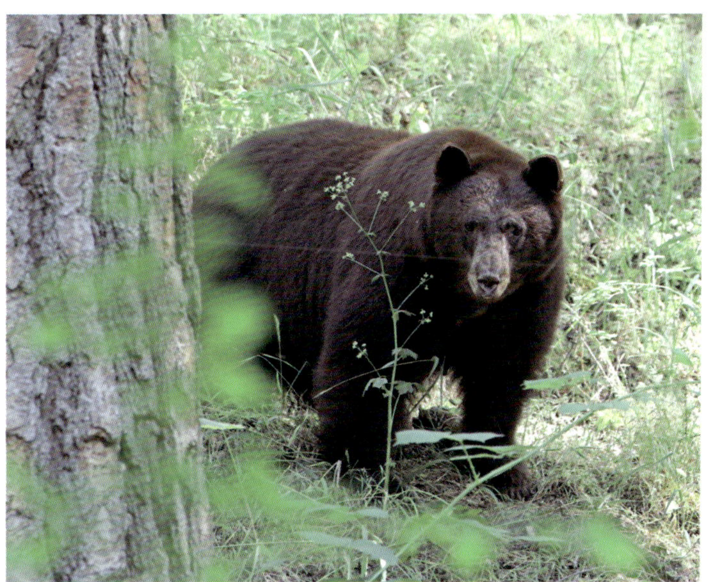

Black bear. *Photo by Dan Elster.*

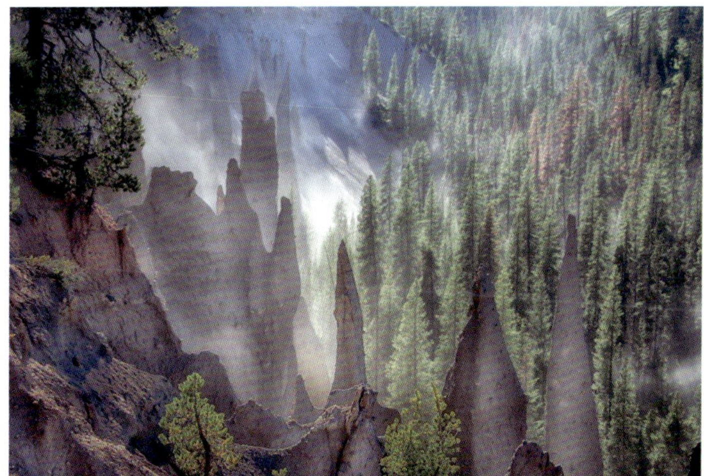

The Pinnacles at Crater Lake National Park. *Photo by Barbara Tricarico.*

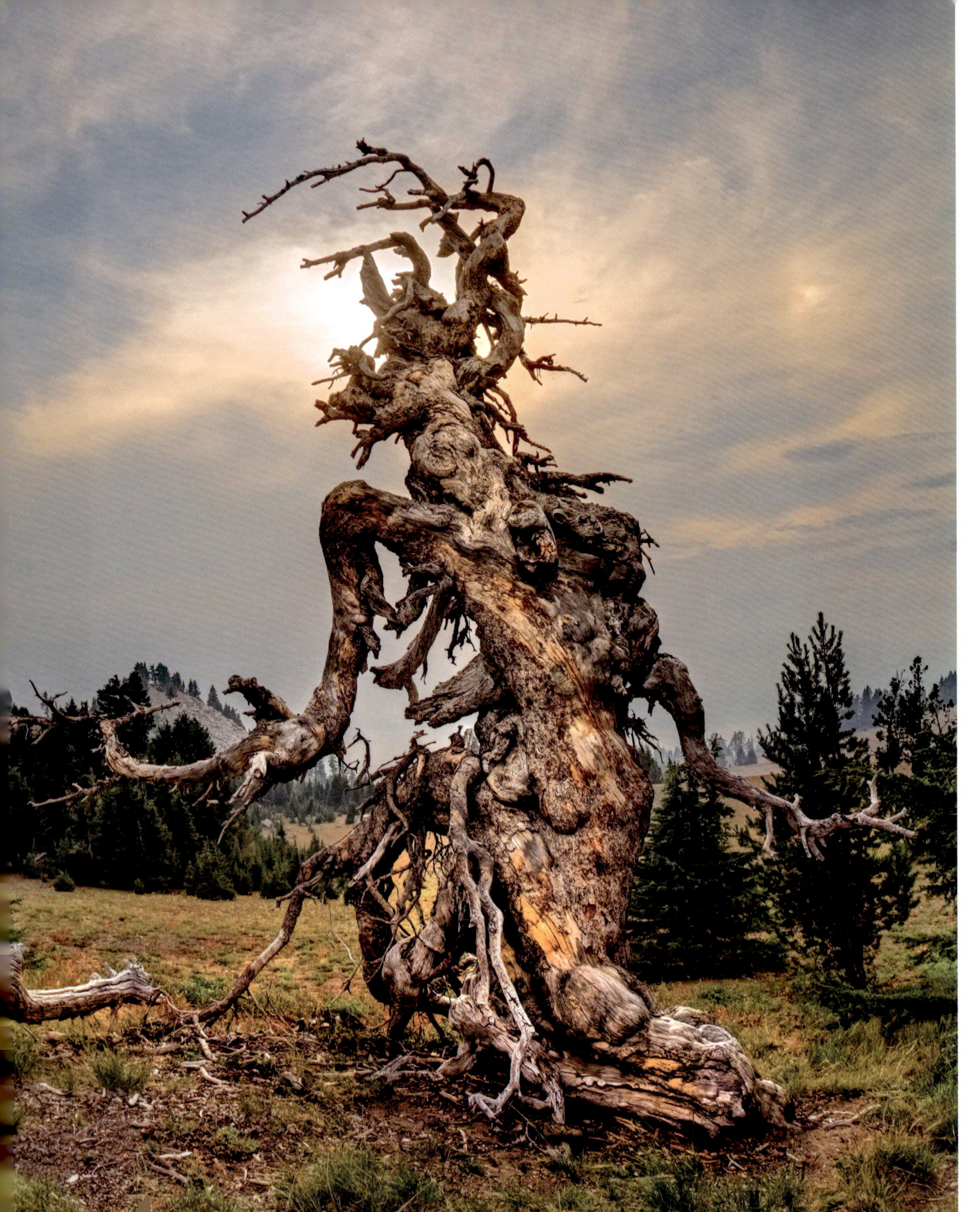

The Goddess Tree across from the Watchman Peak trailhead, Crater Lake. *Photo by Sue Newman.*

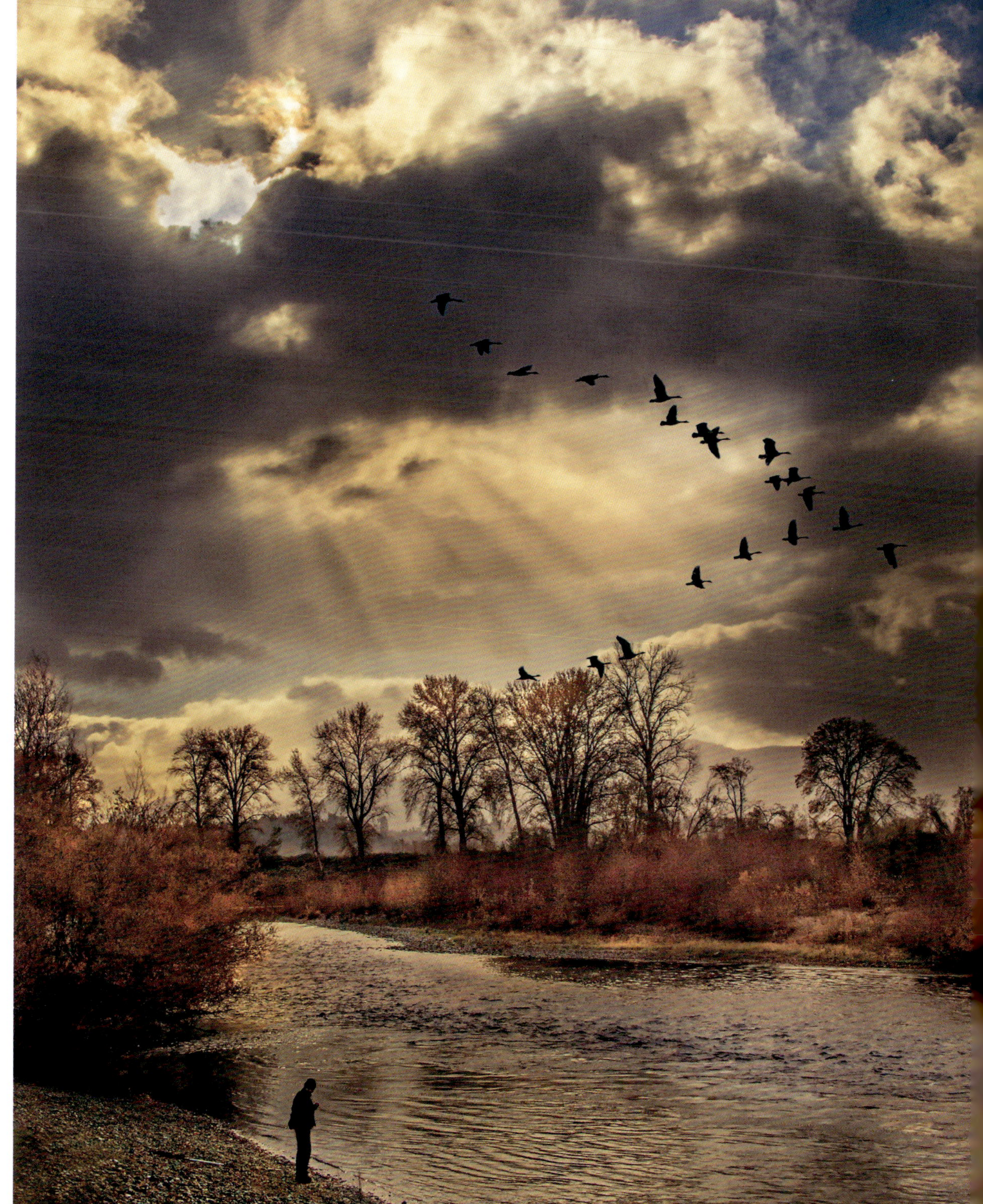

Rogue River, Grants Pass.
Photo by Neal R. Thompson.

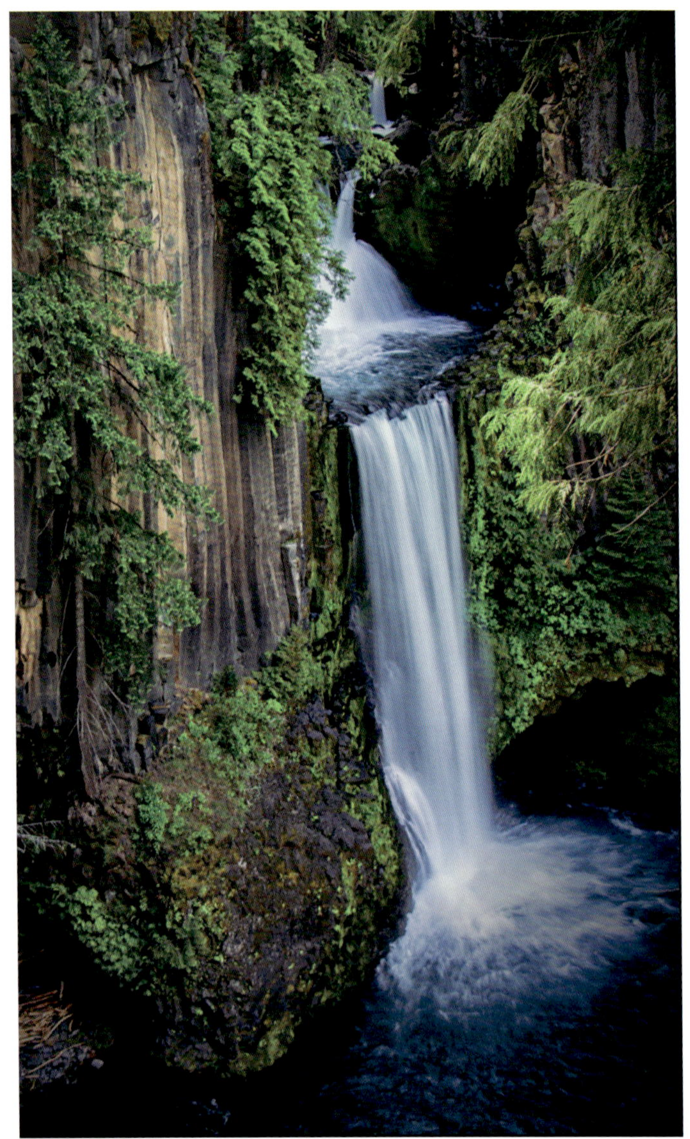

Toketee Falls. *Photo by Alana Lynn Starkweather.*

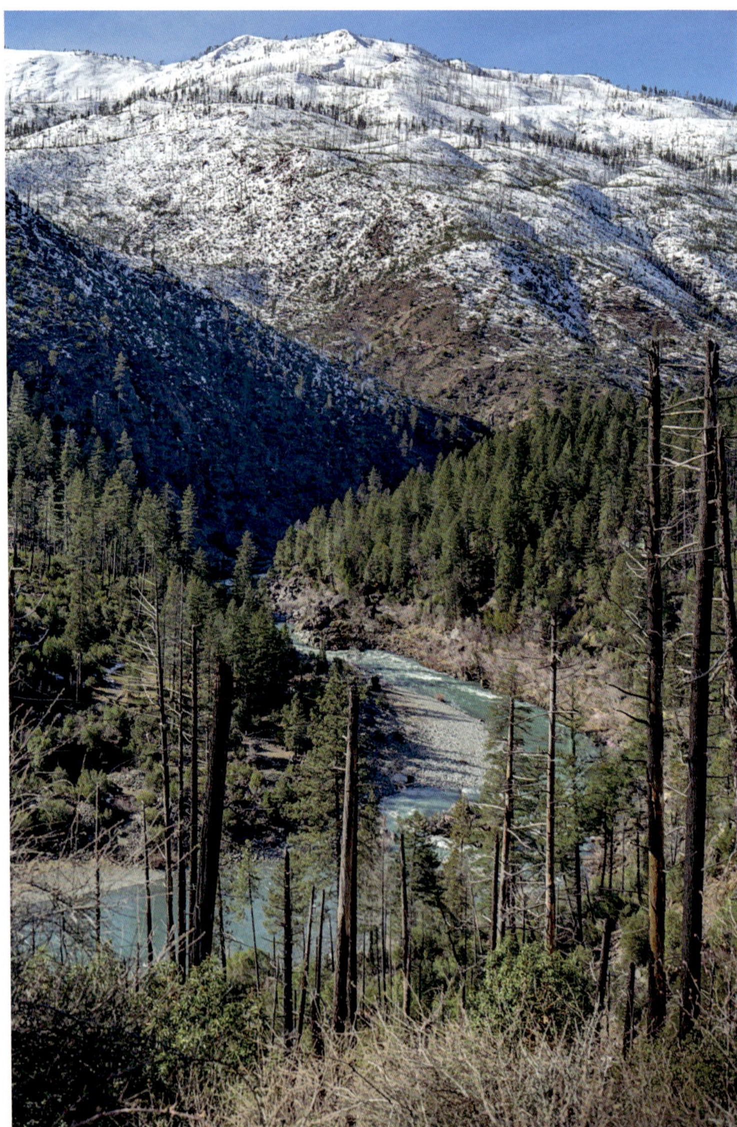

Illinois River. *Photo by Alana Lynn Starkweather.*

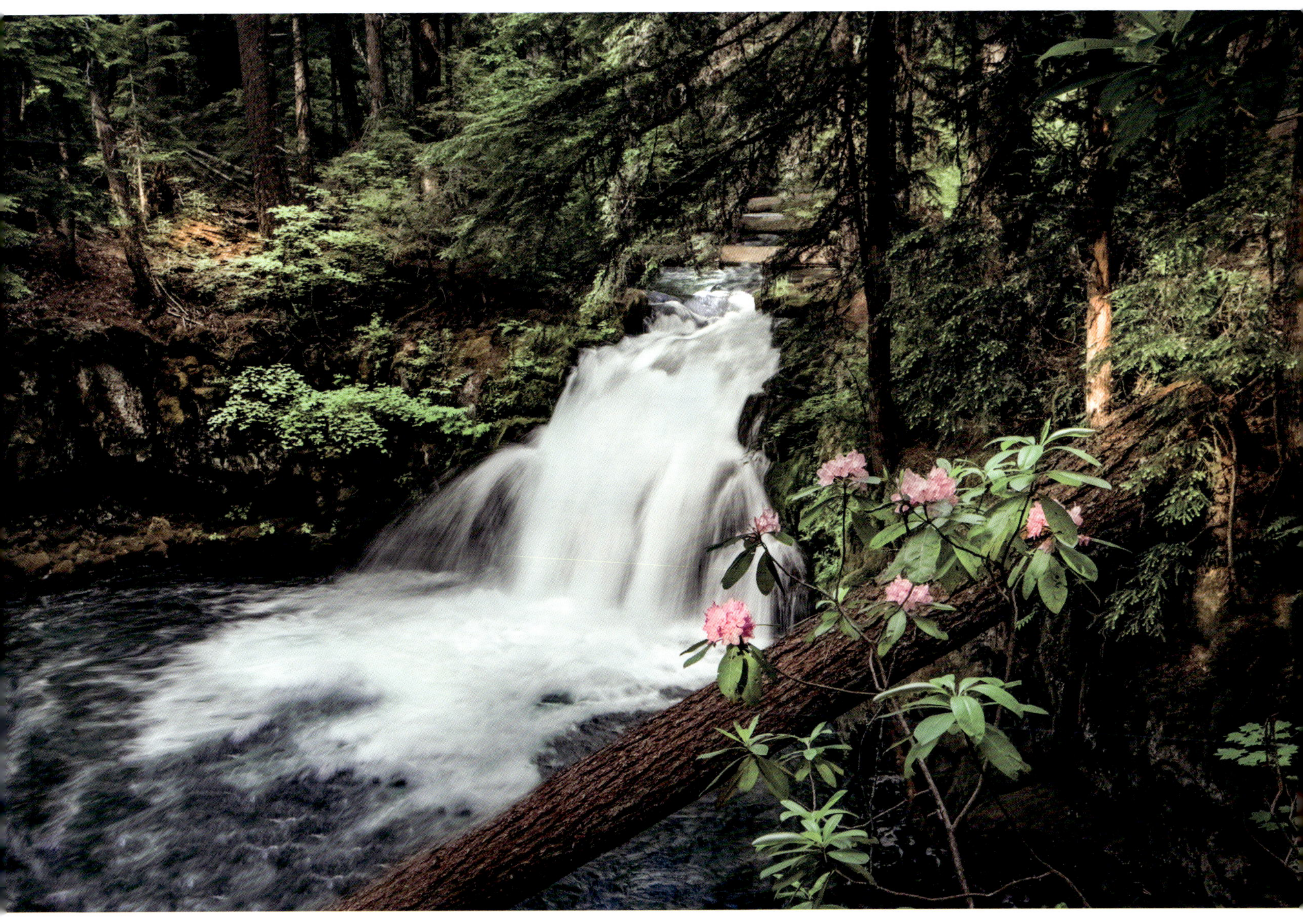

Whitehorse Falls, Umpqua National Forest. *Photo by Sue Stendebach.*

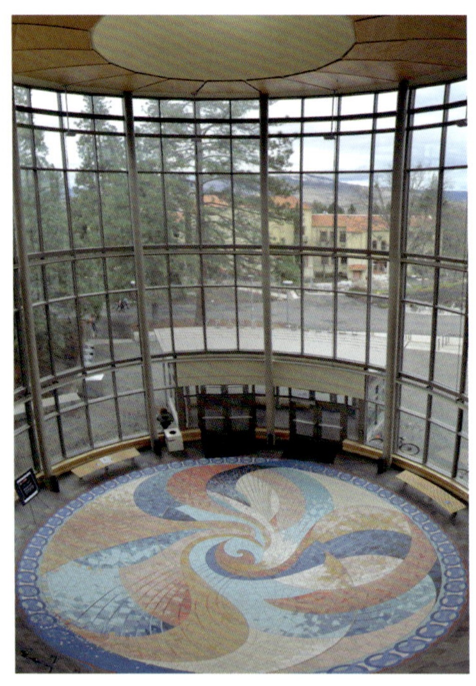

Hannon Library rotunda, Southern Oregon University, Ashland. *Resonance & Dispersion* mosaic by Robert Stout and Stephanie Jurs. *Photo by Barbara Tricarico.*

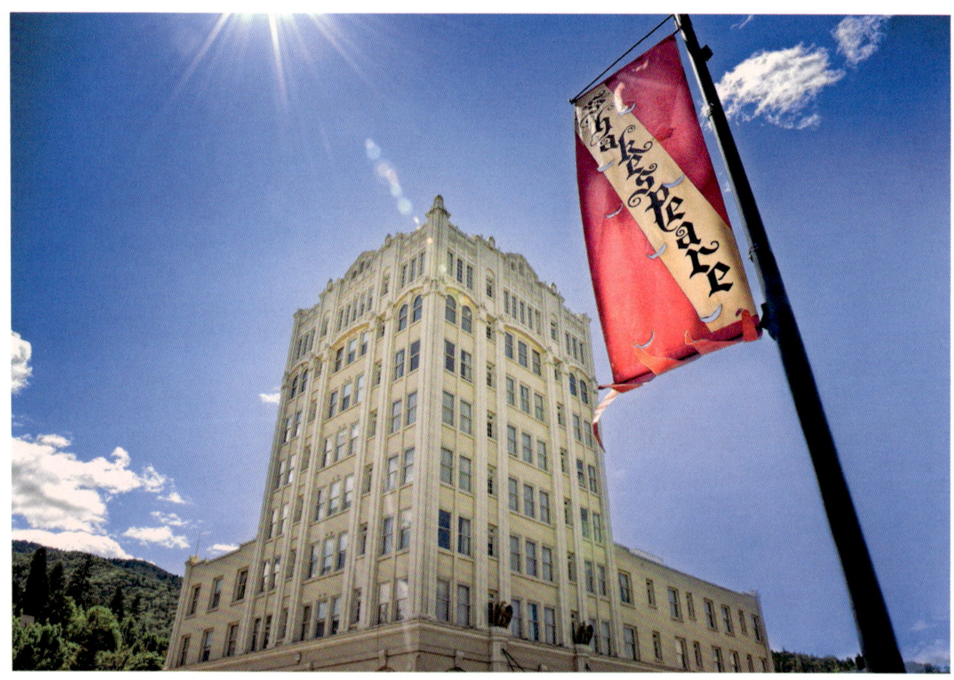

Ashland Springs Hotel, Ashland, built in 1925. *Photo by Barbara Tricarico.*

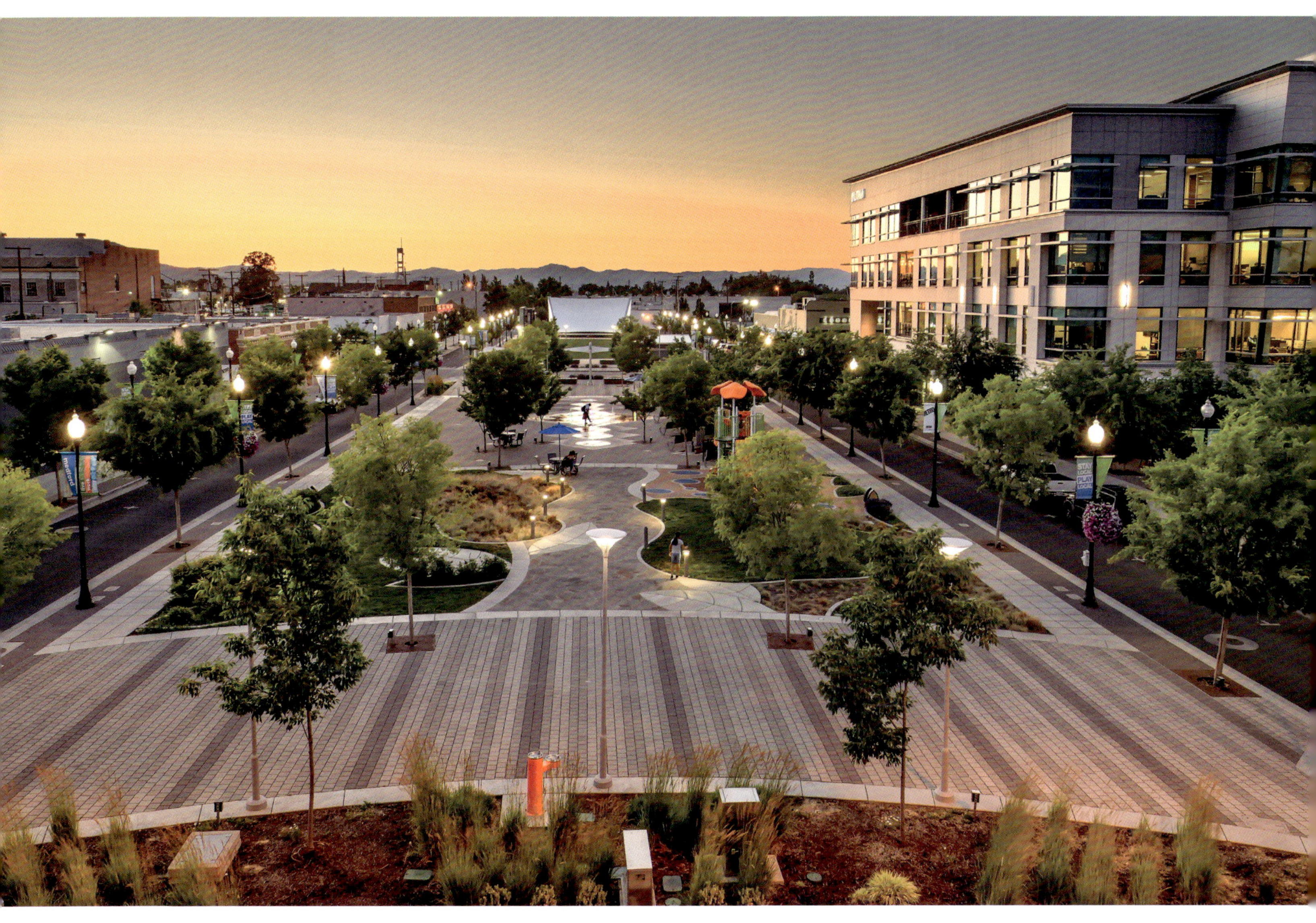

Pear Blossom Park is a vibrant gathering spot in Medford. It hosts music concerts, a Christmas tree lighting, rallies, and community events. *Photo by Jim Craven.*

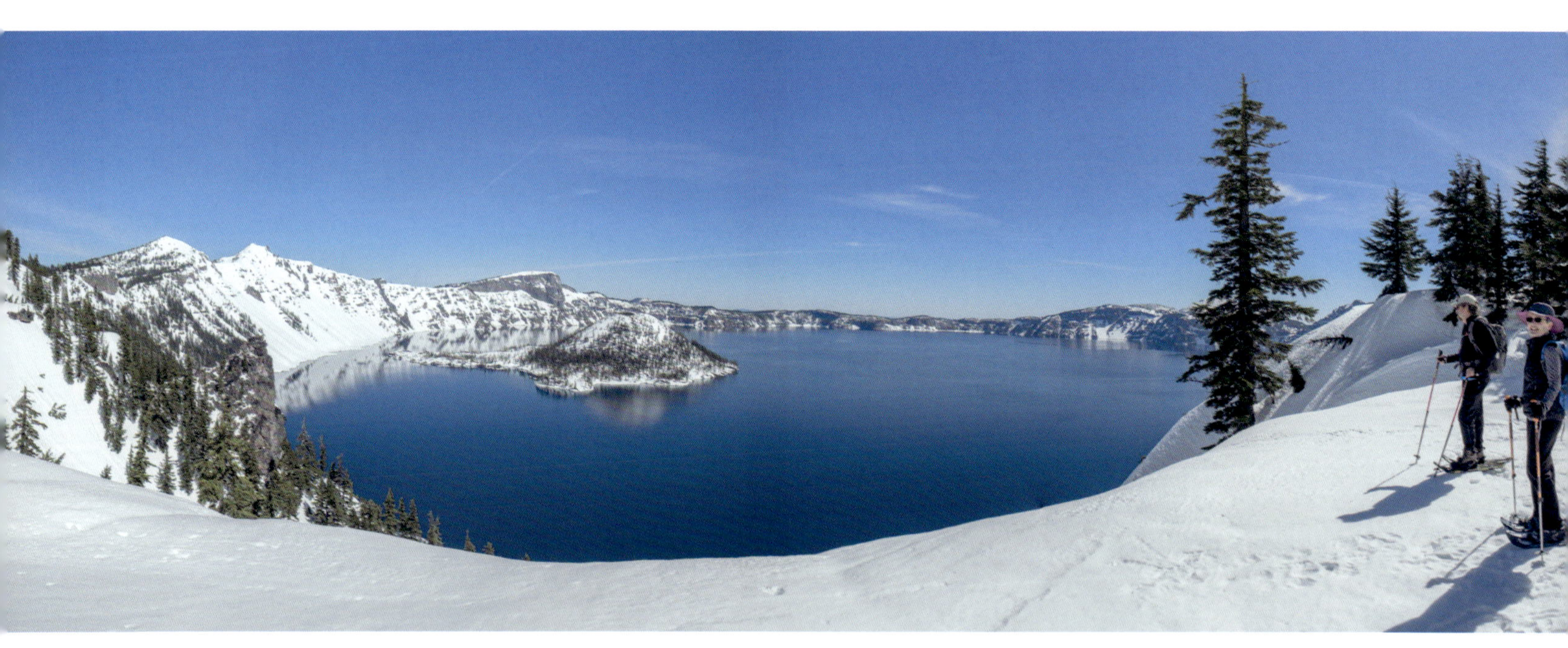

 Crater Lake. *Photo by Bob Palermini.*

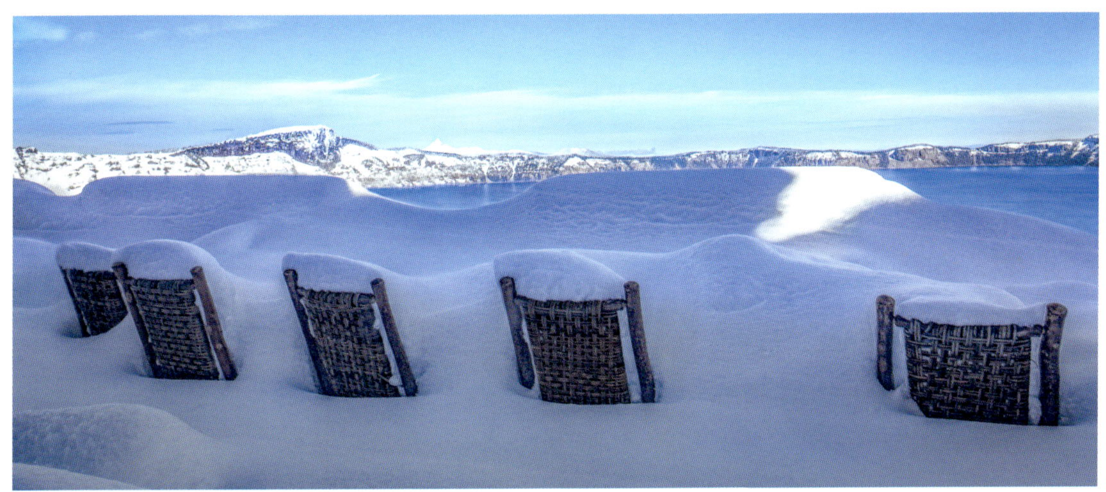

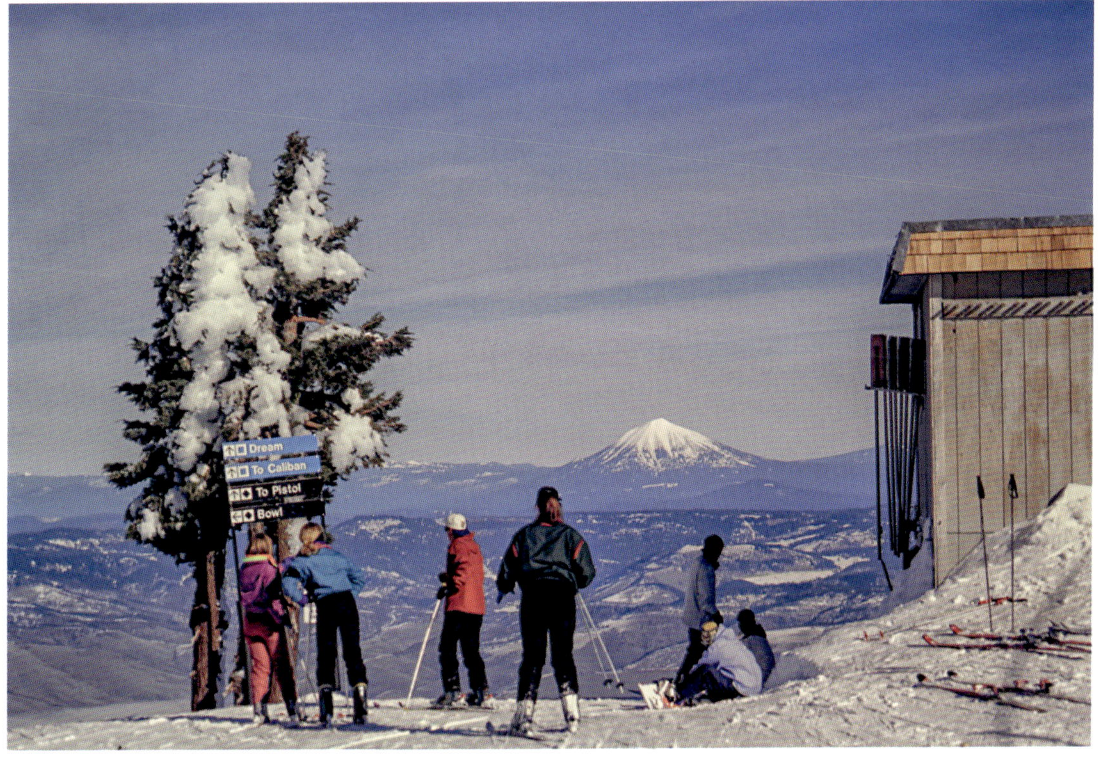

(Top) Winter view from Crater Lake Lodge. *Photo by Sue Stendebach.* • (Bottom) Mount Ashland skiers, with Mount Shasta in the distance. *Photo by Ken Deveney.*

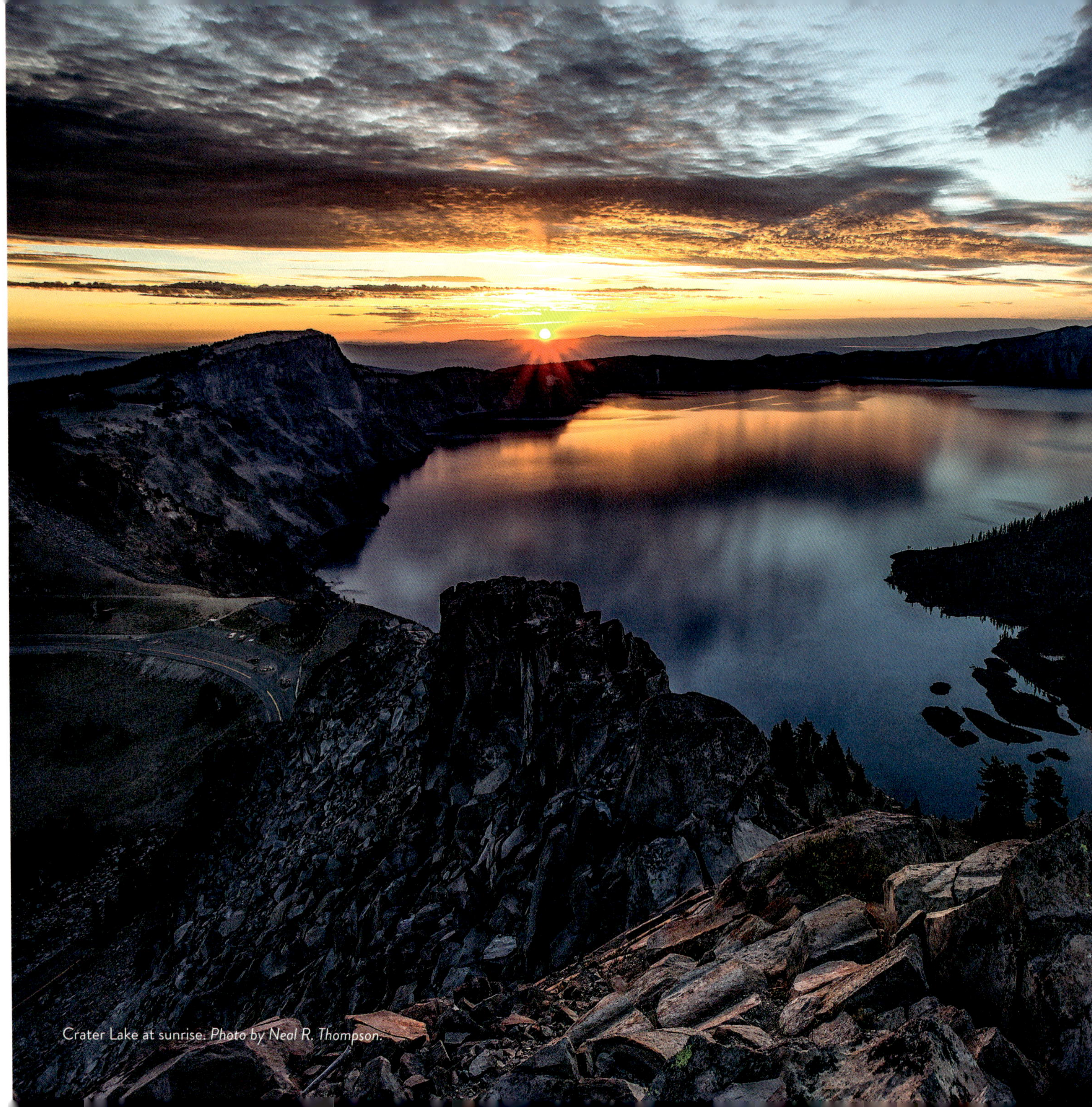

Crater Lake at sunrise. *Photo by Neal R. Thompson.*

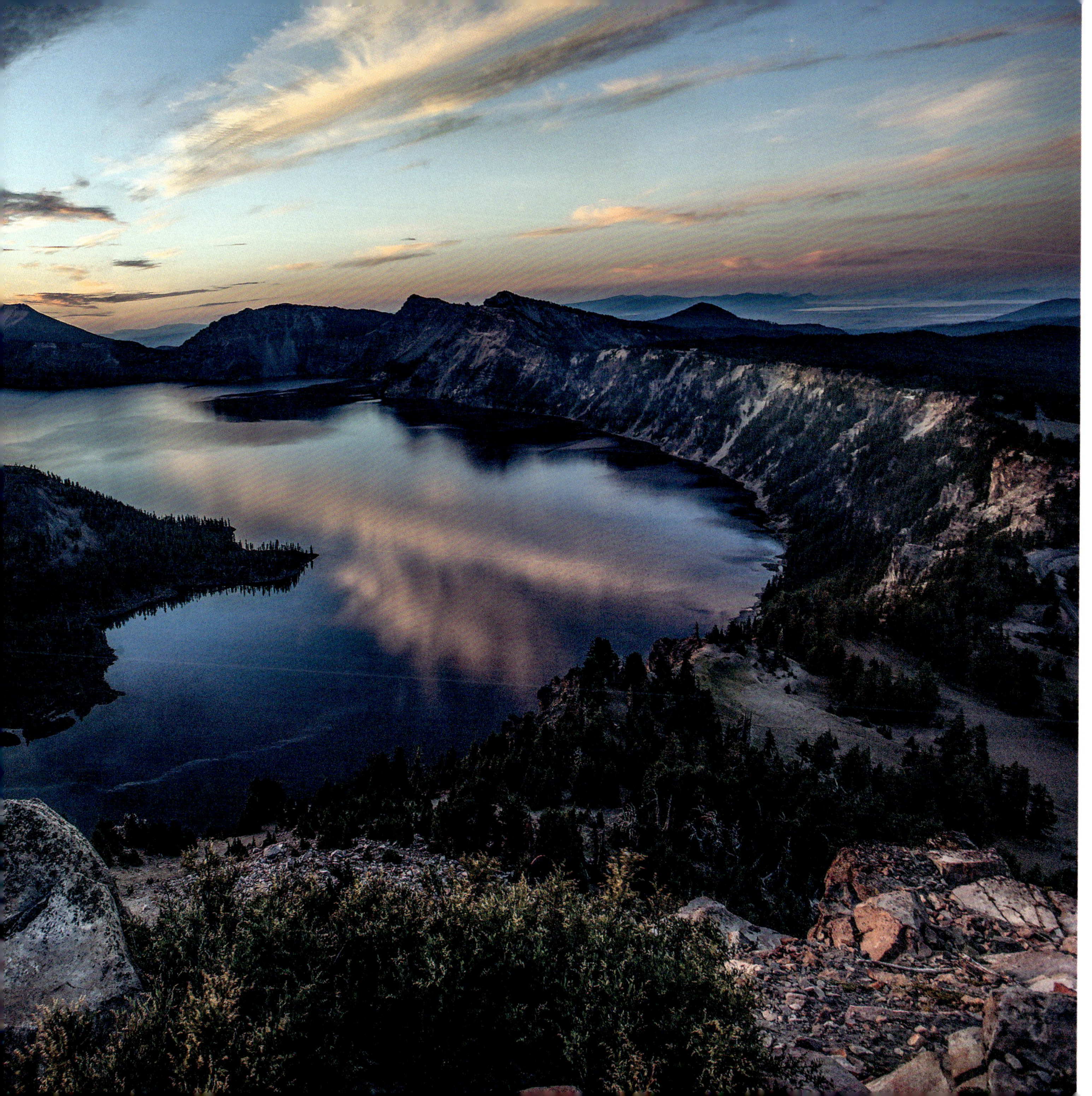

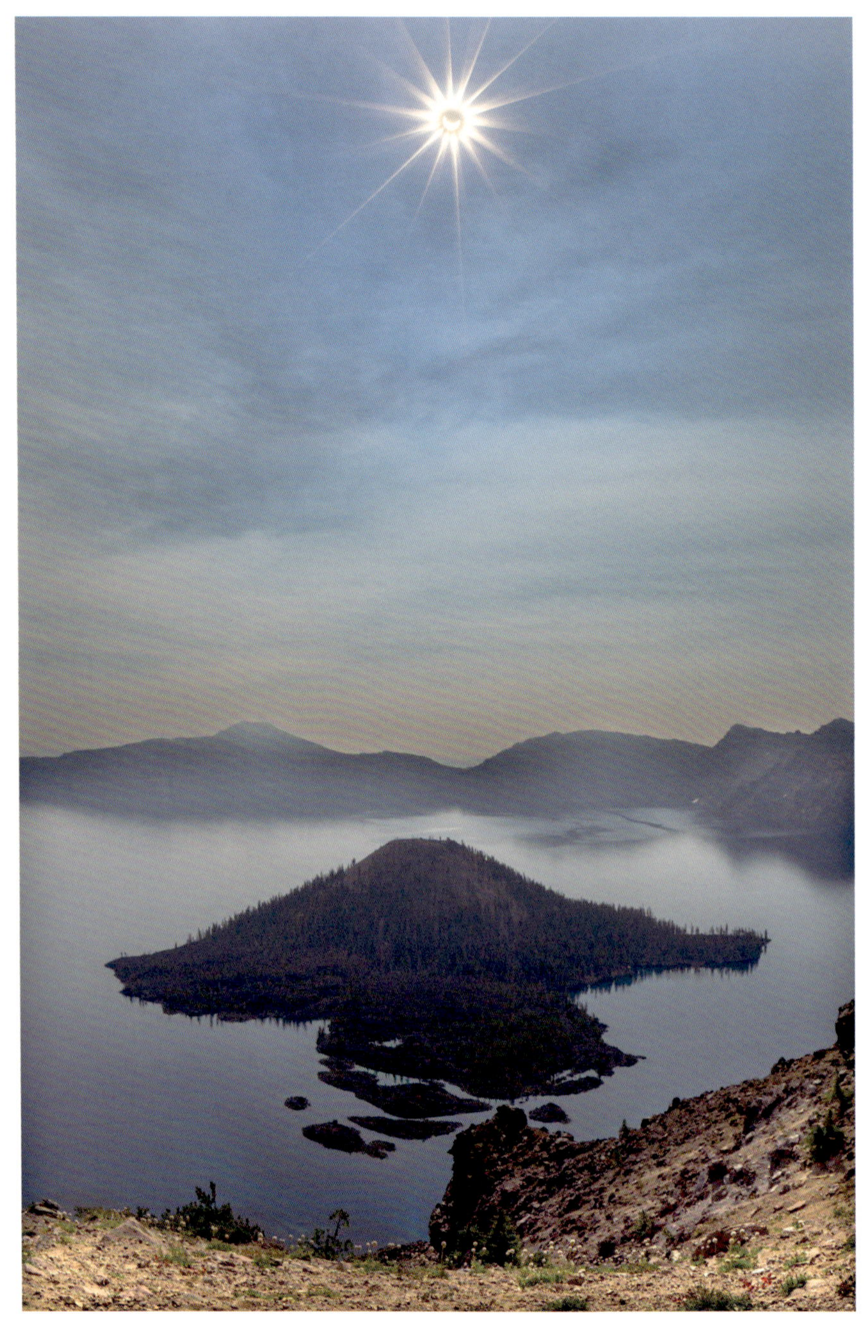

 Solar eclipse over Wizard Island, Crater Lake. *Photo by Sue Newman.* • (Opposite) Phantom Ship at Crater Lake. *Photo by Neal R. Thompson.*

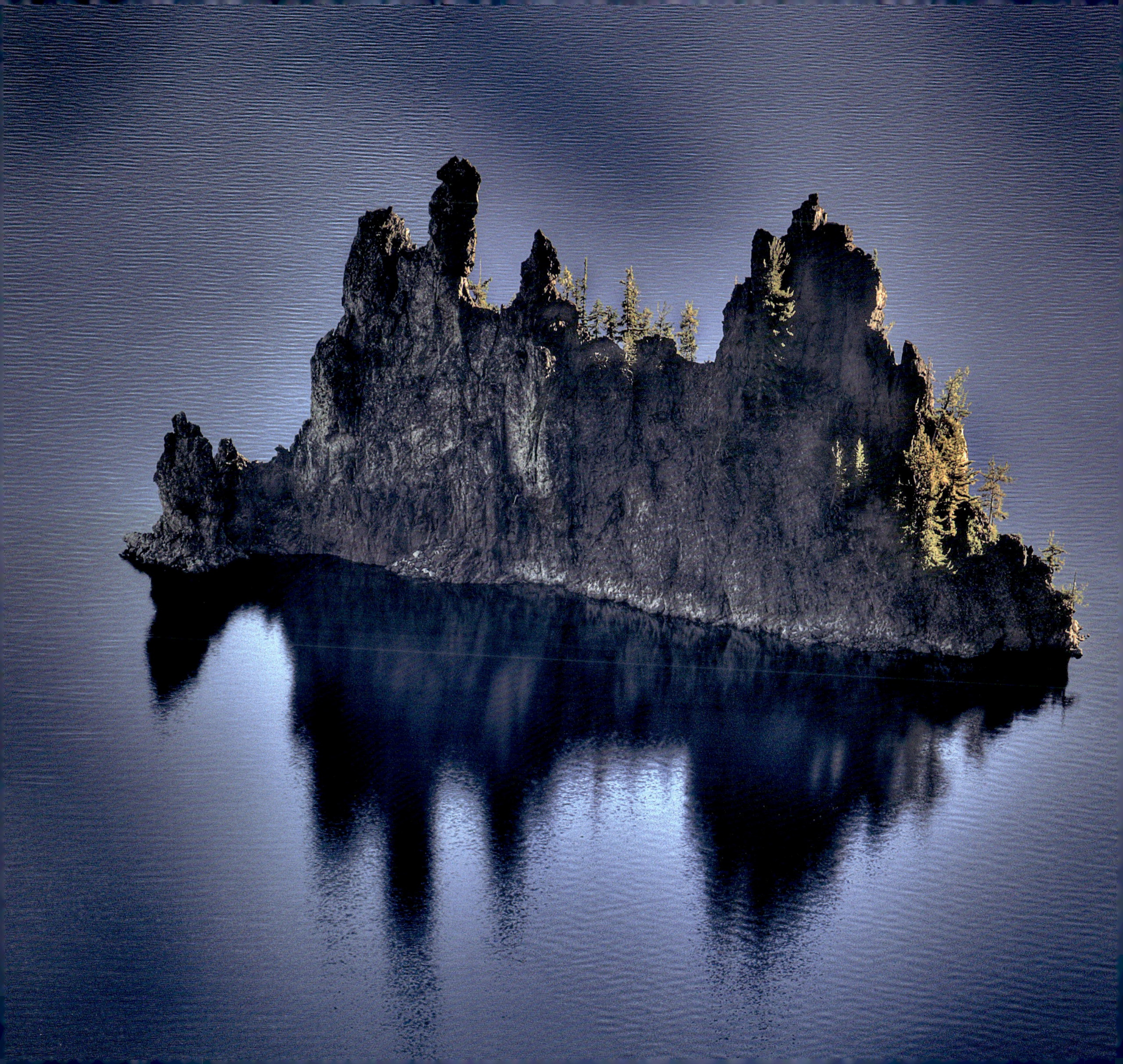

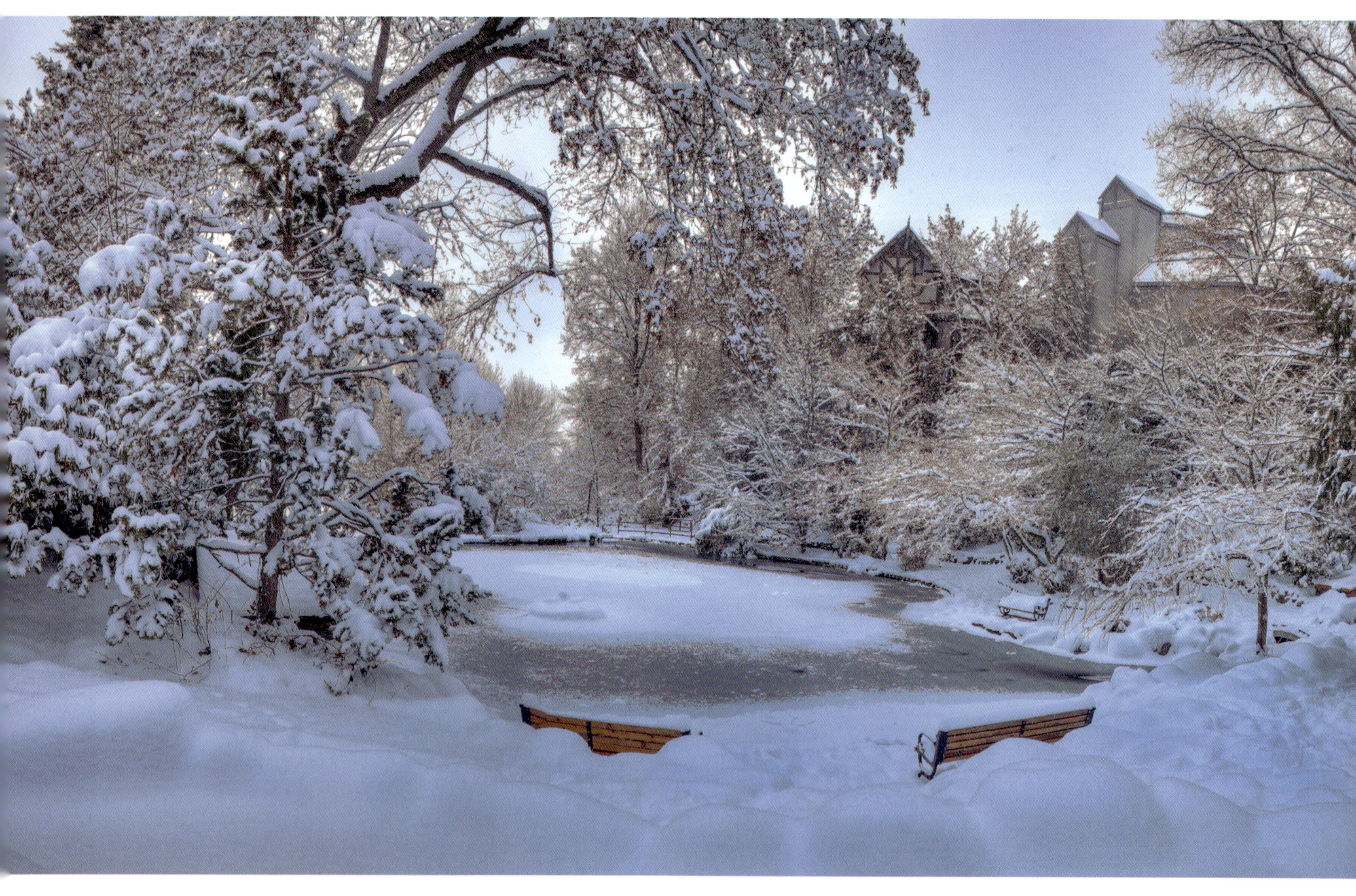

Lithia Park's Lower Duck Pond, with Oregon Shakespeare Festival's Elizabethan Theatre in background, Ashland. *Photo by Neal R. Thompson.*

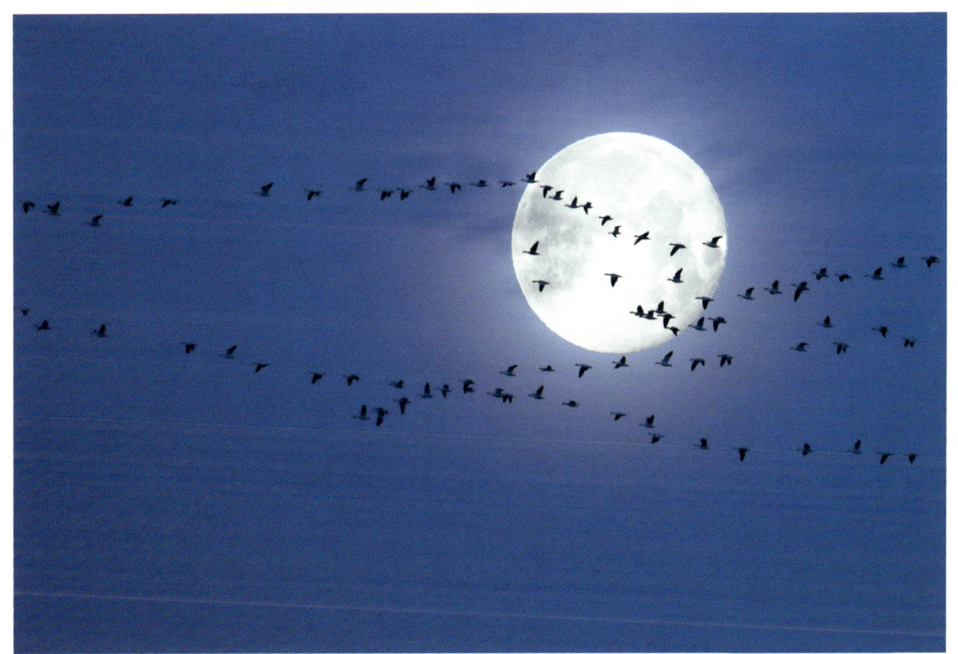

Snow geese and moon. *Photo by Dan Elster.*

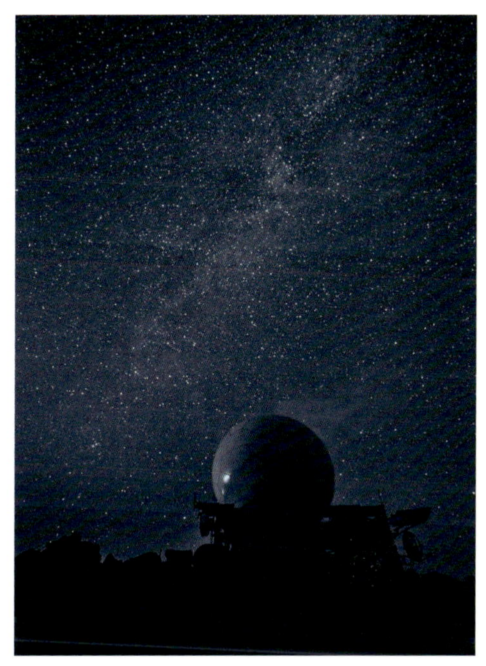

Mount Ashland Radar Sphere and Milky Way.
Photo by Neal R. Thompson.

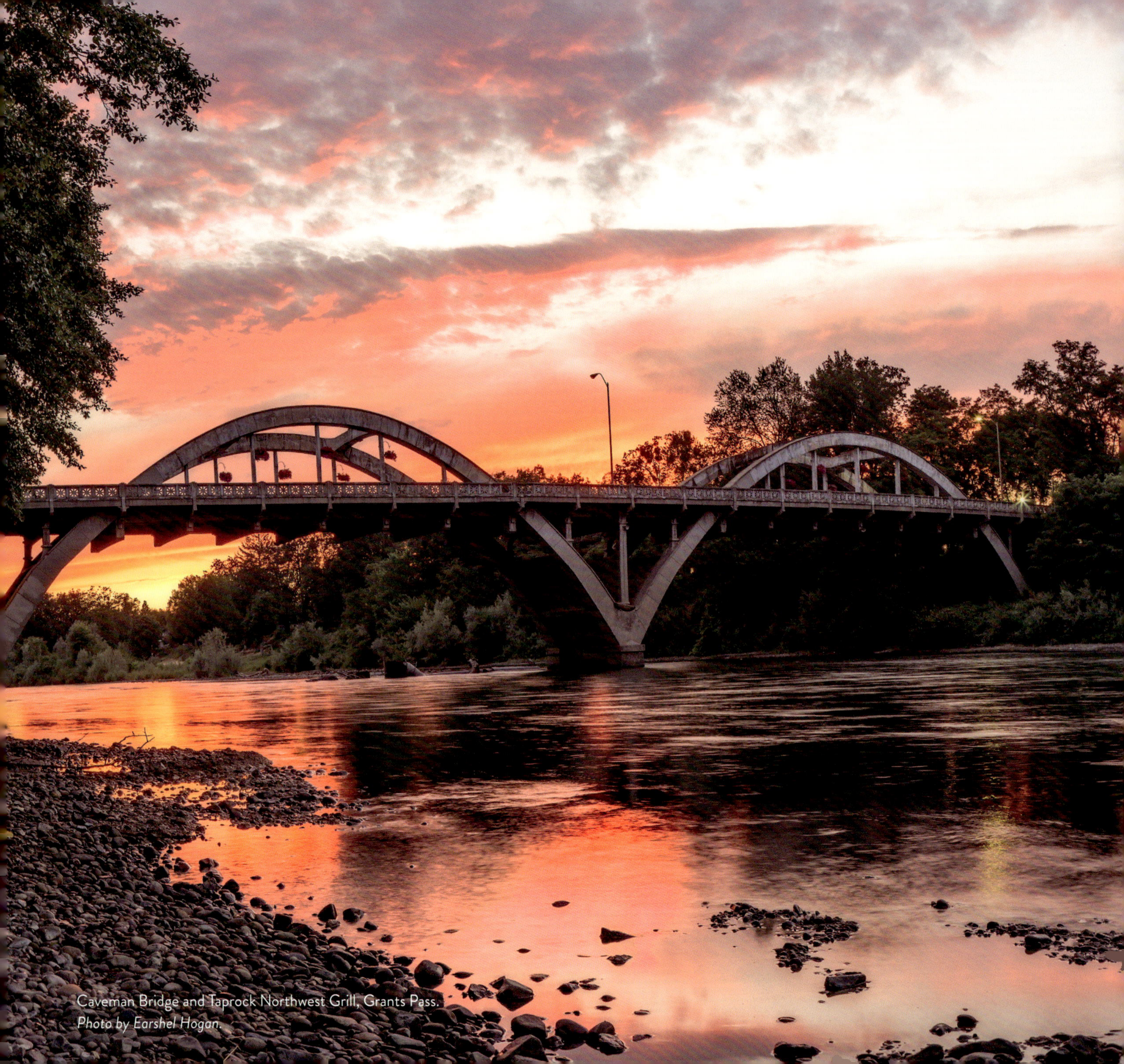

Caveman Bridge and Taprock Northwest Grill, Grants Pass.
Photo by Earshel Hogan.

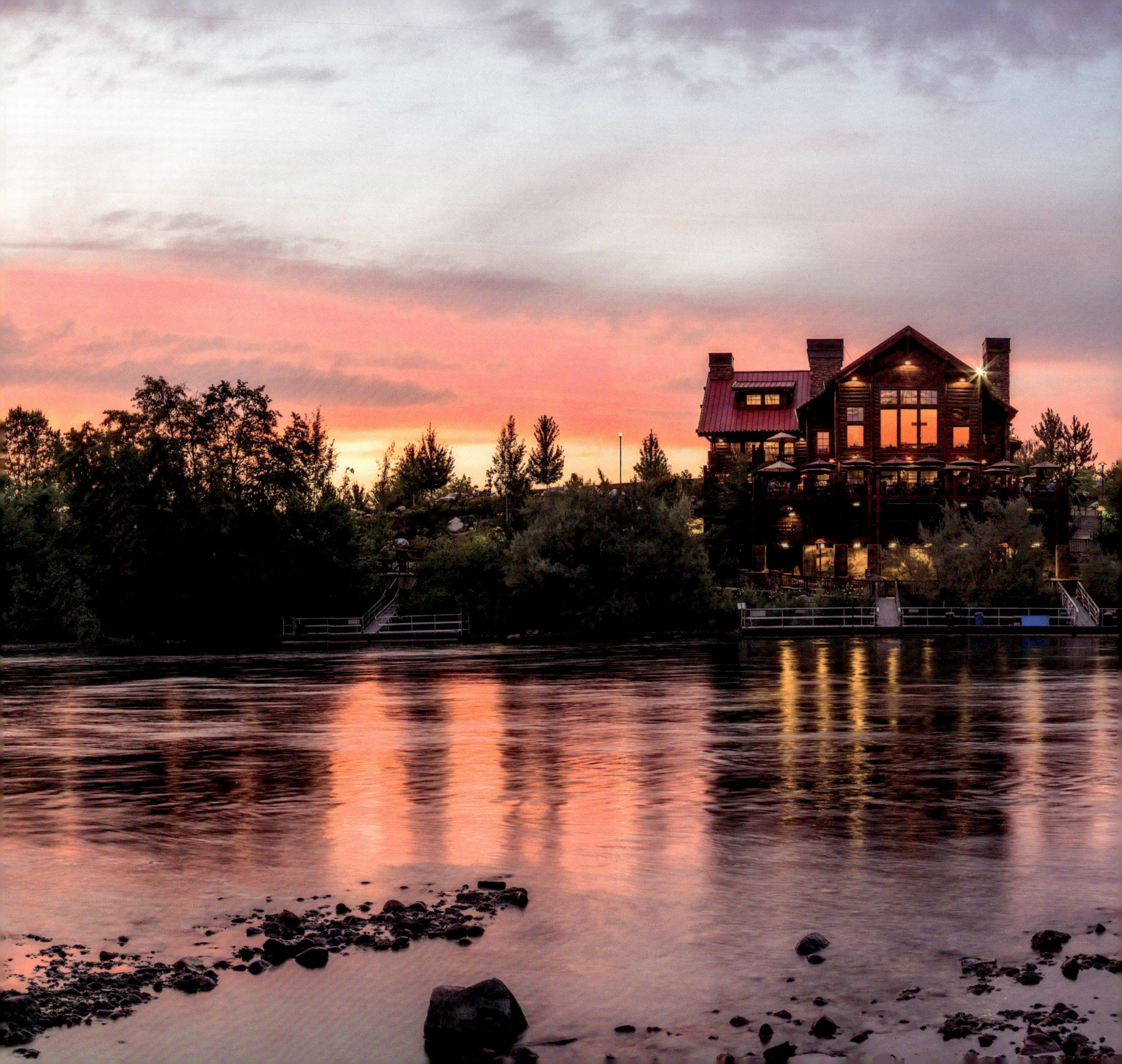

EASTERN OREGON

A trip to eastern Oregon is like stepping back in time. Wild West movies from the 1950s come to mind, with arid towns, covered wagons, free-range cattle, pronghorn antelope, wild mustangs, and abundant tumbleweeds. The region is sparsely populated, primarily agricultural, and boasts several of the state's more than 250 ghost towns.

Here you'll find remarkable, untouched geological formations such as the Painted Hills, Steens Mountains, Alvord Hot Springs and Desert, and Leslie Gulch in the Jordan River Valley. The Snake River has carved the deepest river gorge in North America at Hells Canyon, with more than 215,000 acres of wilderness to explore.

Once home to the Nez Perce tribe, the Wallowa Mountain area, near La Grande, became home to settlers in 1861 and was a prominent logging community. The 360,000-acre Eagle Cap Wilderness is the largest—and some say the most beautiful—wilderness area in Oregon. A gondola near Joseph climbs 3,700 feet from the floor of the Wallowa River Valley to the peak of Mount Howard. The Wallowas are considered one of the Seven Wonders of Oregon.

The expansive John Day Fossil Beds National Monument offers three unique areas to explore: the Painted Hills Unit, Clarno Unit, and Sheep Rock Unit. This landscape was once the home of woolly mammoths and saber-tooth tigers. Plan a stop at the Thomas Condon Paleontology Center in the Sheep Rock Unit to learn about the region and see more than 500 fossils. The Painted Hills are also considered one of the Seven Wonders of Oregon (and one of the most picturesque and often-visited areas of eastern Oregon). Don't blink or you'll miss the town of Mitchell (population approximately 120), with its general store, quaint diners, rustic accommodations, and walkable main street.

The Malheur National Wildlife Refuge, south of Burns, is a nature lover's paradise with approximately 320 known bird species and fifty-eight mammal species. Created in 1908 by Theodore Roosevelt to protect wildlife and migratory birds, the refuge offers 293 square miles of protected land to explore.

The tiny town of Frenchglen (population approximately twelve) is home to the historic Frenchglen Hotel, a state heritage site built in 1924. It is conveniently located between the Malheur National Wildlife Refuge and the Steens Mountain. In the remote southeastern part of Oregon, Steens Mountain has an elevation of 9,733 feet. The single mountain stretches fifty miles north to south, covering 98,859 acres, with a total of 170,166 acres in the Steens Mountain Wilderness. There you'll see wild horses, sagebrush, and, nearby, the parched and isolated Alvord Desert.

Owyhee Canyonlands are called "the last great unprotected expanse of the American West." With only three paved roads cutting across the territory, adventure seekers can camp, hike, raft, visit bubbling hot springs, and enjoy wildlife.

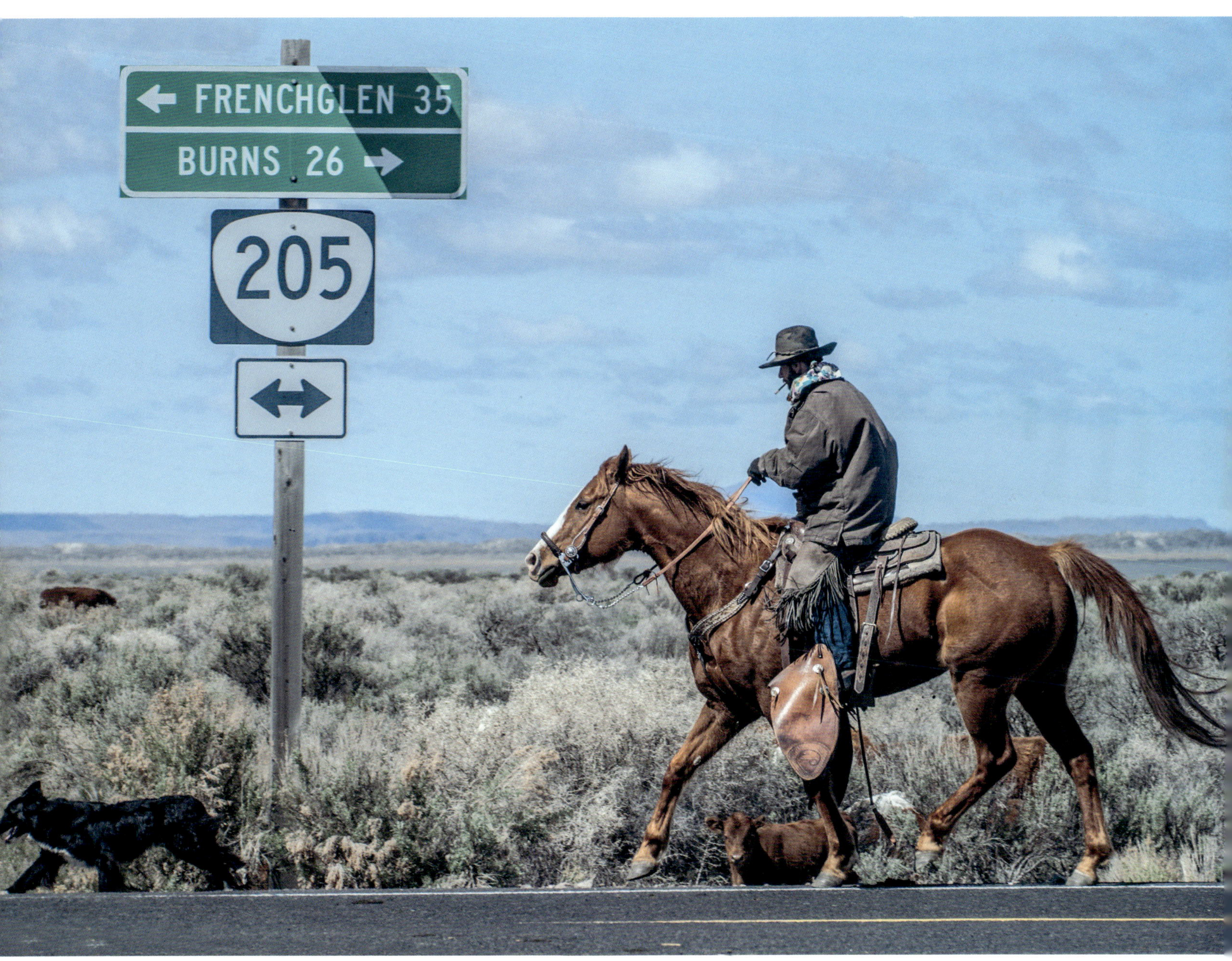

Cowboy on Route 205, Malheur. *Photo by George F. Peterson.*

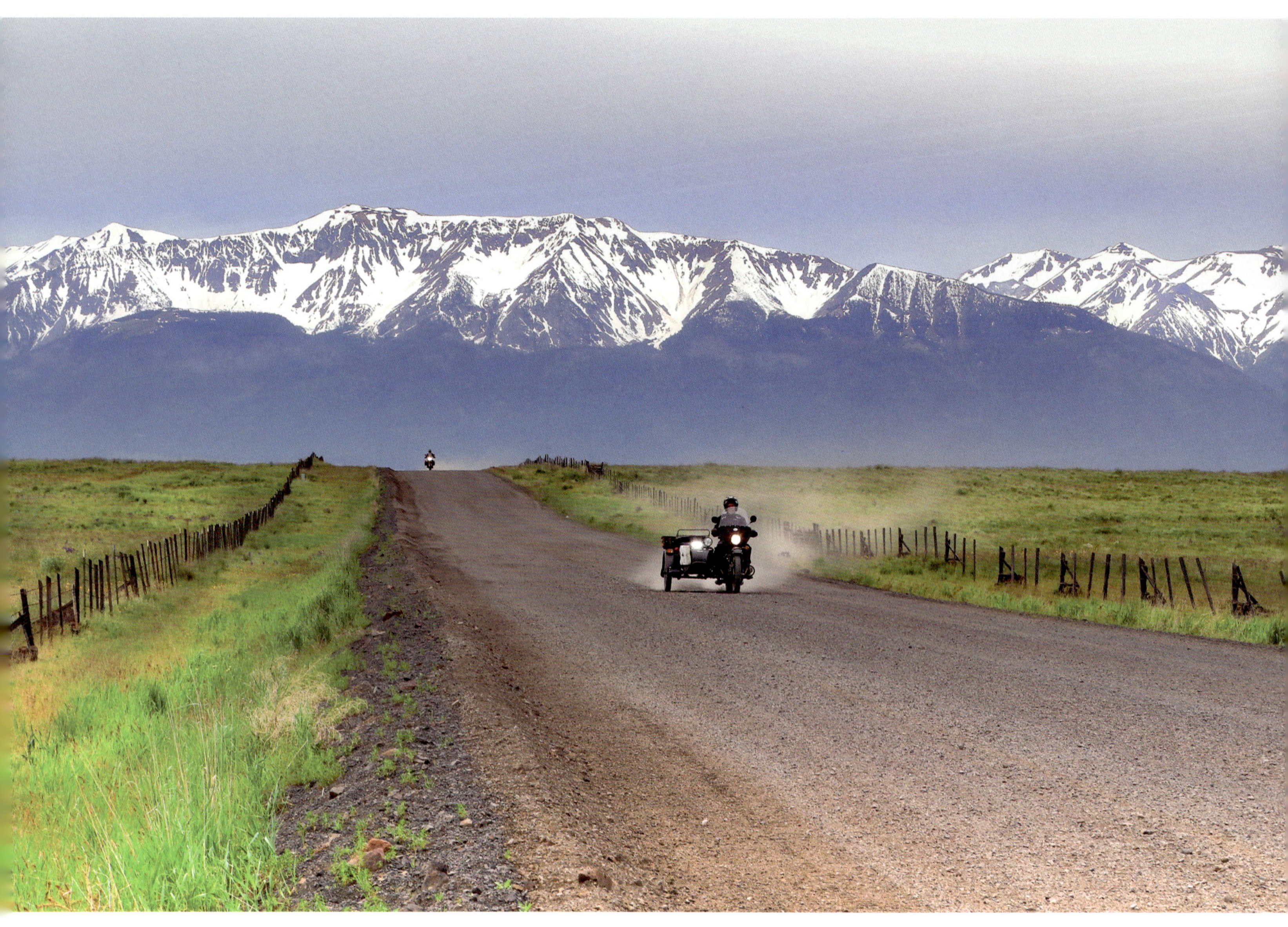

Motorcycles near Wallowa Mountains. *Photo by Terry Fisher.*

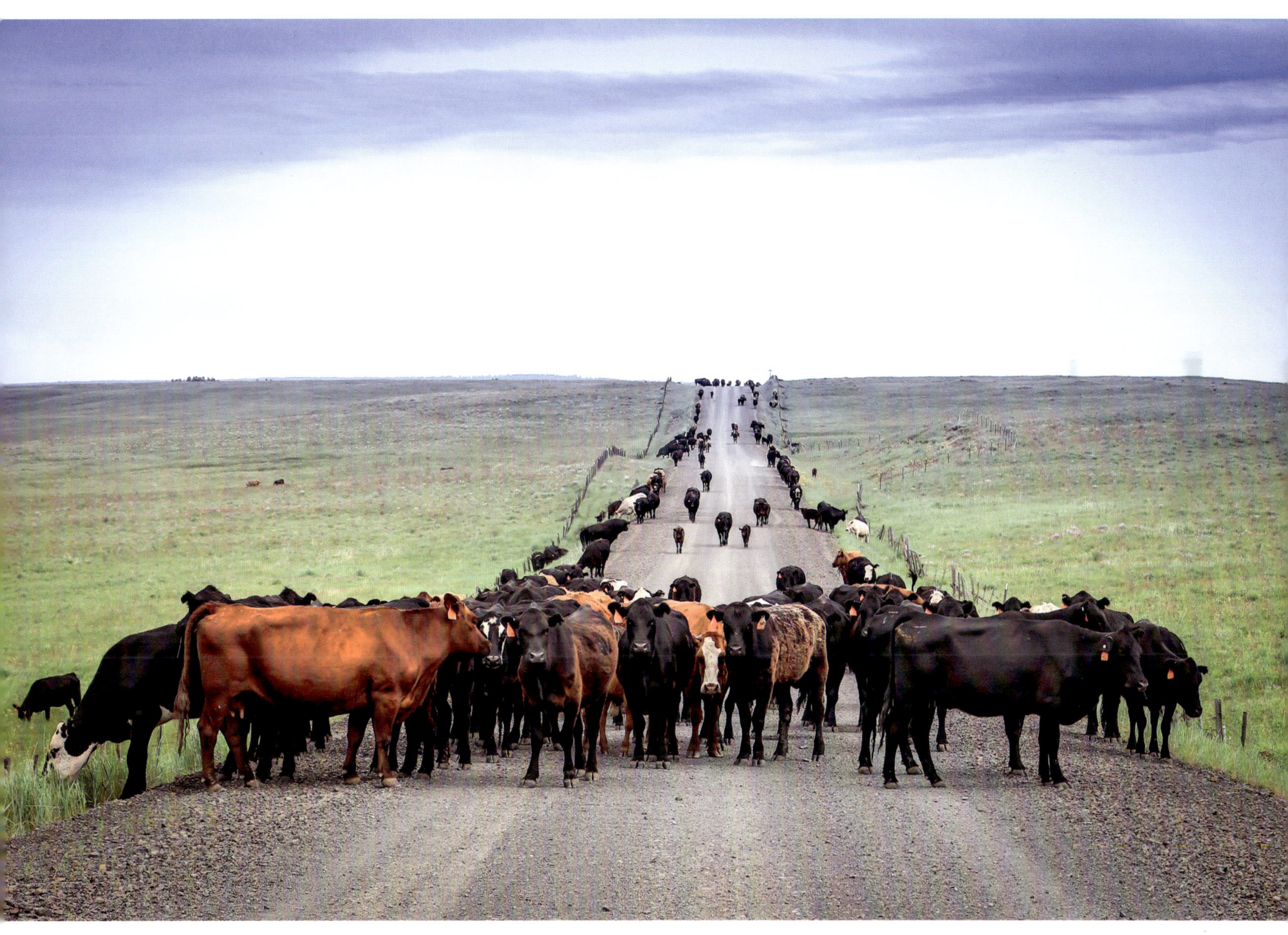

Cattle drive on Zumwalt Prairie Road near Joseph. *Photo by Terry Fisher.*

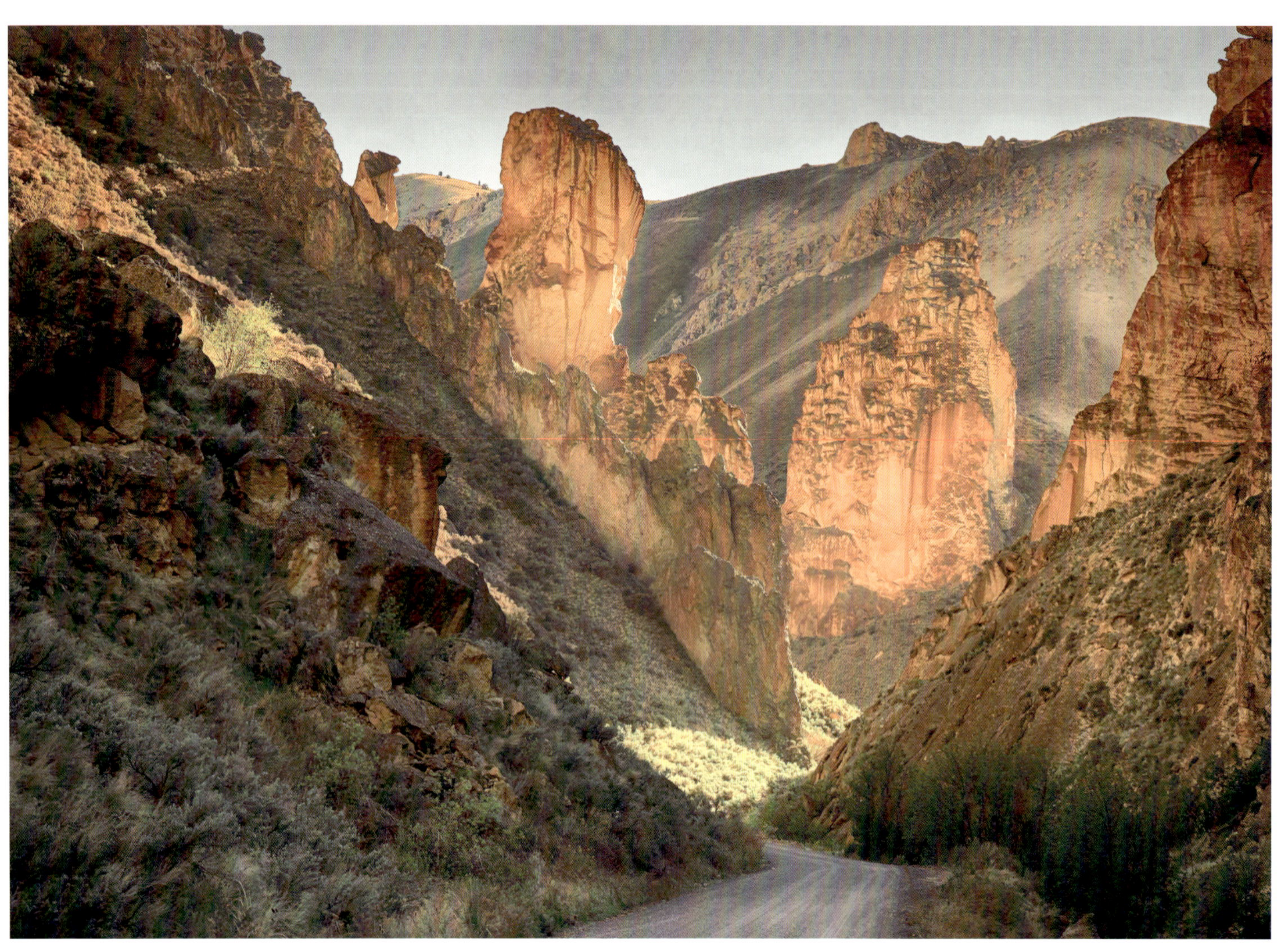

Leslie Gulch is a canyon in Malheur County with rock formations made of tuff. *Photo by John Kirk.*

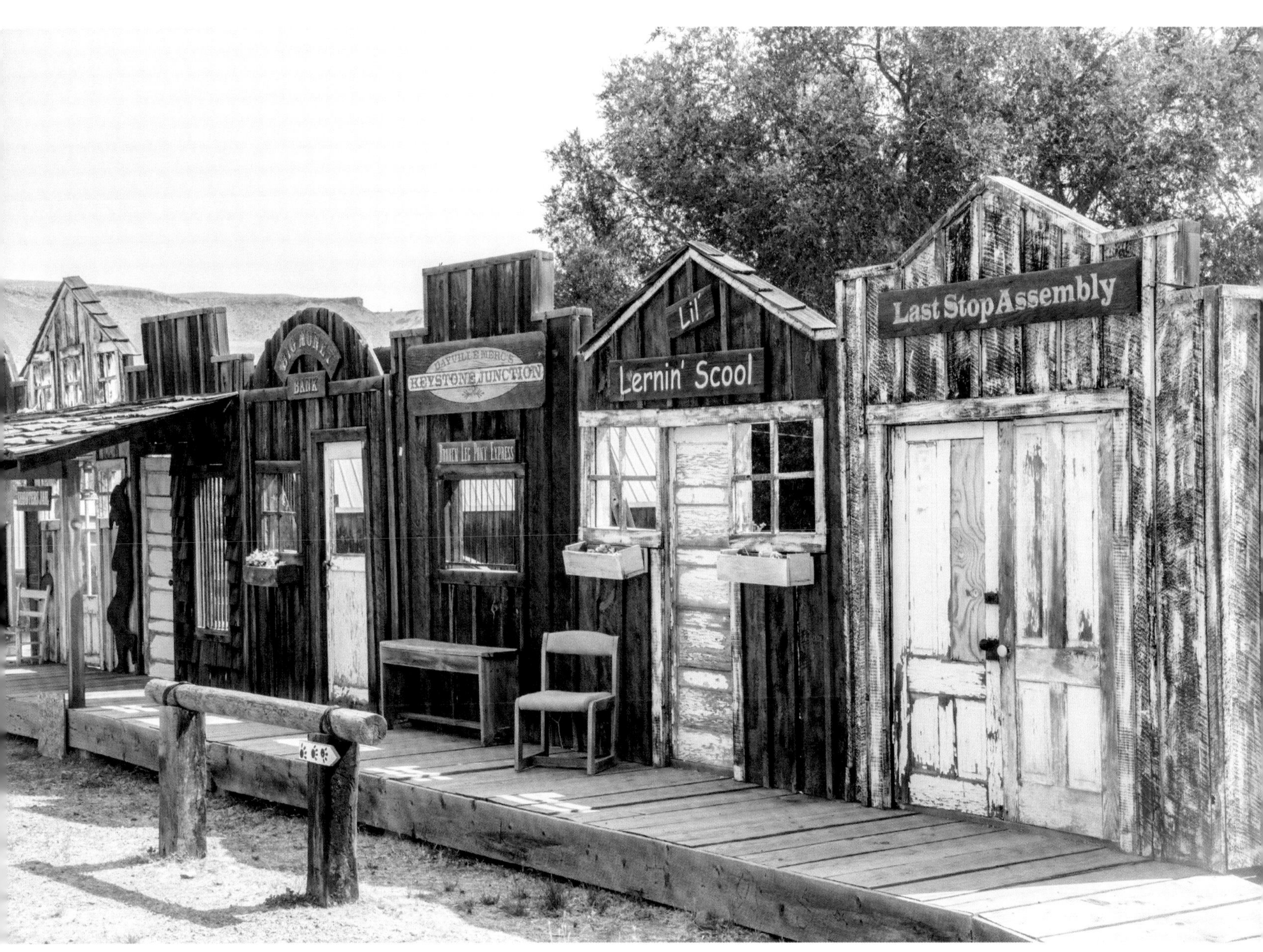

Dayville. *Photo by Diana Standing.*

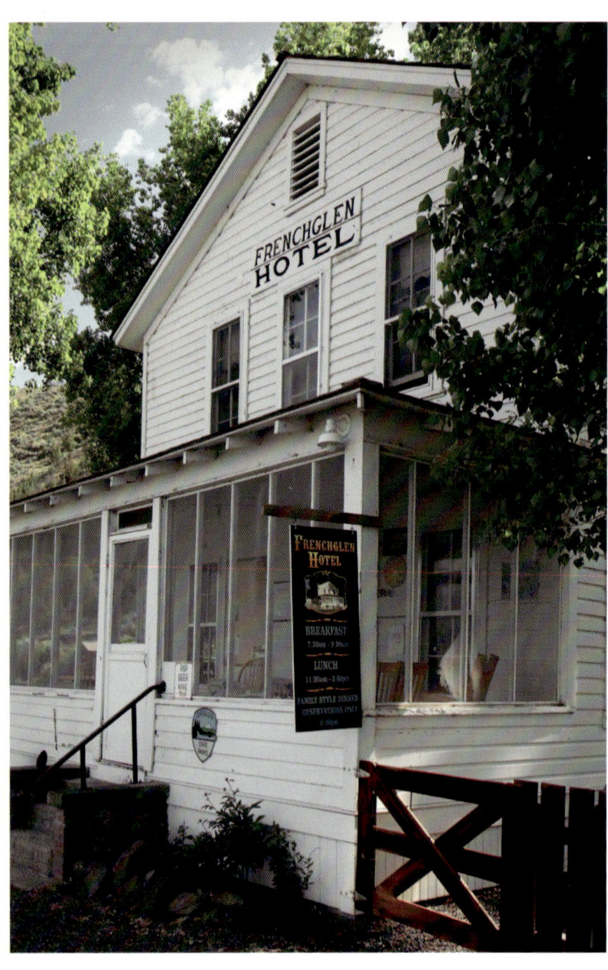

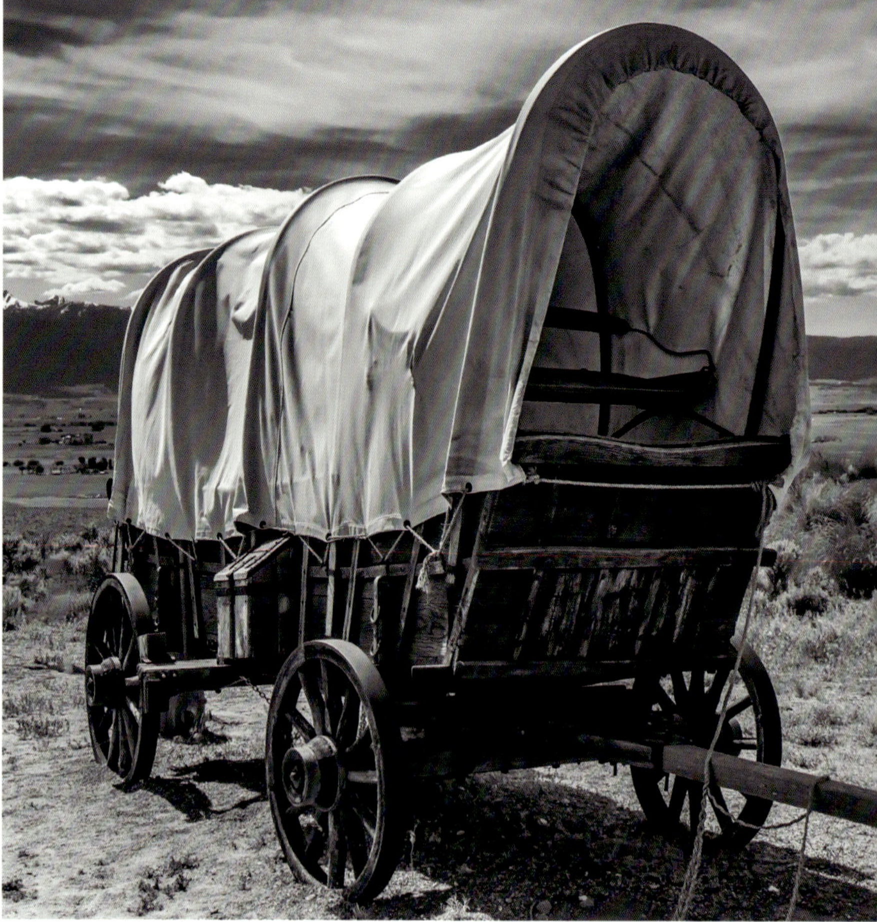

 Frenchglen Hotel, Steens Mountain. Situated in the tiny town of Frenchglen (population of twelve), this hotel was built in 1924. *Photo by John Kirk.*

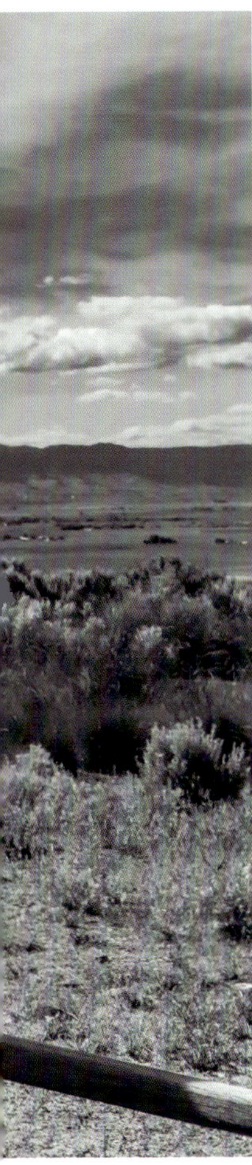

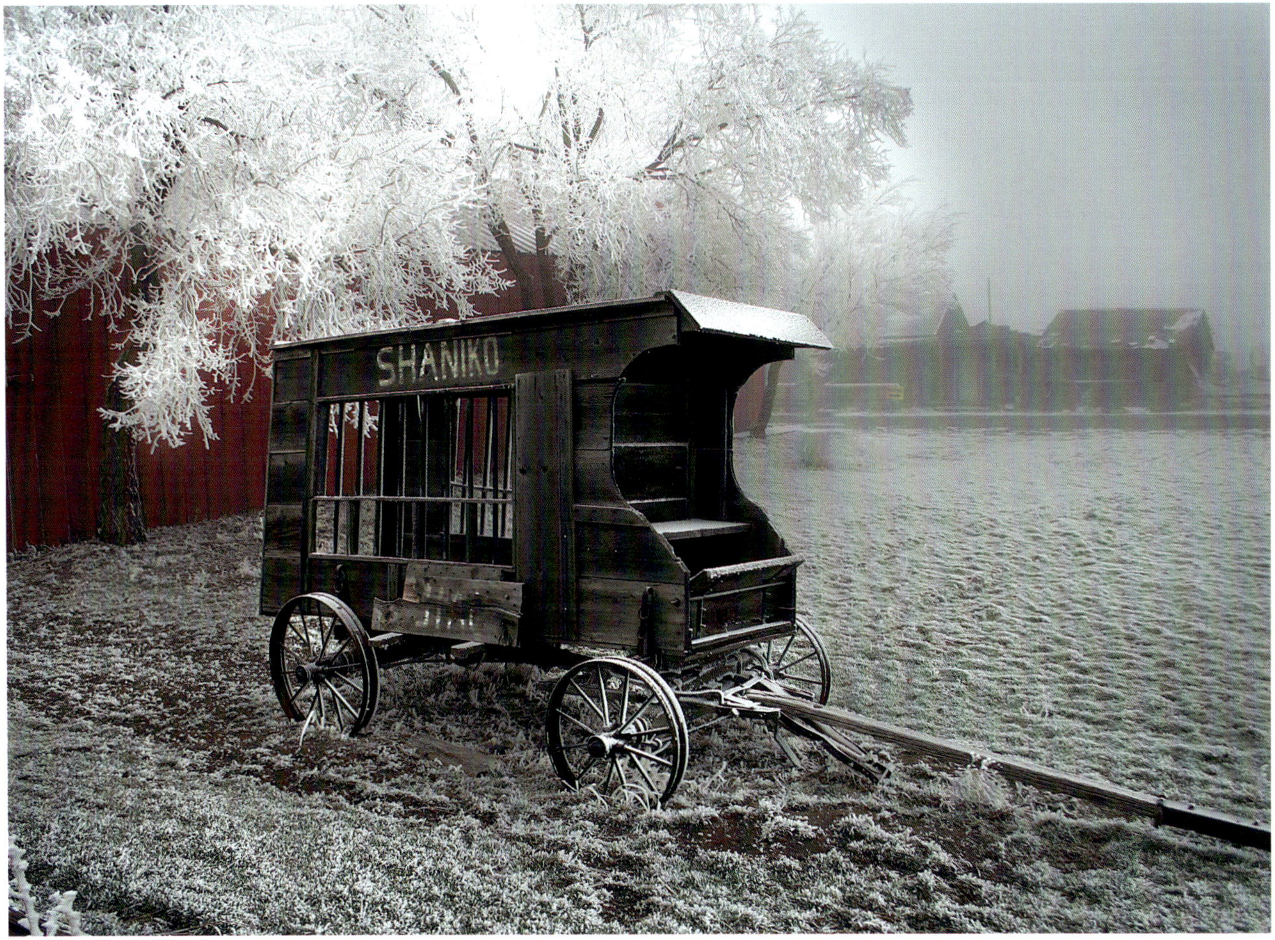

(Middle) Covered wagon at the Oregon Trail Interpretive Center. *Photo by Alan Ingersoll.* • (Right) Stagecoach in Shaniko. *Photo by Neal R. Thompson.*

83

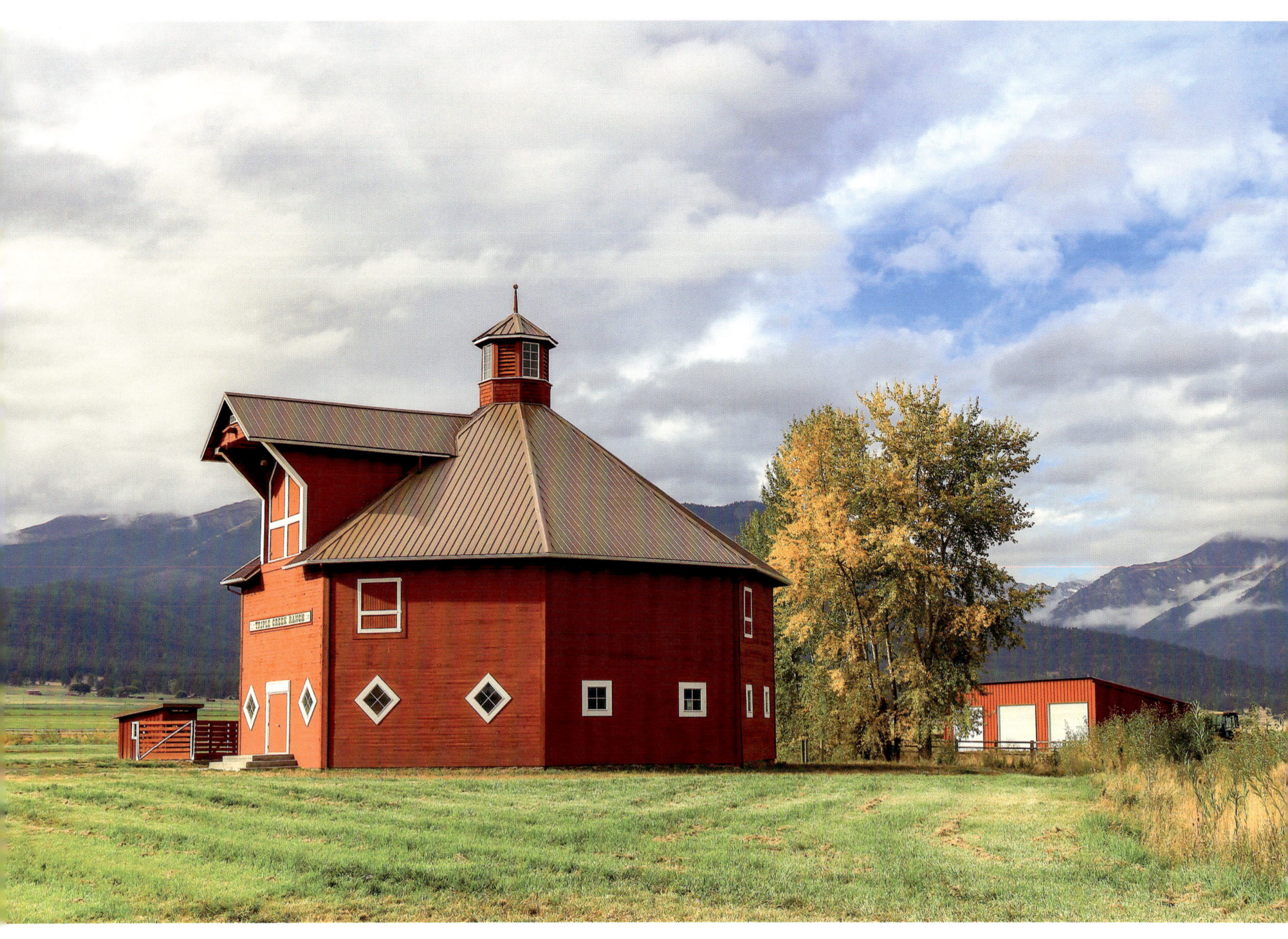

84   Round barn. *Photo by Neal R. Thompson.*

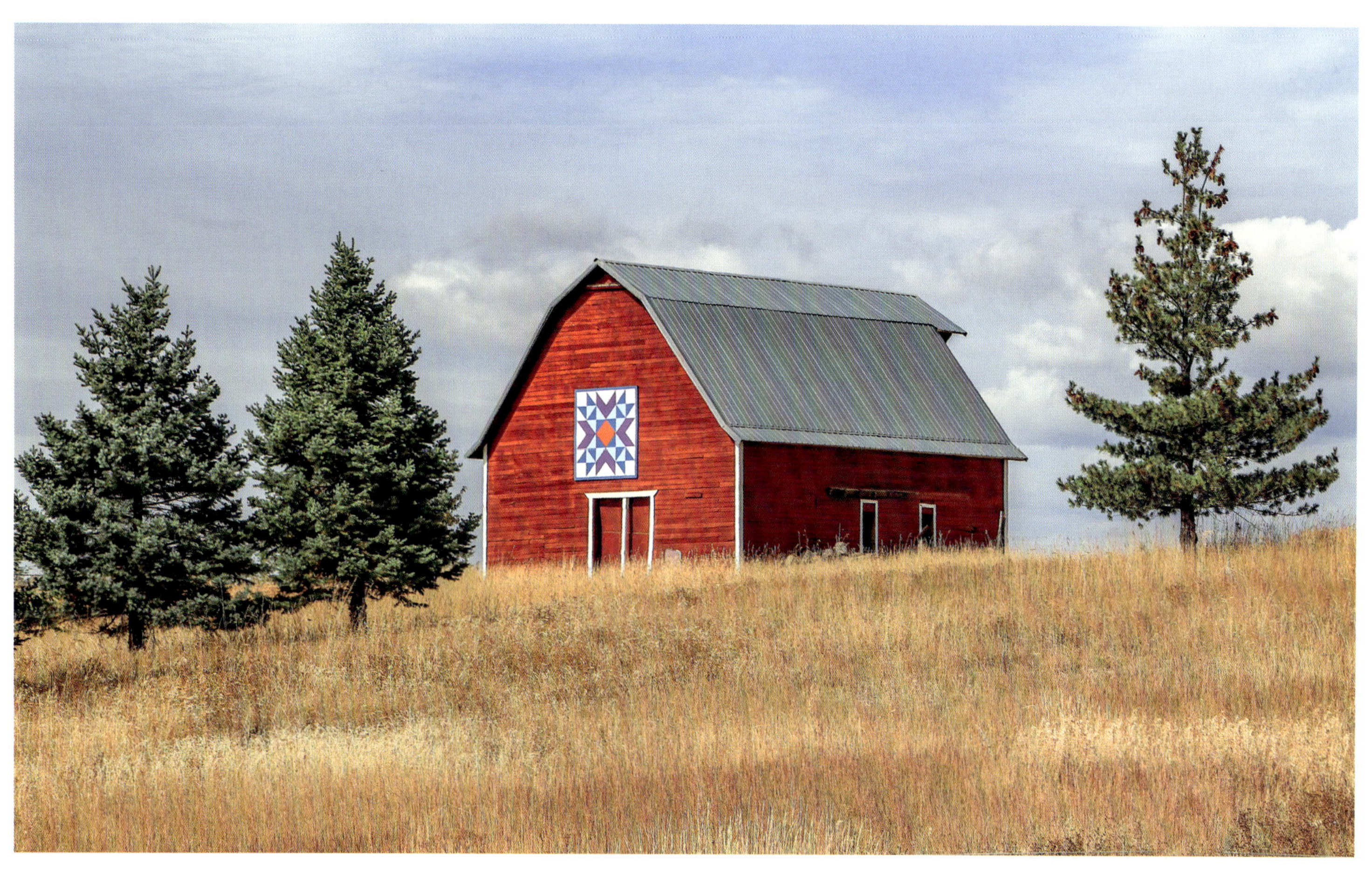

Barn with painted quilt square near Flora. The American Quilt Trail began as a grassroots effort in 2001. More than 7,000 quilt blocks have now been added to barns across the United States. *Photo by Terry Fisher.*

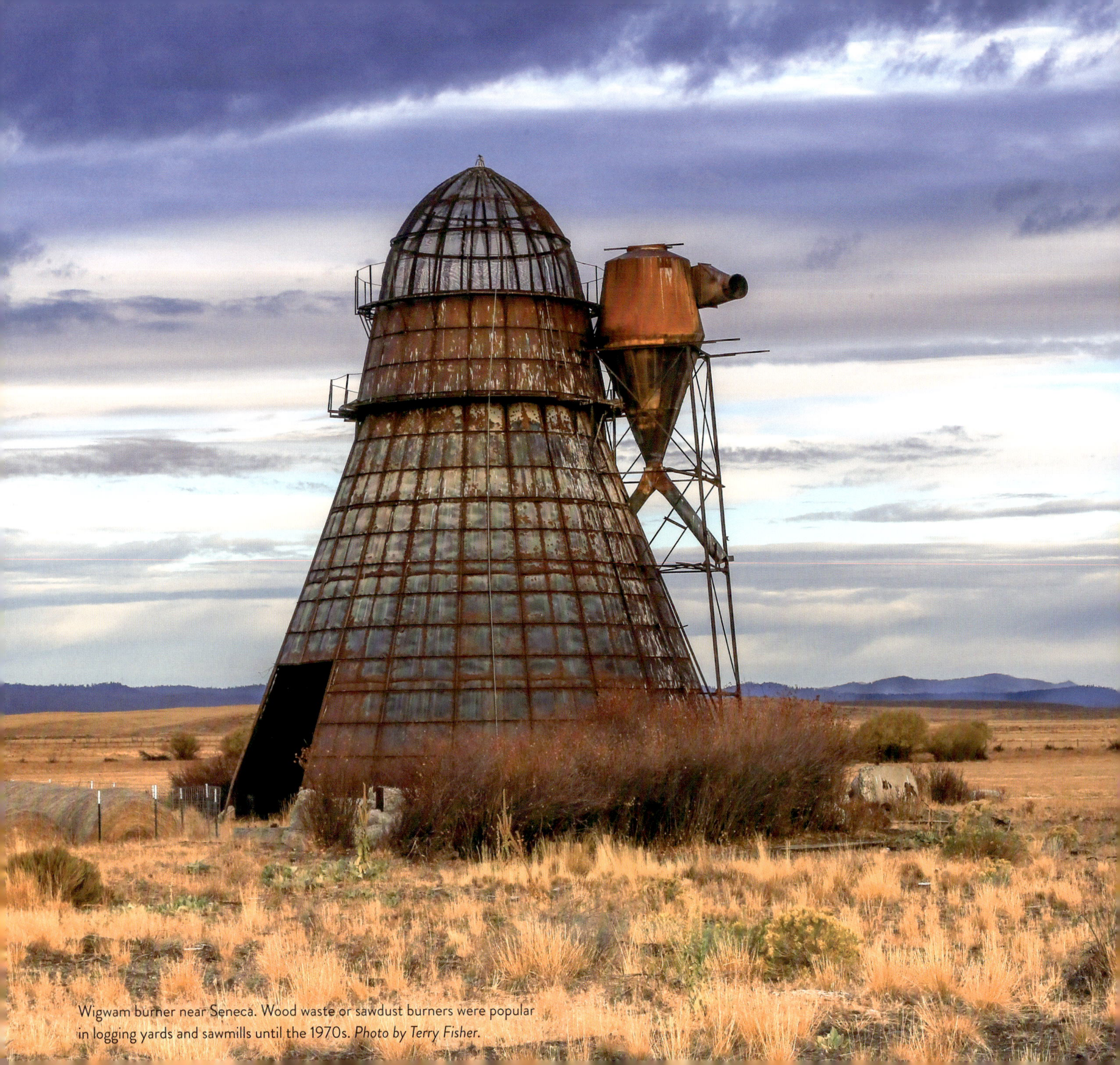

Wigwam burner near Seneca. Wood waste or sawdust burners were popular in logging yards and sawmills until the 1970s. *Photo by Terry Fisher.*

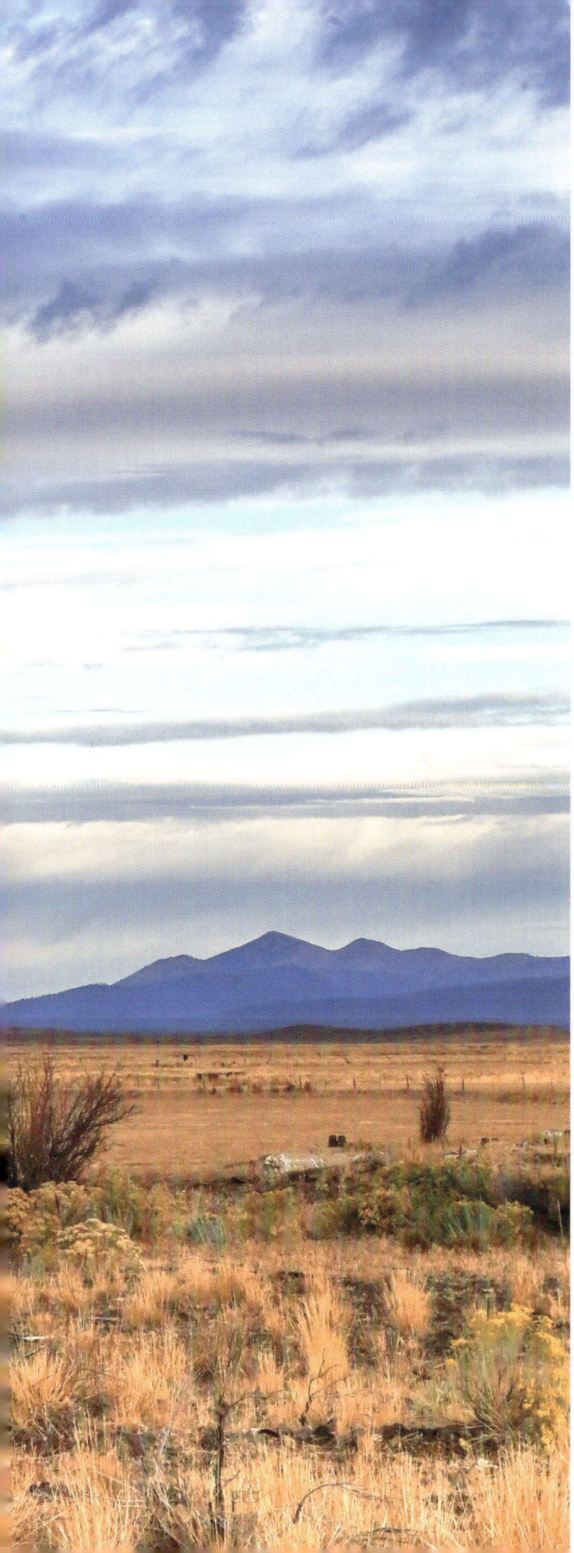

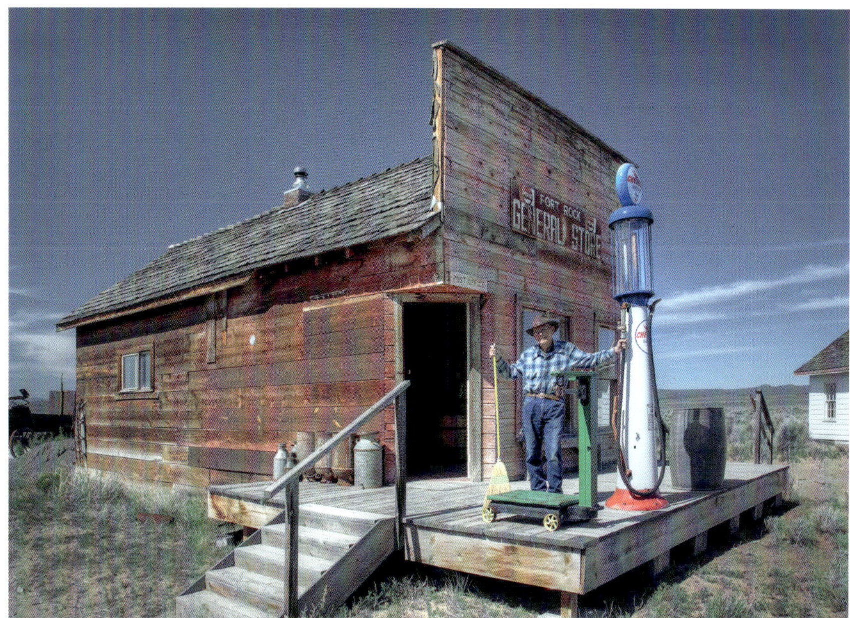

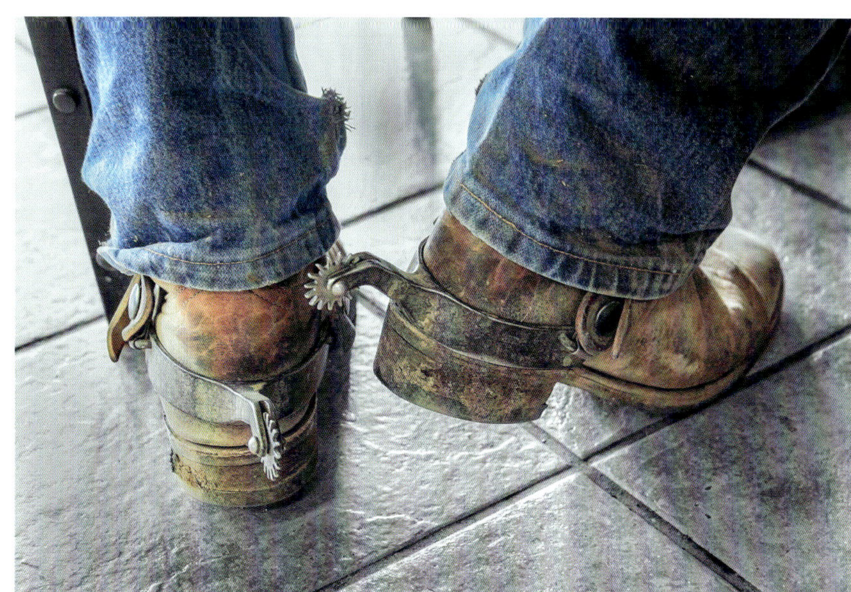

(Top) Fort Rock General Store, opened in the early 1900s. *Photo by John Kirk.*
(Bottom) Cowboy boots. *Photo by Neal R. Thompson.*

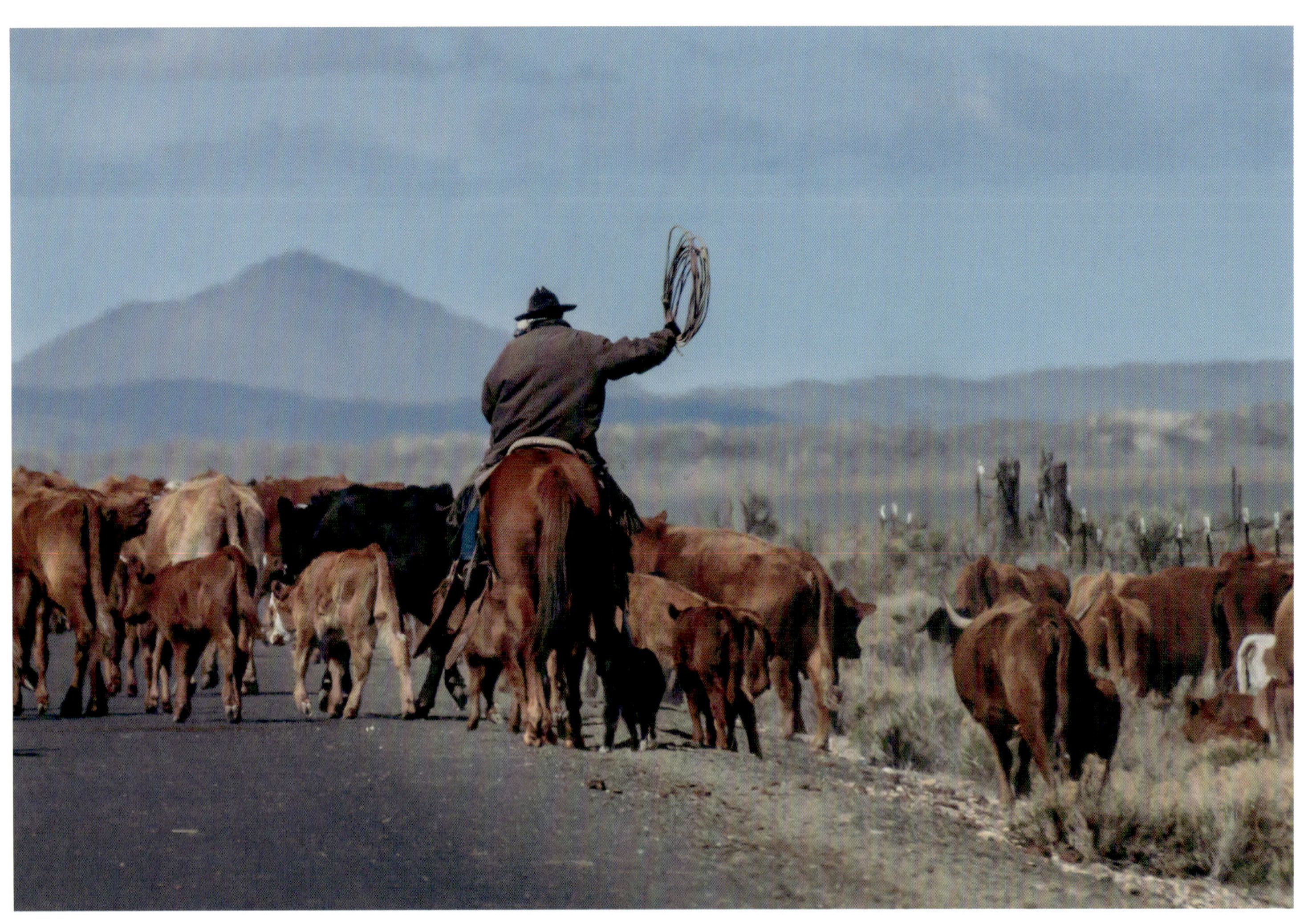

    Cattle rancher near Malheur National Wildlife Refuge. *Photo by George F. Peterson.*

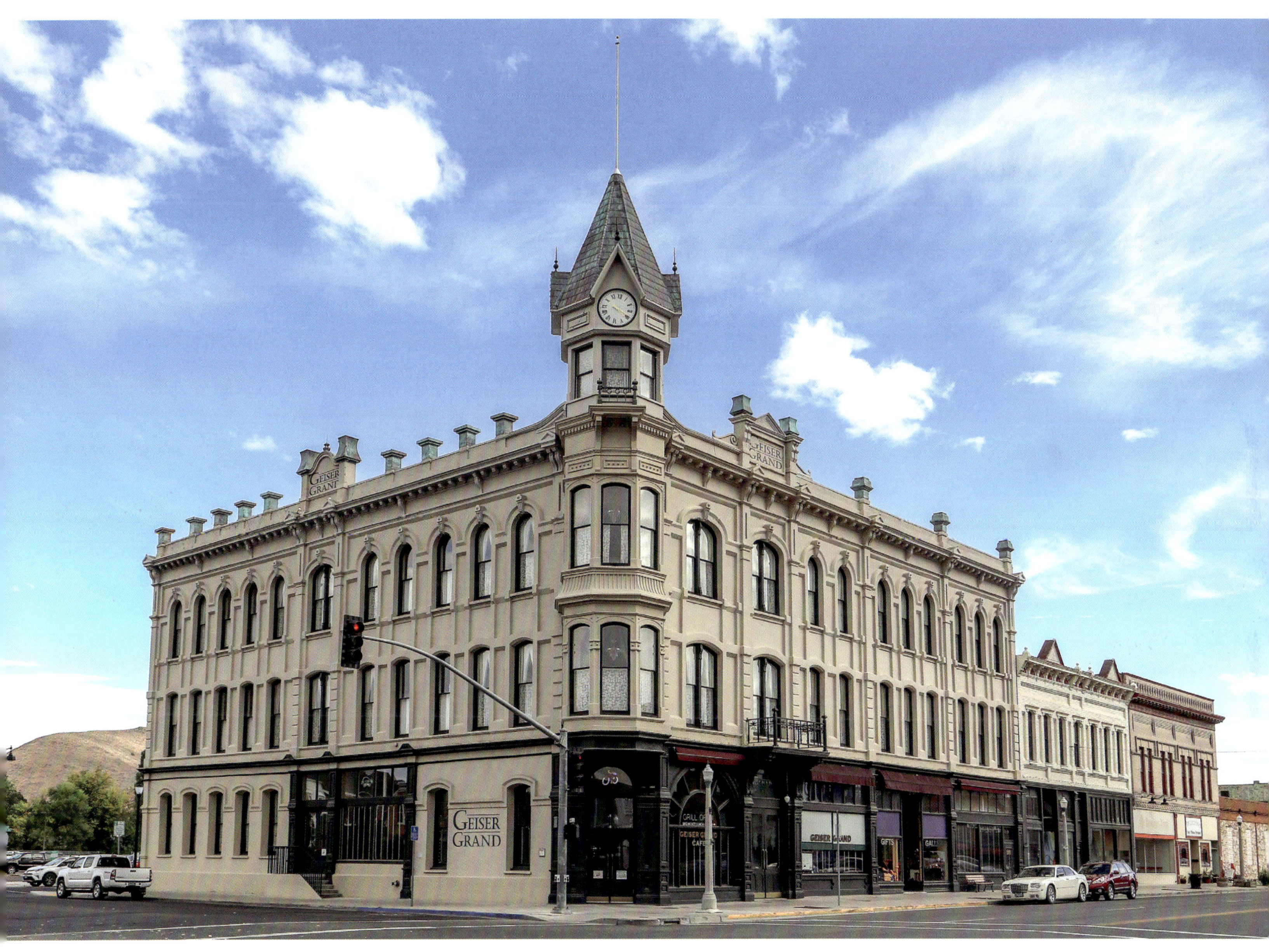

Geiser Grand Hotel, Baker City. Once the finest hotel between Portland and Salt Lake City, this hotel, built in 1893, is said to be haunted. *Photo by Terry Fisher.*

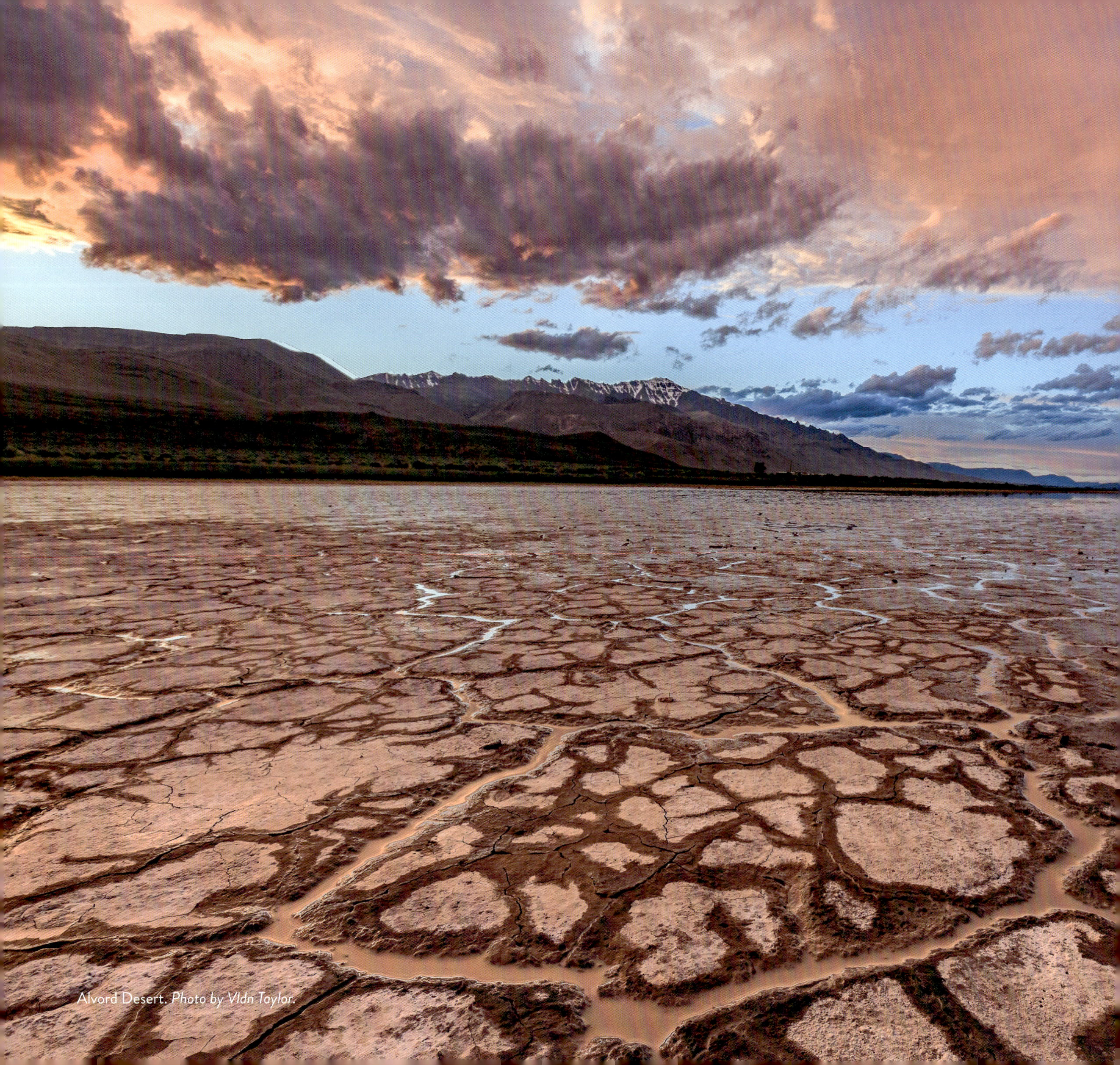

Alvord Desert. Photo by Vldn Taylor.

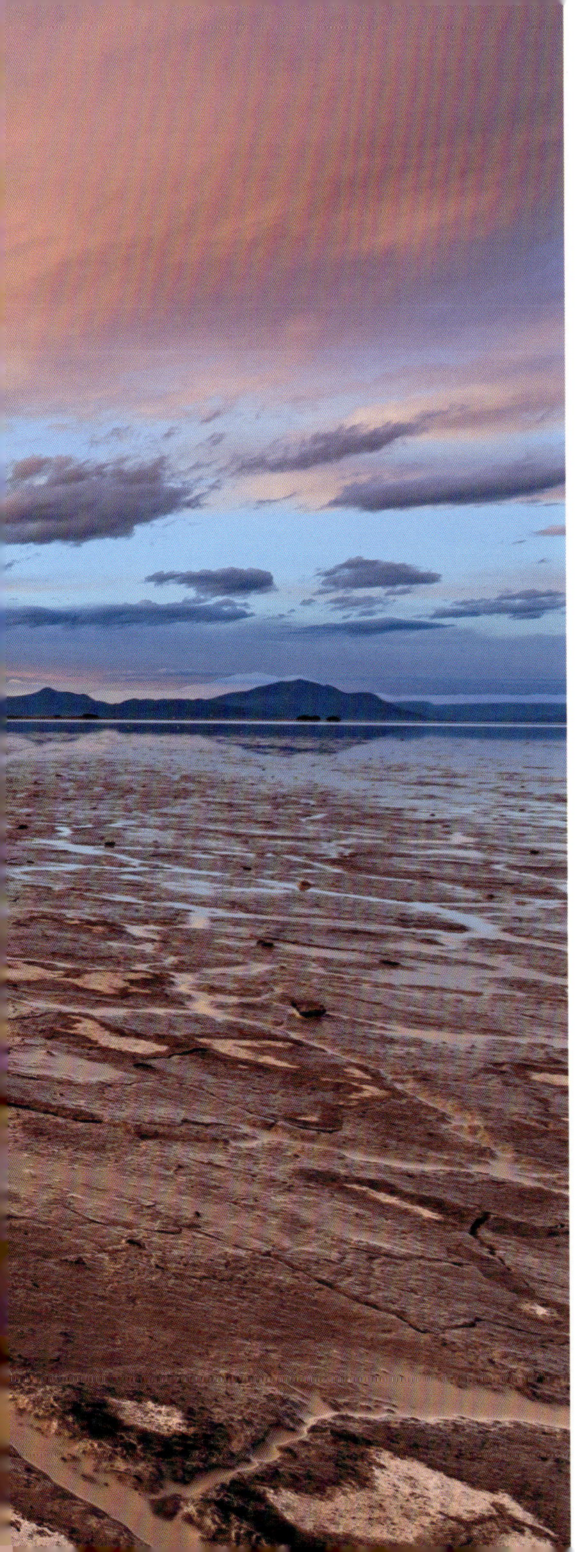

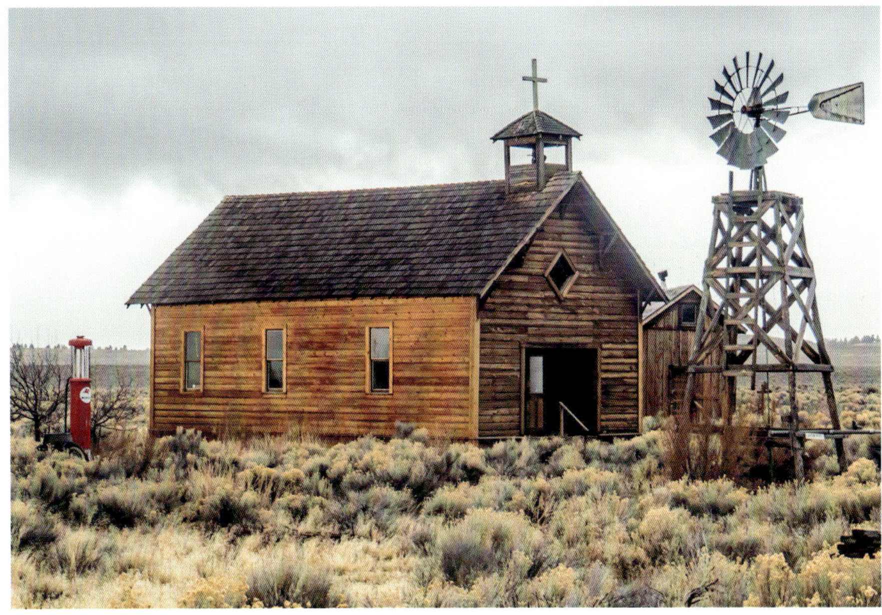

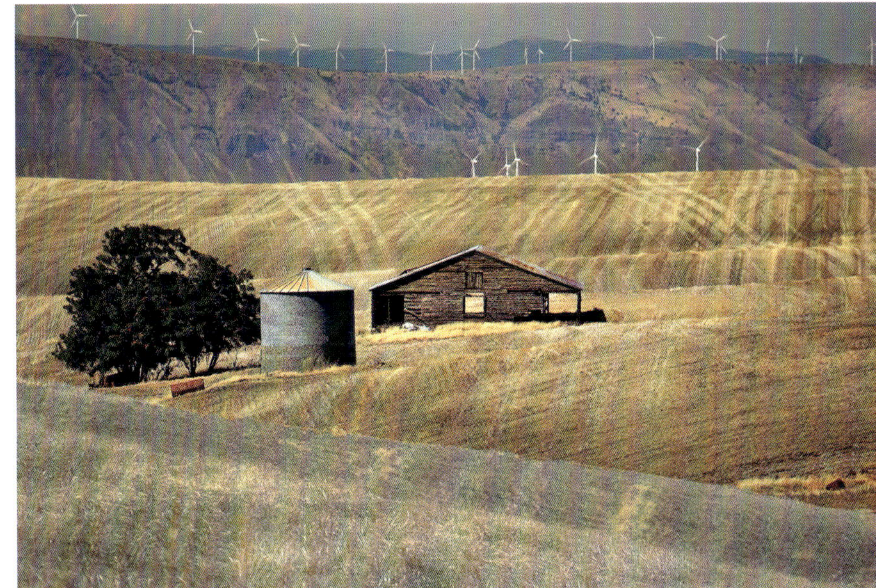

(Top) Fort Rock. The museum features a collection of historic buildings that were moved onto the grounds from remote locations. *Photo by Randy Bryan.*
(Bottom) Wheat fields in Wasco. *Photo by Neal R. Thompson.*

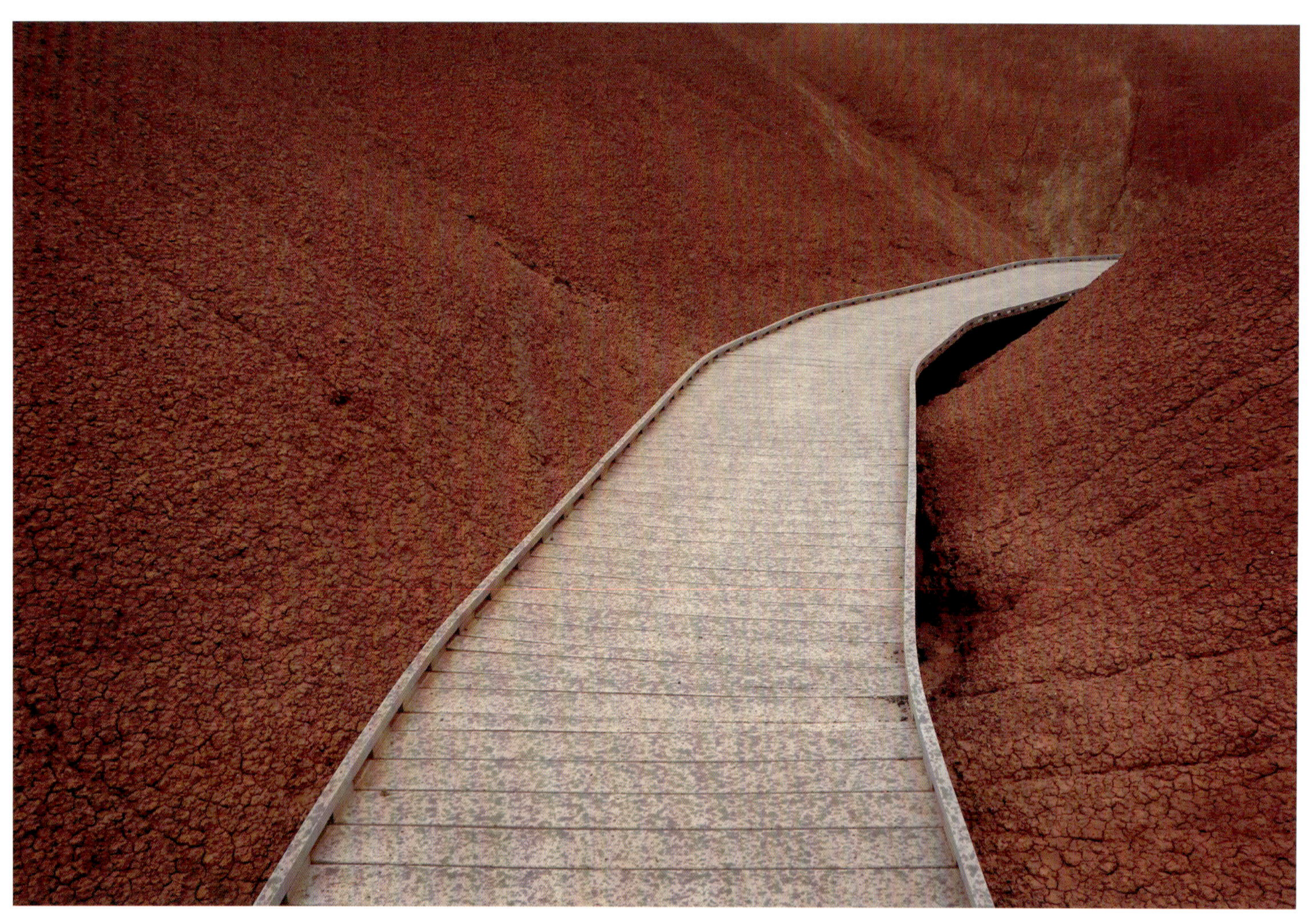

92   John Day Fossil Beds National Monument boardwalk at Painted Cove Overlook. *Photo by John Kirk.*

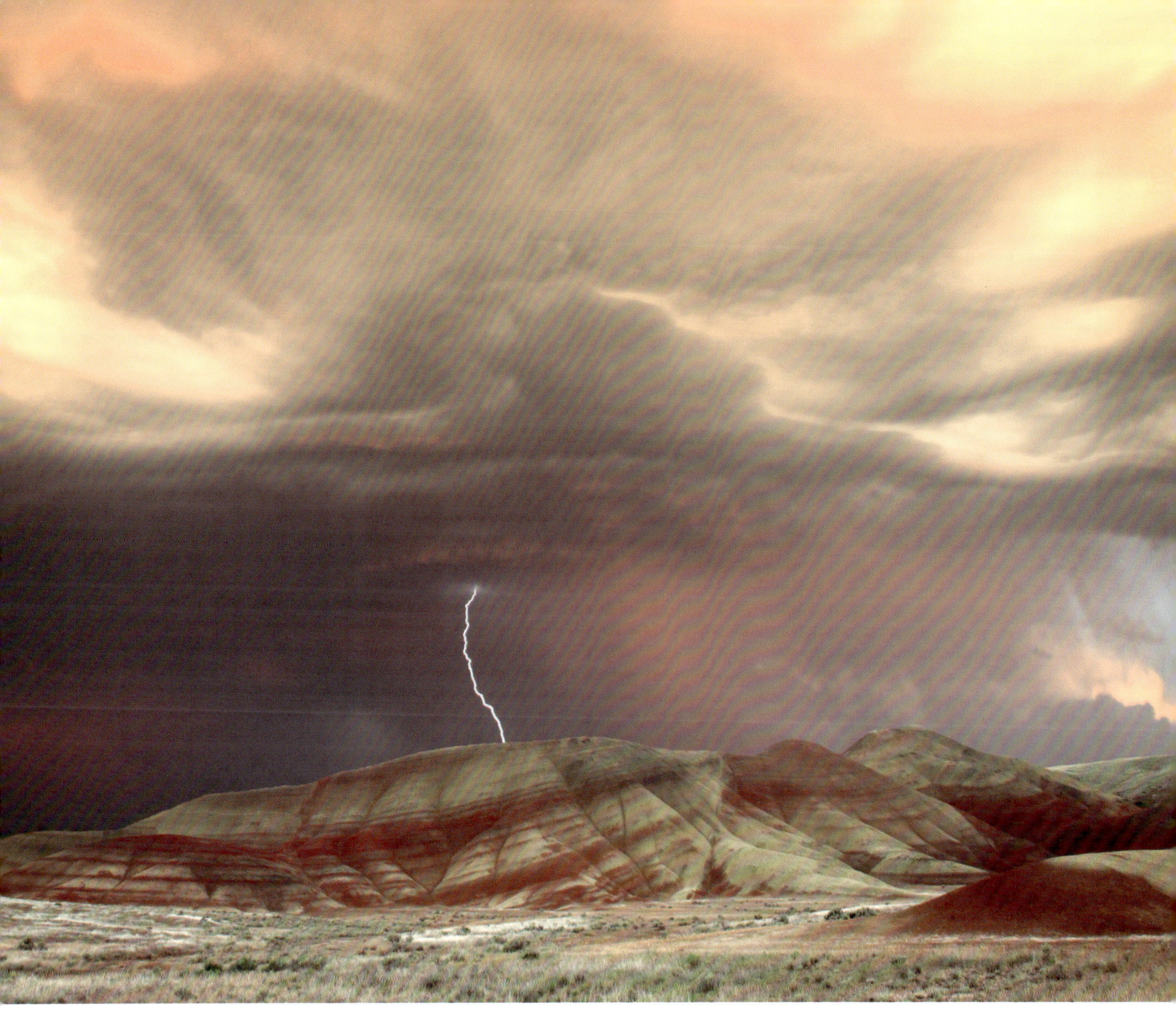

Painted Hills storm. *Photo by John Kirk.* 93

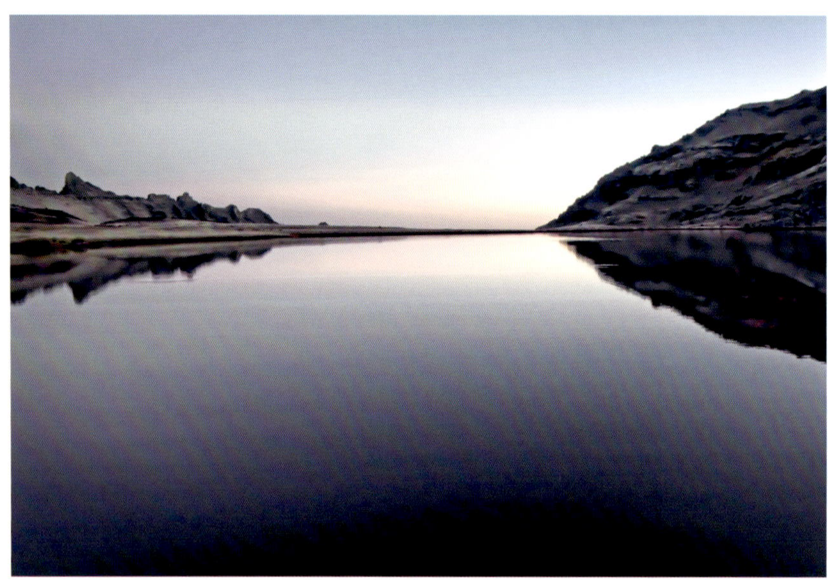

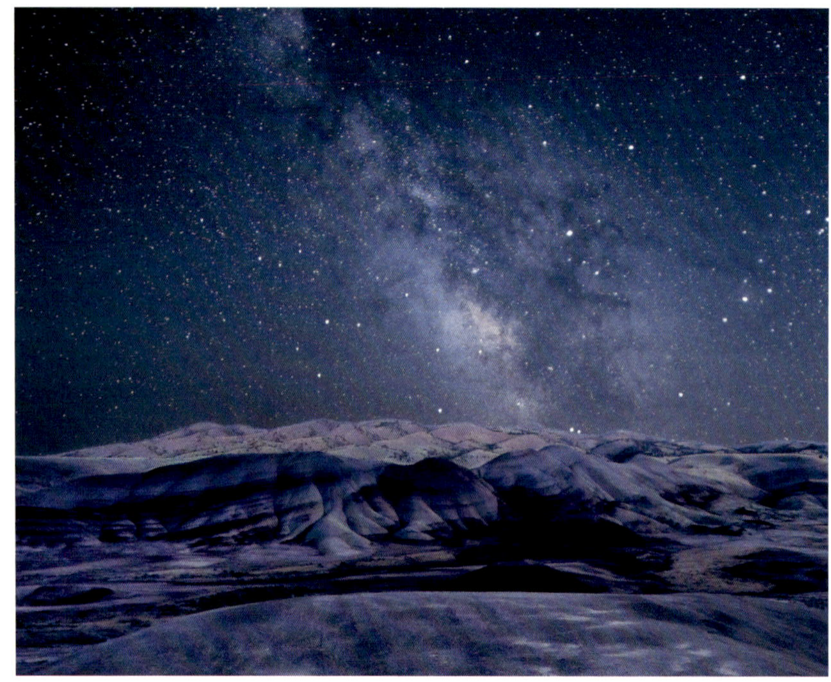

 (Top) Wildhorse Lake at dawn, Steens Mountain. *Photo by Matt Witt.* • (Bottom) Milky Way over Painted Hills. *Photo by Clem Paslack.*

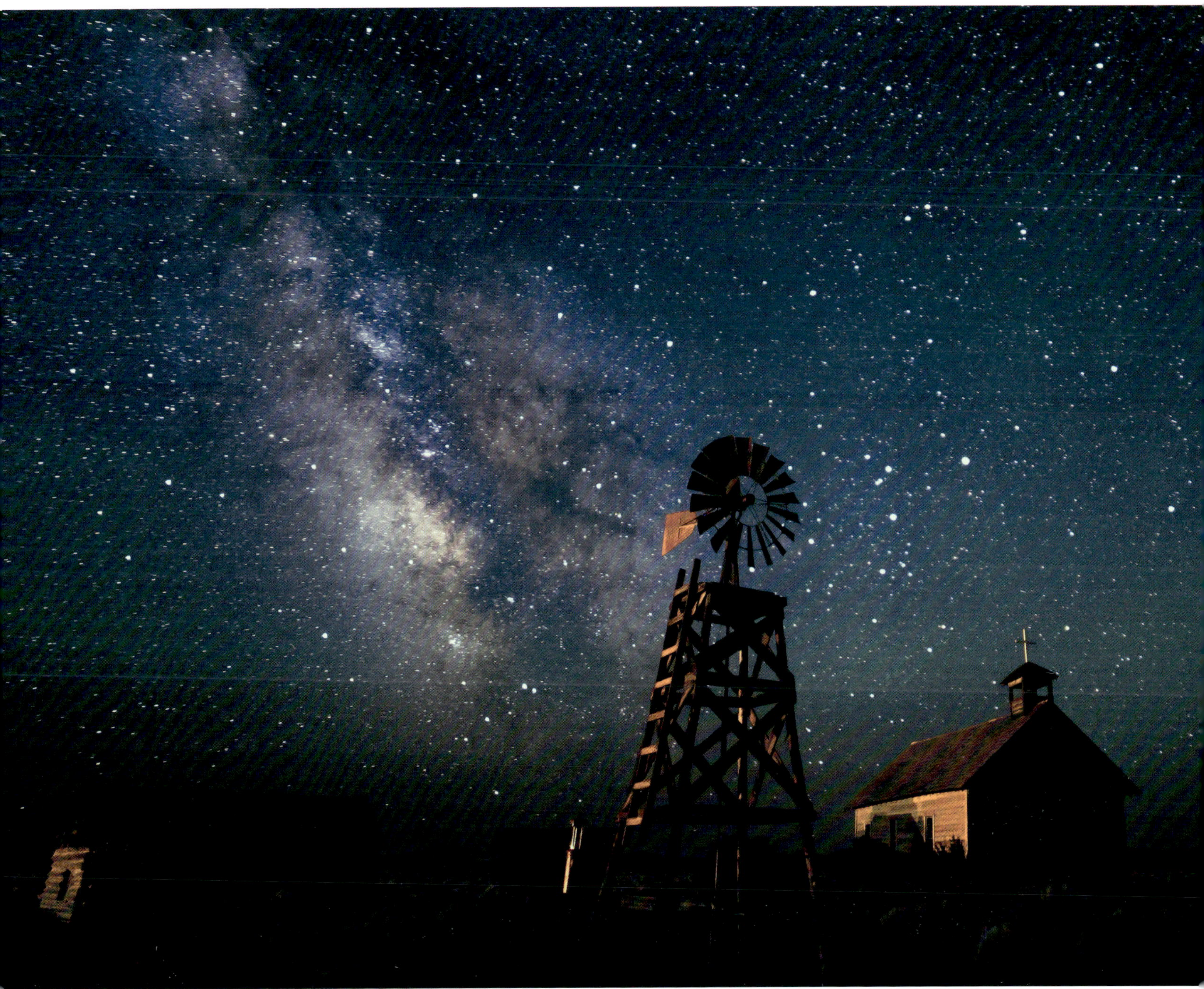

Milky Way over Fort Rock Museum. *Photo by Clem Paslack.*   95

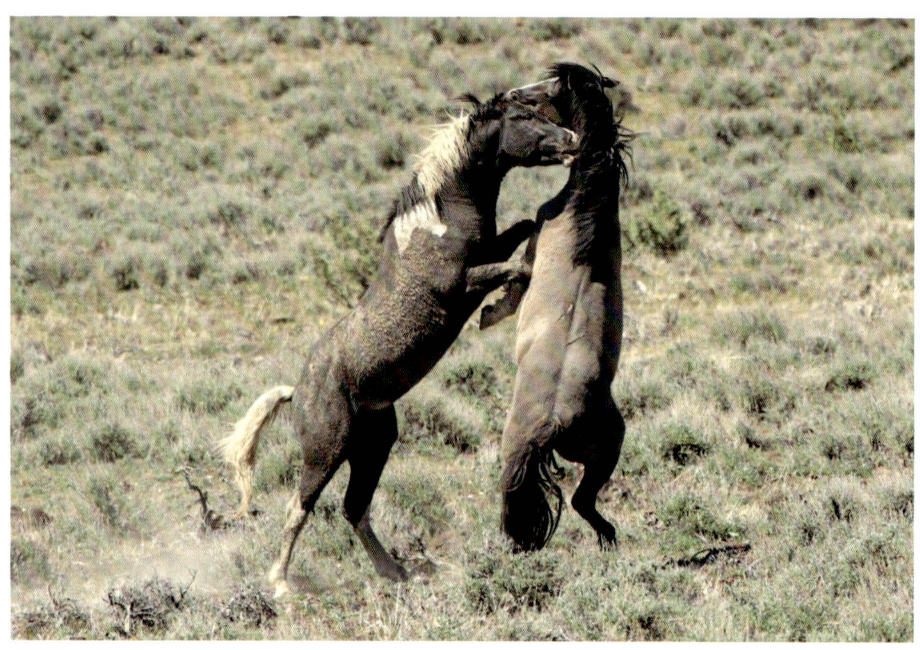

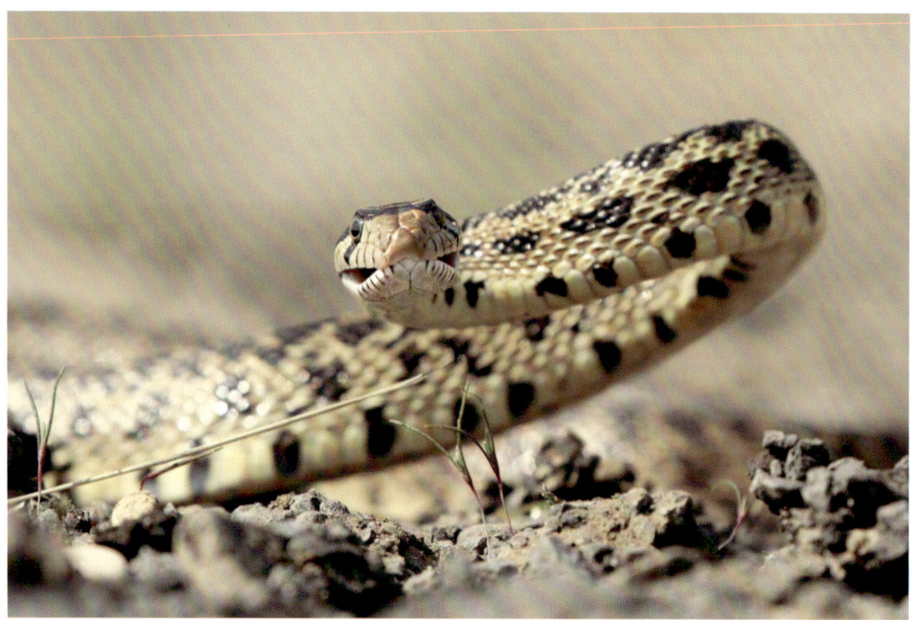

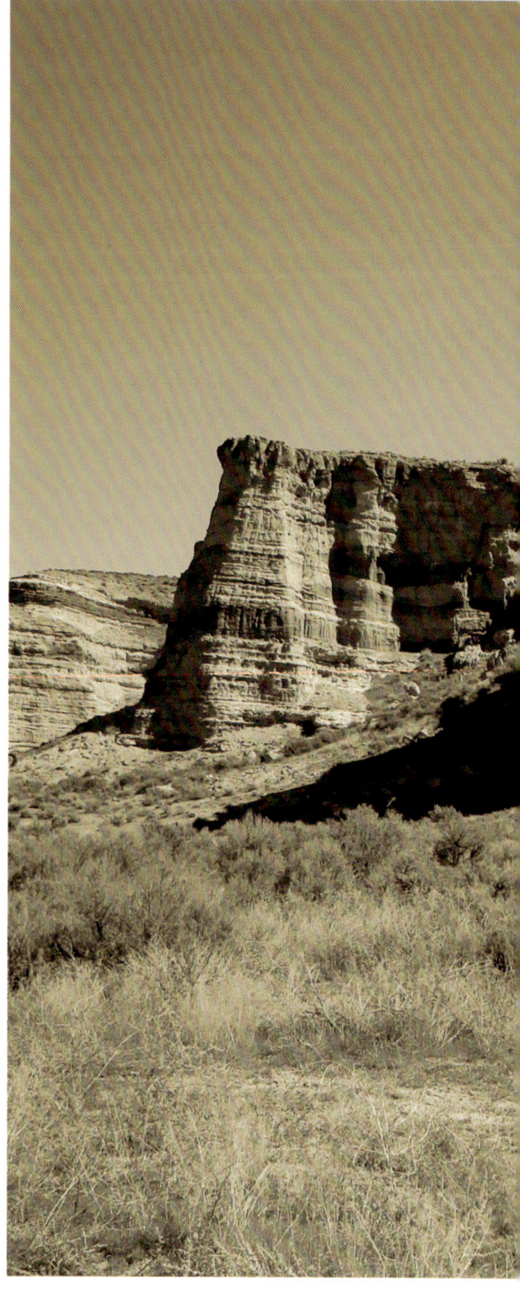

  (Top) Wild mustangs, Steens Mountains. *Photo by Dan Elster.* • (Bottom) Gopher snake. *Photo by Dan Elster.*

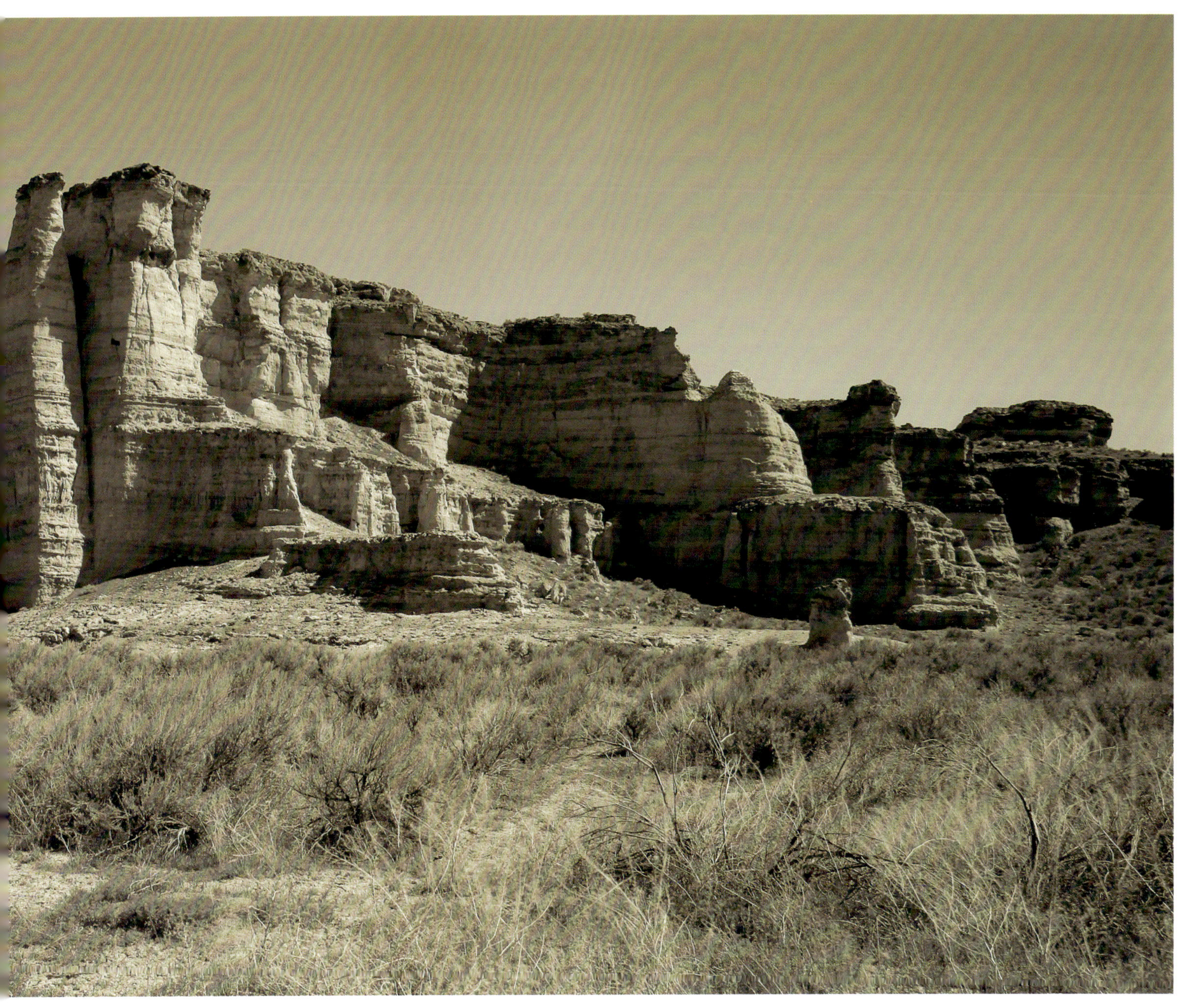

Pillars of Rome, Owyhee. These 100-foot-high formations measure about five miles long and two miles wide. *Photo by John Kirk.*

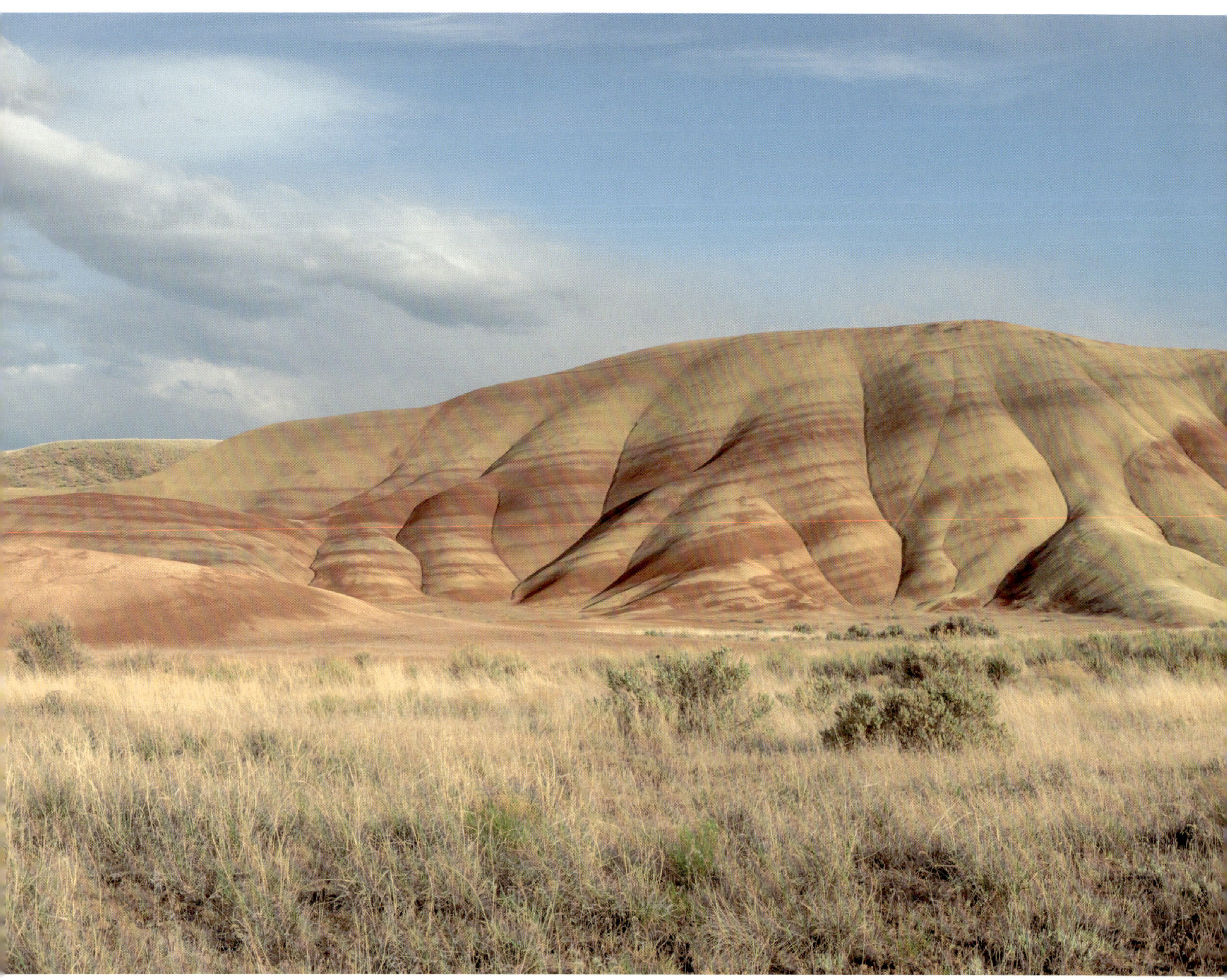

Painted Hills, considered one of the Seven Wonders of Oregon. *Photo by Barbara Tricarico.*

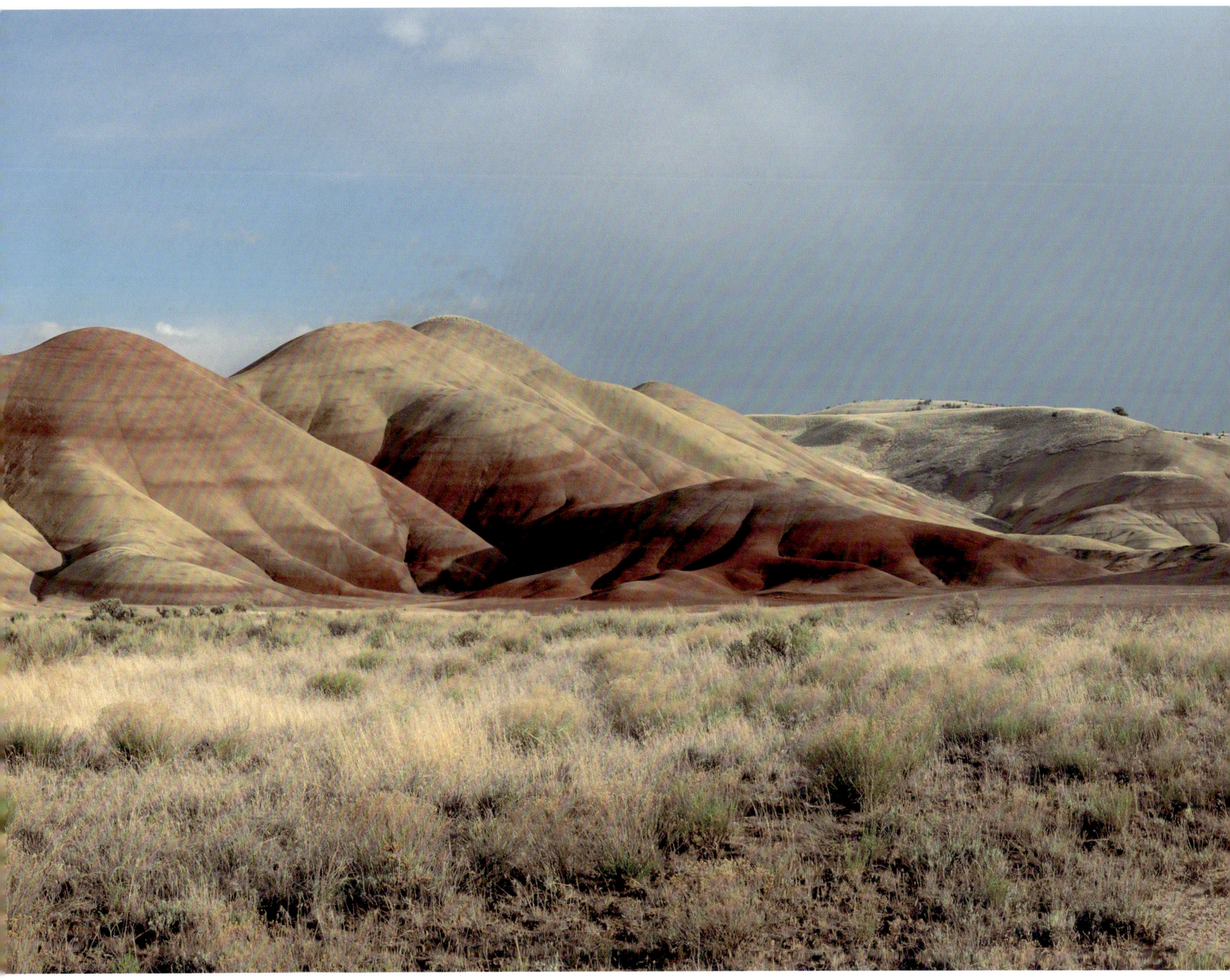

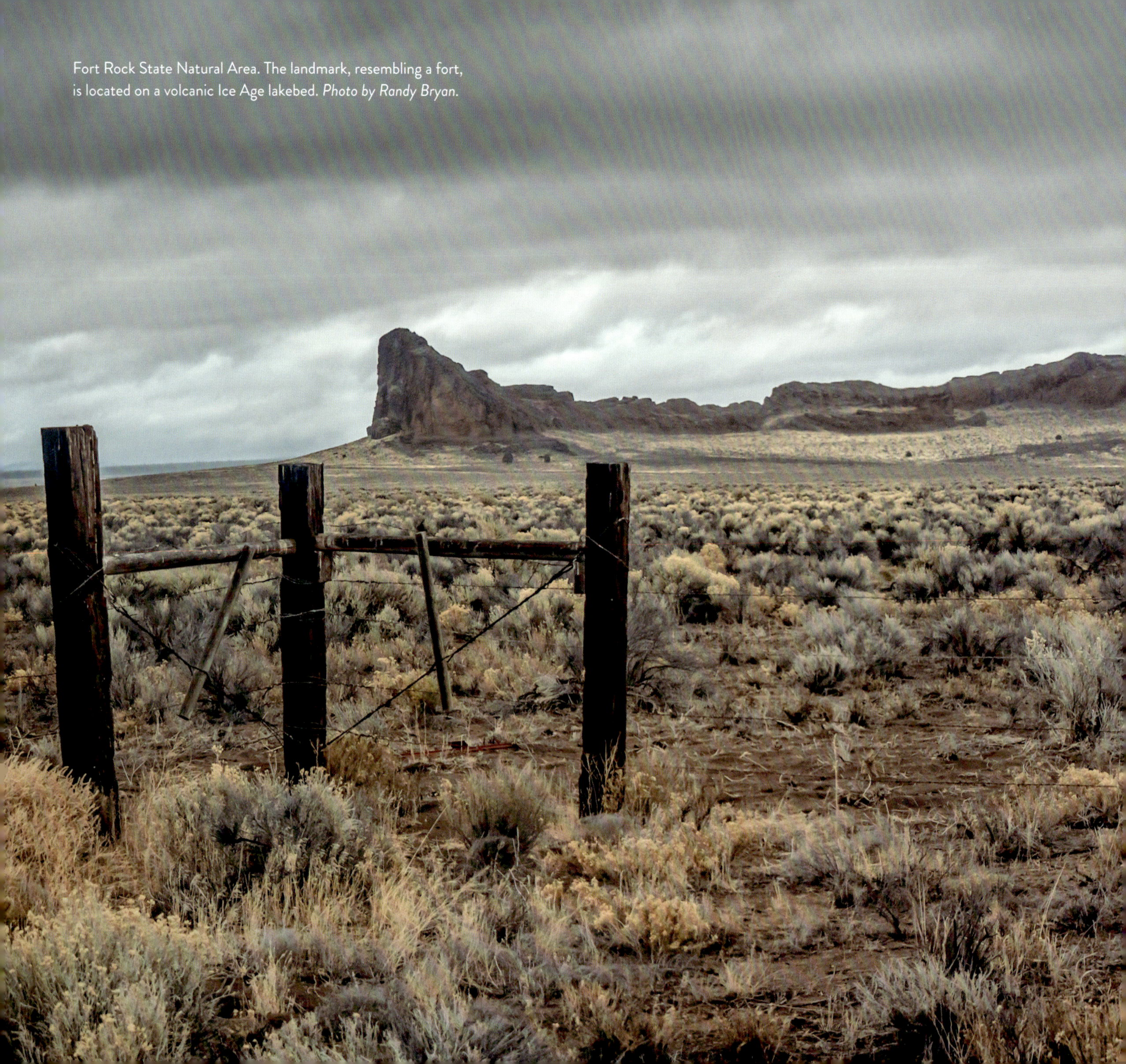

Fort Rock State Natural Area. The landmark, resembling a fort, is located on a volcanic Ice Age lakebed. *Photo by Randy Bryan.*

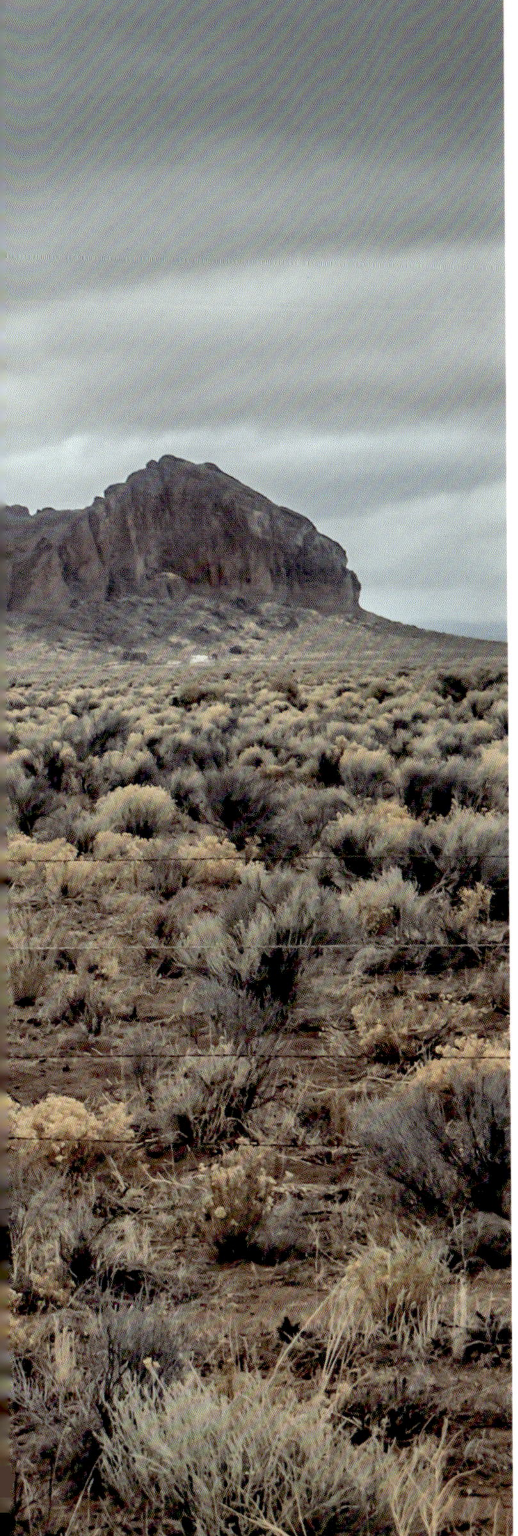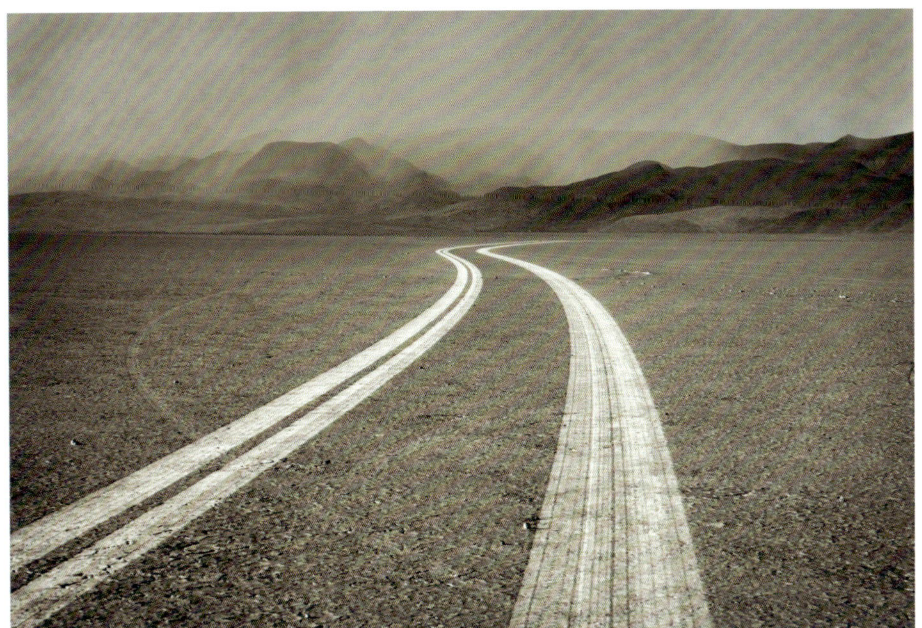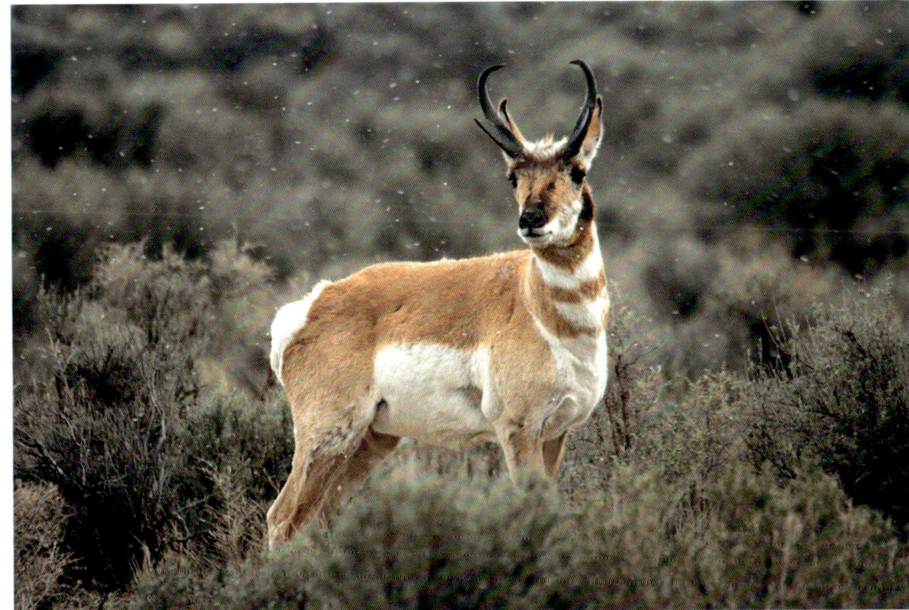

(Top) Alvord Desert. *Photo by John Kirk.* • (Bottom) Pronghorn in the snow. *Photo by Dan Elster.*

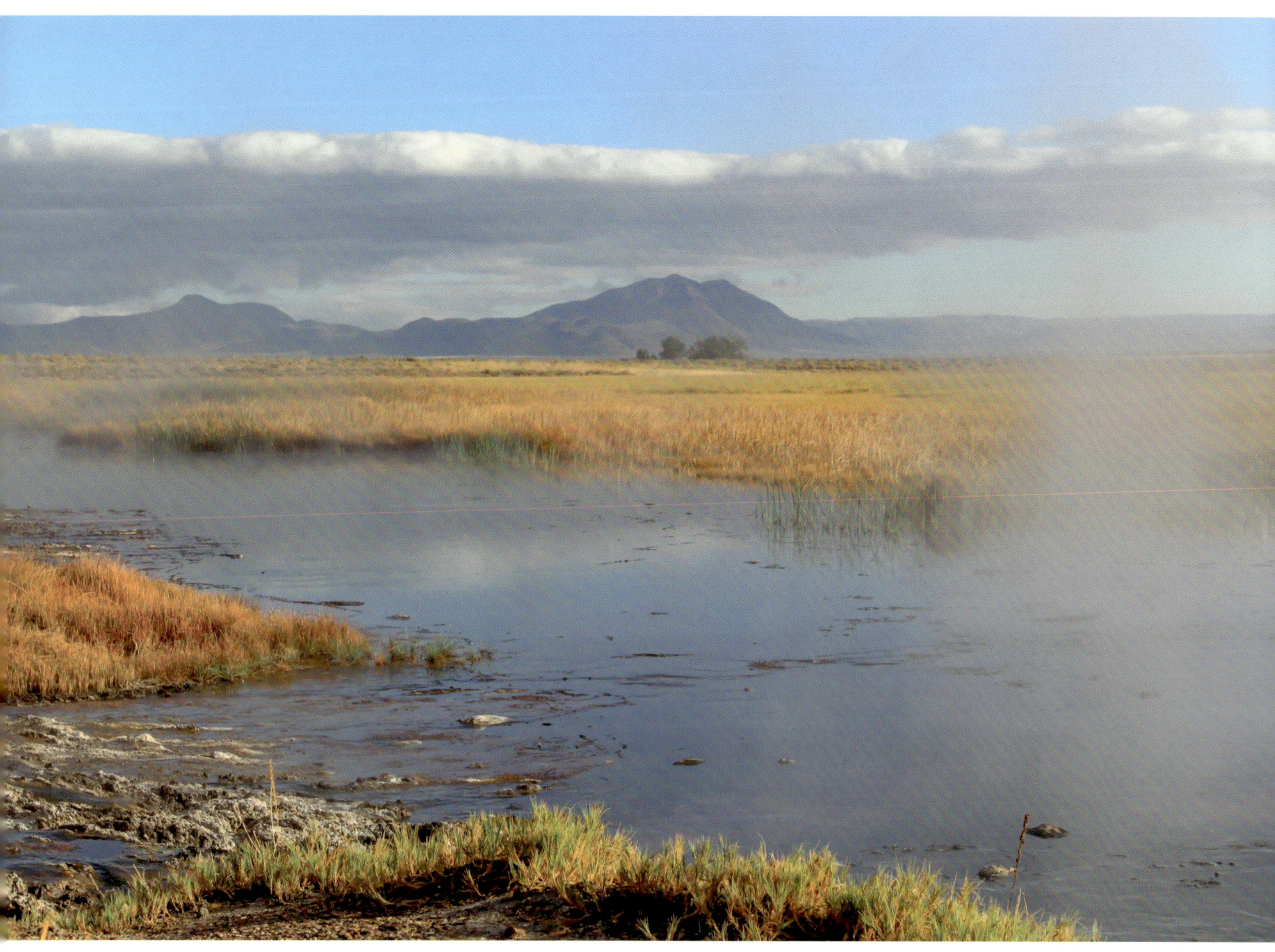

 Alvord Hot Springs. *Photo by Diana Standing.*

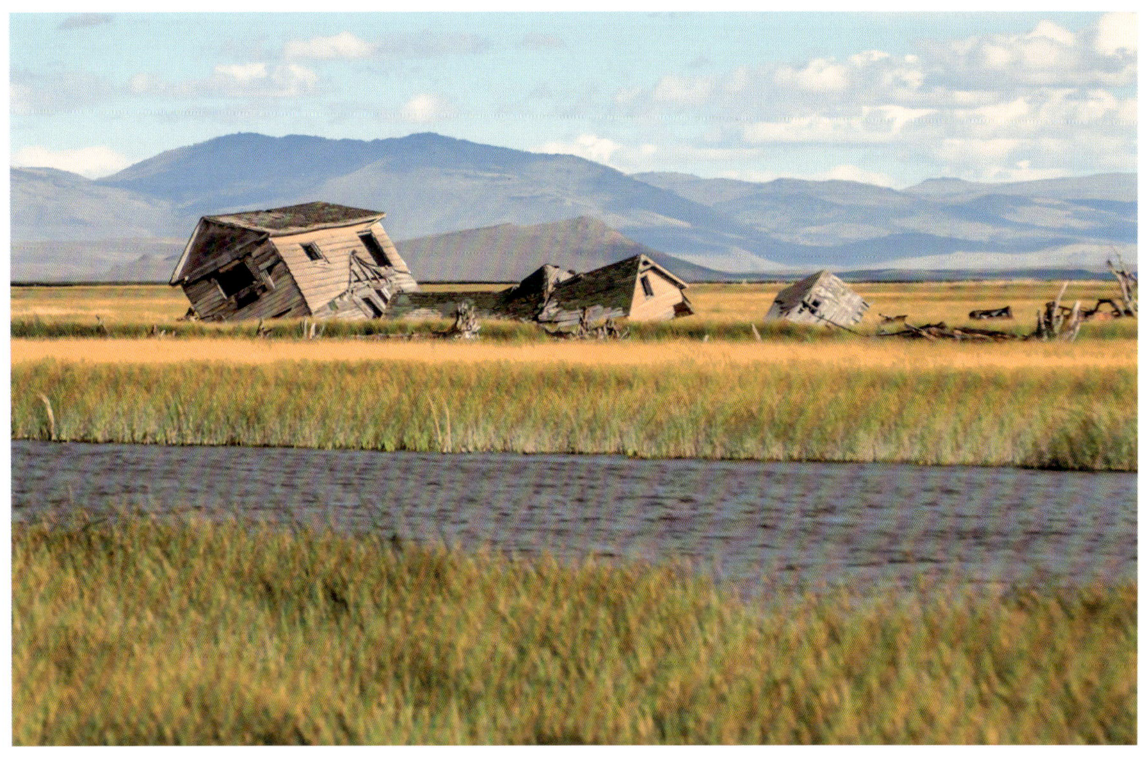

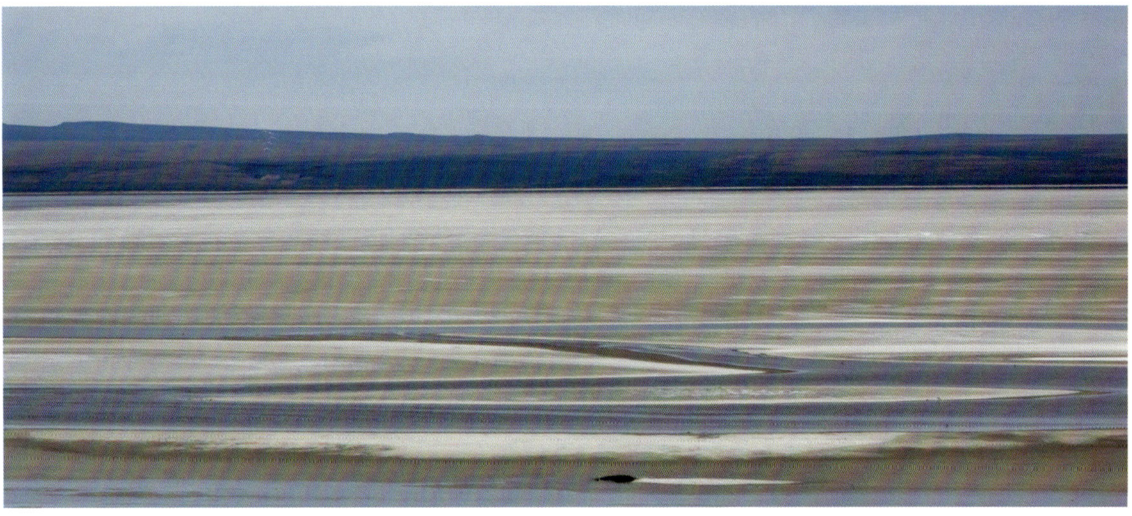

(Top) Abandoned buildings near Malheur National Wildlife Refuge. *Photo by George F. Peterson.* • (Bottom) Lake Abert. *Photo by Vivian McAleavey.*

CENTRAL OREGON

Whether you like the great outdoors or prefer a small town, Central Oregon has something for everyone during all four seasons of the year. Bordered by the Cascade Range and the Deschutes River, the climate is dry and sunny. The river provides recreational activities for the cities of Bend and Sunriver. Rafting, boating, paddleboarding, tubing, kayaking, swimming, and fly fishing are popular. Colorful tubes dot the landscape from Riverbend Park to Drake Park—a relaxing, hour-long summer activity. Winter brings snow to Central Oregon, perfect for skiing at Mount Bachelor or Hoodoo ski resorts.

In addition to the 1,800,000-acre Deschutes National Forest, Deschutes has the distinction of being the most cave-rich county in Oregon, with more than 500 lava tubes. Ancient volcanic activity formed much of the area. Not only did astronauts train on the Oregon lava fields in the 1960s in preparation for their journey to the moon, but a small piece of Oregon lava rock was left on the moon by astronaut Jim Irwin. The Newberry National Volcanic Monument has more than 54,000 acres of lakes and lava flows, much of it viewable from Pauline Peak (elevation 7,984 feet). Newberry Volcano (actually a crater) is the largest in the Cascades volcanic arc. A trip to Central Oregon is not complete without visiting the High Desert Museum to explore regional wildlife, culture, art, and natural resources.

The expansive Ochoco National Forest has a number of campgrounds that draw hikers and bikers. If you're lucky, you might see wild horses! Whether you're an adventurer or spectator, Smith Rock State Park, just outside Redmond in Terrebonne, is a sight to behold with its jagged peaks and red canyon walls. Smith Rock is considered one of the

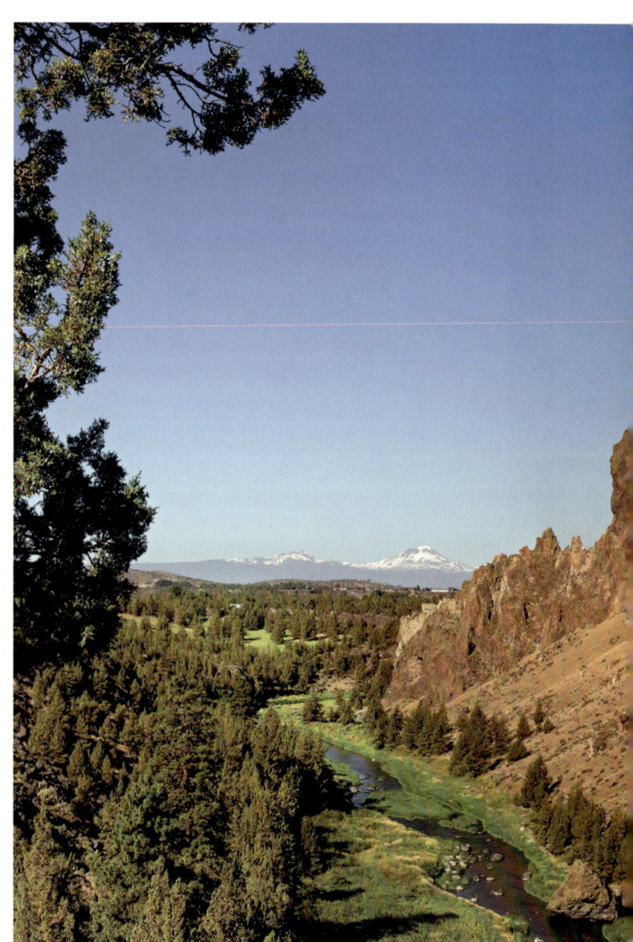

Seven Wonders of Oregon. There you'll find rock climbers, hikers, bikers, and even slackliners walking 350 feet in the air into the mouth of the unusual Monkey Face rock formation.

Bend, one of the state's fastest-growing cities, is Central Oregon's centerpiece. Craft beer festivals and breweries dot the landscape, and Bend has been dubbed "Beer Town USA!" The Deschutes Brewery and the Bend Brewing Company, as well as dozens of other microbreweries in the area, are on the Bend Ale Trail and considered world-class breweries.

The little town of Sisters (population 2,573) graciously opens its doors to a number of annual festivals that draw tens of thousands of visitors yearly from all over the world. Since 1941, the town has hosted events such as the Sisters Outdoor Quilt Festival (the world's largest outdoor quilt show, with more than 10,000 attendees), the Sisters Rodeo, the Sisters Glory Daze Car Show, and the Sisters Folk Festival. The town is framed by the picturesque Three Sisters Mountains, which draw hikers and rock climbers.

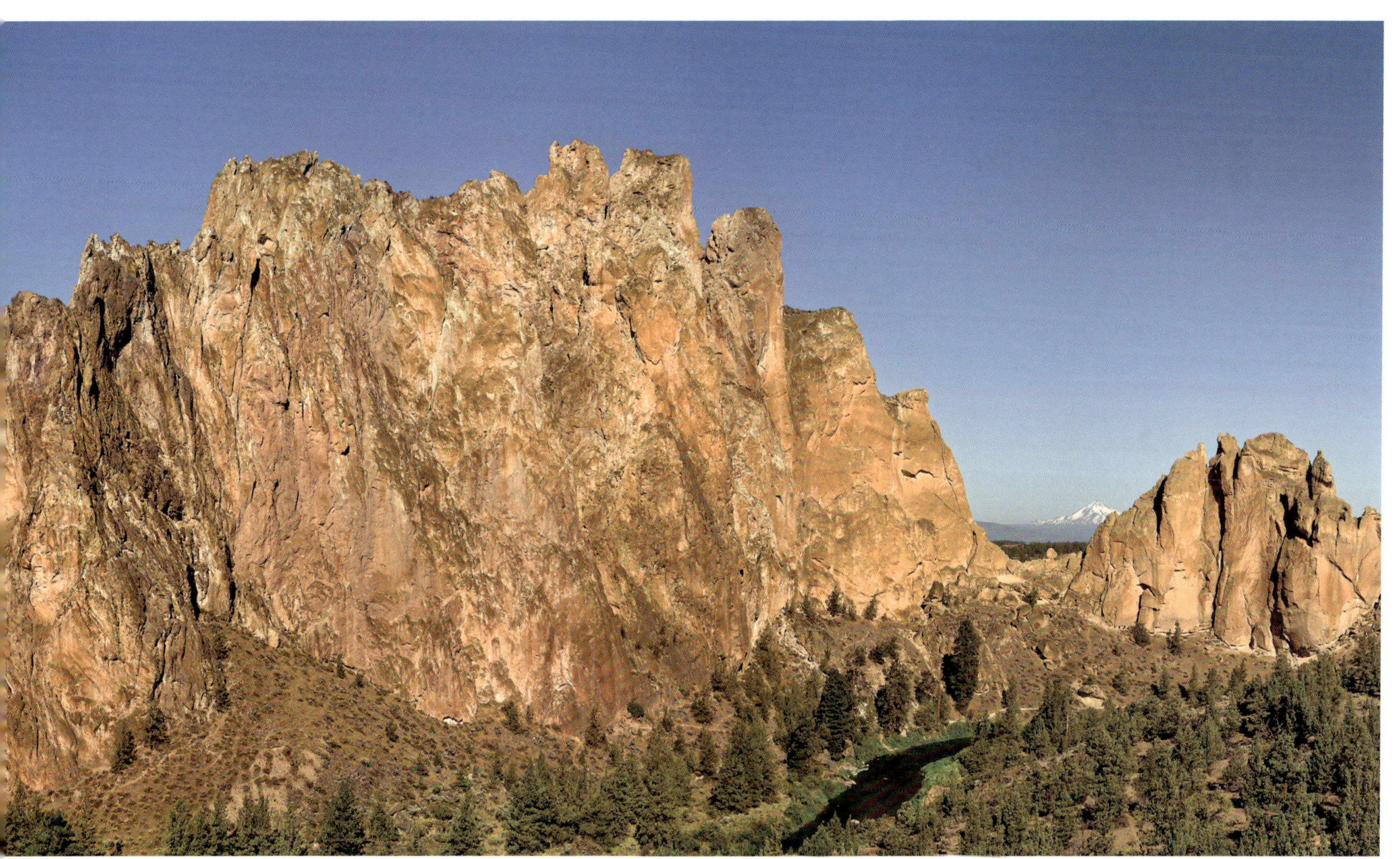

Smith Rock. *Photo by John Christer Petersen.*

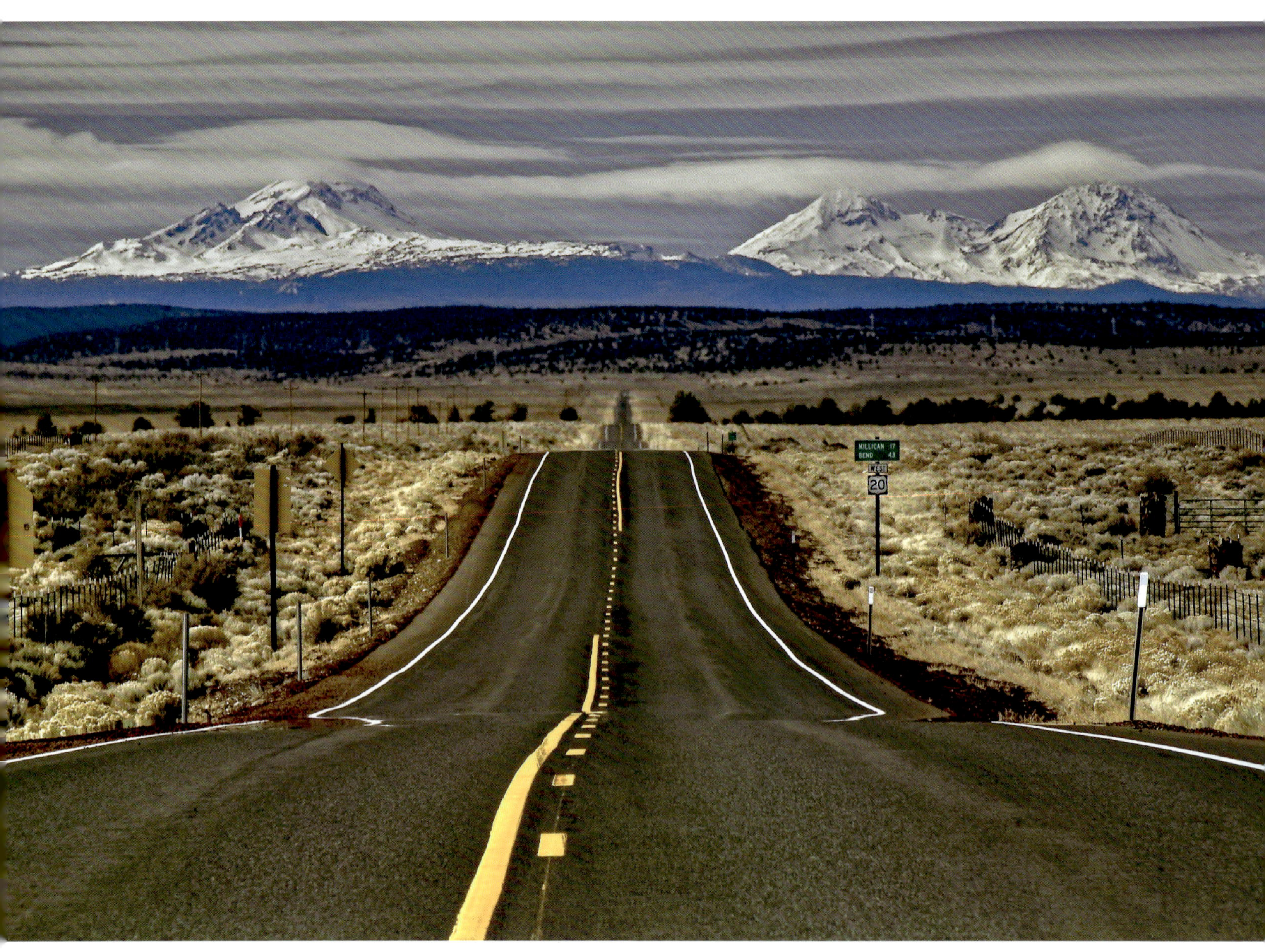

    Highway 20, with views of Middle Sister, North Sister, and Broken Top Mountains. *Photo by Jay Newman.*

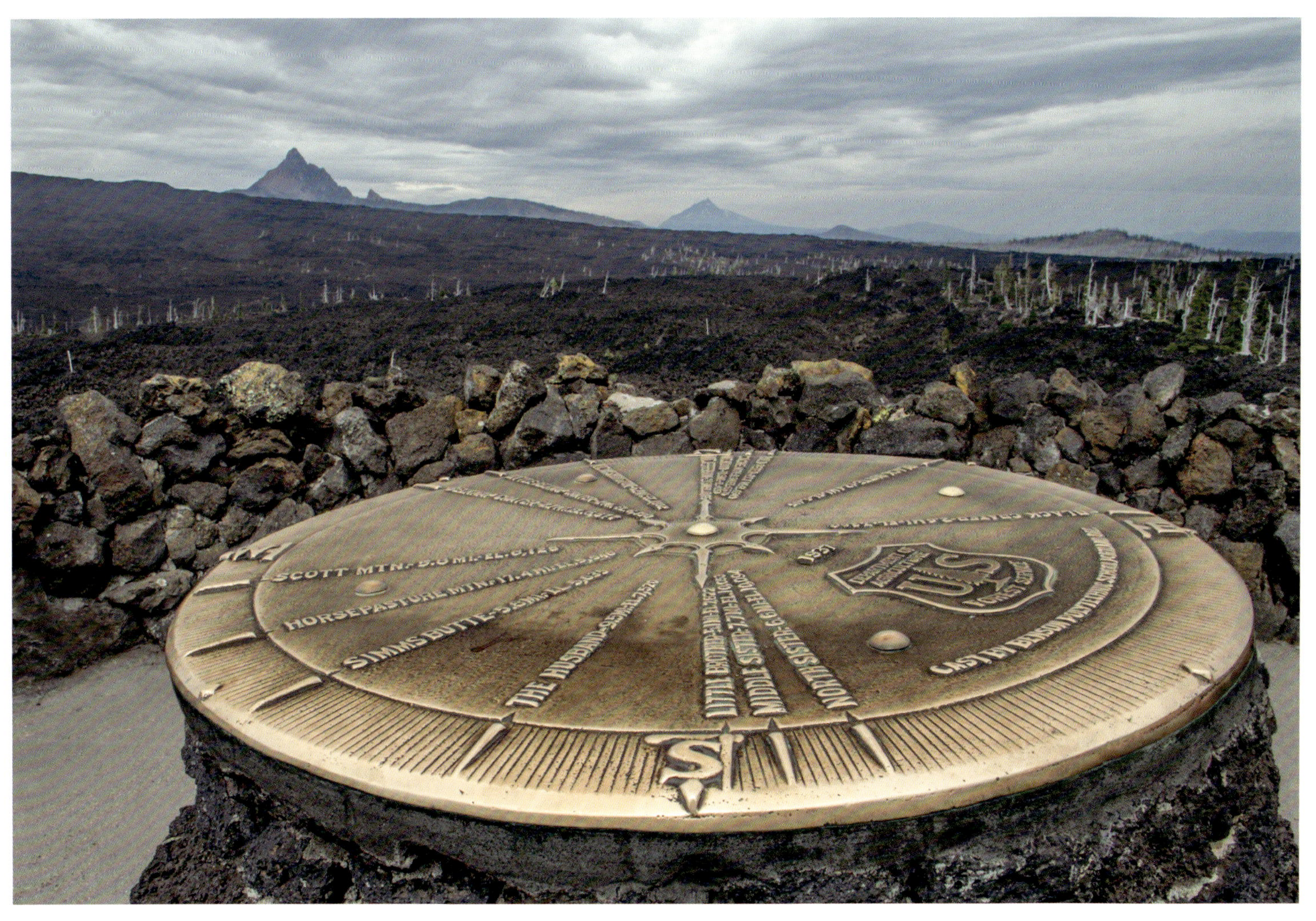

Dee Wright Observatory Pointer in the Deschutes National Forest at the McKenzie Pass. The Civilian Conservation Corps built the observatory during the Great Depression. Mount Washington is in the background on the left. *Photo by Howard Hunt.*

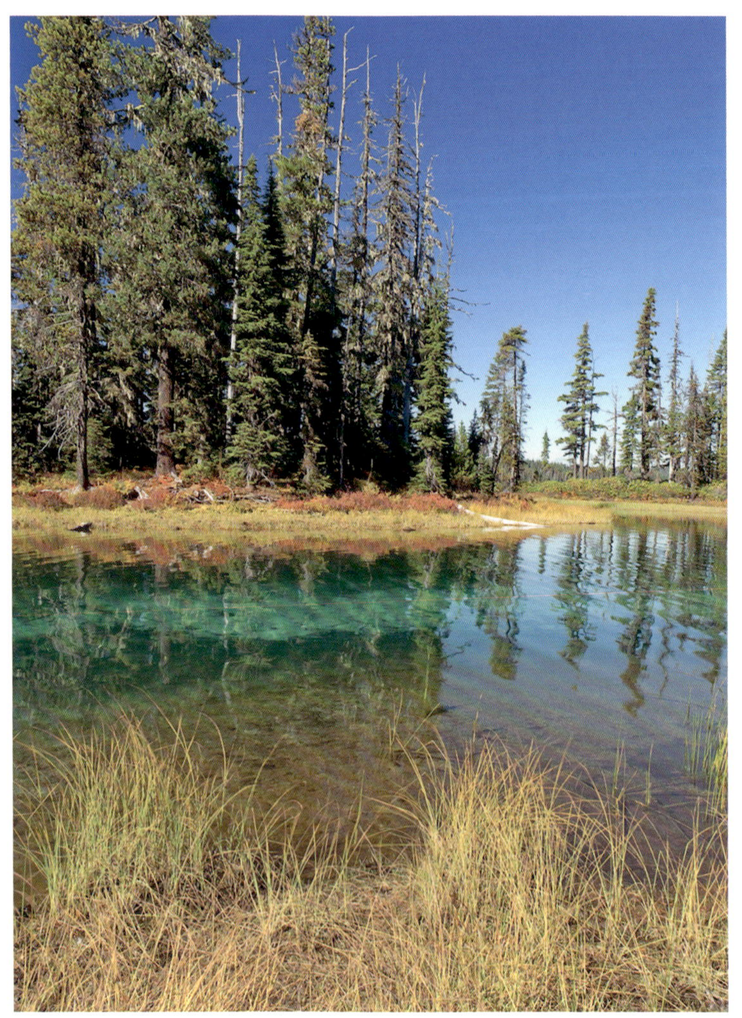

Waldo Lake, in the Cascade Mountains, is the second-deepest lake in Oregon after Crater Lake. *Photo by Vivian McAleavey.*

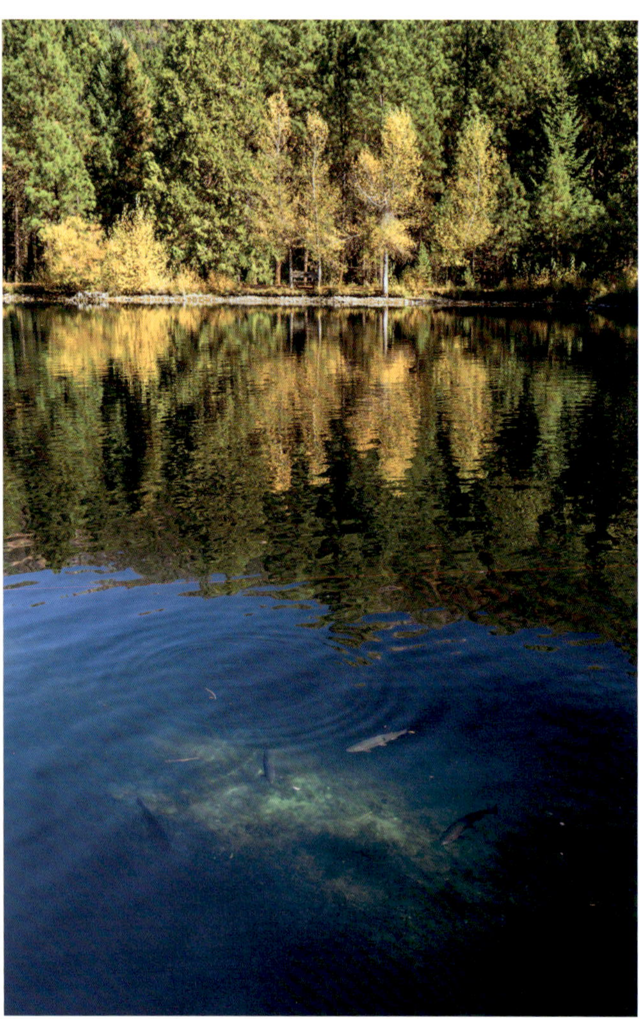

Wizard Falls Fish Hatchery in Sherman. Fish raised are rainbow trout, kokanee salmon, spring chinook, and summer steelhead. *Photo by Jay Newman.*

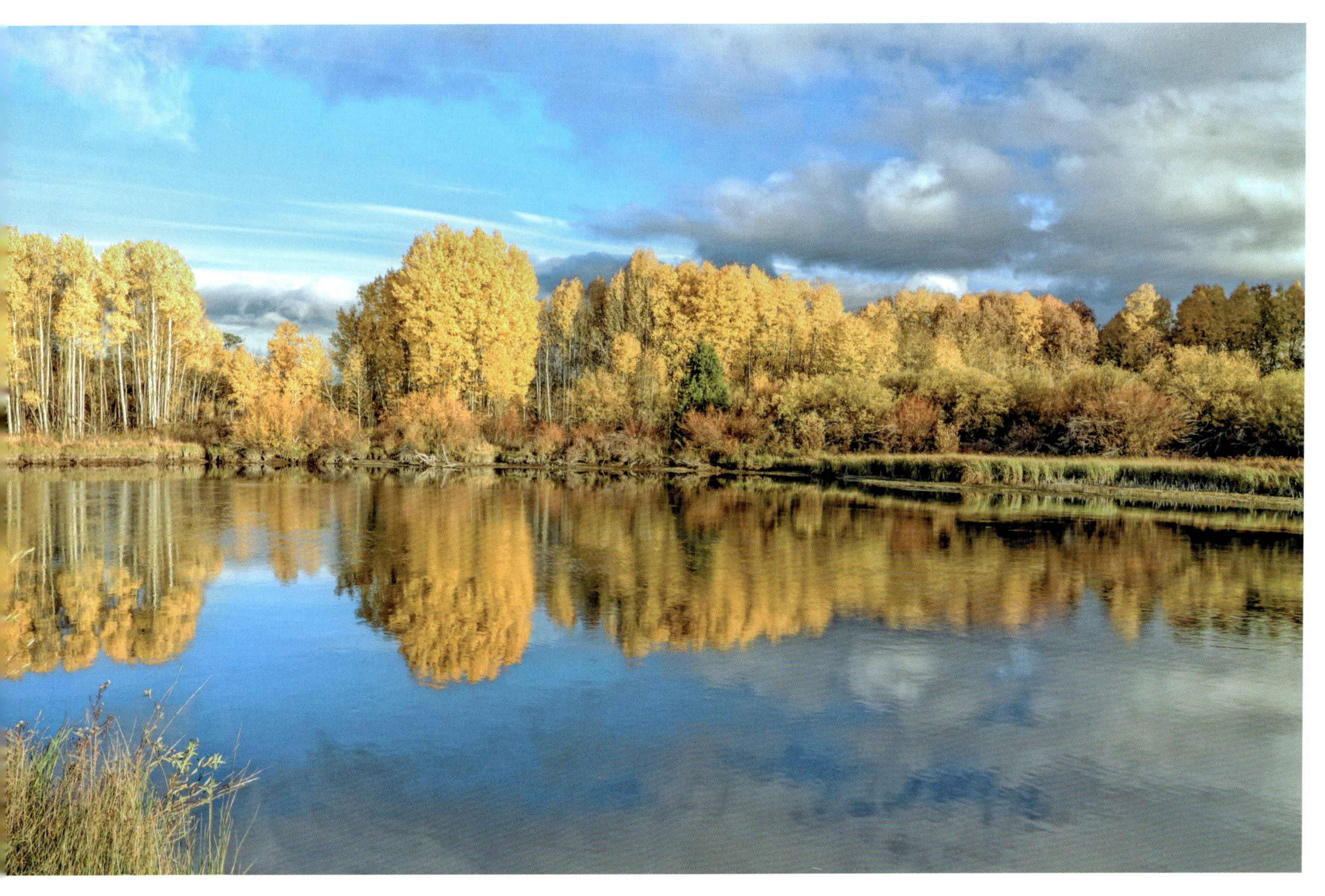

Deschutes River aspens in Bend. *Photo by Barbara Tricarico.*

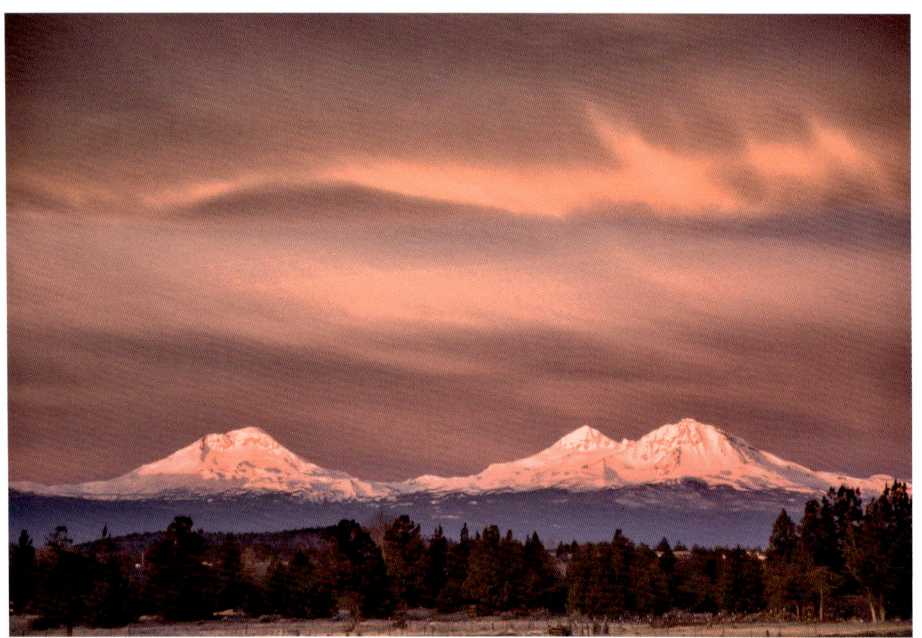

Three Sisters Mountains. Seen for miles around, these volcanic mountains are the third-, fourth-, and fifth-highest peaks in Oregon, each at over 10,000 feet in elevation. *Photo by Hans Stroo.*

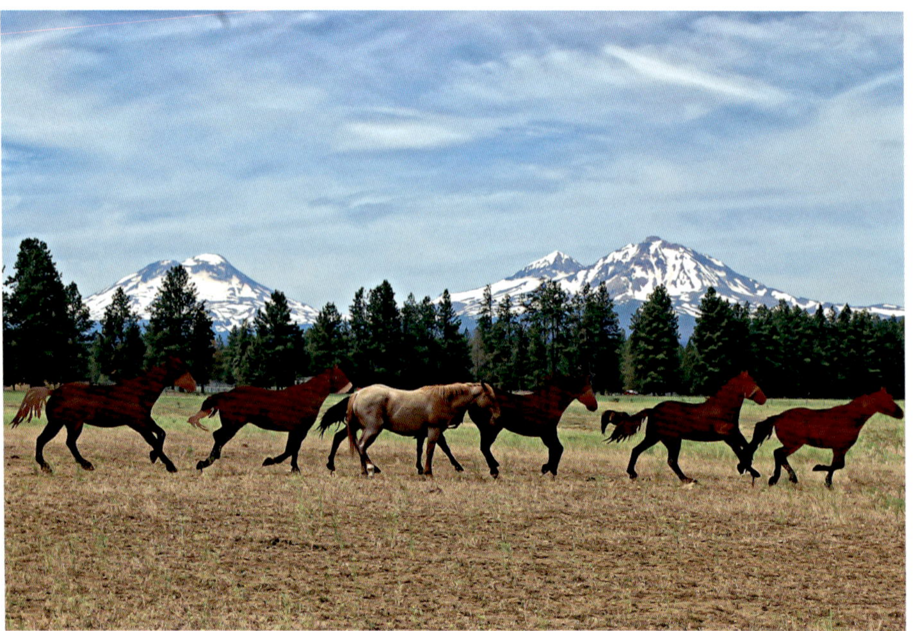

Lone horse on Highway 20. The Three Sisters Mountains are the backdrop for these metal horse sculptures created by Brian Bain, commissioned by Sisters to commemorate the town's ranching and equestrian heritage. *Photo by Barbara Tricarico.*

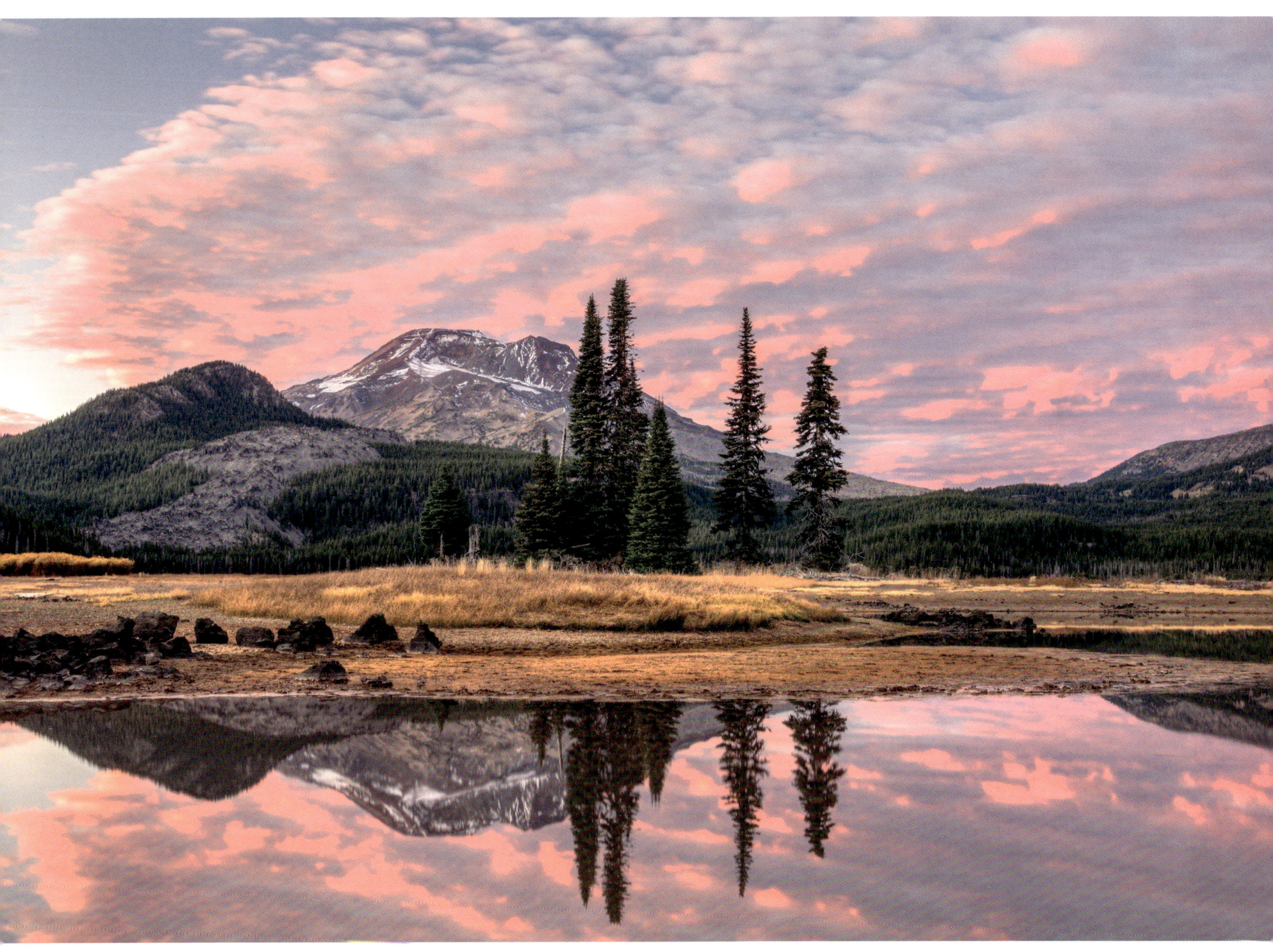

Sparks Lake is twenty-five miles west of Bend. *Photo by Sue Newman.* 111

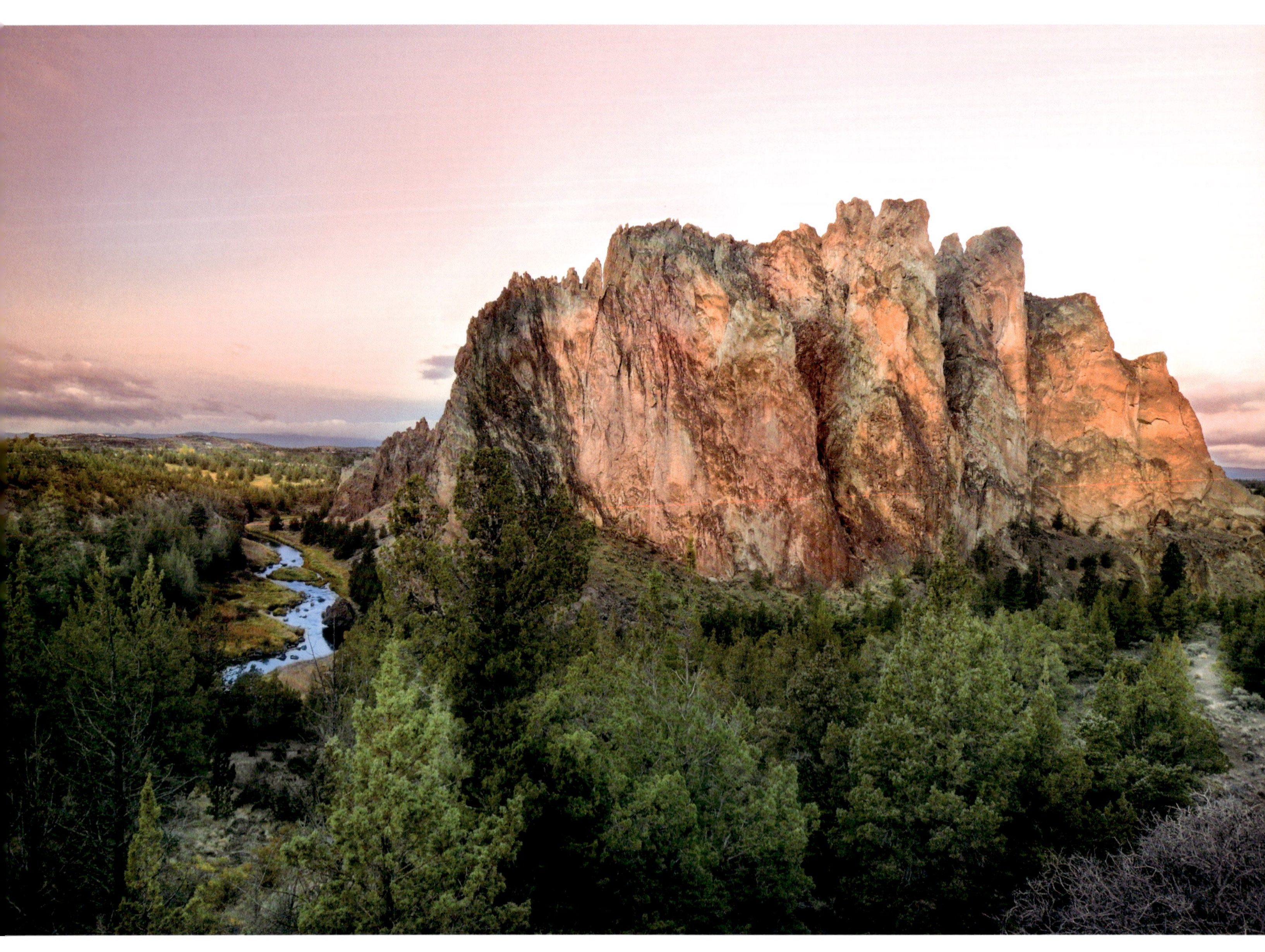

Smith Rock and Crooked River at sunrise. Near the cities of Redmond, Bend, and Sisters, Smith Rock State Park is a popular destination. *Photo by Barbara Tricarico.*

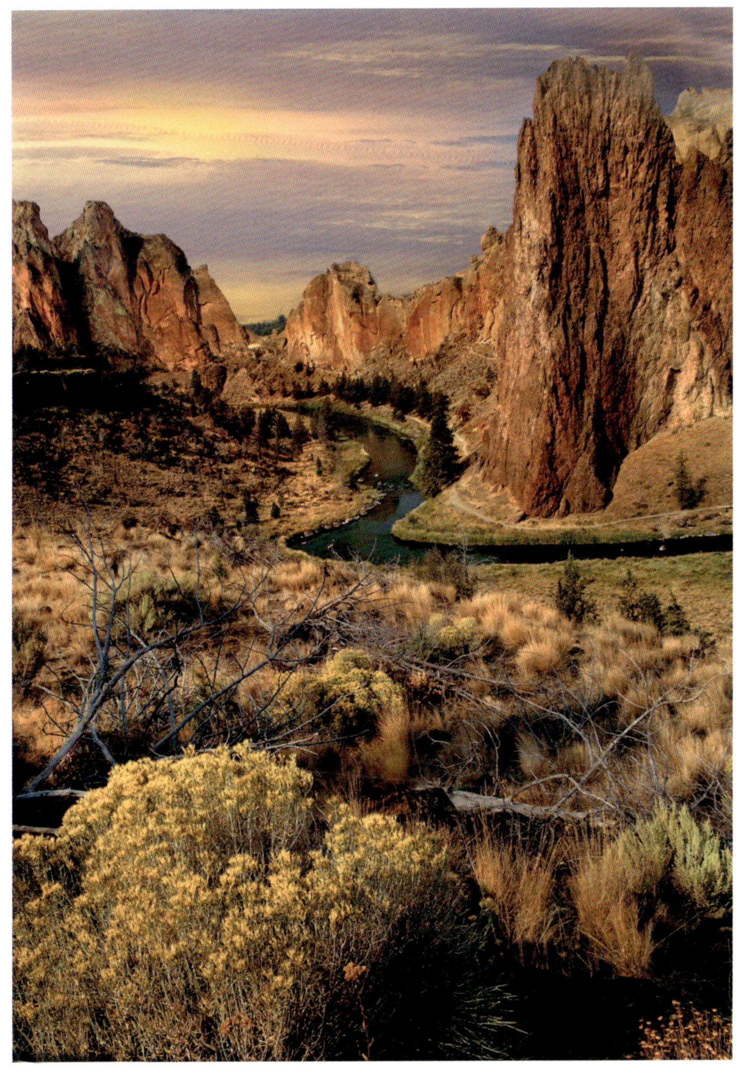

Smith Rock and Crooked River. *Photo by Neal R. Thompson.*

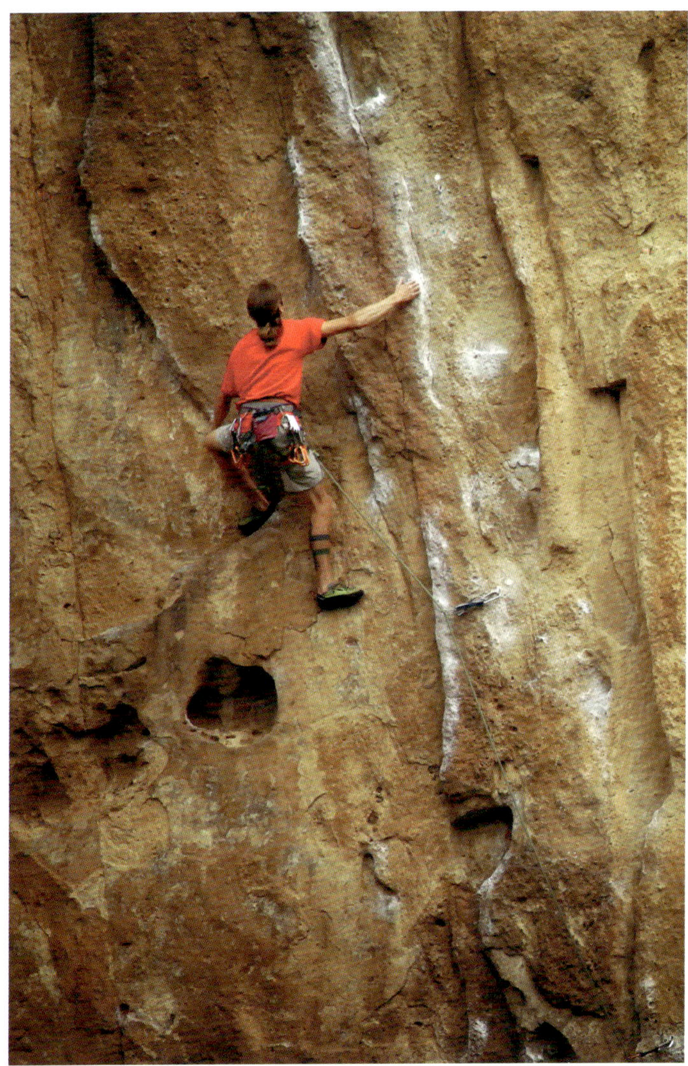

Rock climber, Smith Rock State Park. *Photo by John Kirk.*

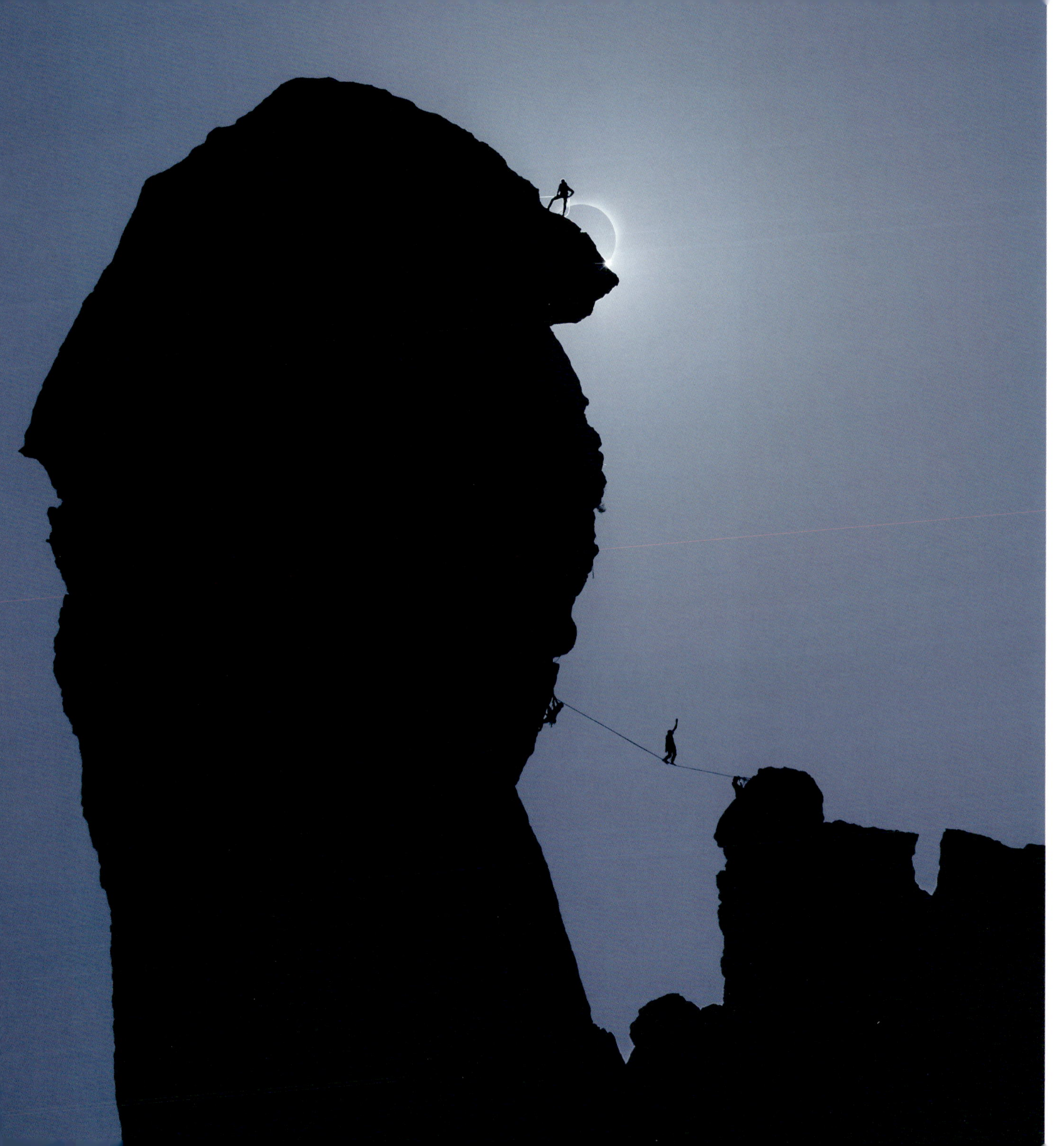

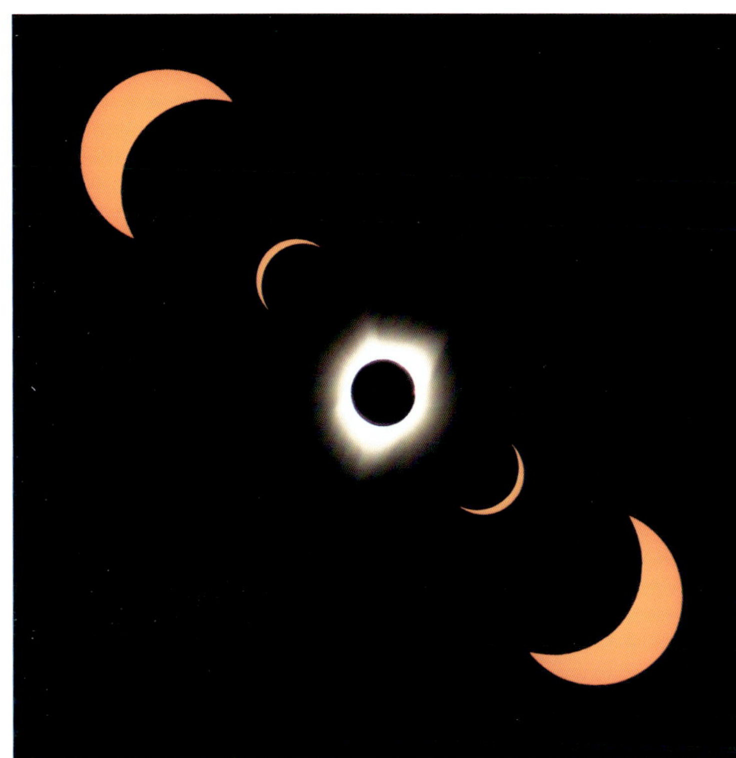

Total solar eclipse composite. *Photo by Alan Ingersoll.*

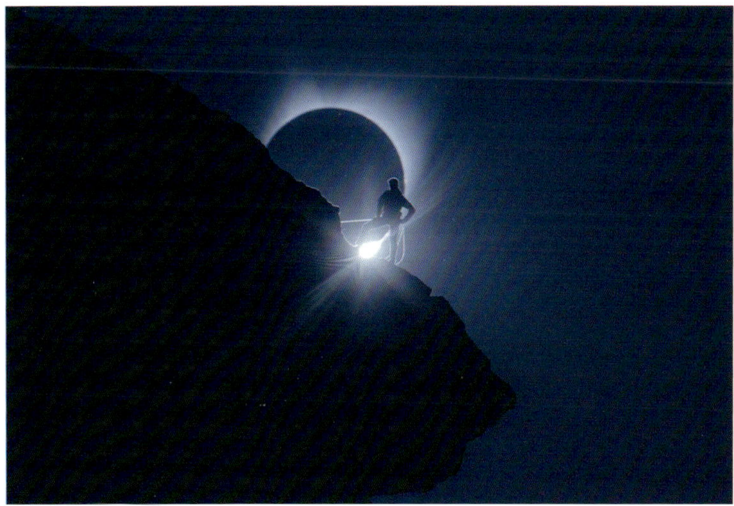

Total solar eclipse. Rock climber Tommy Smith was dramatically captured against a total eclipse at Smith Rock State Park on August 21, 2017. The event lasted less than two minutes. *Photo by Andrew Studer.*

(Opposite) Slackliner Ryan Robinson walks from Springboard into the "mouth" of Monkey Face at Smith Rock State Park, while Tommy Smith poses from above. The backdrop is a total solar eclipse, which occurred on August 21, 2017. *Photo by Andrew Studer.*

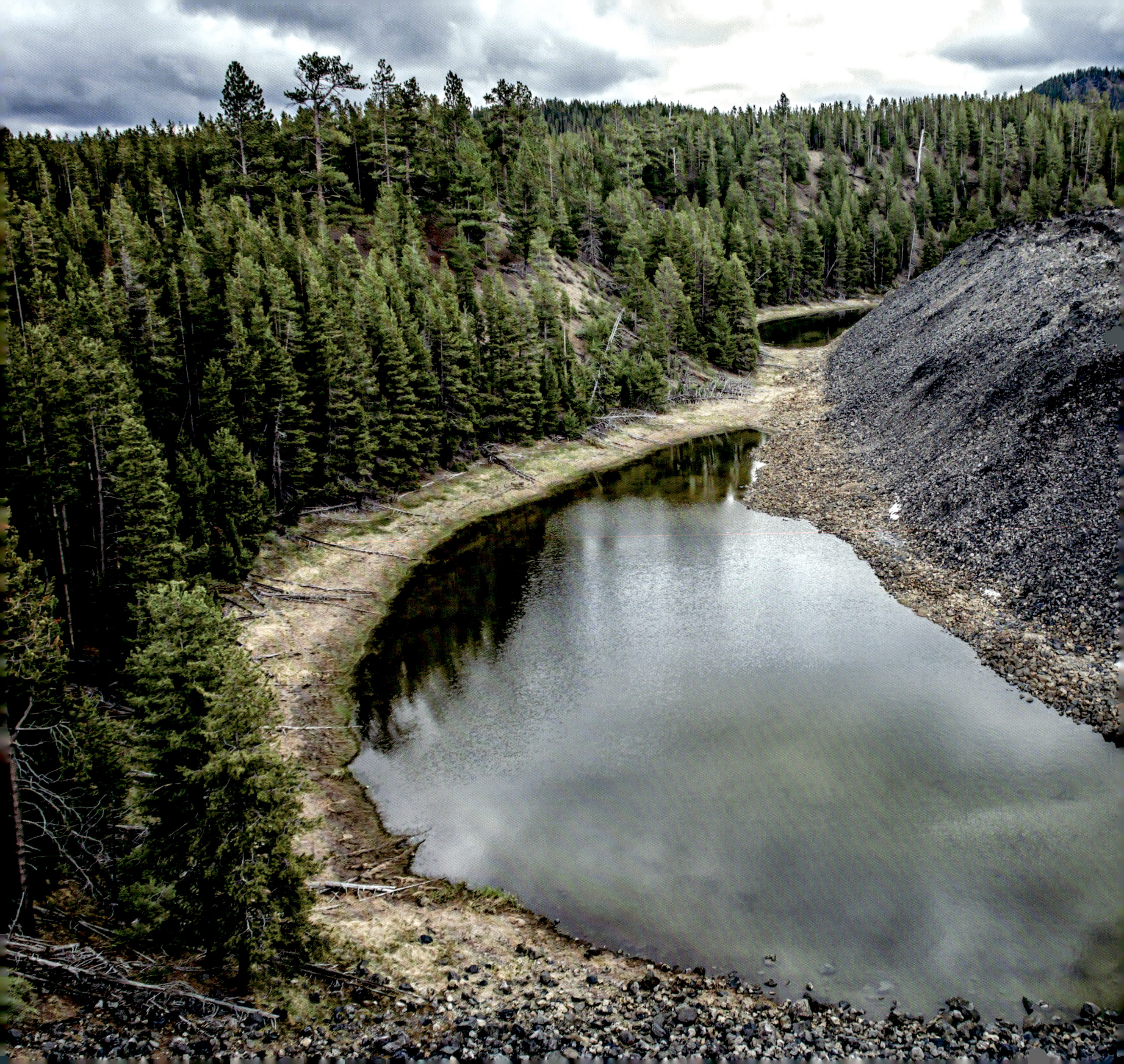

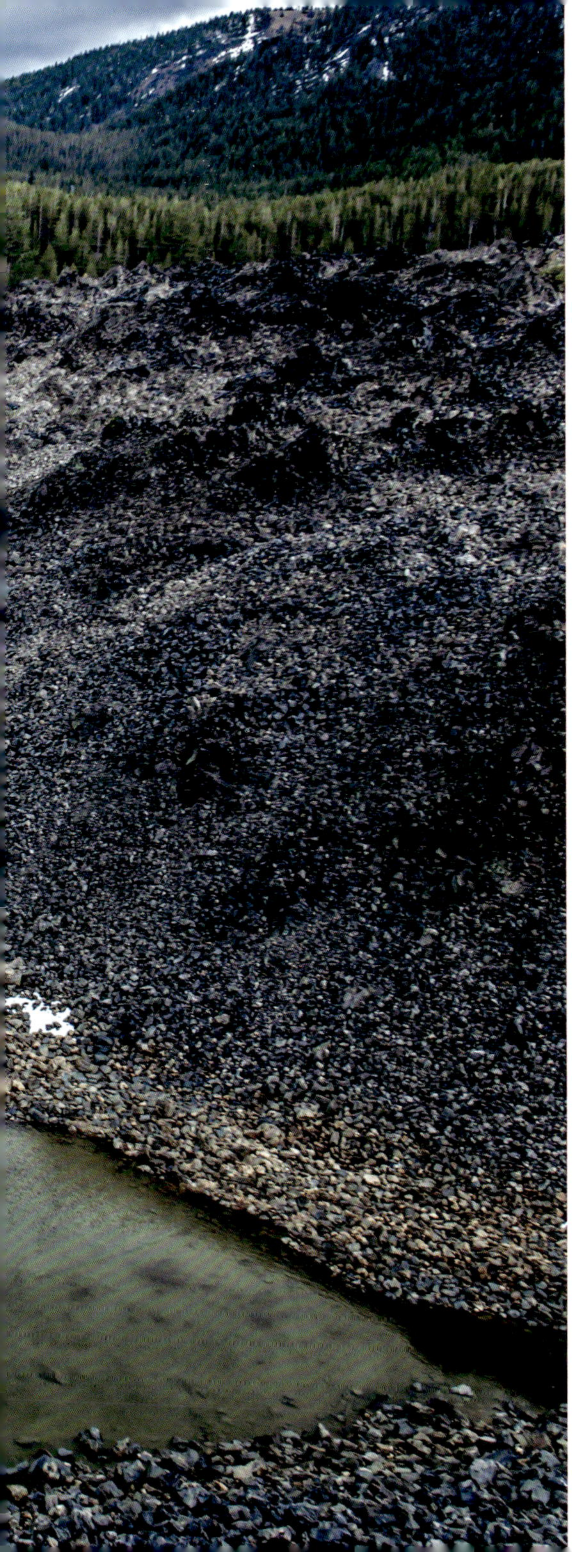

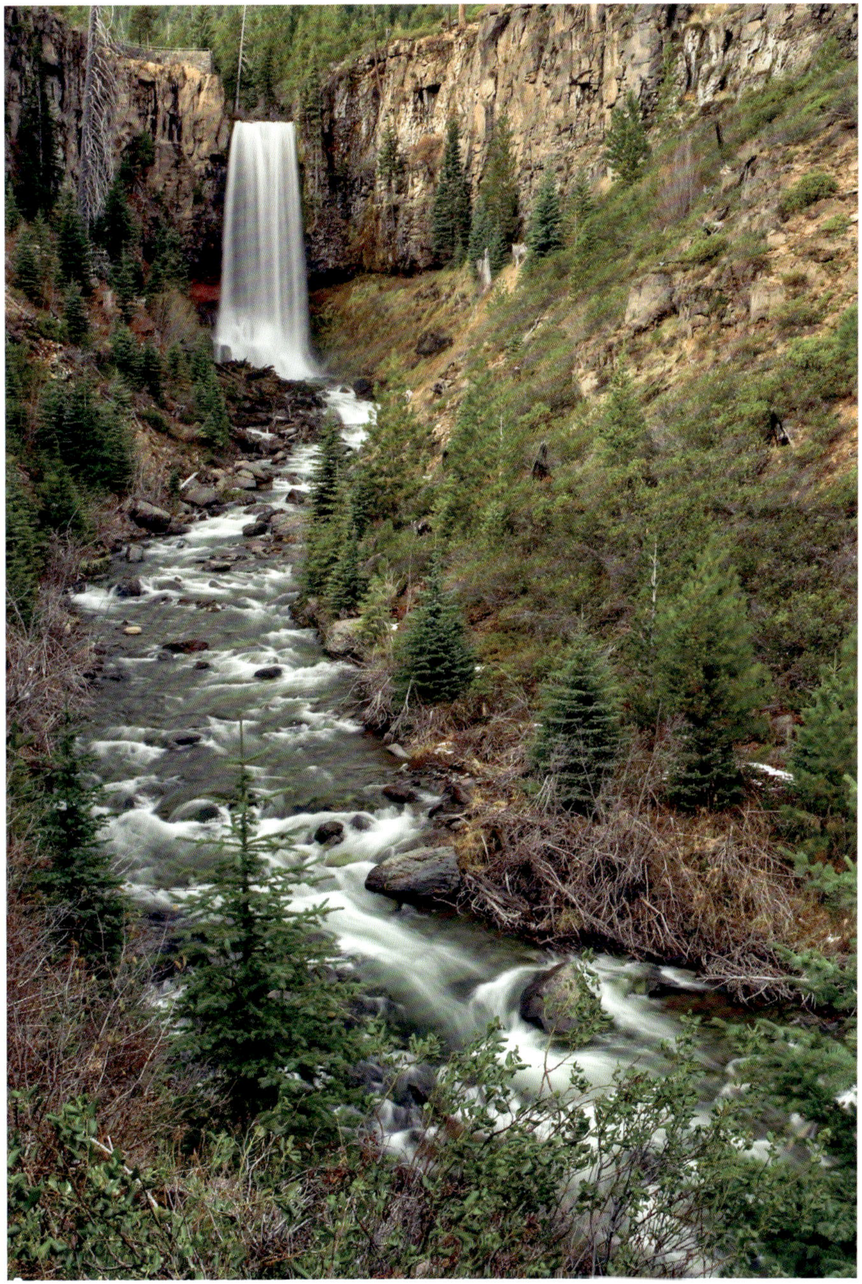

Tumalo Falls is a 97-foot waterfall near Bend. *Photo by Jay Newman.*
(Opposite) Big Obsidian Flow, Newberry National Volcanic Monument. *Photo by Barbara Tricarico.*

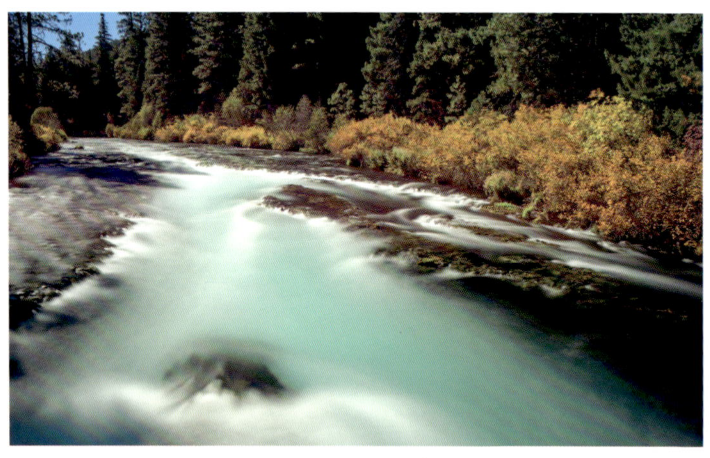

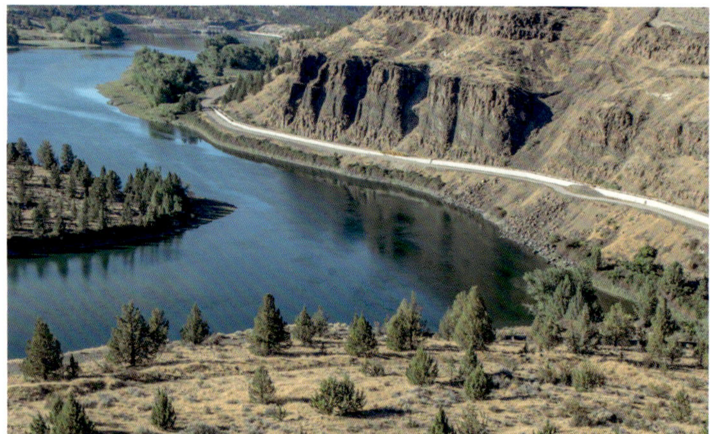

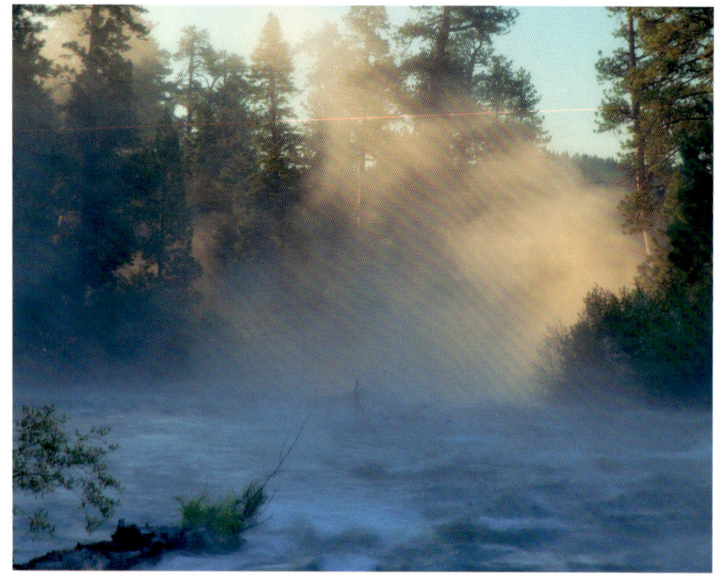

(Above) A tributary of the Deschutes River near Sisters, the Metolius River is popular for fly-fishing. *Photo by Jay Newman.*

(Top right) Warm Springs Reservation near Madras. The area is occupied and governed by the Confederated Tribes of Warm Springs. *Photo by George F. Peterson.*

(Bottom right) Early dawn, Deschutes River. *Photo by John Christer Petersen.*

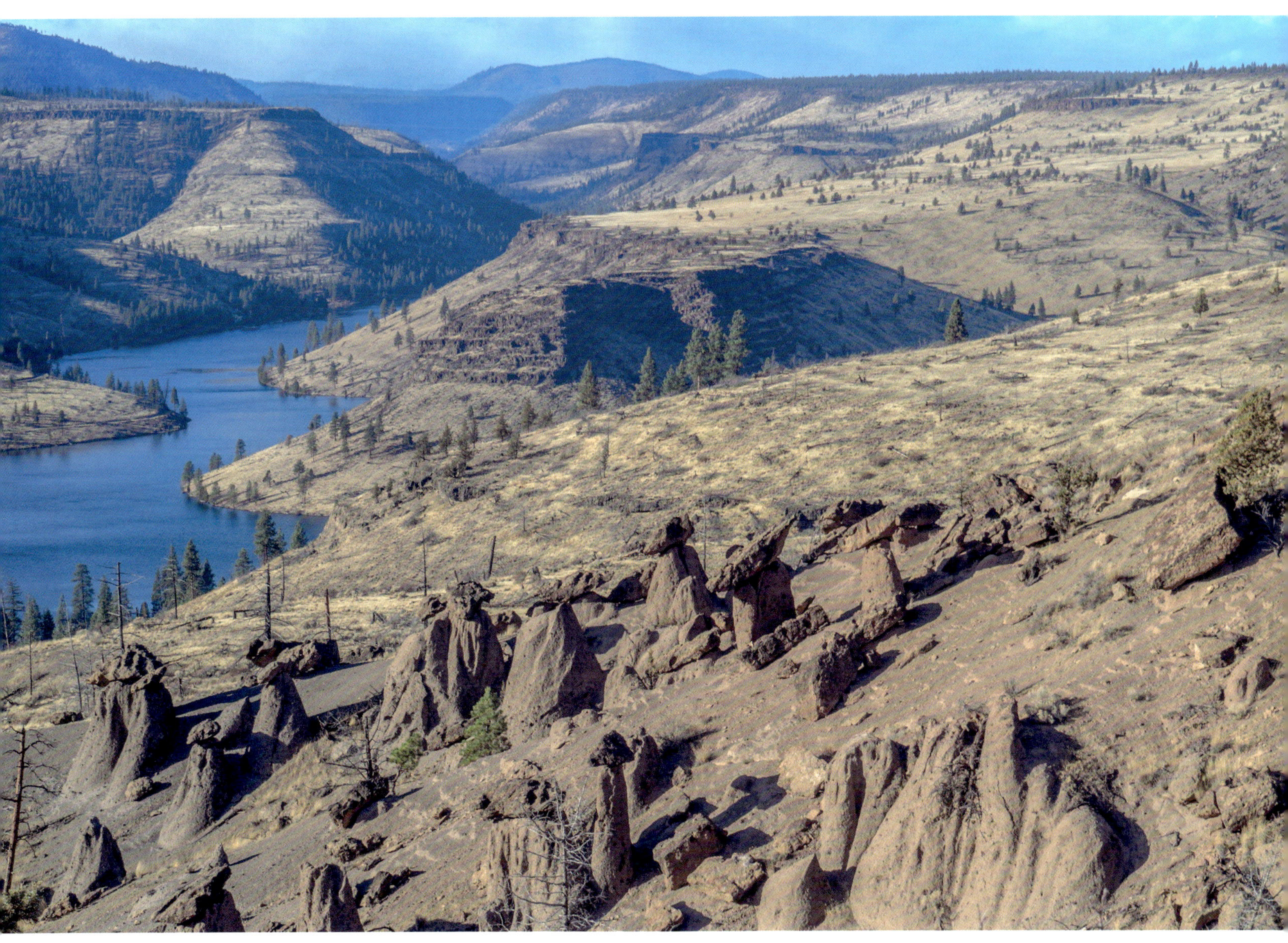

Balancing Rocks are natural rock formations on the Metolius River near the Deschutes National Forest. *Photo by Randy Bryan.*   119

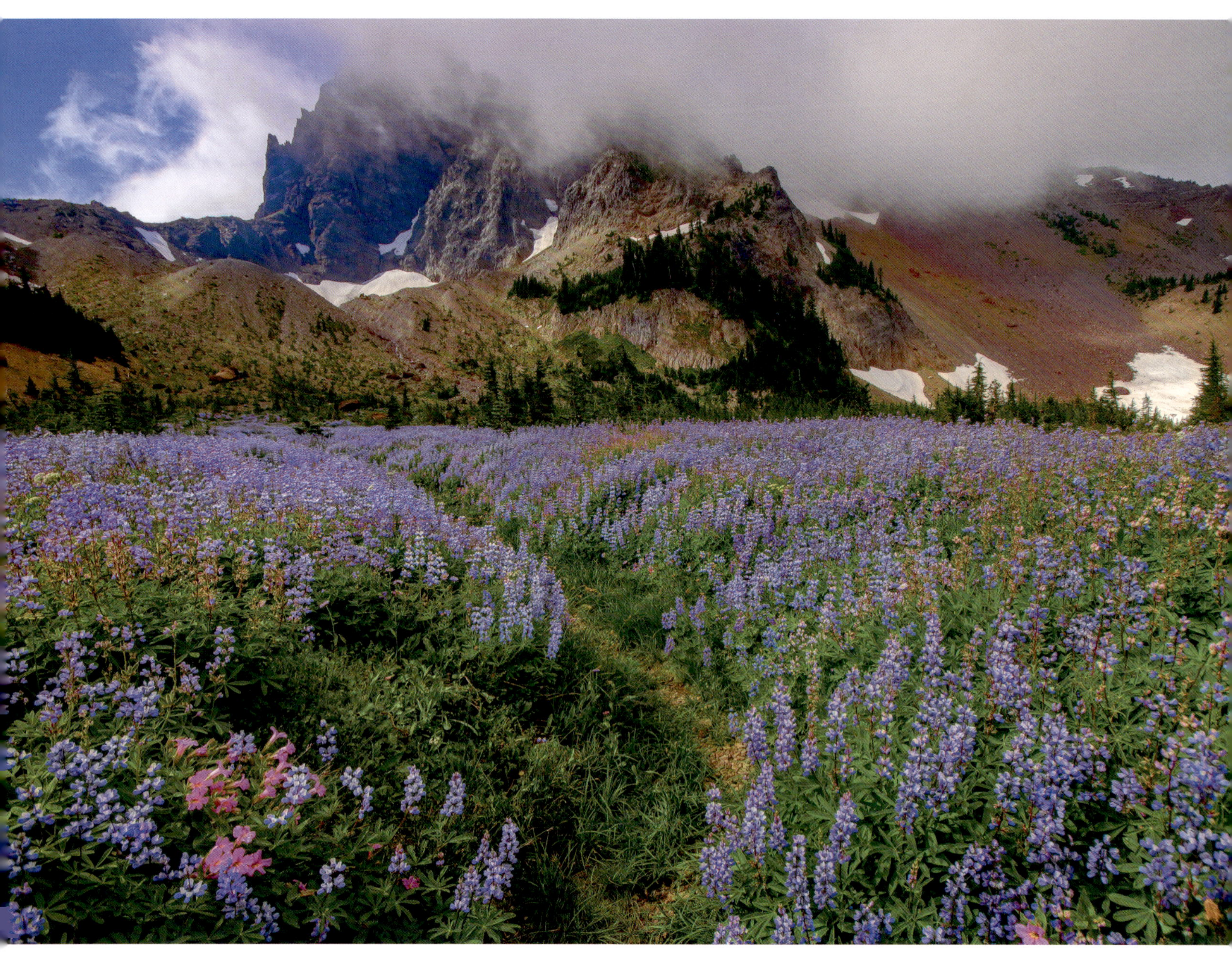

Meadow near Three Finger Jack. Named for an outlaw in the Old West, this area in the Cascade Range is an inactive, glaciated volcano. *Photo by Clem Paslack.*

120

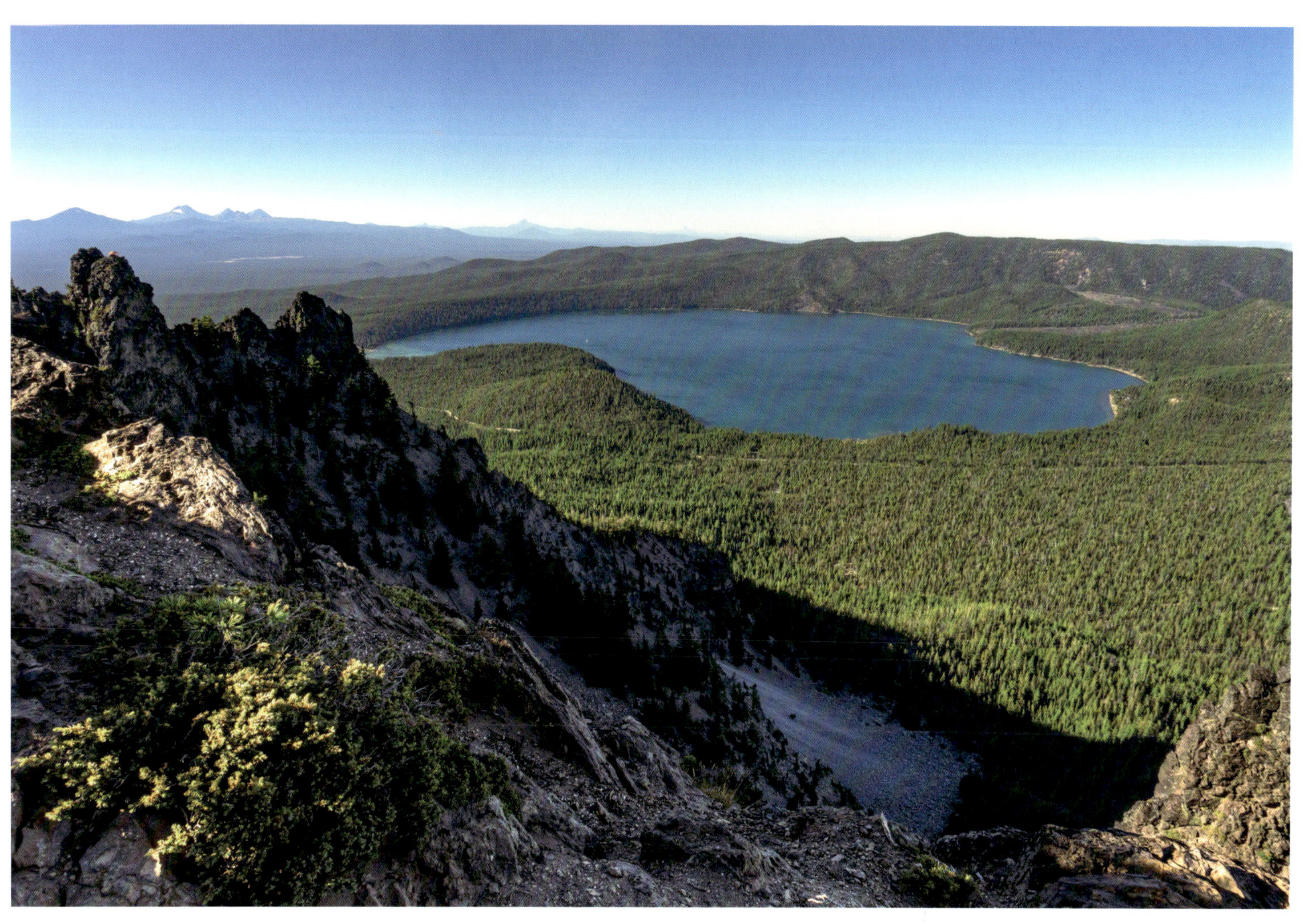

Paulina Lake seen from Paulina Peak. The lake was formed by 500,000 years of volcanic activity and sits within Newberry Caldera. *Photo by Sue Newman.*

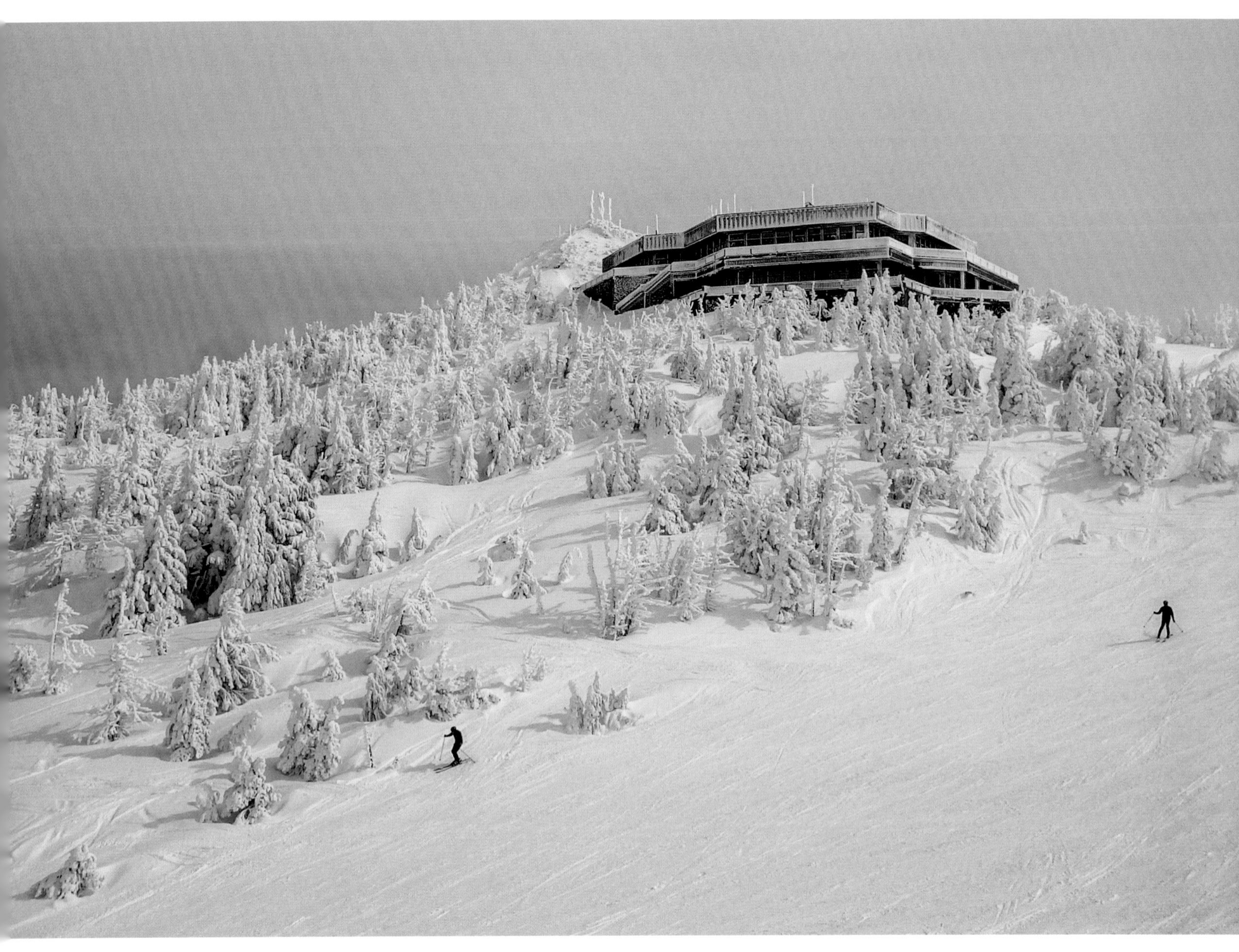

    Mount Bachelor ski lodge. *Photo by George F. Peterson.*

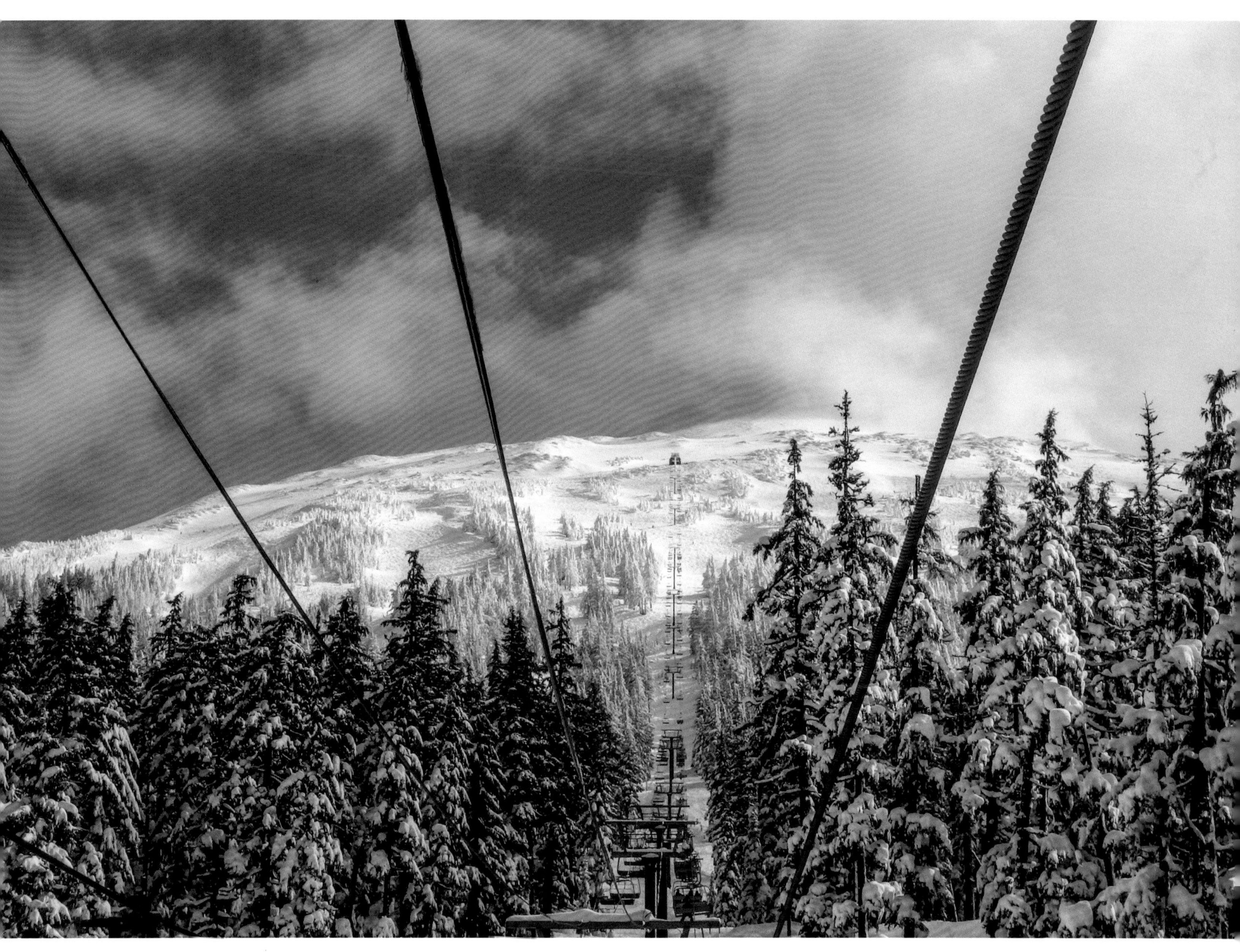

Mount Bachelor ski lift. Located twenty-two miles outside of Bend, 9,068-foot Mount Bachelor is a popular ski destination with 3,683 acres of skiable area. It is the only Cascade volcano with a chairlift to the summit. *Photo by George F. Peterson.*

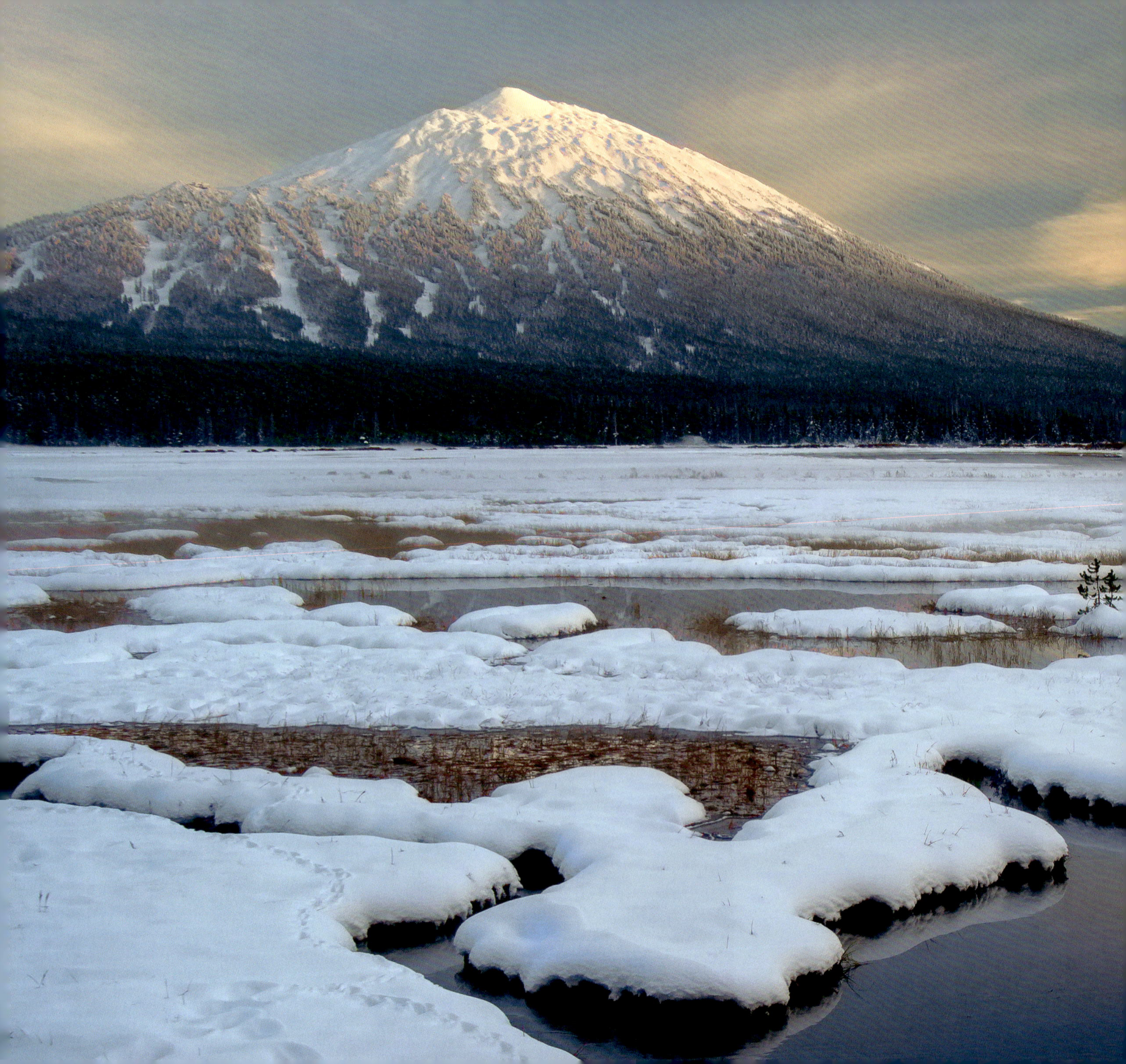

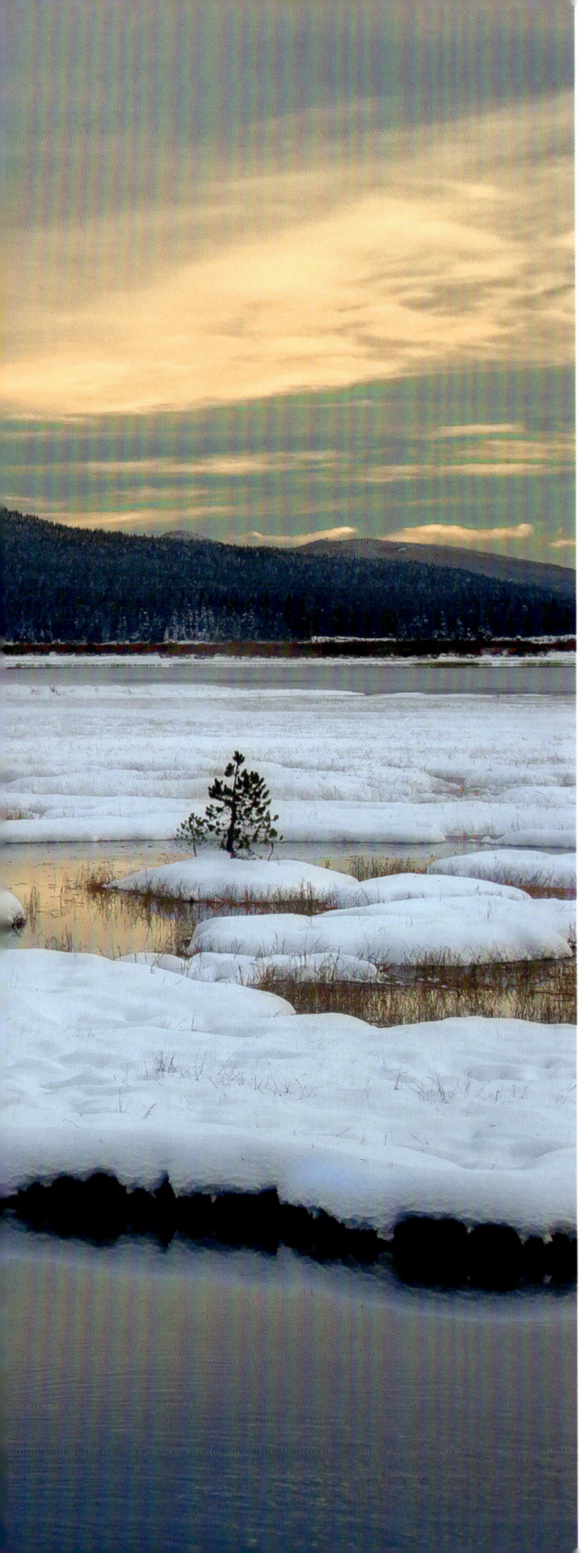

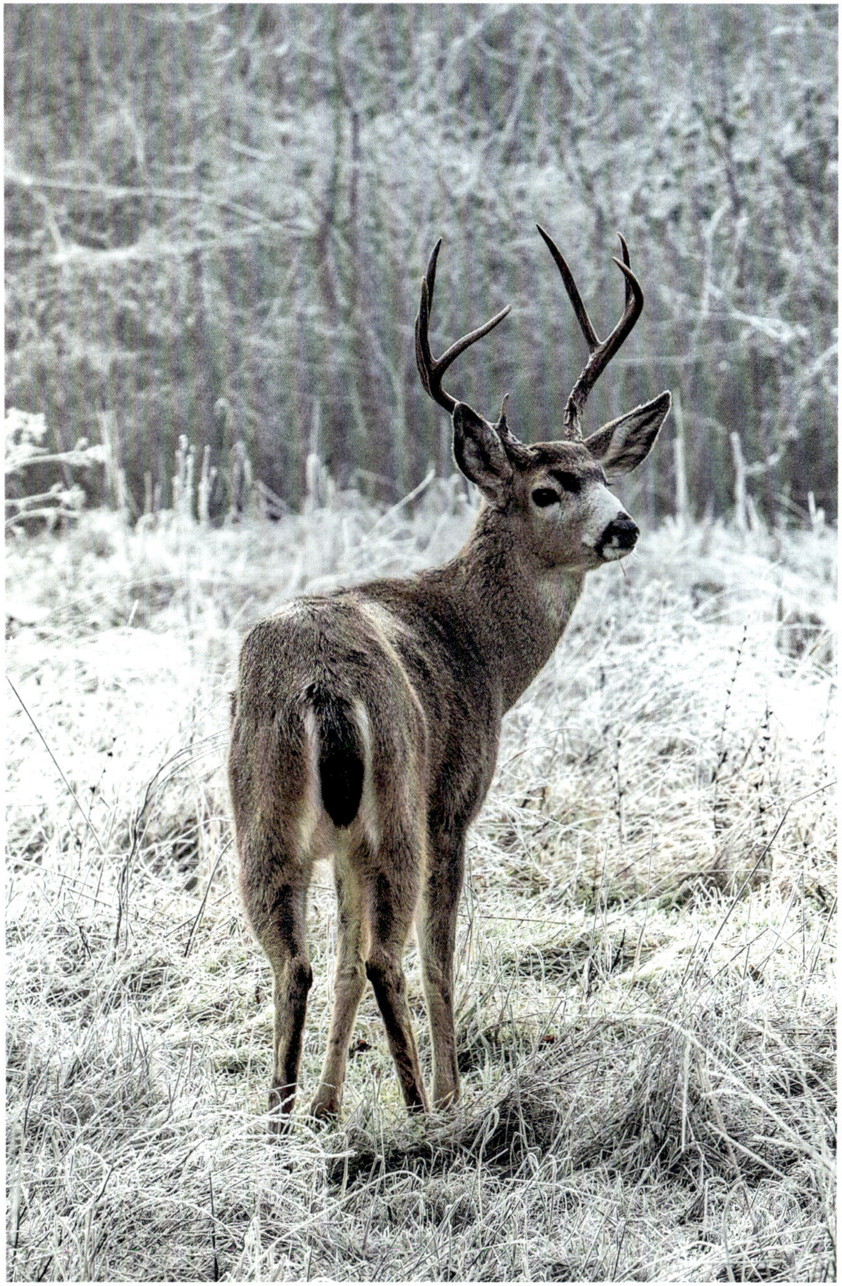

Black-tailed buck. *Photo by Nick Viani.* 125
(Opposite) Mount Bachelor from Sparks Lake. *Photo by Clem Paslack.*

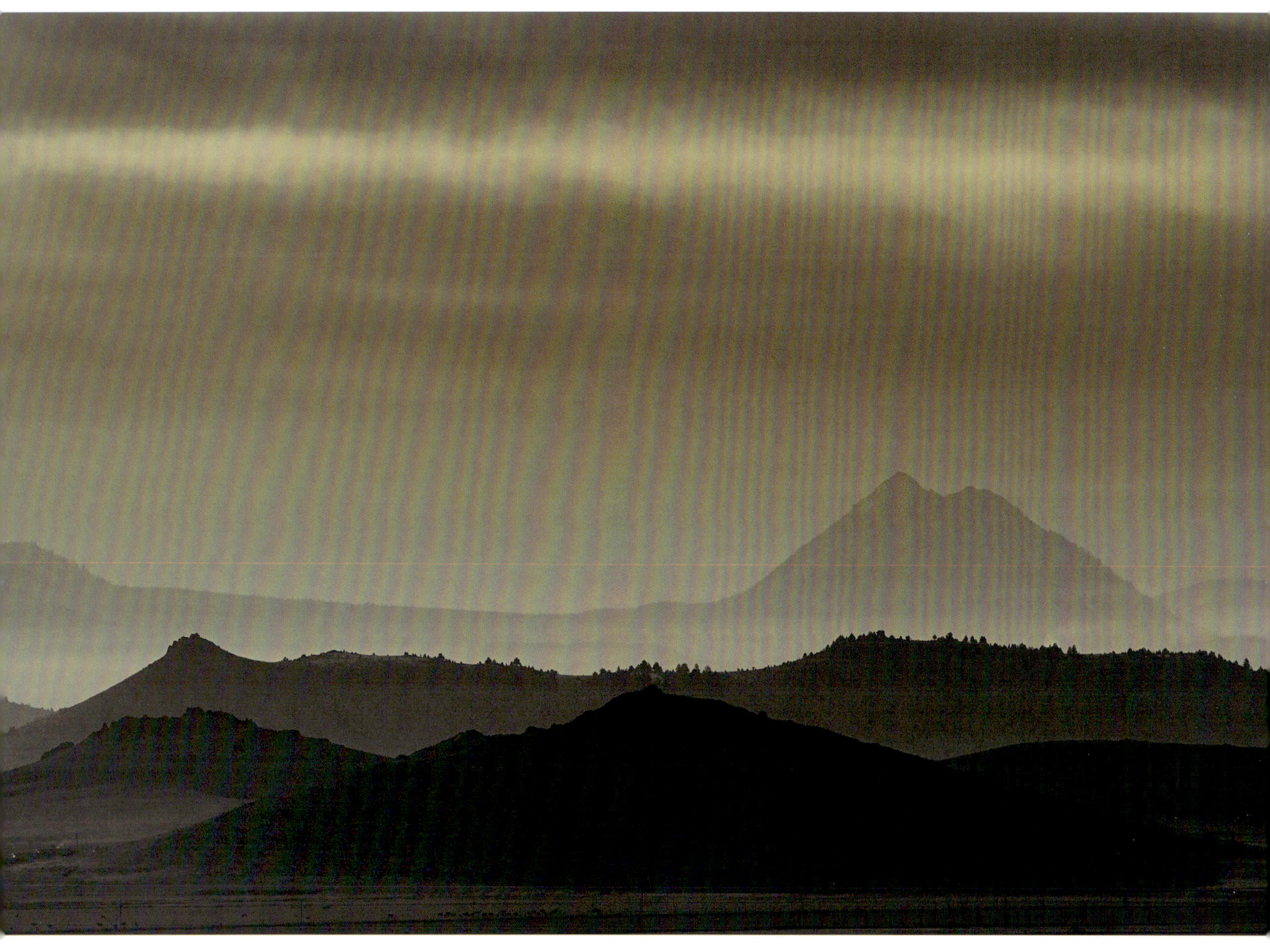

126   Black Butte landscape. Black Butte is an extinct volcano and a popular hiking location. *Photo by David Lorenz Winston.*

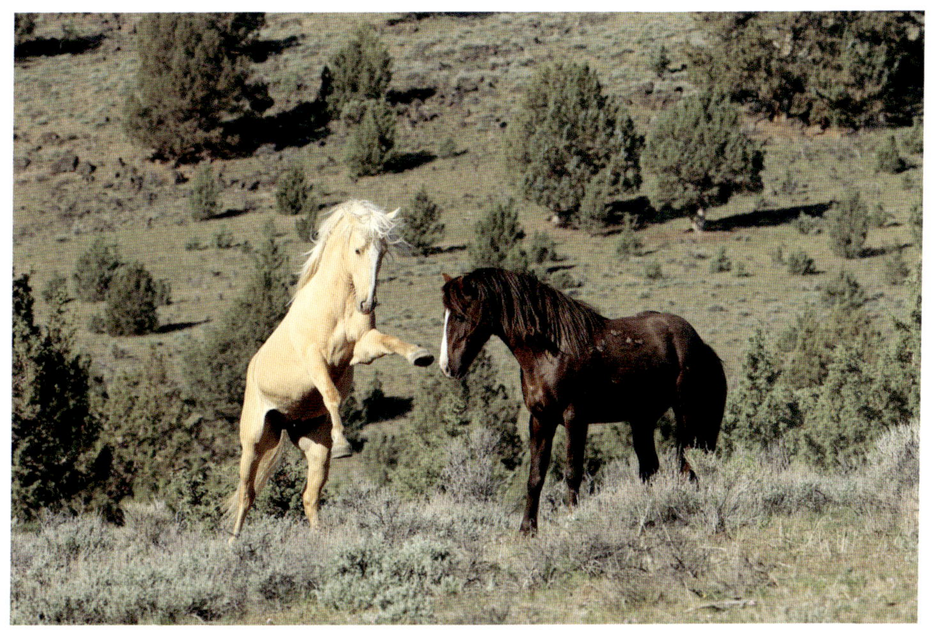

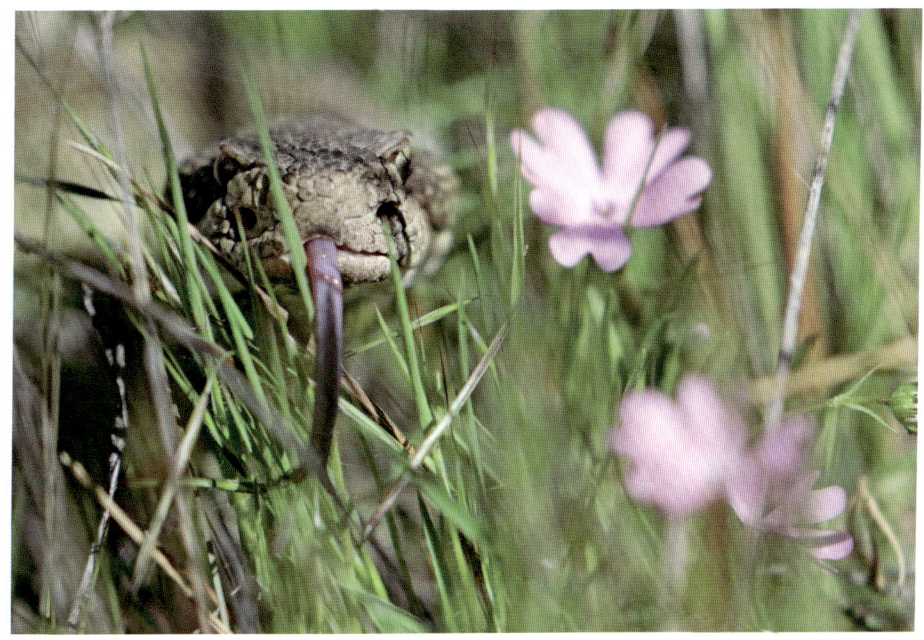

(Top) Wild horses. *Photo by Dan Elster.* • (Bottom) Northern Pacific rattlesnake. *Photo by Dan Elster.*

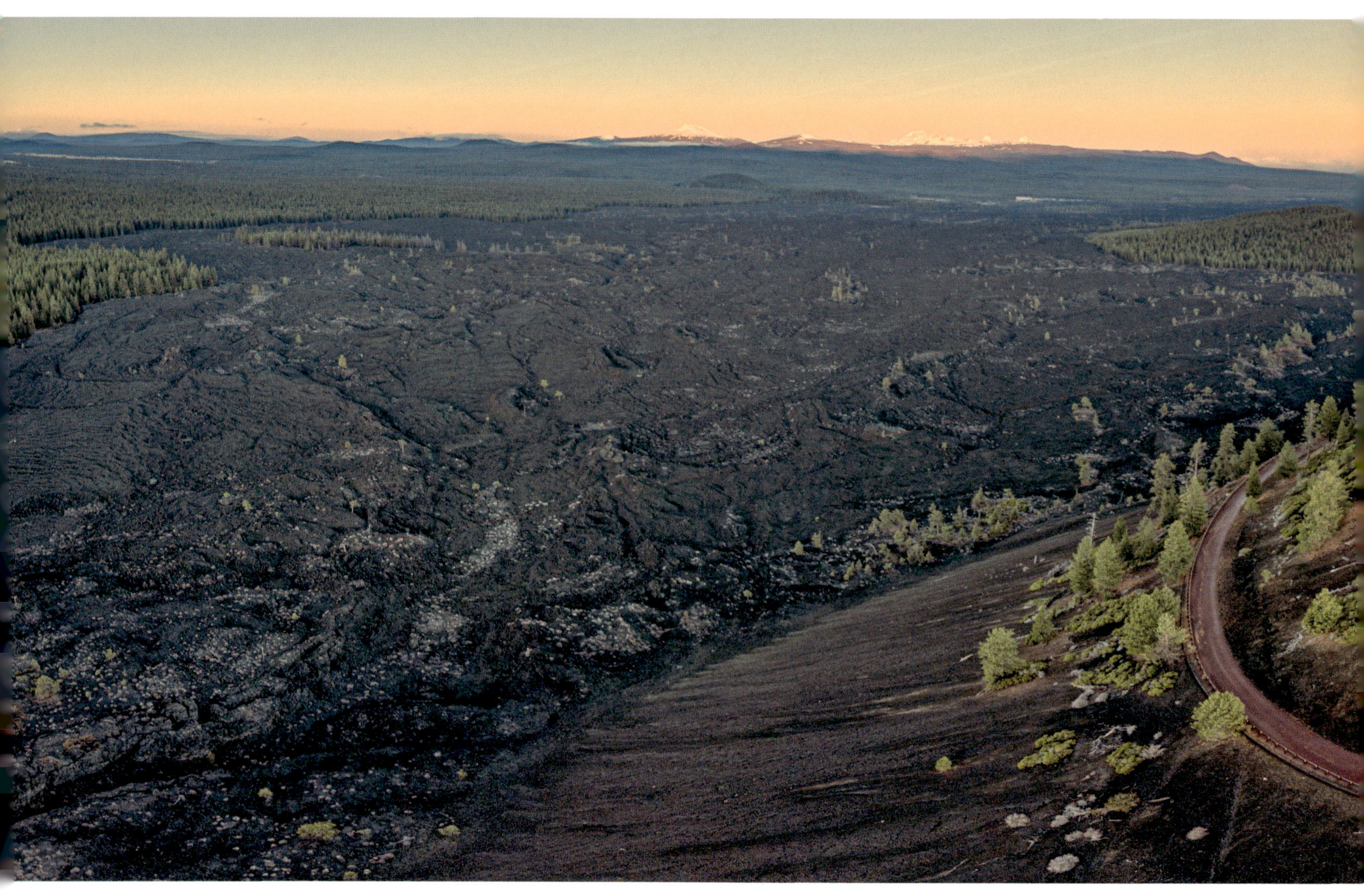

Lava Butte. Near Sunriver and Bend, Lava Butte is a cinder cone and part of the Newberry National Volcanic Monument. It was caused by an eruption about 7,000 years ago. At the top of the spiral road is a US Forest Service lookout tower built in 1931. In 1966, astronauts trained here for the moon landings. *Photo by Mason Marsh.*

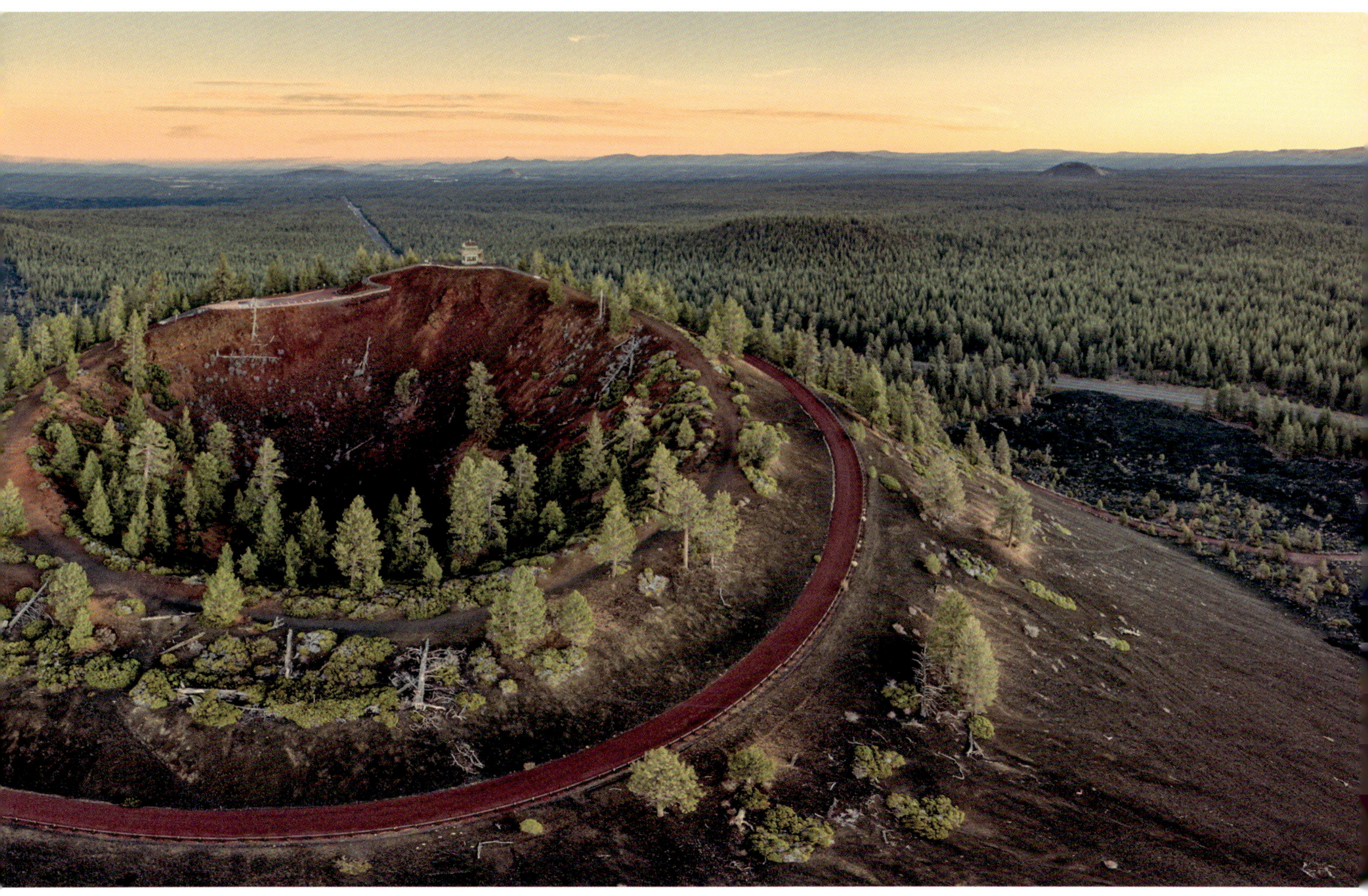

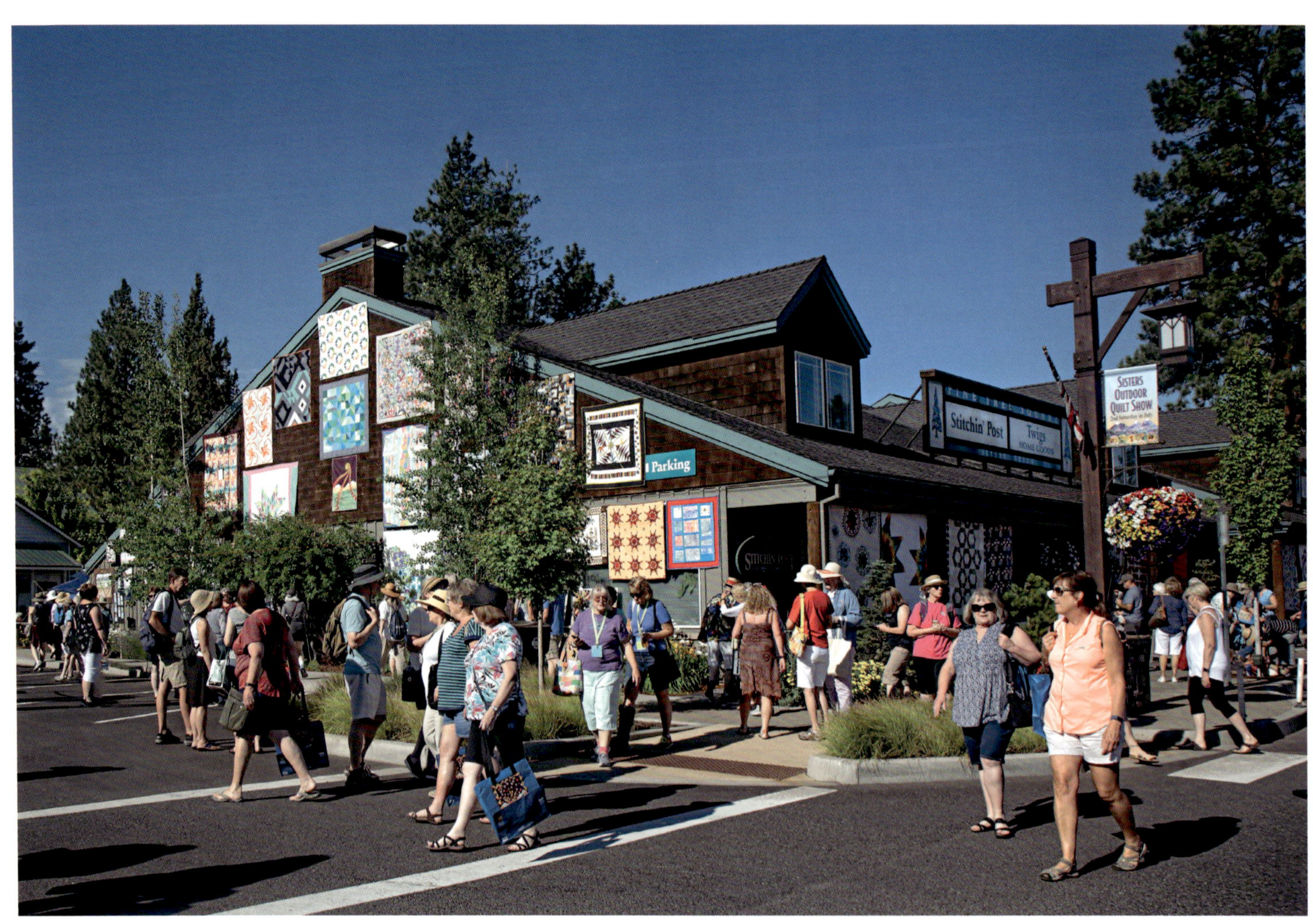

Sisters Outdoor Quilt Show. Operating every year since 1975, this event attracts more than 10,000 visitors from all over the world to the small town of Sisters, population 2,500. It is recognized as the world's largest outdoor quilt show and sale, with weeklong classes and workshops. *Photo by Barbara Tricarico.*

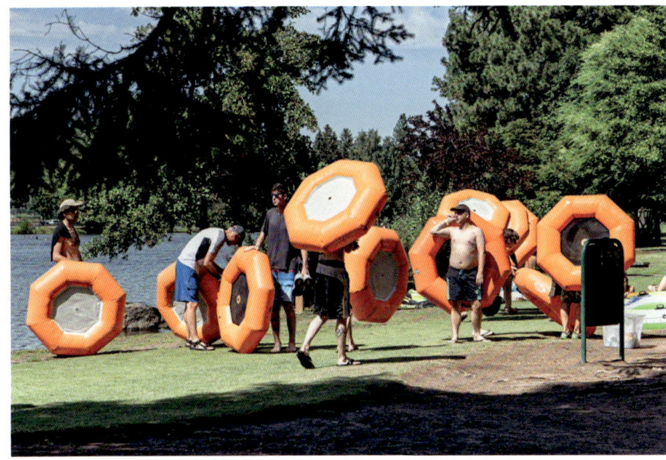

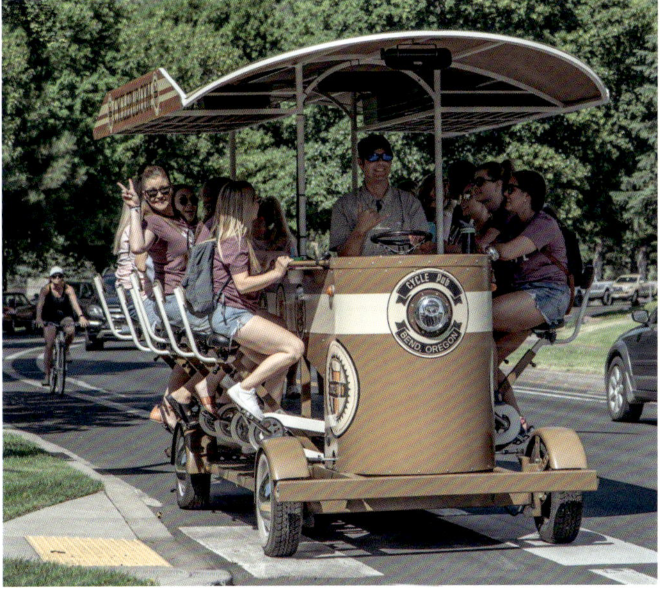

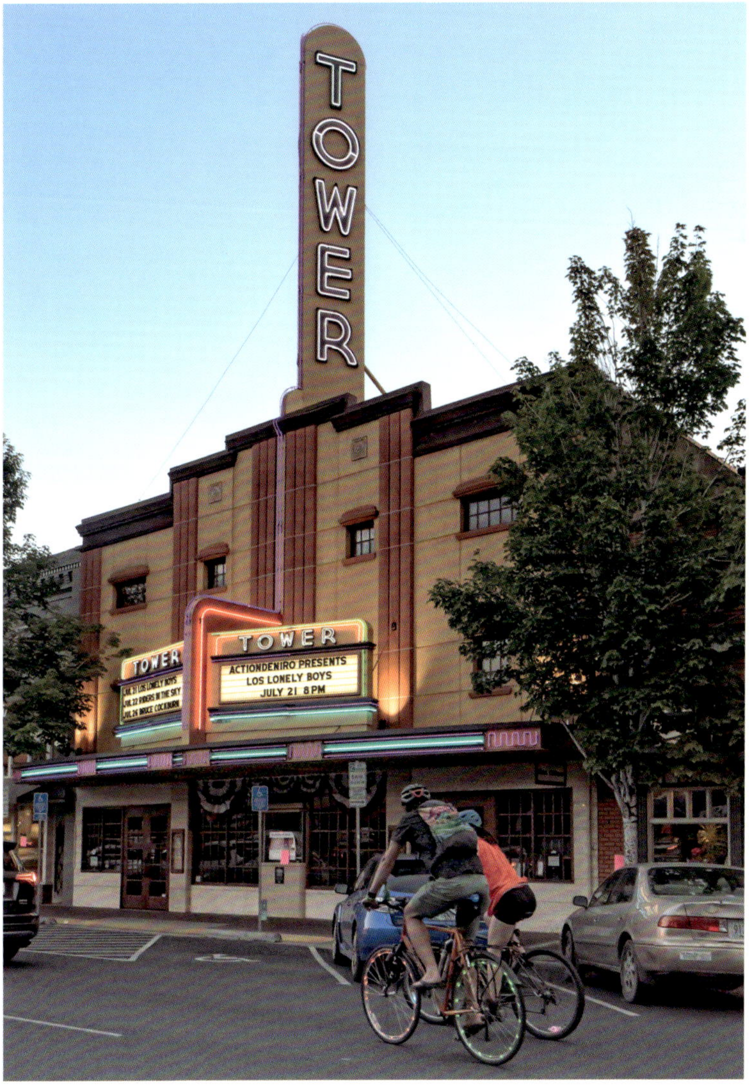

Tubing the Deschutes River is a popular summertime activity at Drake Park in Bend. *Photo by Barbara Tricarico.*

Rolling pub on wheels. "The Official Bend Ale Trail" features the town's many world-class craft breweries. *Photo by Barbara Tricarico.*

Tower Theatre, Bend. The theater was built in 1940. *Photo by Barbara Tricarico.*

5

WILLAMETTE VALLEY

History buffs are familiar with the Willamette River Valley's rich Native American history and early settler heritage. In the 1830s, the 170-mile Oregon Trail brought emigrants in covered wagons from the East and Midwest. The last stop was Oregon City.

The verdant Willamette Valley, known historically as "the land of milk and honey," is synonymous with Oregon Wine Country. The valley stretches 150 miles and includes more than 750 vineyards and 500 wineries. It has become one of the foremost pinot noir–producing areas in the world. The valley's lushness is attributed to the Willamette River, which is surrounded by three mountains and runs from Portland to Eugene.

Gardens and flower farms produce a riot of color each spring and summer. Why go to Holland when you can visit the annual Wooden Shoe Tulip Festival in Woodburn in March and April? Not far away, in Silverton, is the beautiful 80-acre Oregon Gardens, open 365 days a year and host to an annual Christmas in the Garden event. On the grounds is Oregon's only Frank Lloyd Wright structure, the Gordon House.

Silver Falls State Park near Silverton is the largest in the Oregon state parks system, with more than 9,000 acres. It is often called Oregon's "crown jewel," with ten waterfalls, miles of walking and horse trails, RV sites and campgrounds, and the Silver Falls Lodge and Conference Center.

Salem, once a destination on the Oregon Trail, is the second-most-populated city in Oregon. The heart and soul of the Willamette Valley, Salem became the state capital in 1850. It was the first state capital in the United Sates to produce solar power in 2002. The beautiful Oregon State Capitol houses the House and Senate and offices for the governor, treasurer, and secretary of state.

Outside Salem is the quaint town of Mount Angel, complete with a working glockenspiel at the town center. Settled in 1867 by German and Swiss Catholics, Mount Angel still hosts an annual Oktoberfest. The historic St. Mary's Catholic Church stands regally near the center of town, not far from the Mount Angel Abbey, a Benedictine monastery and university.

McMinnville is called "the Heart of Oregon Wine Country." The historic city, incorporated in 1876, is a beehive of activity year-round. It regularly hosts the International Pinot Noir Celebration on the Linfield College campus, as well as an annual Turkey Rama and UFO Festival. McMinnville is home to the Evergreen Aviation Museum, which houses the famed "Spruce Goose."

Cottage Grove is known as the covered-bridge capital of Oregon. Many beautiful murals can be found on buildings throughout the town, documenting historic events. Its small-town charm is the backdrop of many films, including Buster Keaton's silent film *The General*, *Animal House*, and *Stand by Me*.

Although there are many top-notch colleges and universities throughout Oregon and the Willamette Valley, none are more competitive than the Beavers (Oregon State University in Corvallis) and the Ducks (University of Oregon in Eugene). The popular "Civil War" football game, held annually between the two rivals, began in 1894.

Not far from Corvallis, the Buena Vista Ferry still crosses the Willamette River daily. The cable ferry dates to the 1800s and is one of only three still operating in Oregon (the others are in Canby and Wheatland).

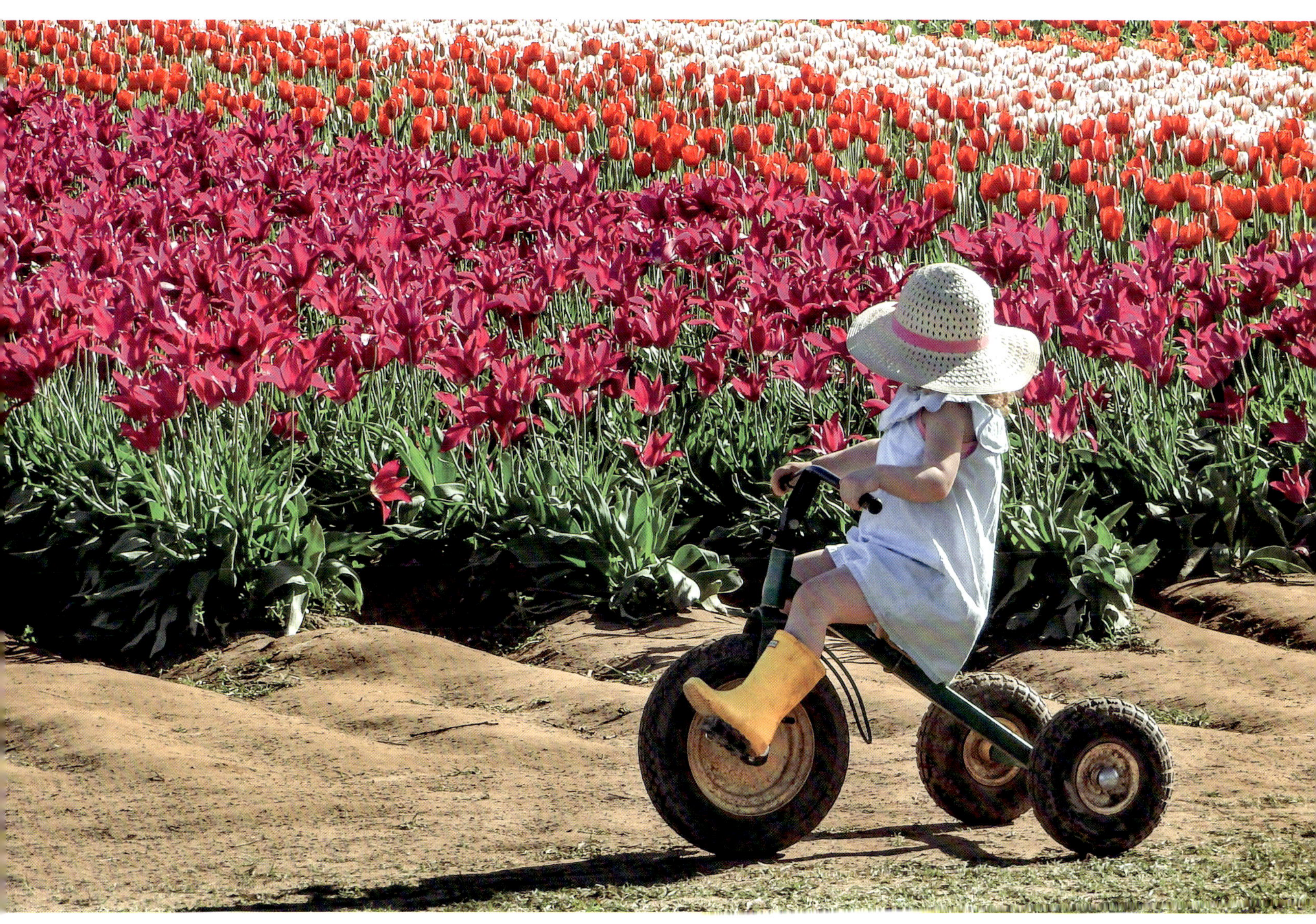

Wooden Shoe Tulip Farm, Woodburn. *Photo by Charles Hillestad.* 133

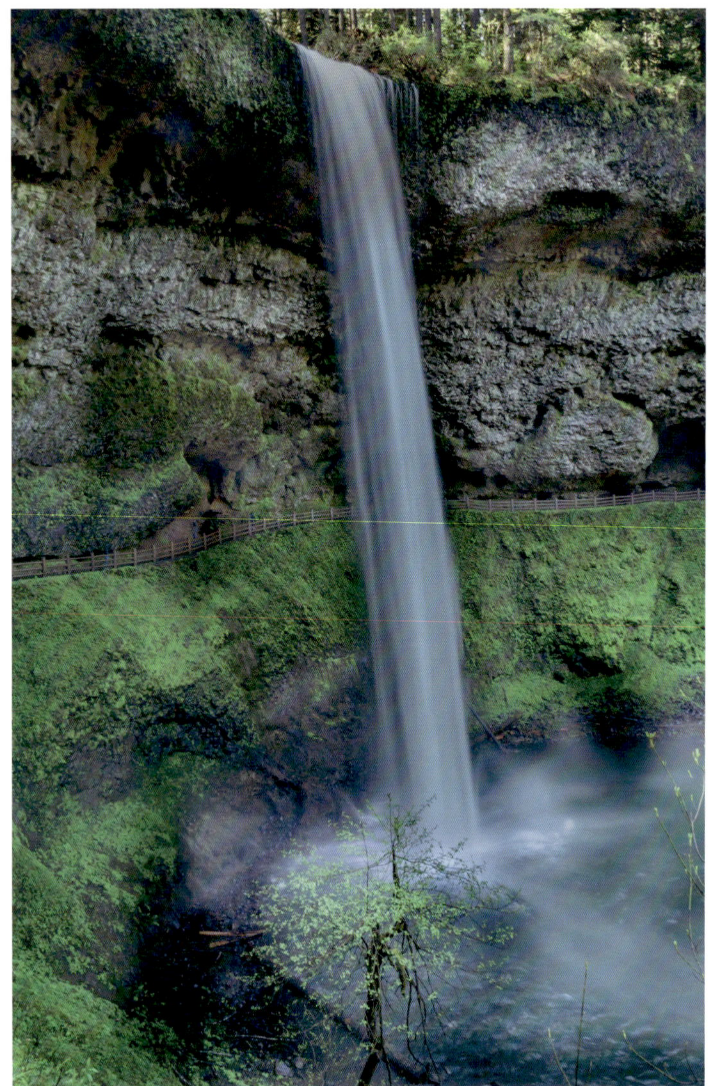 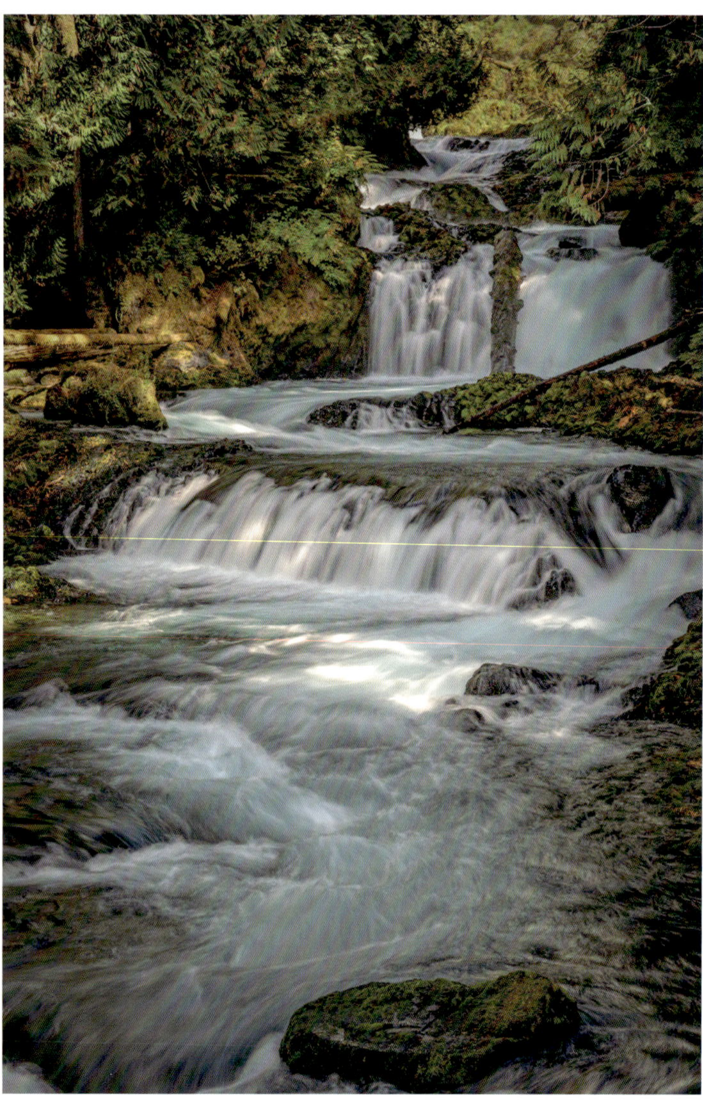

South Falls. Visitors delight in walking behind the 177-foot South Falls. It is one of ten waterfalls in Silver Falls Park, the largest state park in Oregon. *Photo by Gary Hill.*

McKenzie River below Sahalie Falls. *Photo by Alana Lynn Starkweather.*

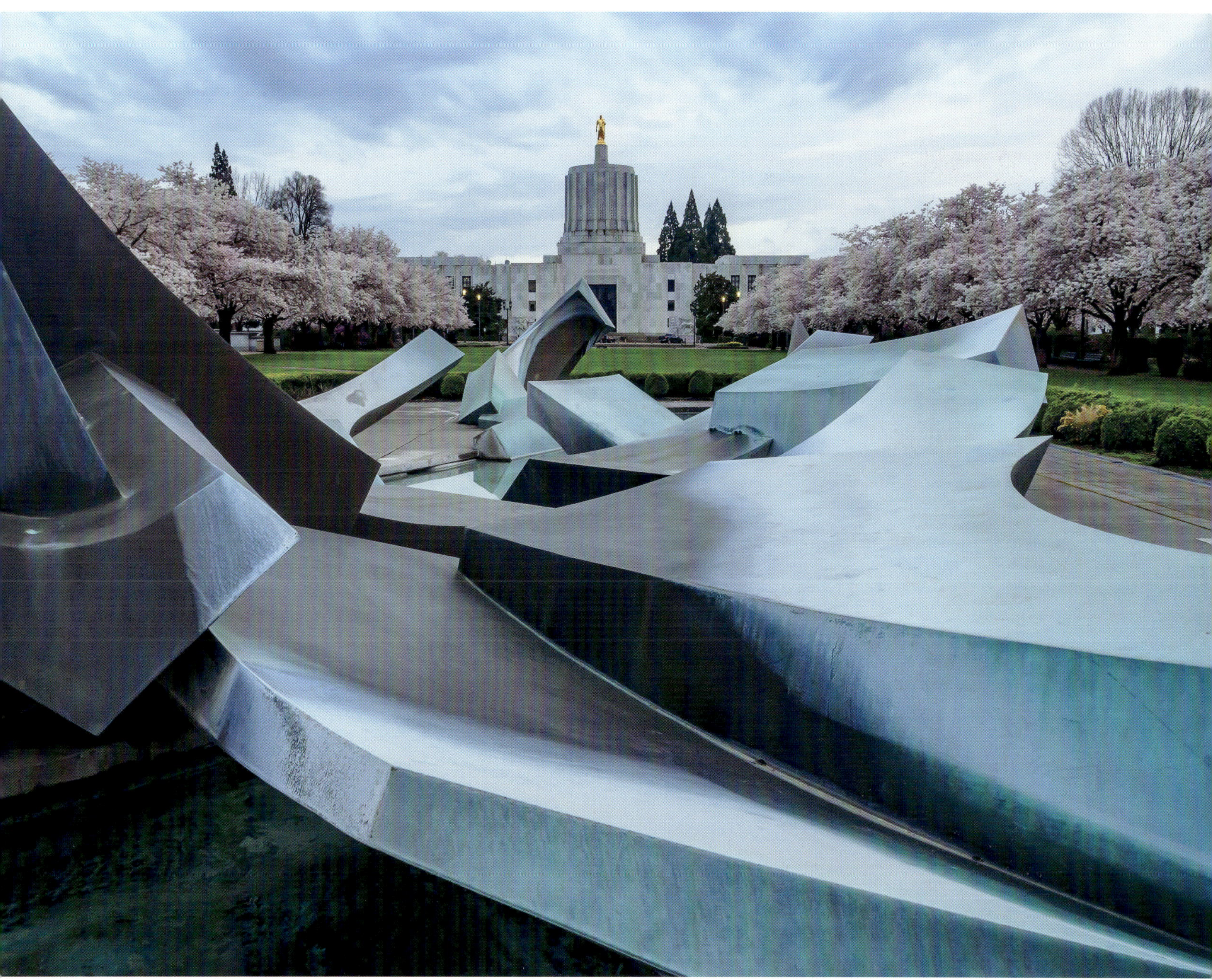

Sprague Fountain at the Oregon State Capitol, Salem. *Photo by Vldn Taylor.* 135

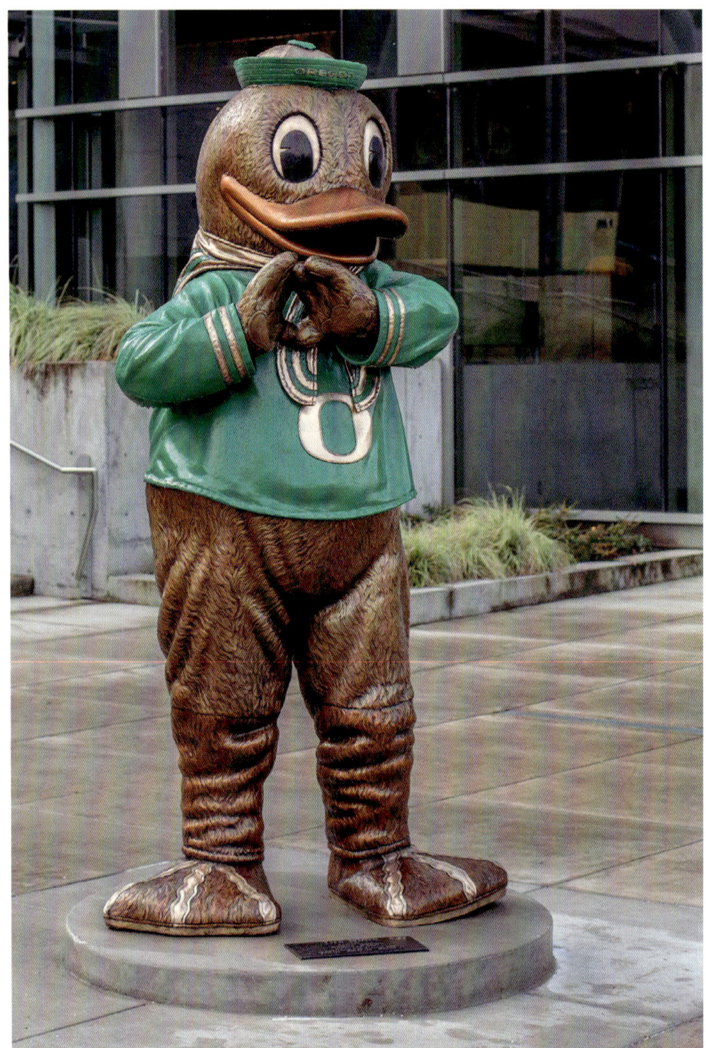

The Oregon Duck, the University of Oregon's mascot. Bronze sculpture completed in 2016 by Oregon native Alison Brown. *Photo by Ellen Ahern.*

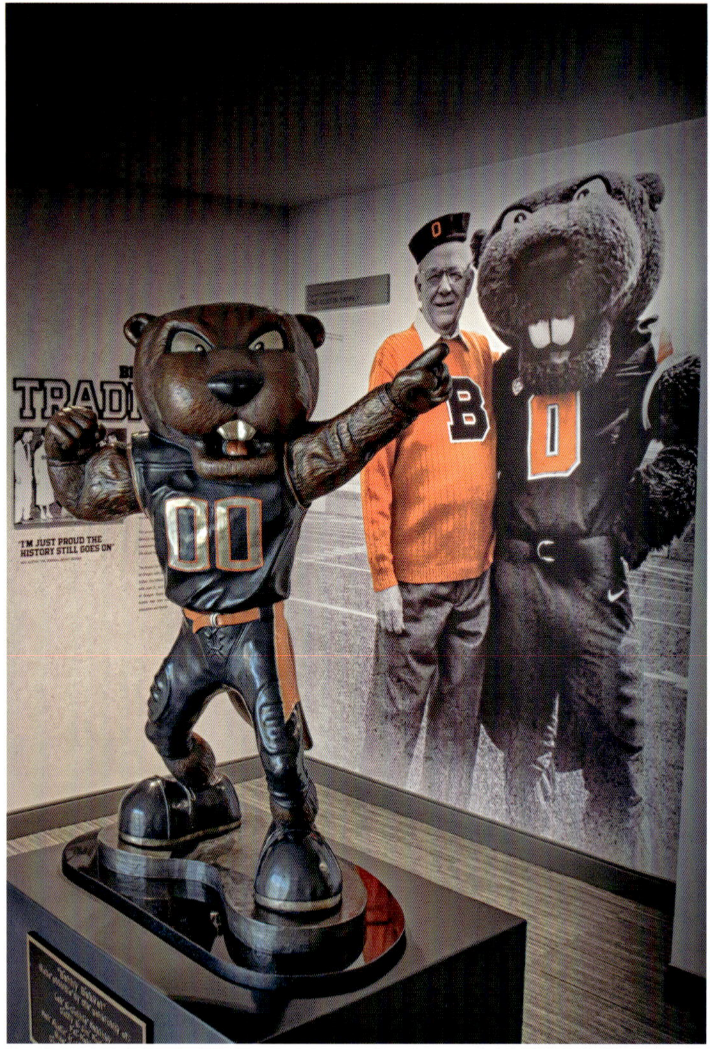

Benny the Beaver, Oregon State University's mascot, Corvallis. Ken Austin was the first Benny the Beaver mascot in 1952. Bronze sculpture completed in 2017 by Oregon native Alison Brown. *Photo by Barbara Tricarico.*

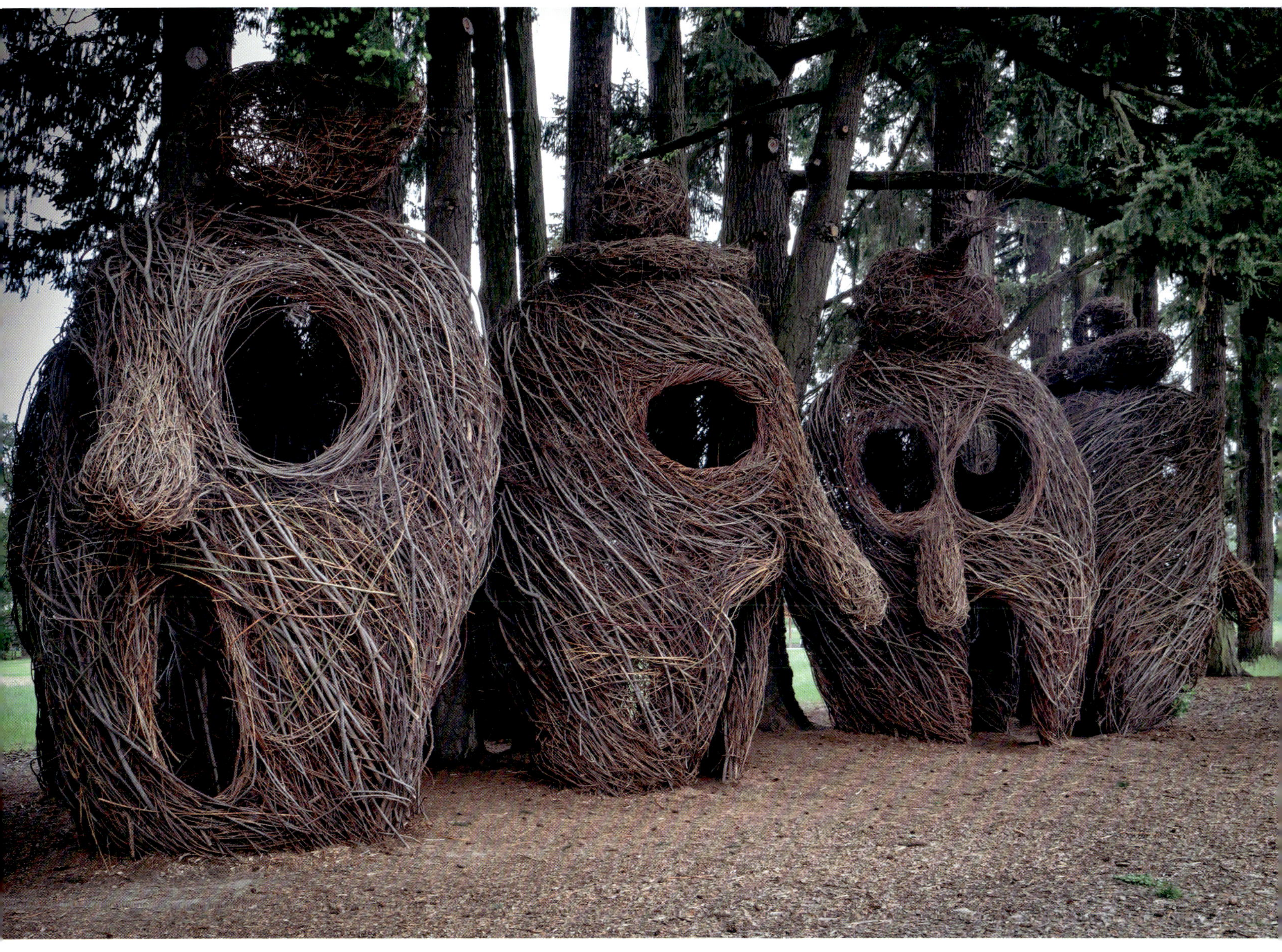

Stickwork sculptures created by artist Patrick Dougherty at Orenco Woods Nature Park, Hillsboro. *Photo by Barbara Tricarico.*   137

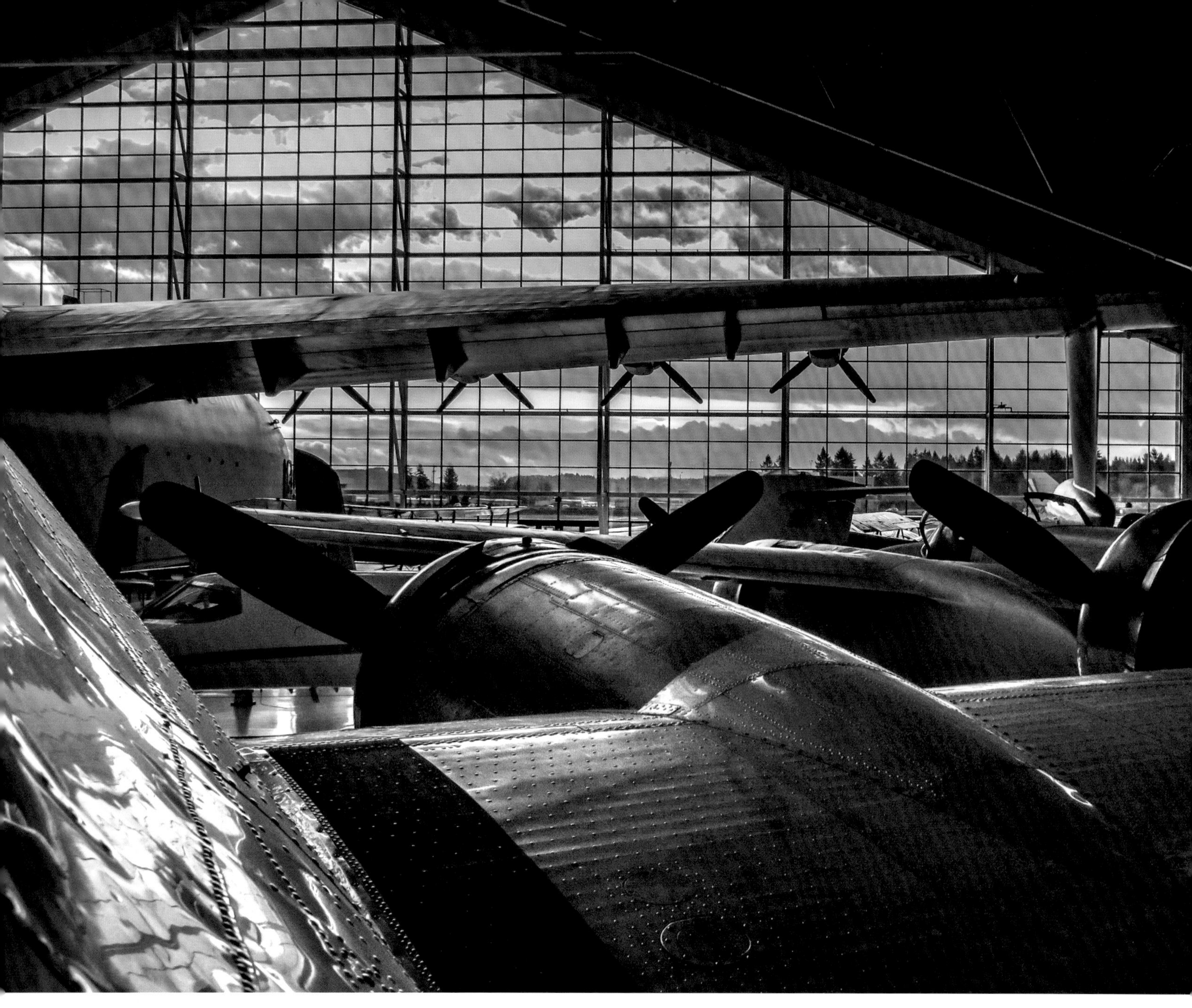

Spruce Goose at Evergreen Aviation Museum, outside McMinnville. The museum was built to house Howard Hughes's gigantic birch airplane, flown only once during World War II. It is the largest wooden airplane ever constructed. *Photo by Charles Hillestad.*

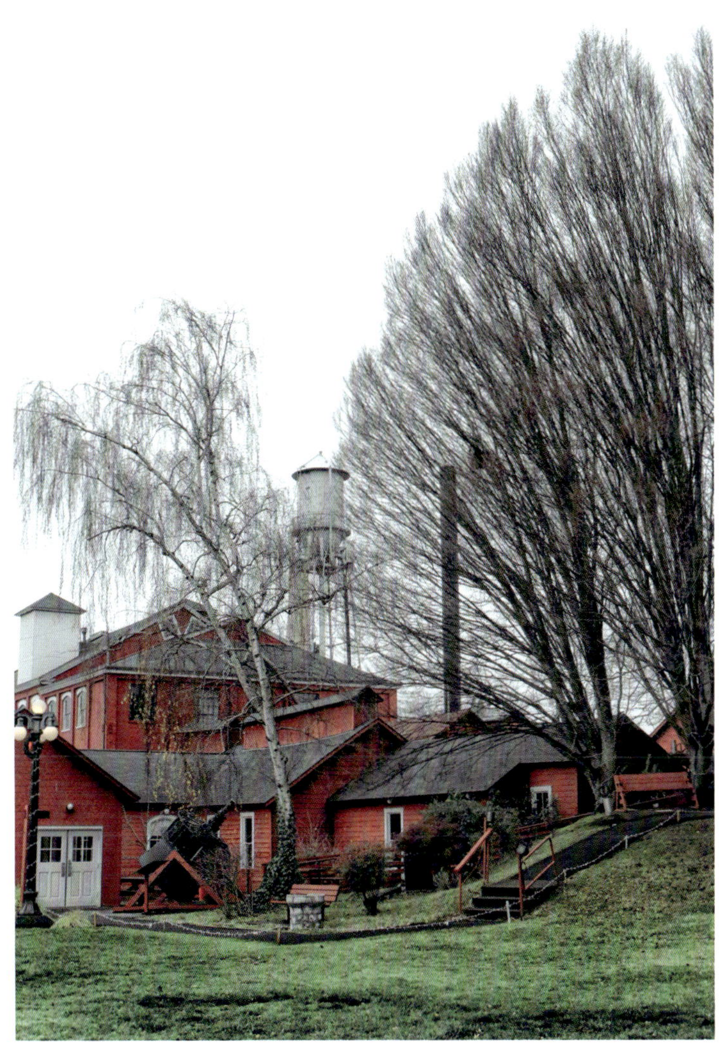

Thomas Kay Woolen Mill buildings at the Willamette Heritage Center in Salem. *Photo by Richard Krieger.*

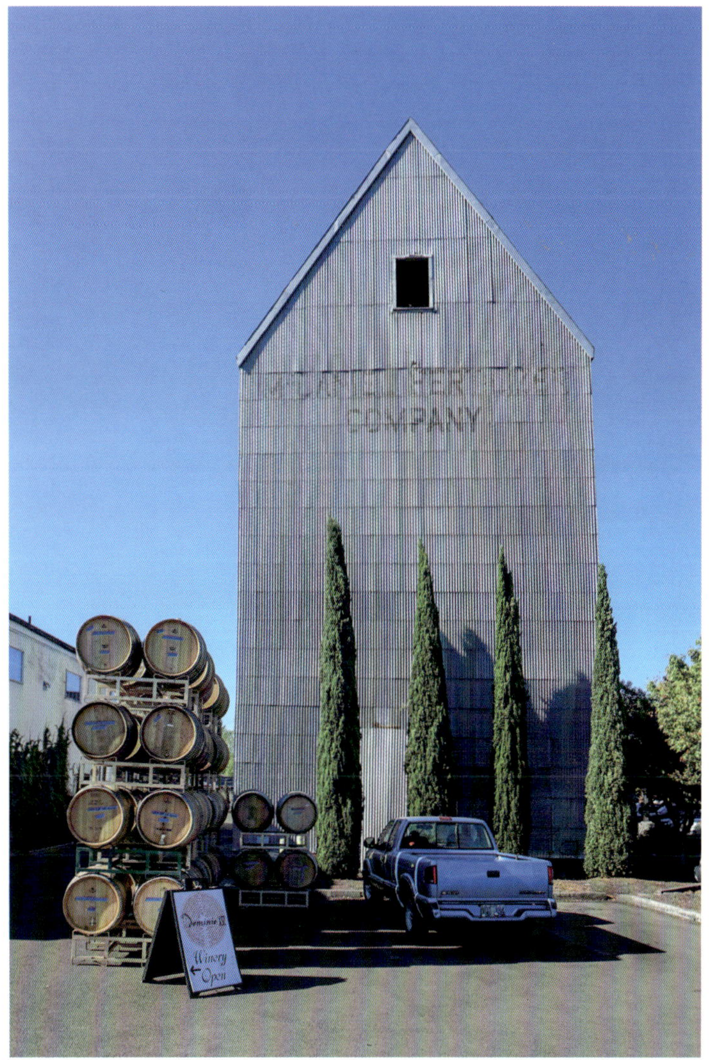

McMinnville's Historic Granary District is a cluster of former grain warehouses that now house urban wineries, breweries, and shops. *Photo by Charles Hillestad.*

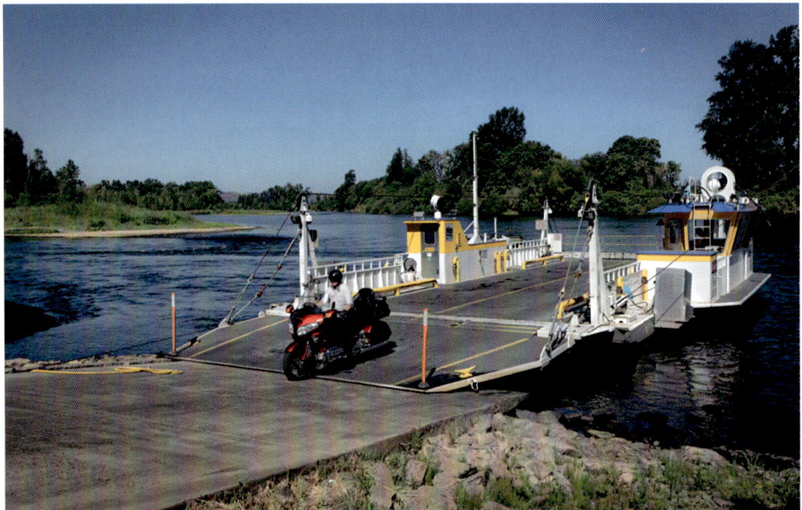

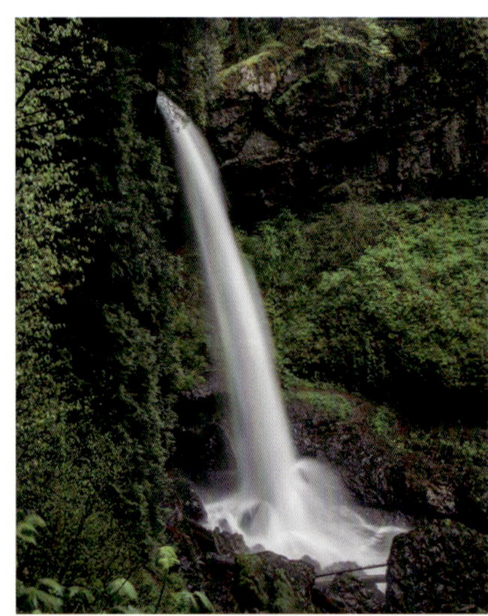

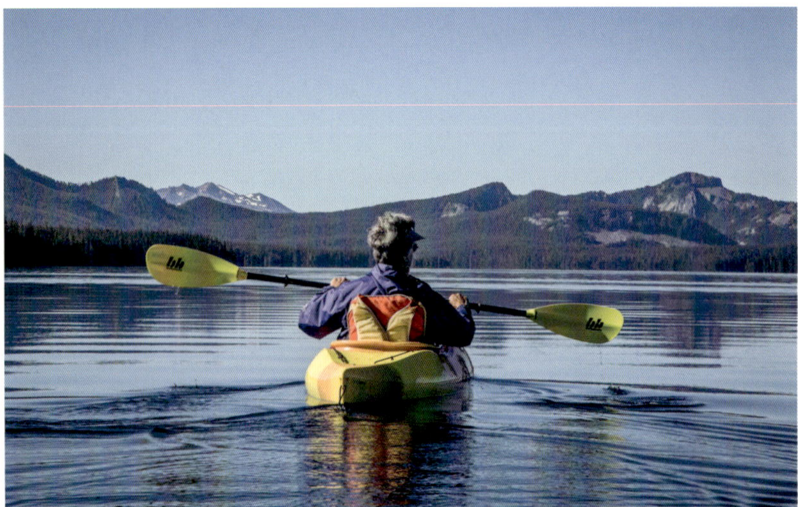

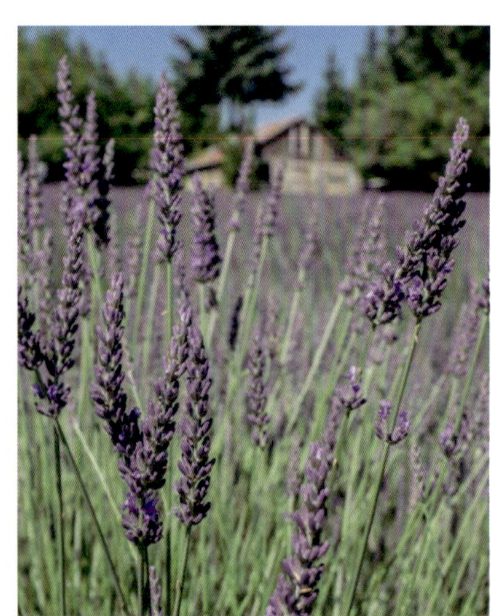

The Buena Vista Ferry connects Marion and Polk Counties. The Willamette River cable ferry has operated since 1852 and is one of three ferries still operating in the state. *Photo by Barbara Tricarico.*

North Falls at Silver Falls State Park. Silver Falls is often called the crown jewel of the Oregon state parks system. *Photo by Alana Lynn Starkweather.*

Waldo Lake. *Photo by Kate Geary.*

Mountainside Lavender Farm, Hillsboro. *Photo by Vivian McAleavey.*

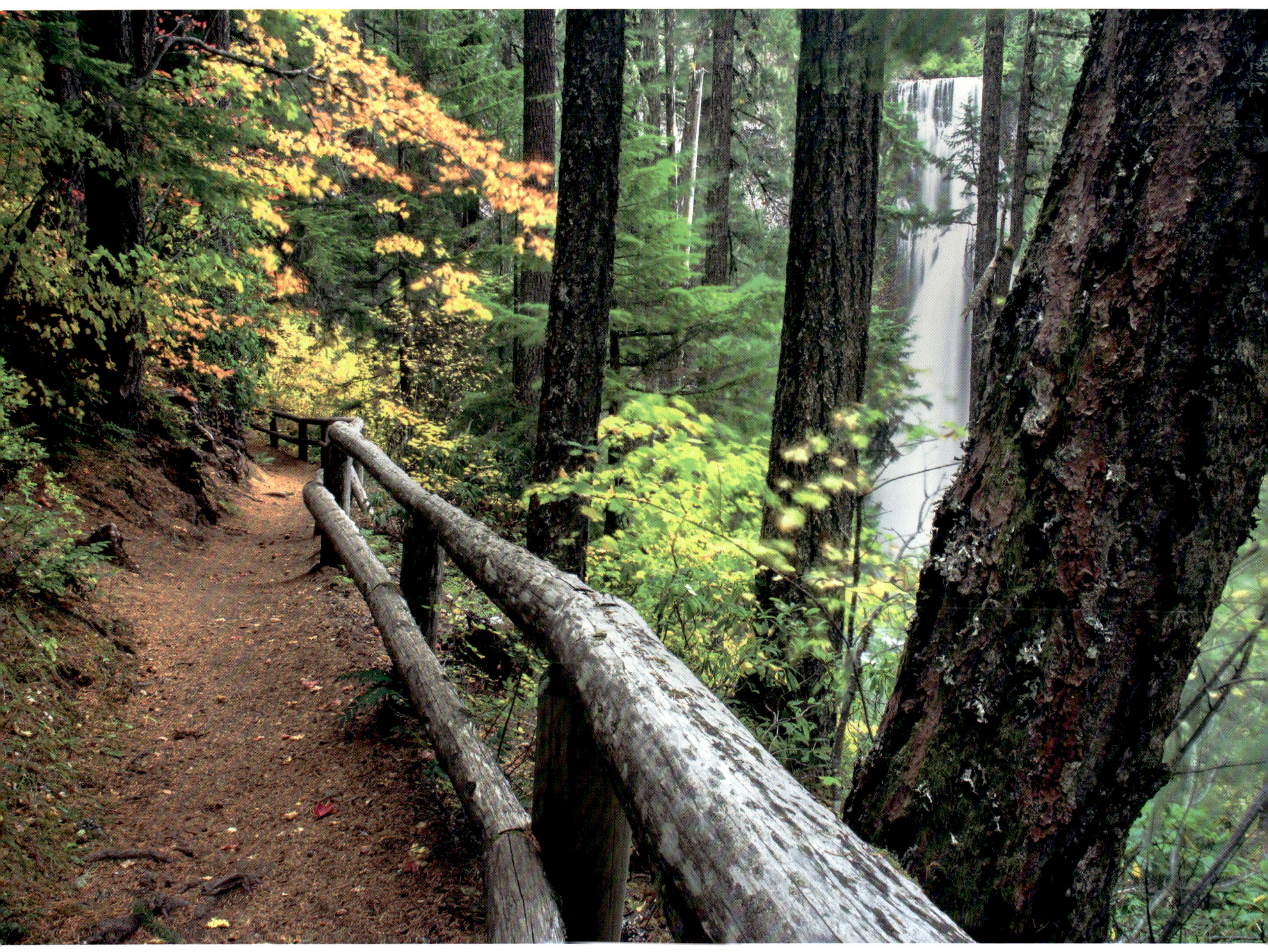

Salt Creek Falls trail, Willamette National Forest. *Photo by Jay Newman.* 141

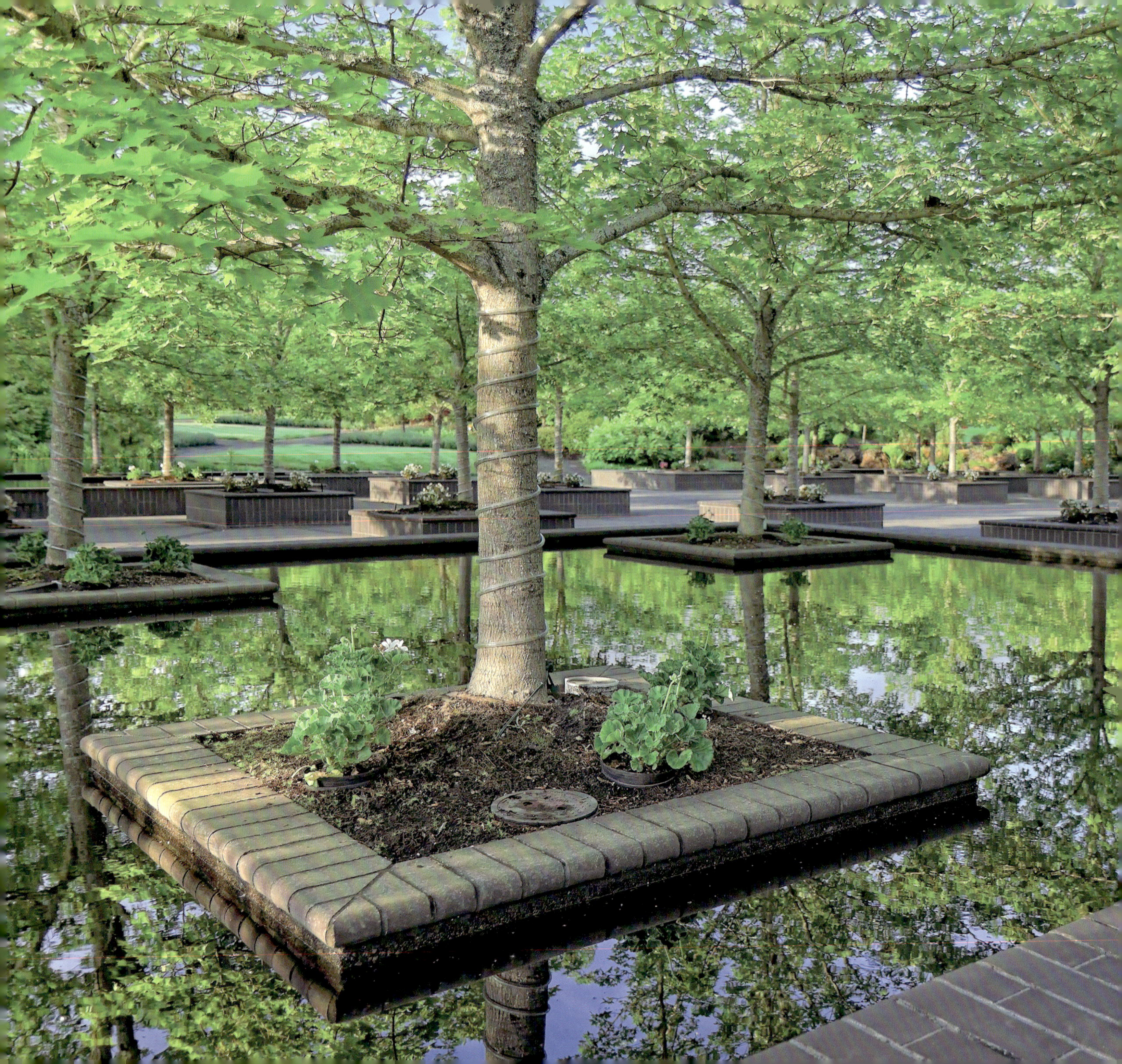

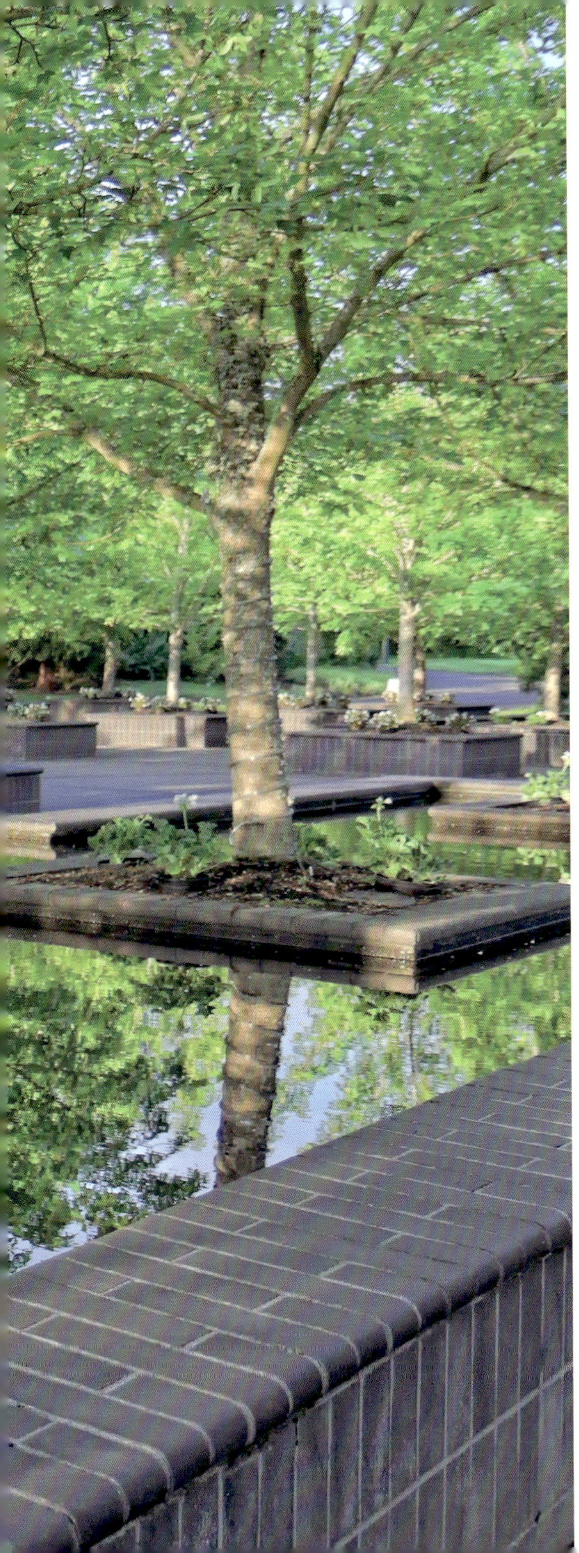

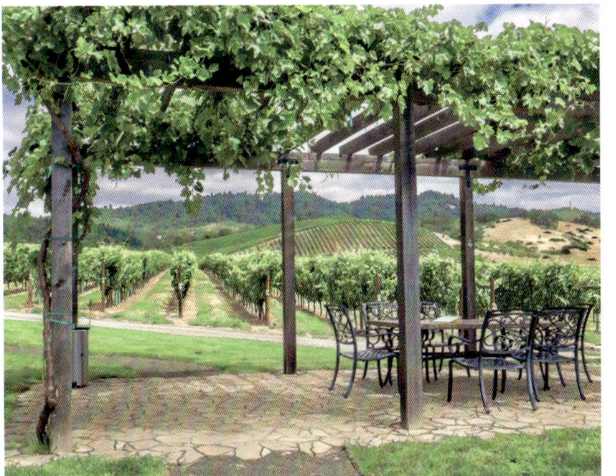

Abacela Winery, Roseburg. *Photo by Vivian McAleavey.*

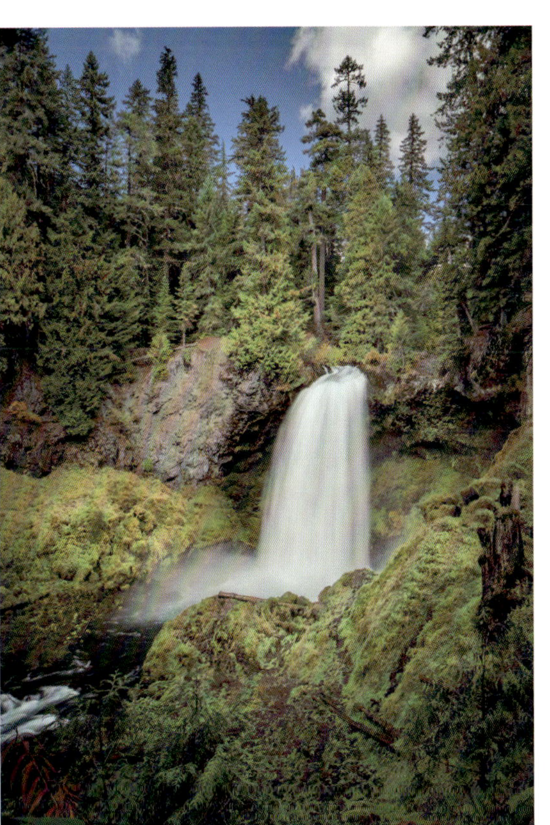

Sahalie Falls. *Photo by Alana Lynn Starkweather.*

(Opposite) Oregon Gardens reflective tree ponds, Silverton. *Photo by John Christer Petersen.*

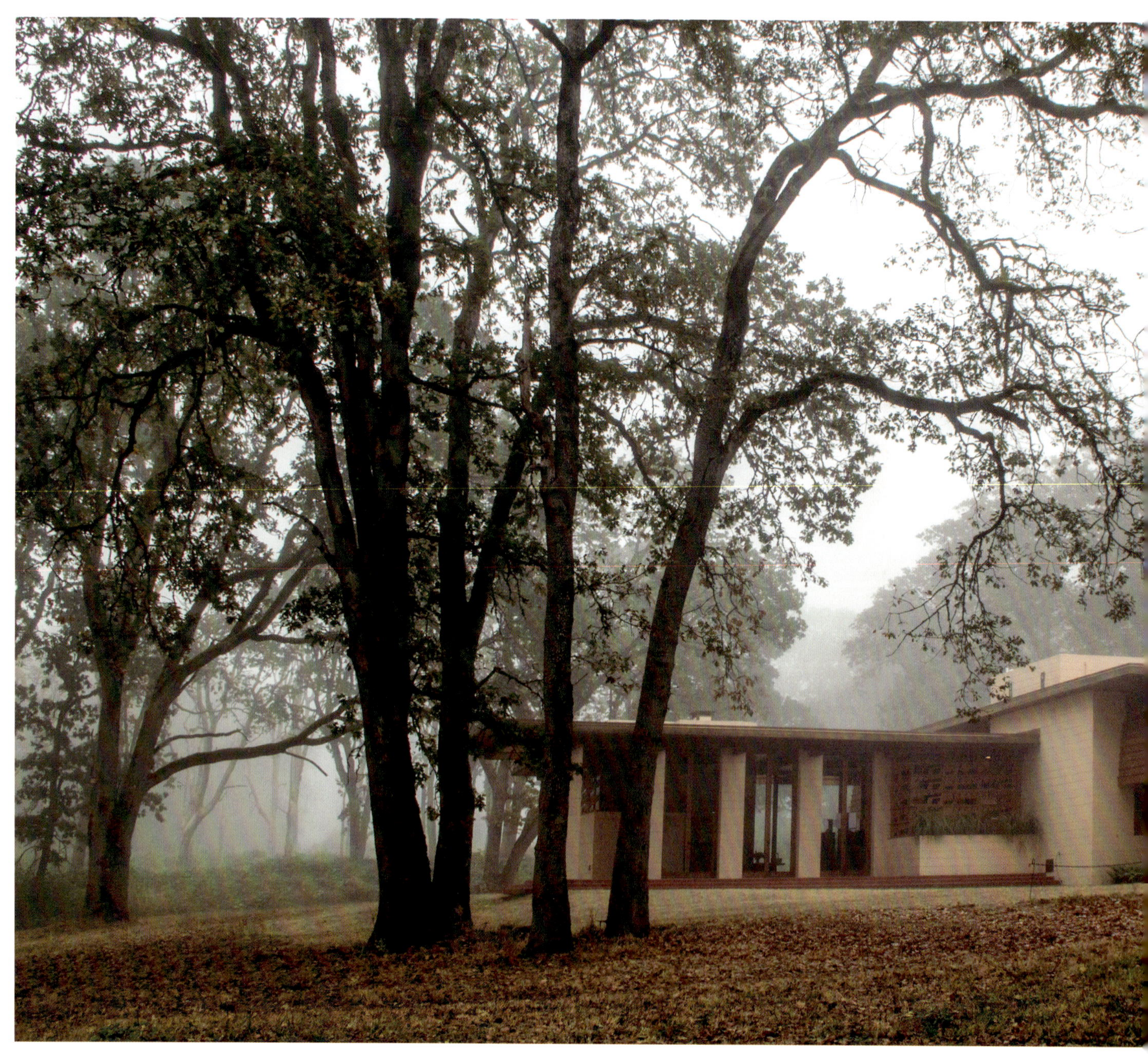

144   The C. E. Gordon House is the only Frank Lloyd Wright house in Oregon. It was built in
1957 in Wilsonville and relocated to Silverton in 2001. *Photo by Howard Hunt.*

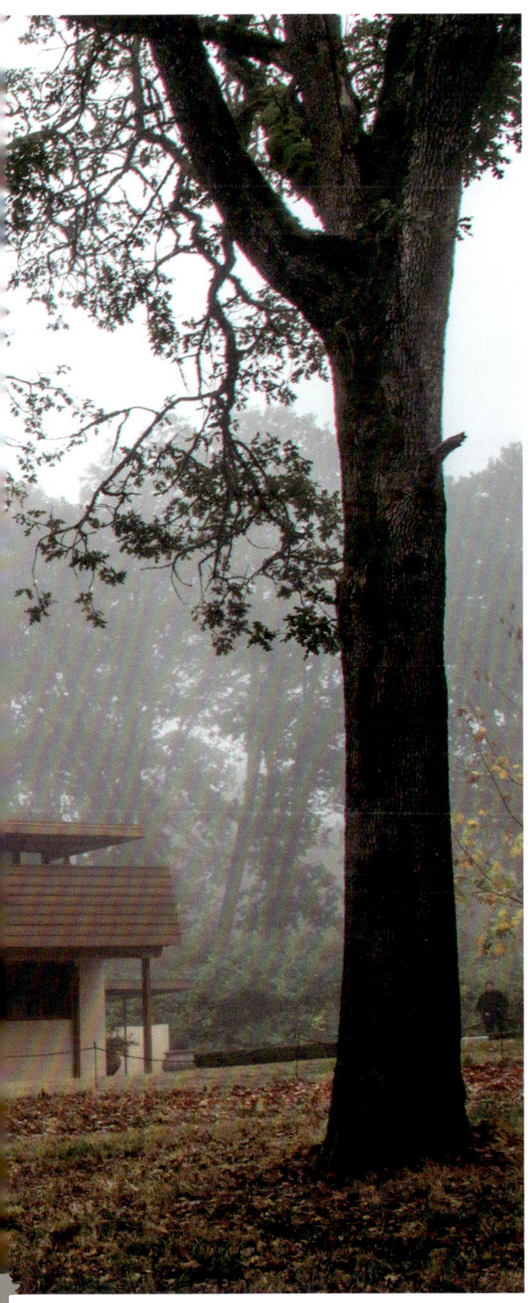

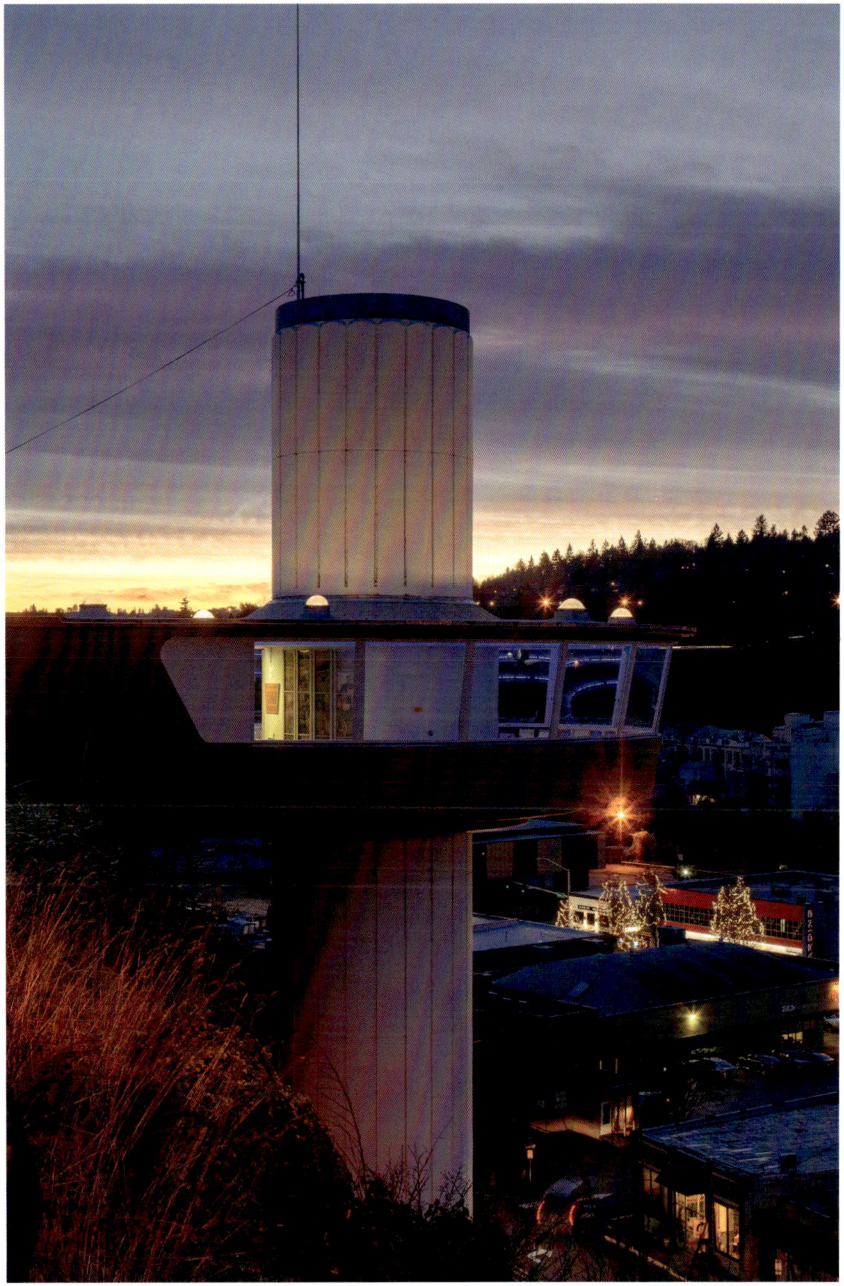

Oregon City Municipal Elevator, first opened in 1915, is the only "vertical street" in North America and one of only four municipal elevators in the world. *Photo by Vldn Taylor.*

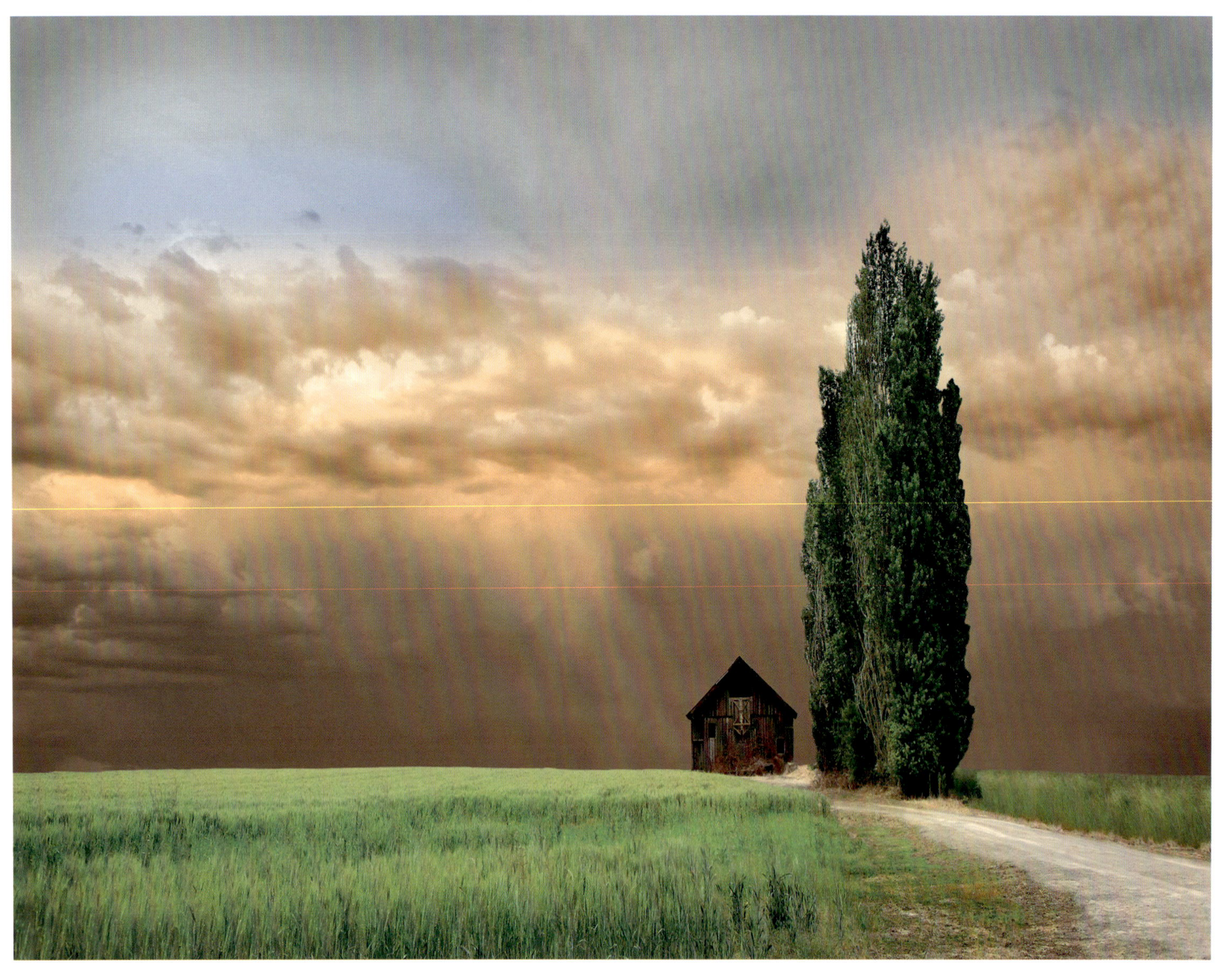

  Willamette Valley farm country. *Photo by John Kirk.* • (Opposite) Wooden Shoe Tulip Farm, Woodburn. Mount Hood in background. *Photo by Vldn Taylor.*

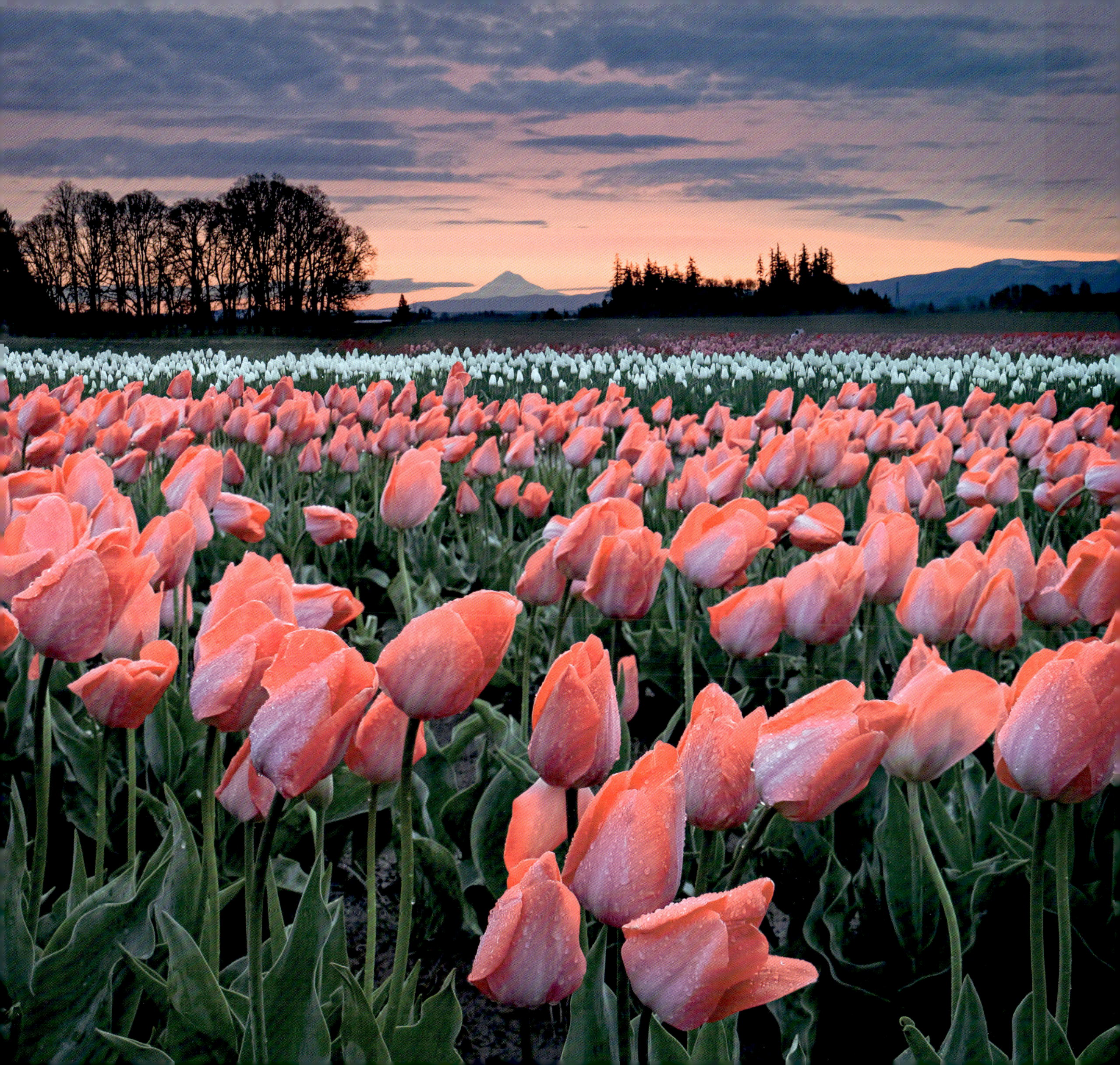

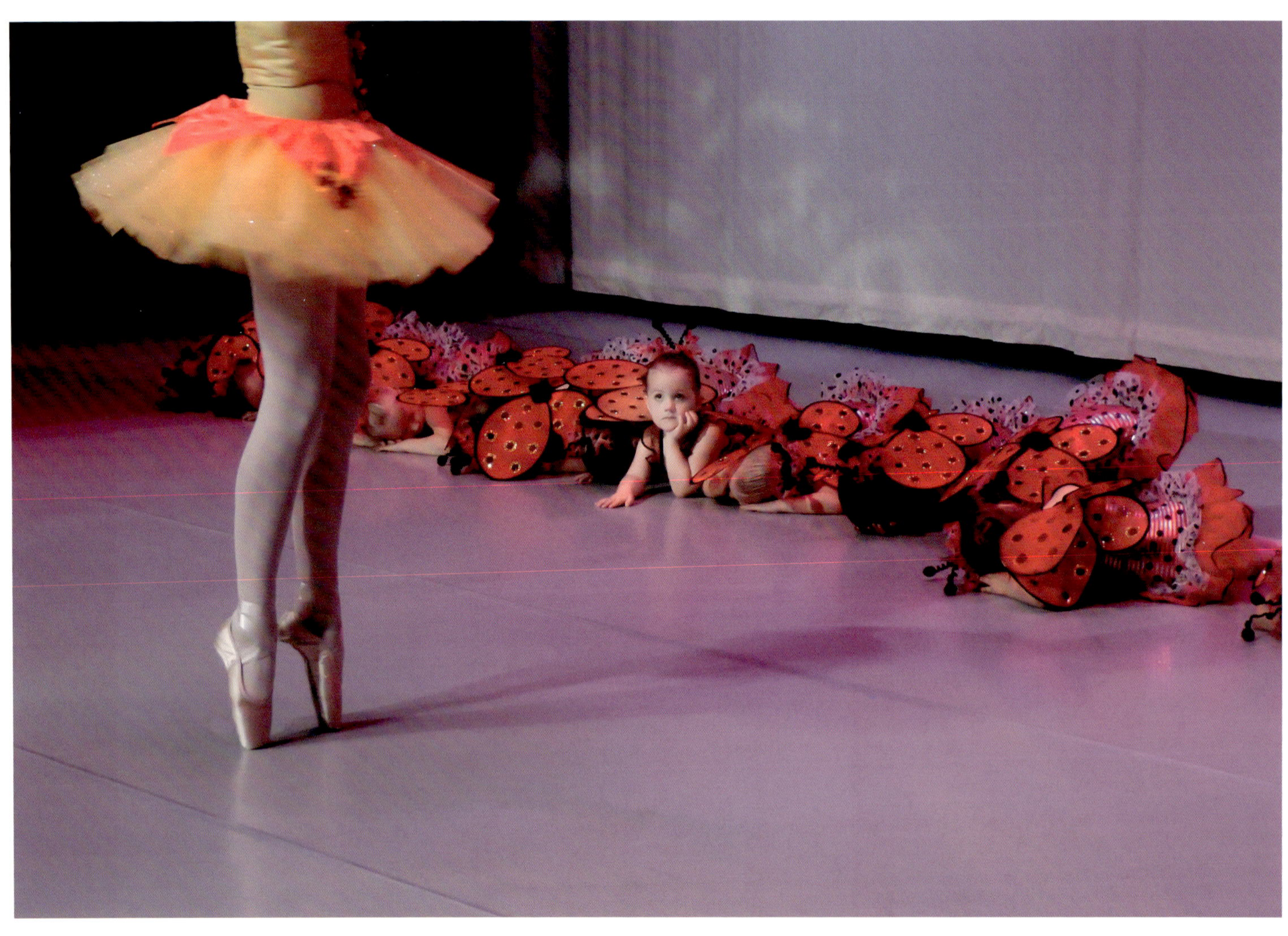

Performance by aspiring dancers at Gallery Ballet & Tap School in McMinnville. *Photo by Charles Hillestad.*

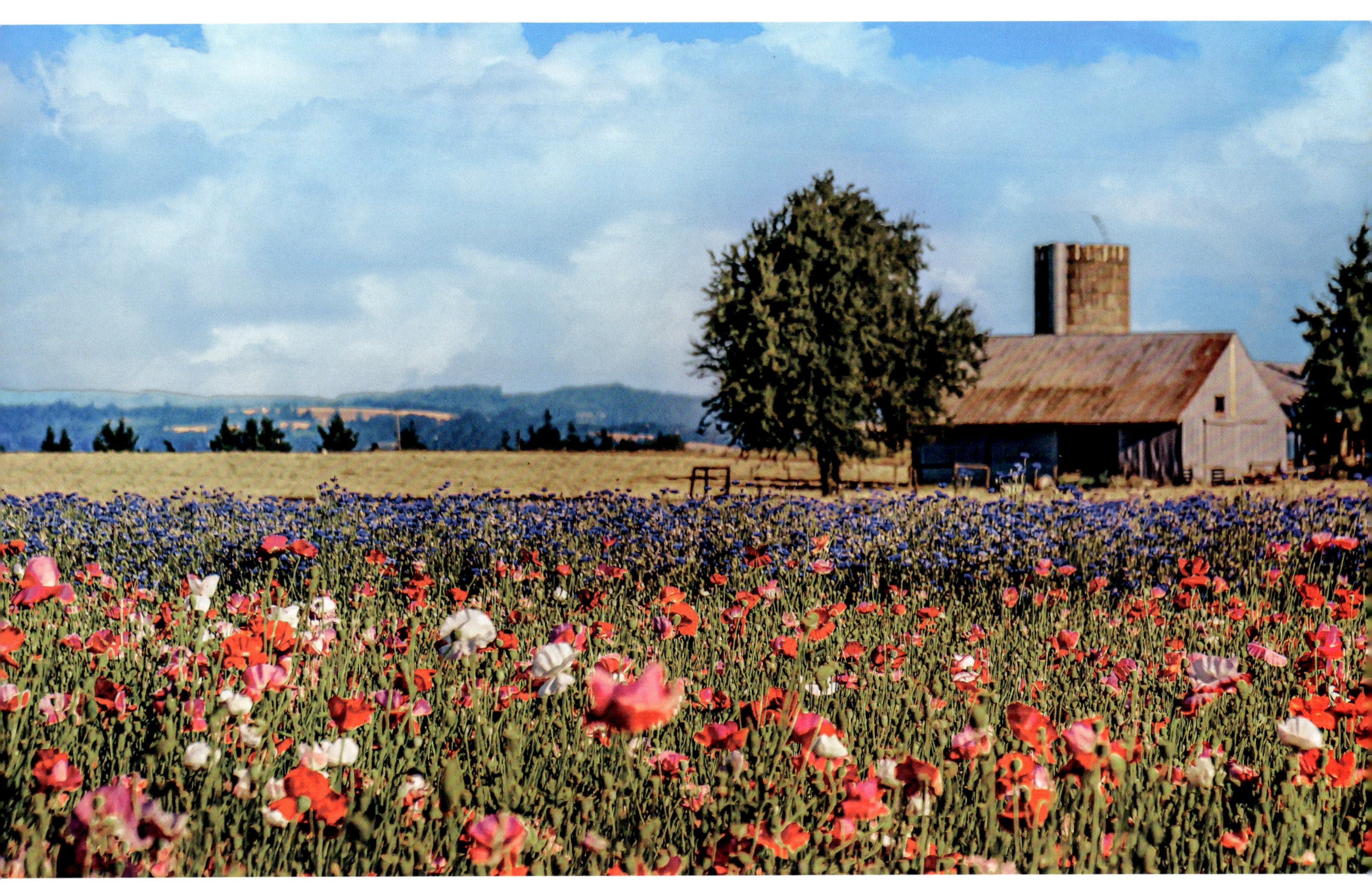

Flower field near Mount Angel. *Photo by Cornelius Matteo.* 149

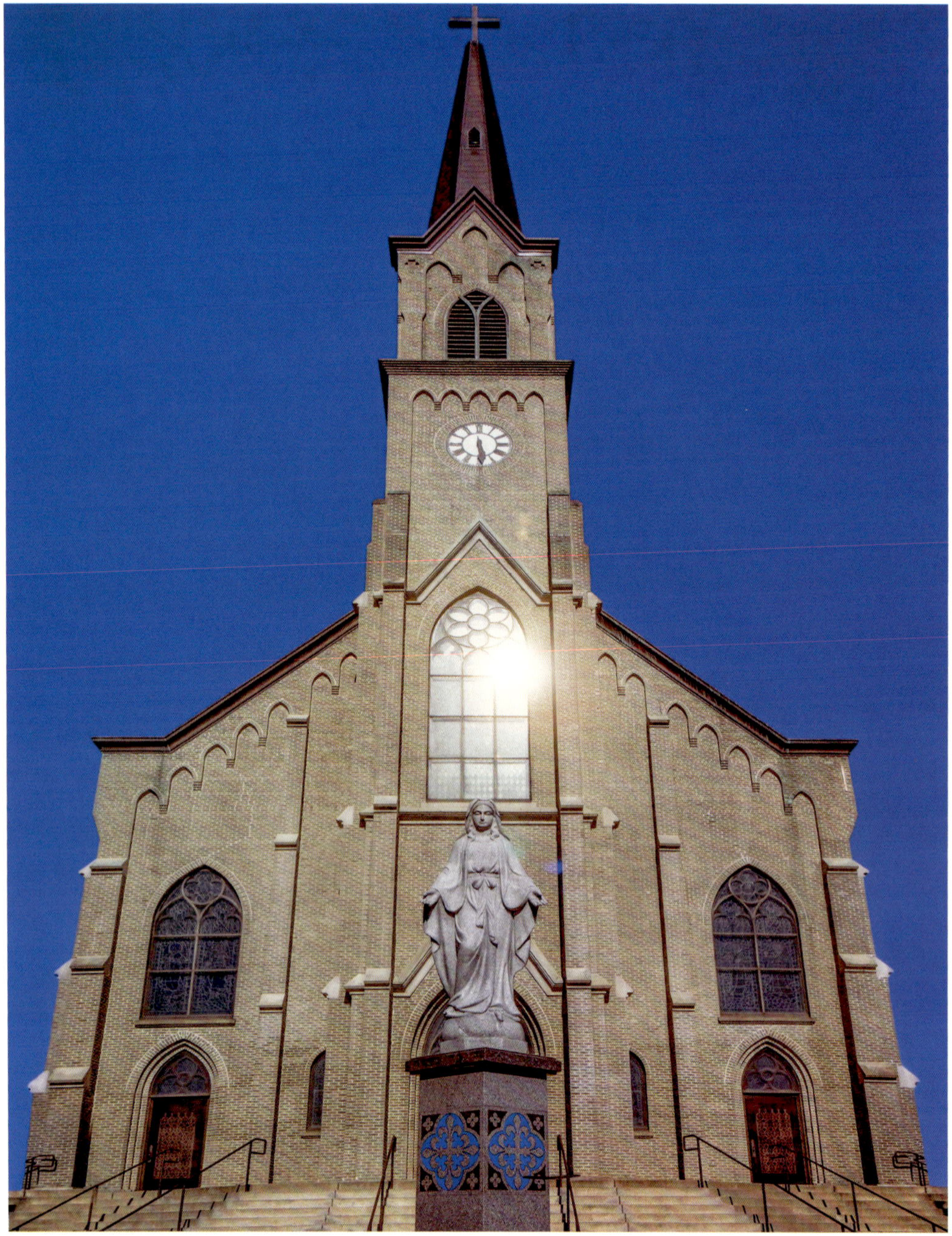

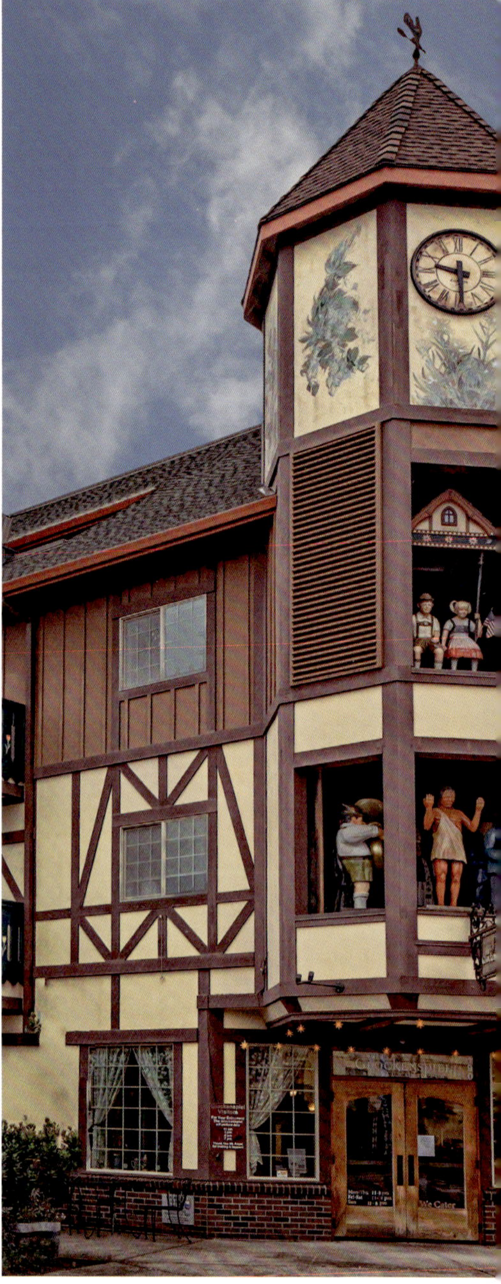

 St. Mary's Church, Mount Angel, built in 1912. *Photo by Cornelius Matteo.*

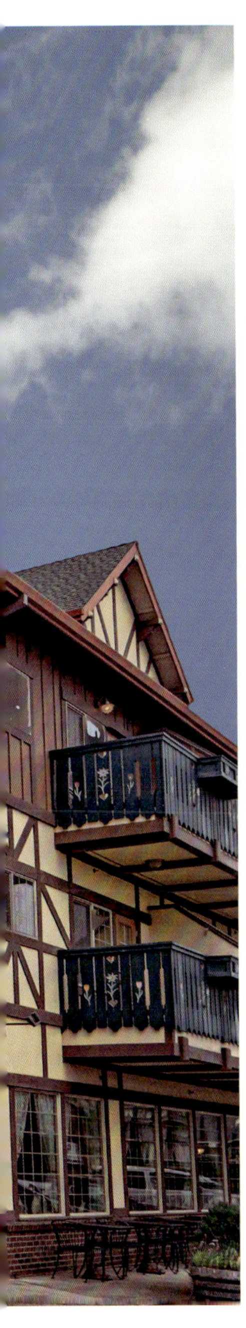

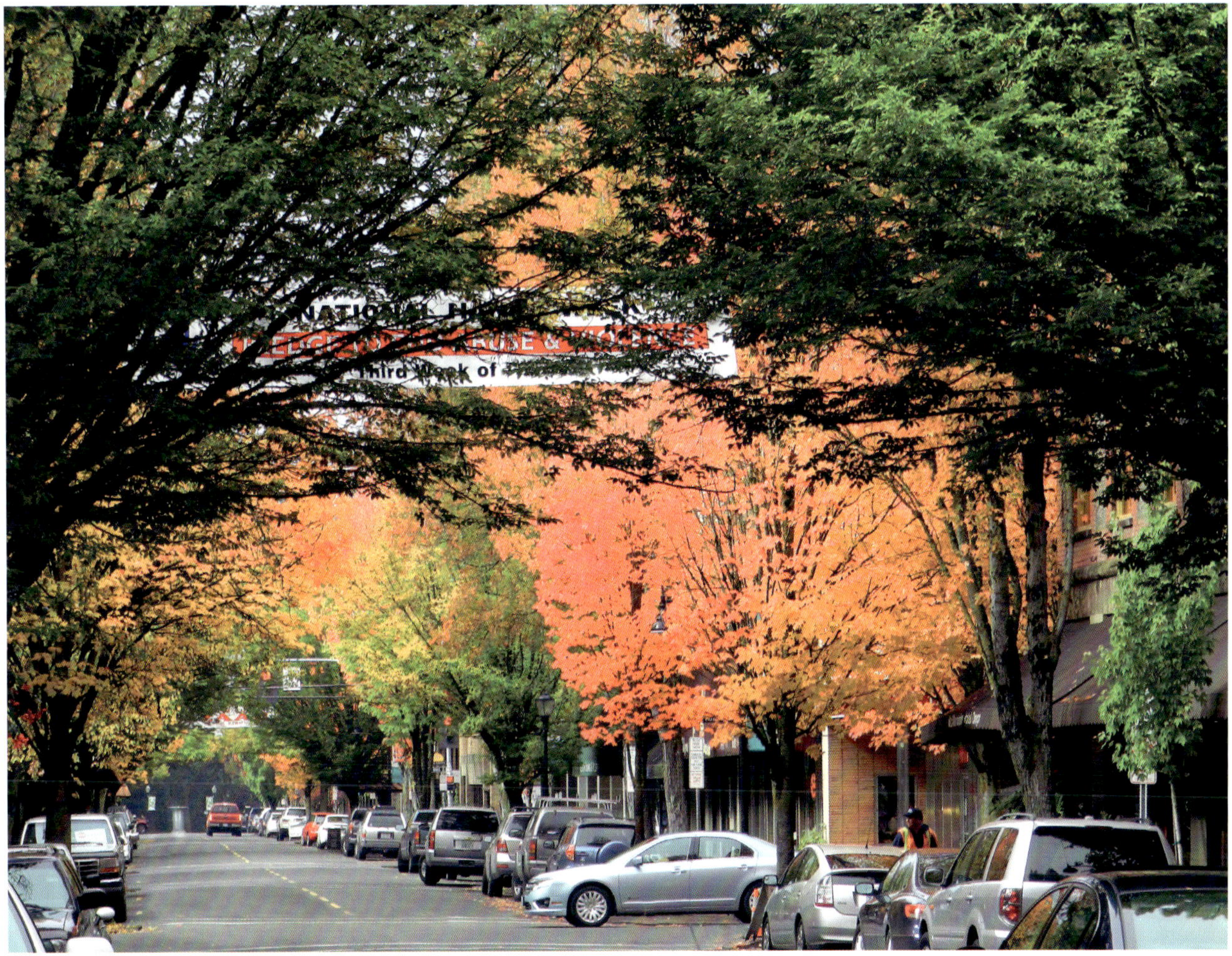

Glockenspiel, Mount Angel. Seven carved-wood characters circle four times daily at America's tallest glockenspiel. Each year, Mount Angel holds an Oktoberfest celebrating its Swiss German heritage. *Photo by Barbara Tricarico.*

Downtown McMinnville's tree tunnel on "Oregon's Favorite Main Street." *Photo by Charles Hillestad.*

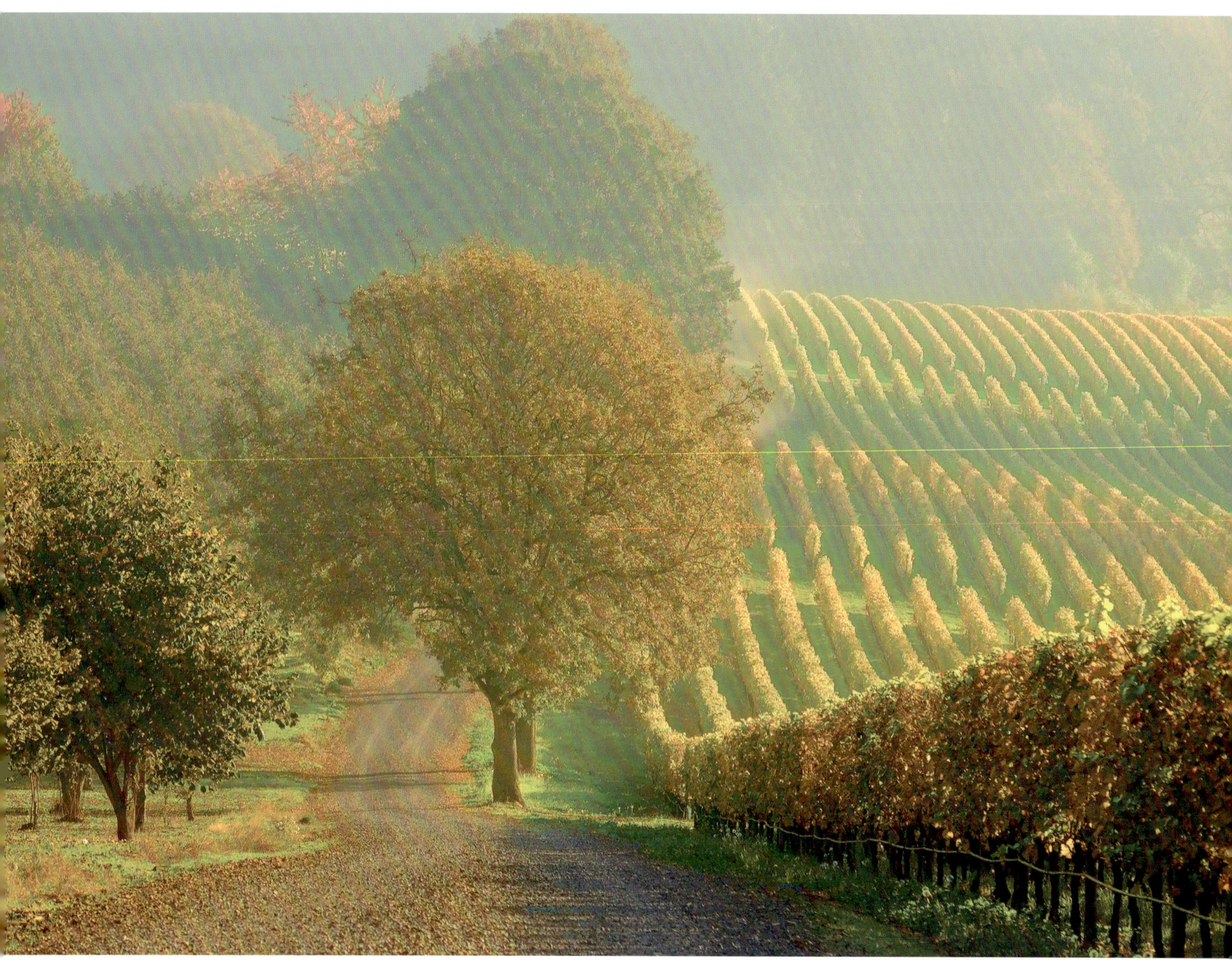

 Autumn in the Dundee Hills vineyards. *Photo by Clem Paslack.*

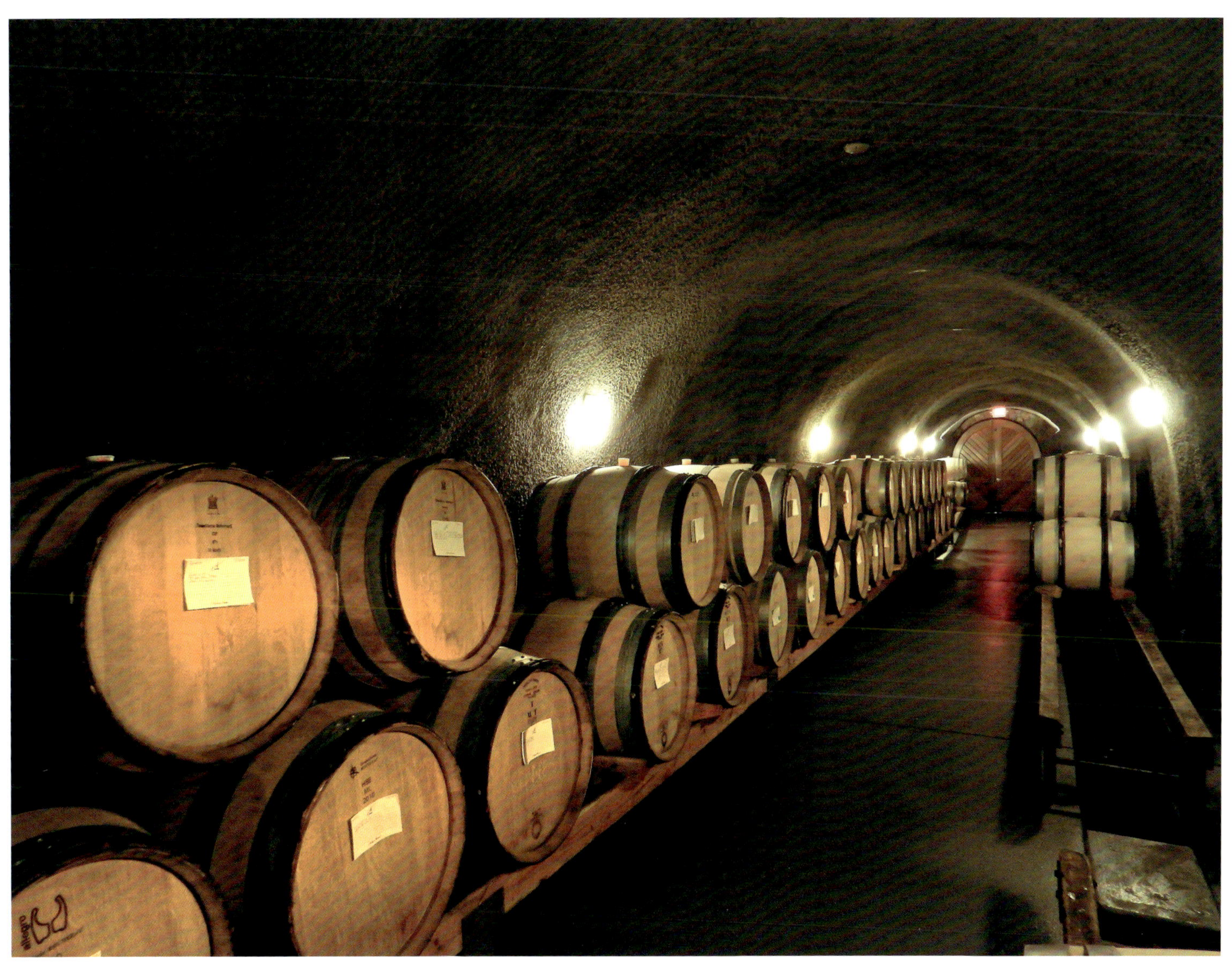

Archery Summit Winery Barrel Cave, Dayton. *Photo by Charles Hillestad.* 153

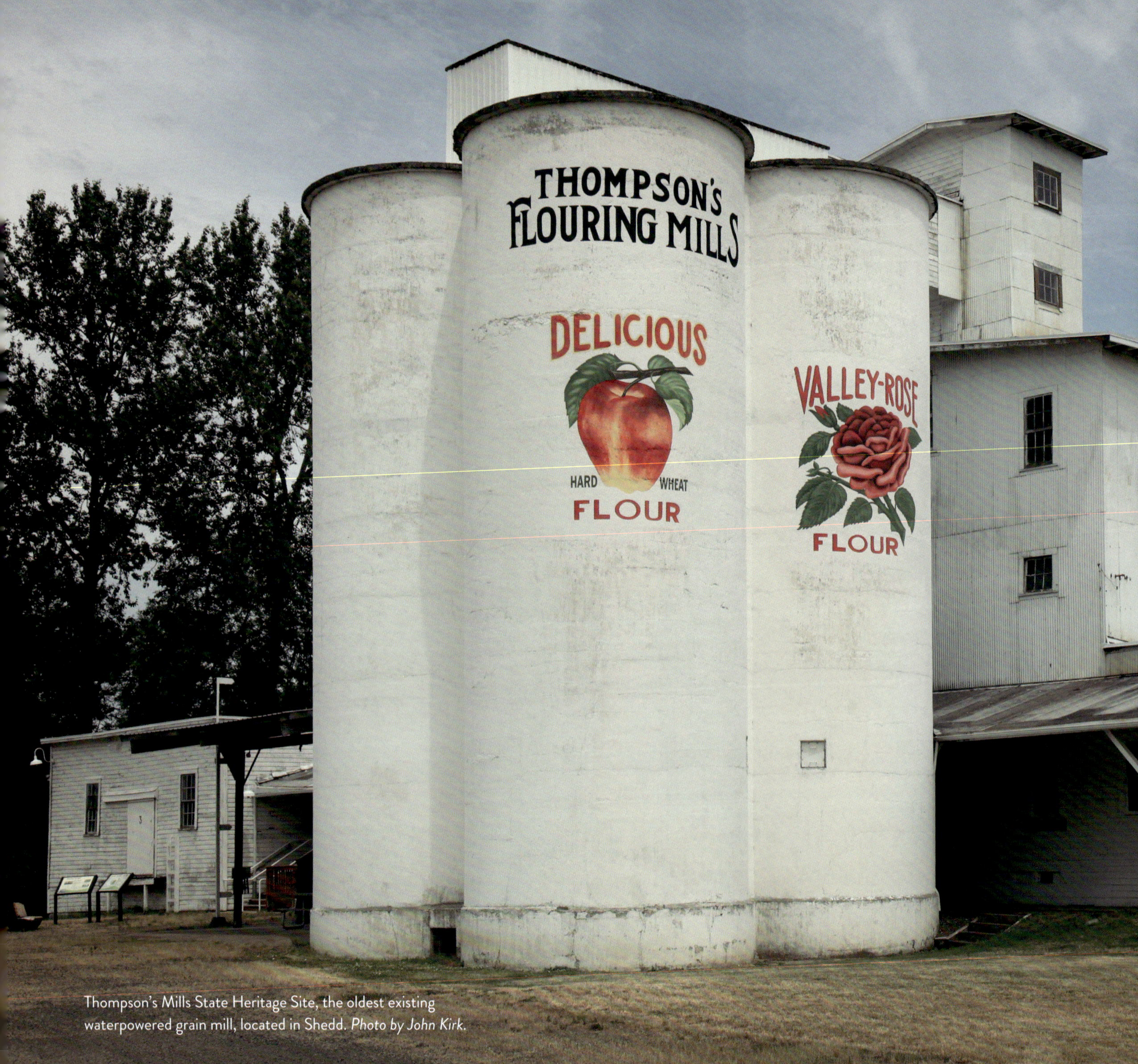

Thompson's Mills State Heritage Site, the oldest existing waterpowered grain mill, located in Shedd. *Photo by John Kirk.*

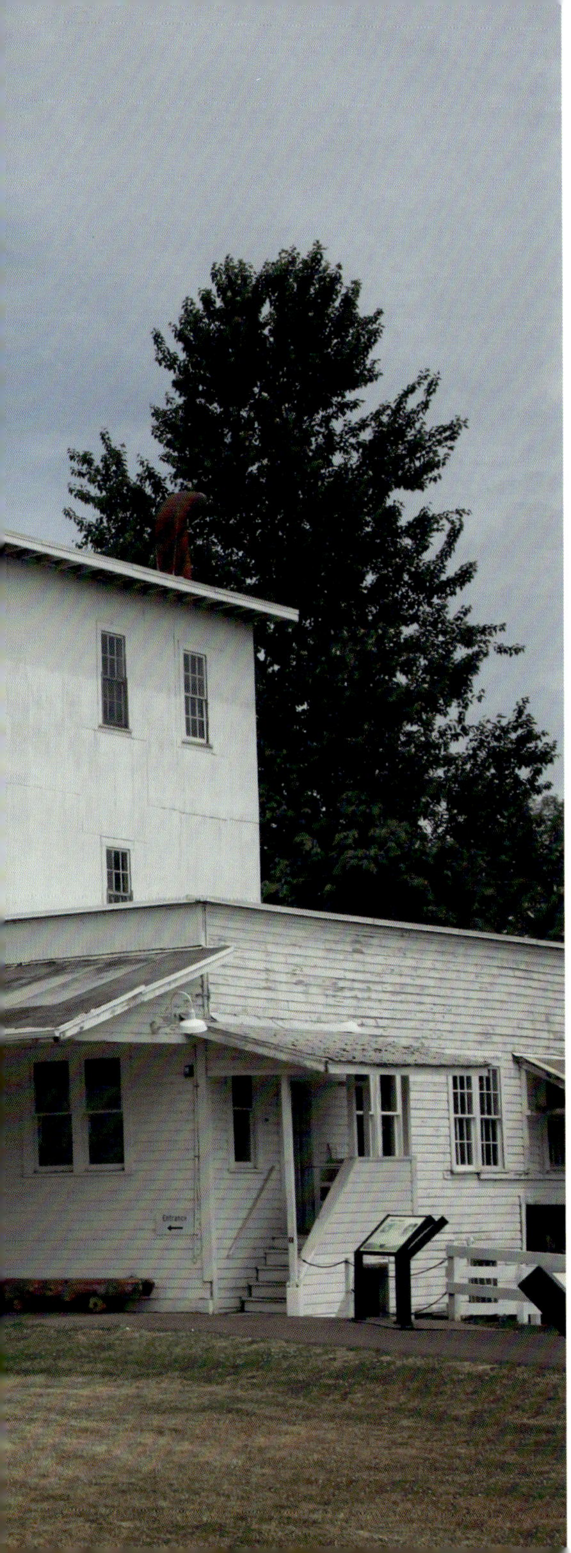

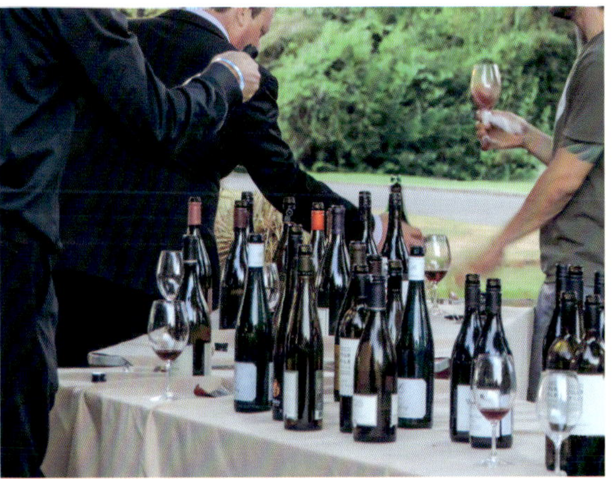

International Pinot Noir Festival at Linfield College, Oak Grove. *Photo by Charles Hillestad.*

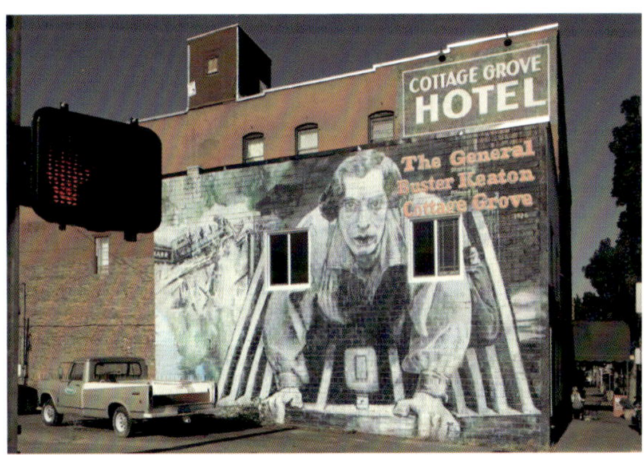

The Buster Keaton film *The General* was filmed in Cottage Grove in 1926. This mural adorns the wall of the hotel where Keaton and the film crew stayed. *Photo by John Kirk.*

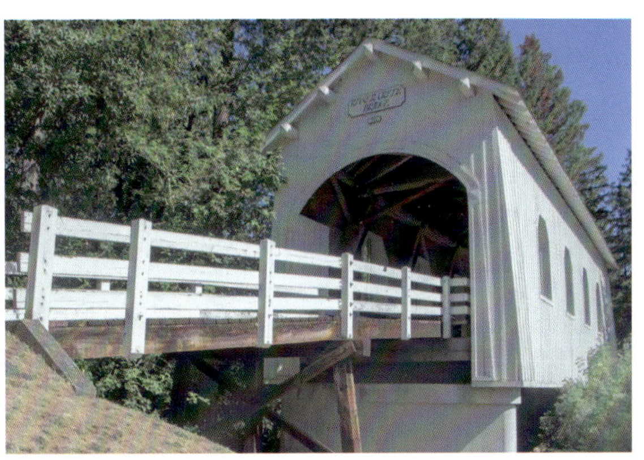

Ritner Creek Covered Bridge, Pedee. Built in 1927, it is the last covered bridge on a state highway in Oregon. There are fifty historic covered bridges in Oregon, down from approximately 450. *Photo by Diana Standing.*

6

OREGON COAST

Oregonians don't go to the beach—they go to the "coast." One of the prettiest drives you'll ever take is along Oregon's 363-mile coastline. Tourists often expect to go swimming, but the water temperature is normally below 50 degrees, with strong currents and riptides.

Striking rock formations define each region along the Oregon Coast. Portlanders flock to Cannon Beach, only ninety minutes away, where you can see elusive puffins nesting on the 235-foot Haystack Rock. Distinctive Face Rock in Bandon features a woman's face in the sunset. Bandon is also well known for Bandon Dunes, a world-class golf course with greens looking out to the Pacific Ocean. The coastal town of Brookings, in a banana belt, yields temperate weather year-round. Travel Oregon named the entire coast one of the Seven Wonders of Oregon.

Oregon's coastal lighthouses once meant safety to both the maritime community and the prosperous timber-shipping industry. While no longer used for navigation, the eleven iconic lighthouses still stand sentinel along the coastline.

In addition to extraordinary rock formations, sea stacks, and scenic coves, the quaint ocean towns of Brookings, Bandon, Lincoln City, and Cannon Beach are great sources for fresh local seafood. The mighty Rogue River empties into the ocean at Gold Beach. It's an area where you can enjoy both river sports and ocean sports in the same day and eat local salmon or crab for dinner. Newport's draw is the 23-acre Oregon Coast Aquarium. Charleston is a working fishing village, and *Architectural Digest* recently named Manzanita the prettiest town in Oregon.

If you visit at high tide, you may witness the natural phenomena of Thor's Well near Yachats and Devil's Punchbowl near Newport or see crashing waves the size of skyscrapers explode against the rocks at Shore Acres.

Walk or dune-buggy along one of the longest dunes in the country at the Oregon Dunes National Recreation Area. Hear and see barking sea lions along Cape Arago or at the Sea Lion Caves near Florence. At low tide along the rocky coast, look for colorful starfish, urchin, and anemone in tidal pools.

While in the Bandon or the Cape Arago areas, visit Shore Acres State Park & Botanical Gardens. Beautiful roses, tulips, rhododendrons, dahlias, water lilies, and plants from all over the world are on display throughout the year, thanks to the mild climate. The estate, originally built in 1906 by Louis J. Simpson, greets more than 250,000 visitors yearly. During the Holiday Lights Display, more than 300,000 L.E.D. lights adorn the mansion and grounds.

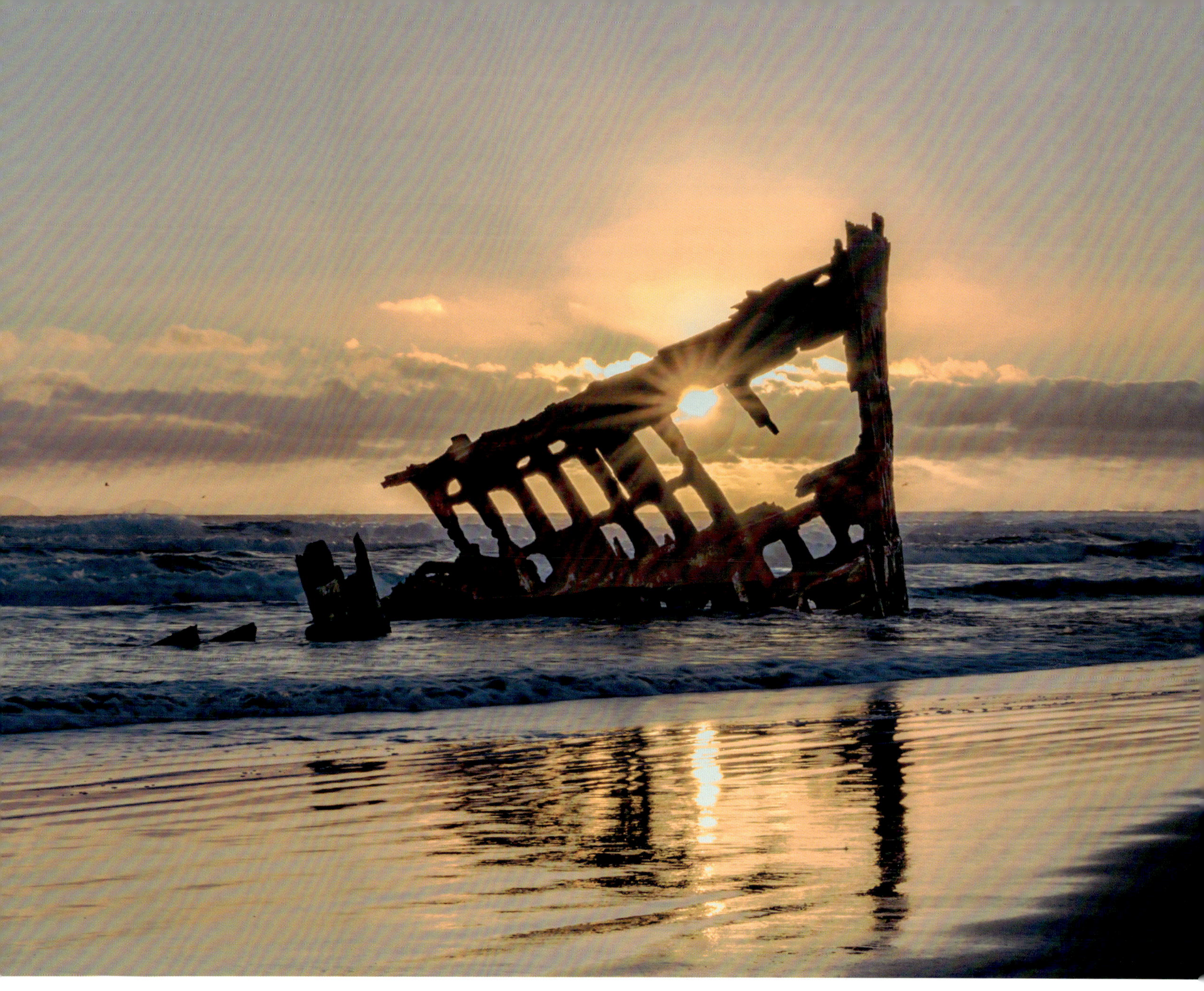

Peter Iredale wreck, Astoria. The sailing ship ran ashore in 1906. Captain H. Lawrence's final toast to his ship was "May God bless you, and may your bones bleach in the sands." *Photo by Doug Farrell.*   157

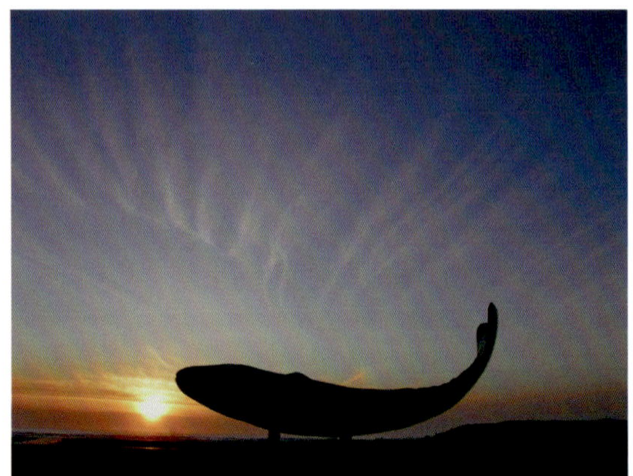

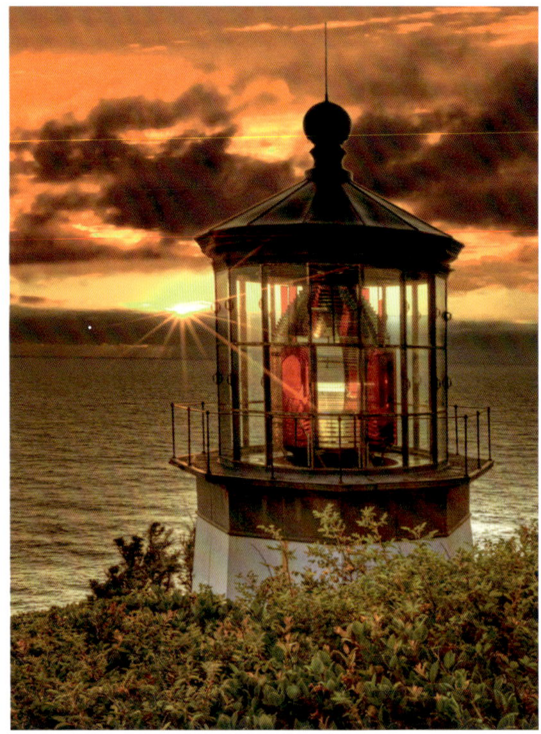

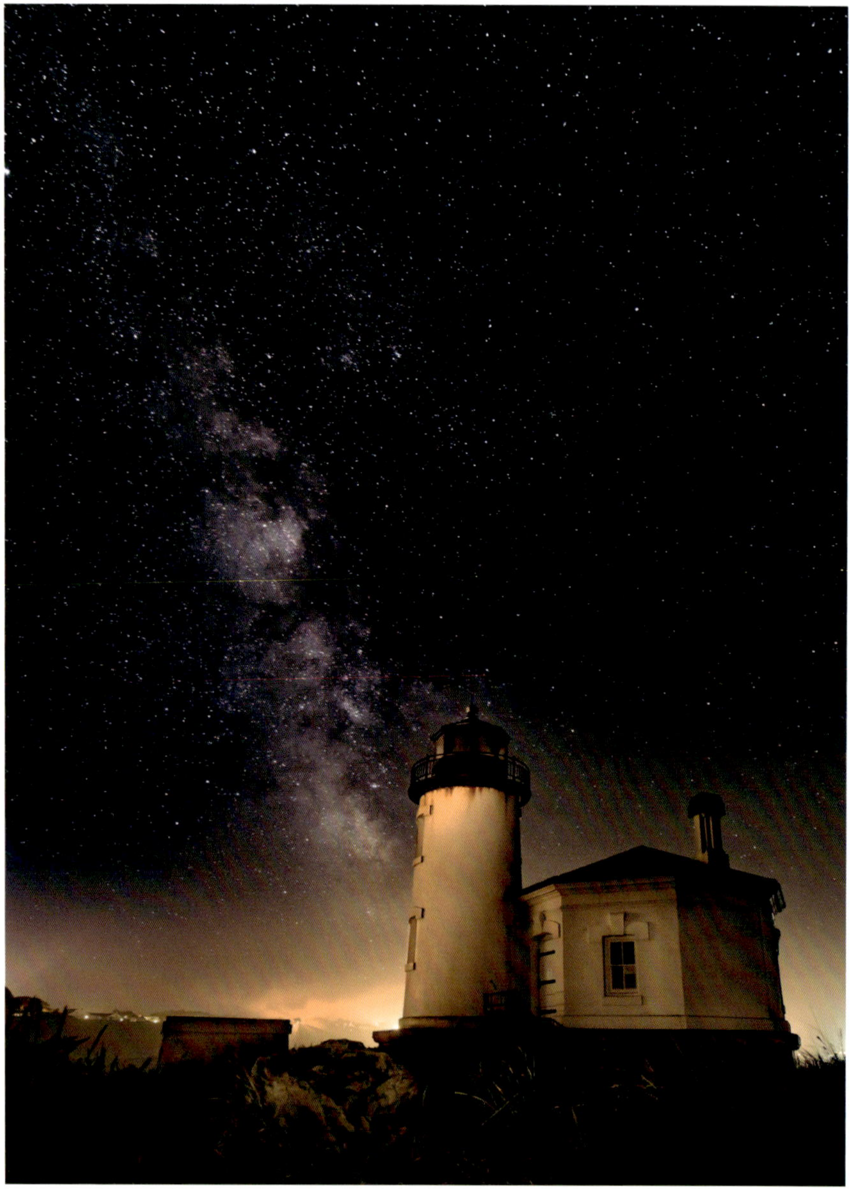

(Top left) Sunset at Whale Park, Cannon Beach. *Whale* is a sculpture that commemorates the discovery of a whale skeleton in January 1806 by the Lewis and Clark expedition. *Photo by Charles Hillestad.* • (Bottom left) Located ten miles west of Tillamook on Cape Meares, this lighthouse was built in 1890. *Photo by Rudy Dierks.* • (Right) Milky Way above Coquille River Lighthouse, Bandon. *Photo by Linda Rodgers.*

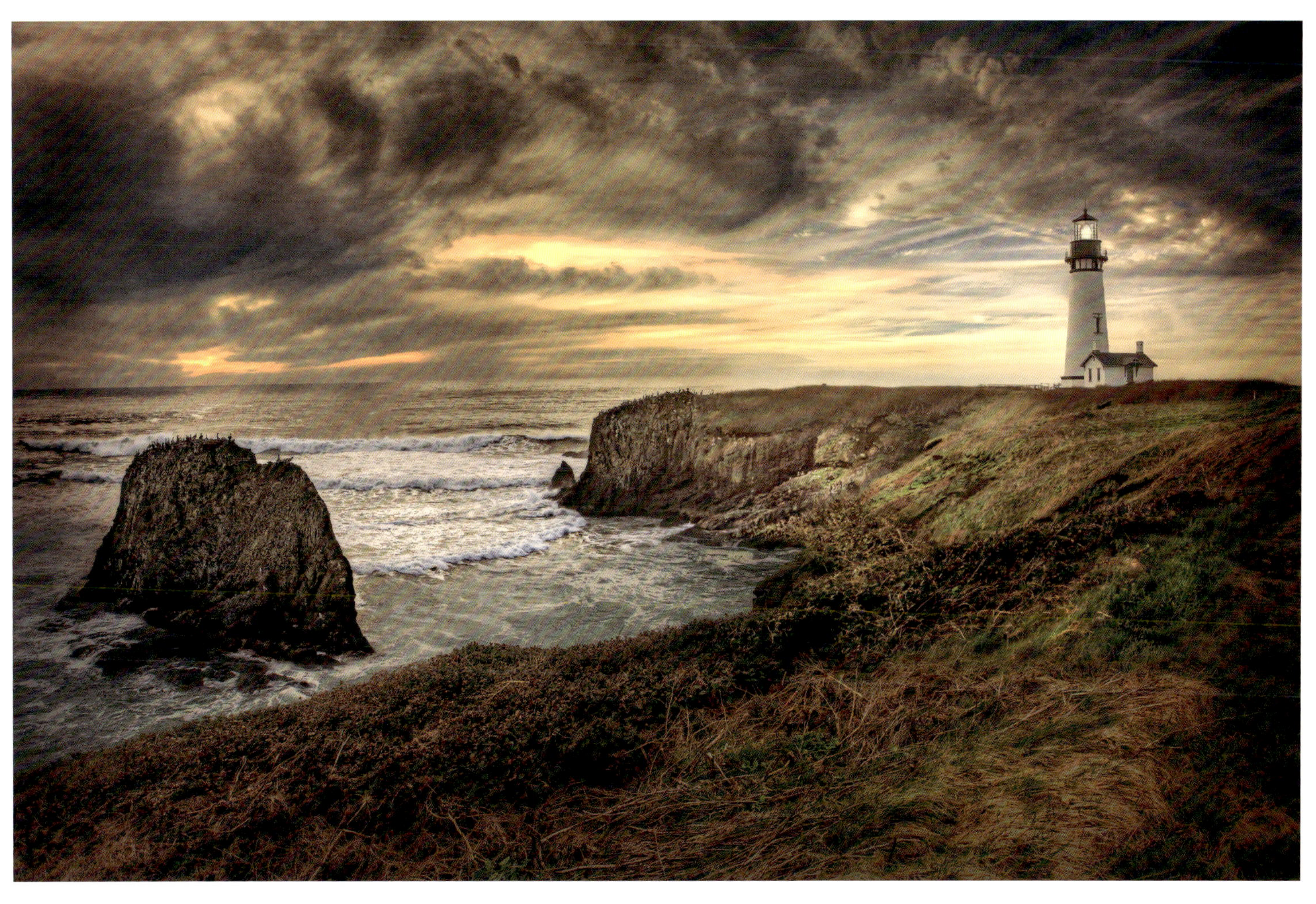

Yaquina Head Lighthouse in Newport is the tallest lighthouse in Oregon and stands 93 feet high. It was first lit in 1873. *Photo by Rudy Dierks.*

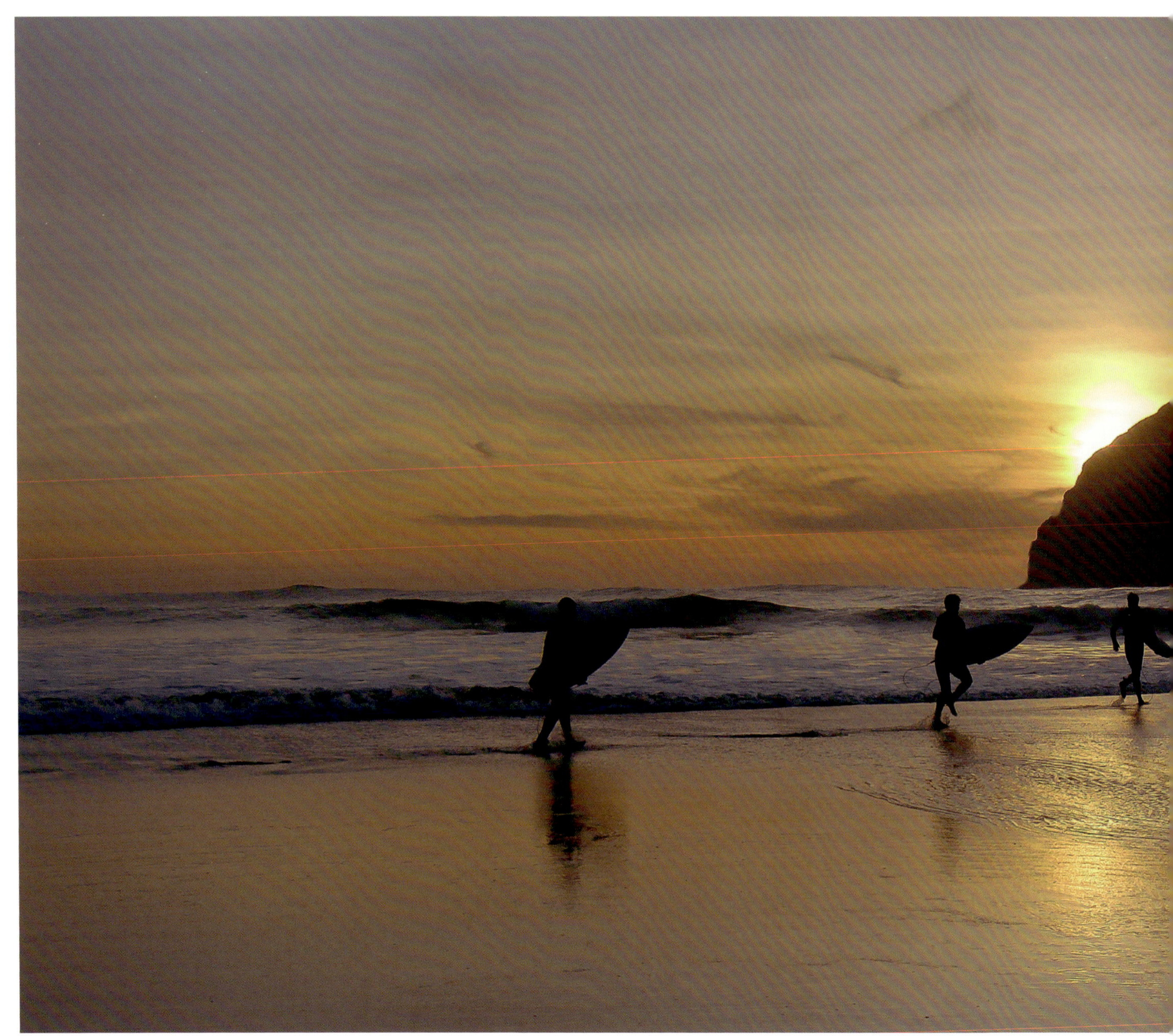

160 Surfers at Pacific City. *Photo by Clem Paslack.*

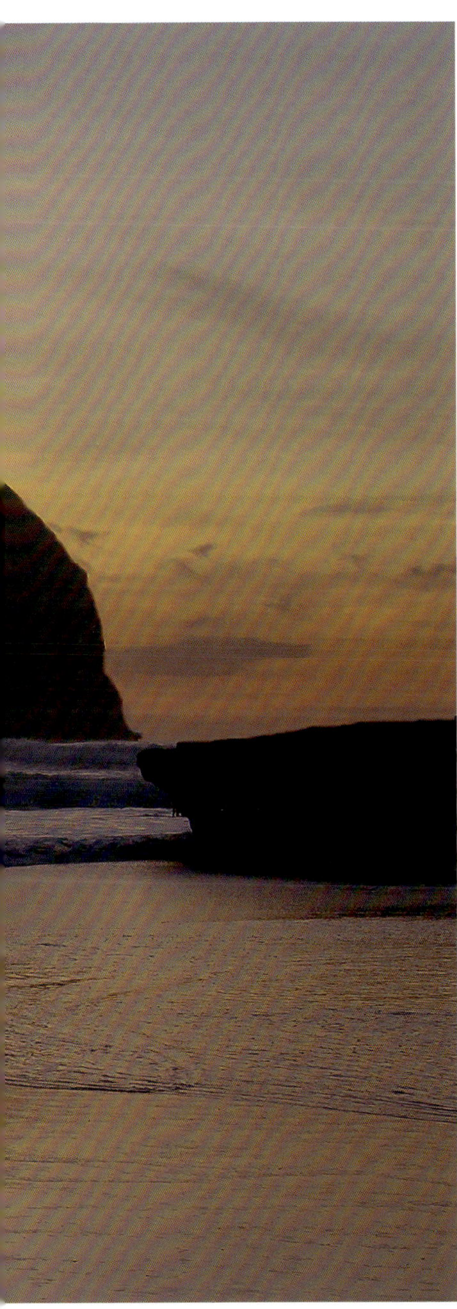

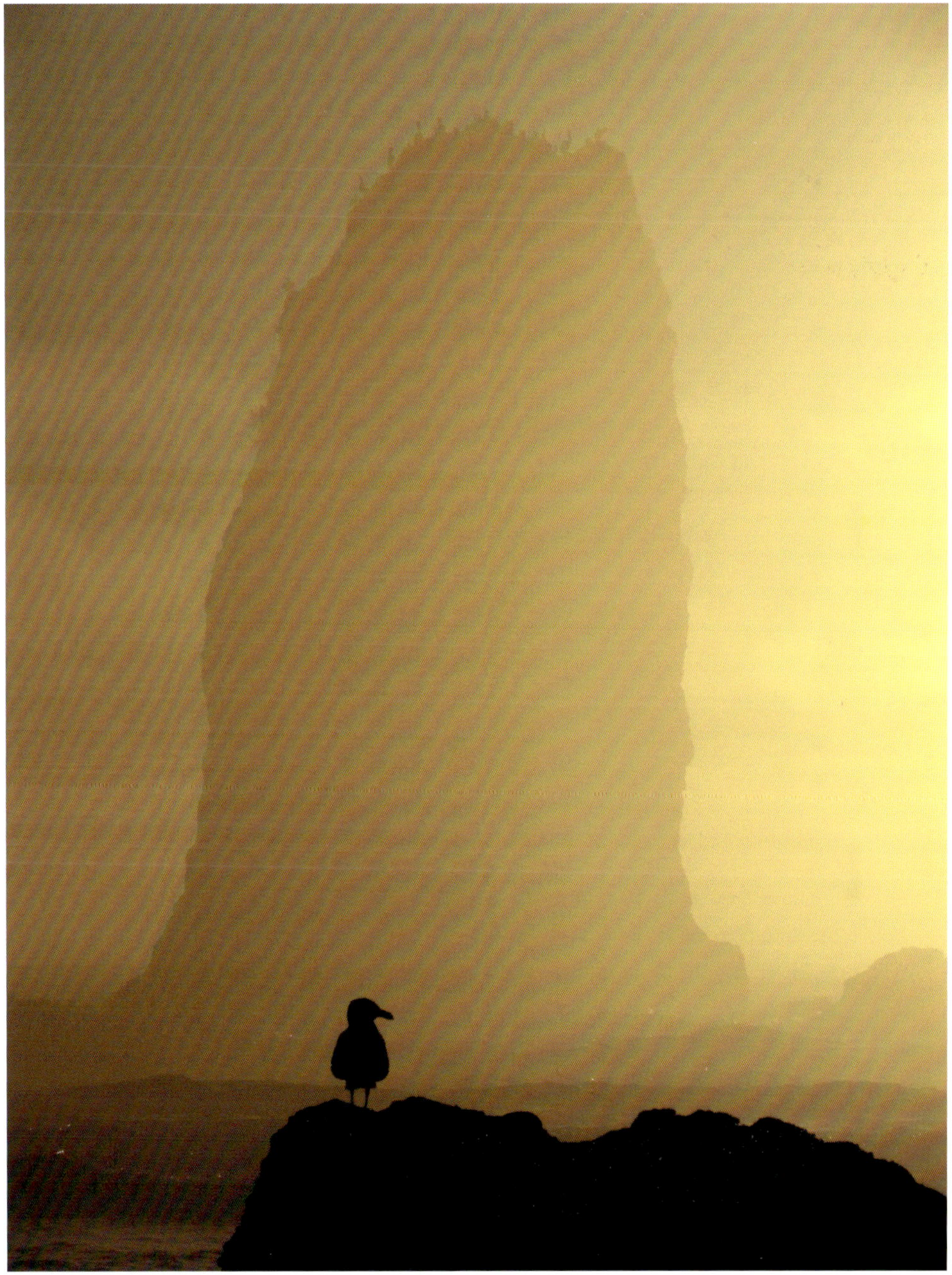

The Needles, Cannon Beach. *Photo by Charles Hillestad.* 161

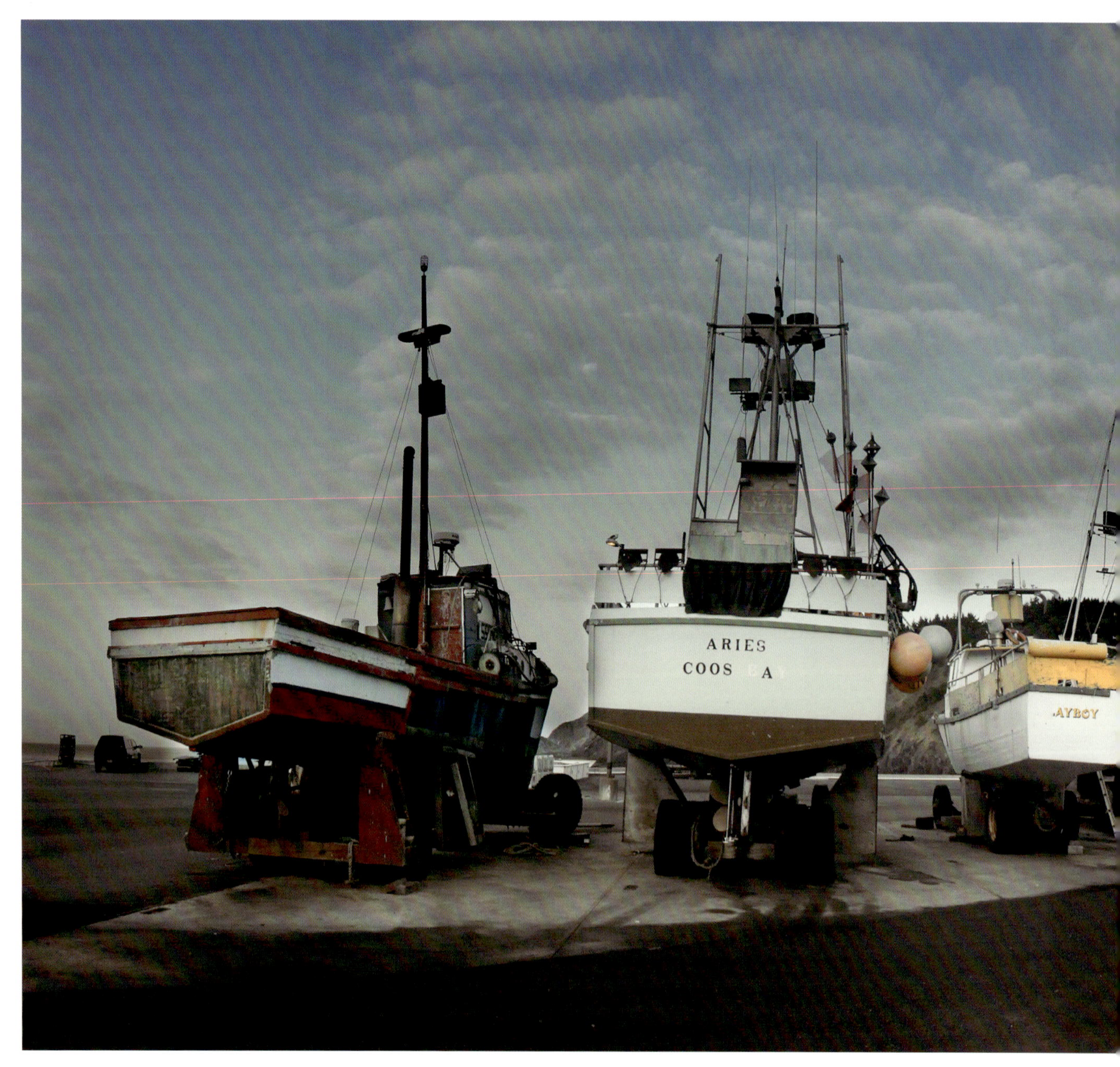

Port Orford's "dolly dock" is one of only two dolly ports in the United States and six in the world. Each boat is
lifted into and out of the open-water dock by cranes and stored on its own dolly. *Photo by John Kirk.*

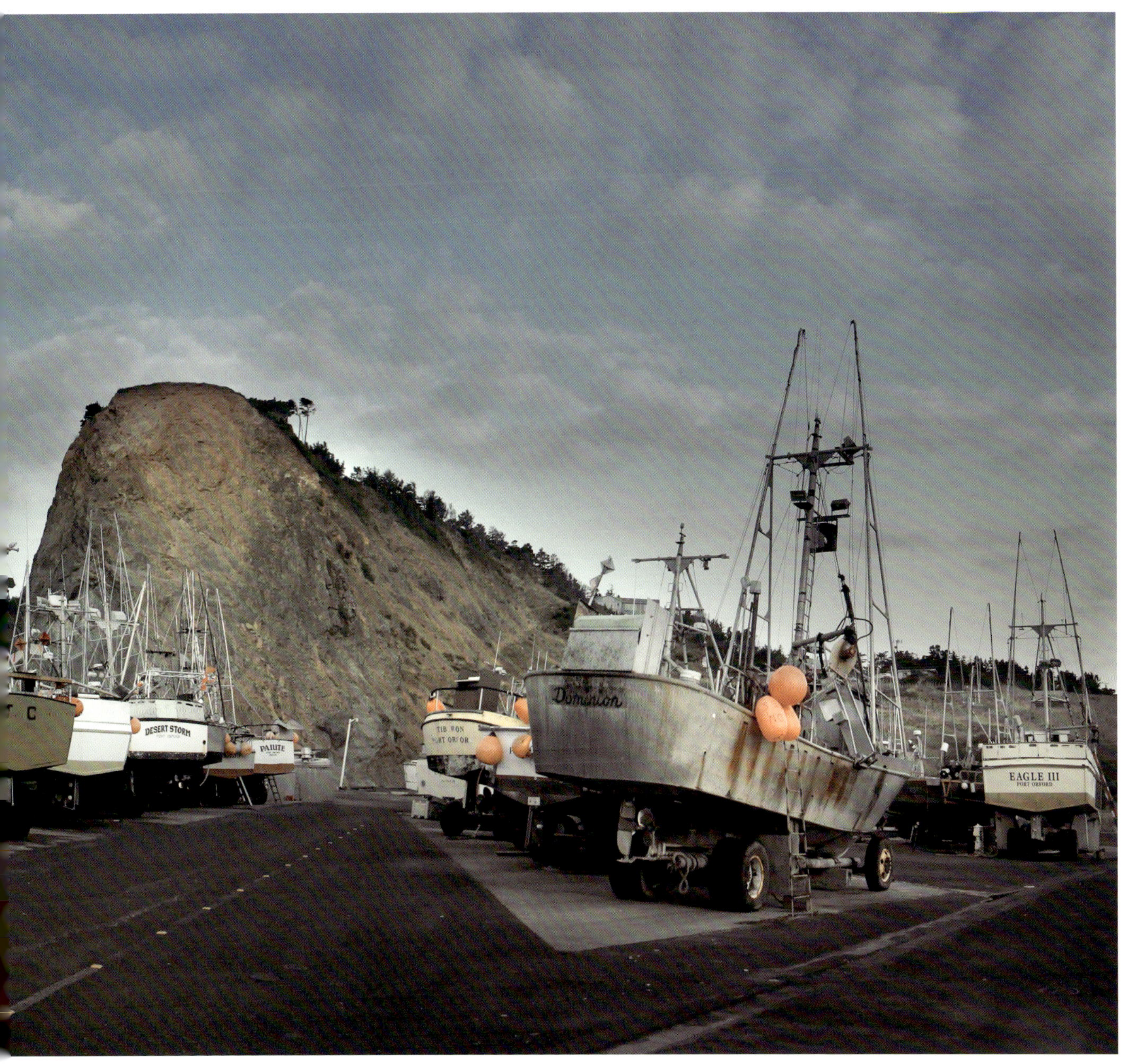

DESERT STORM
PORT ORFORD
PAIUTE
TIB RON
PORT ORFOR
Dominion
EAGLE III
PORT ORFORD

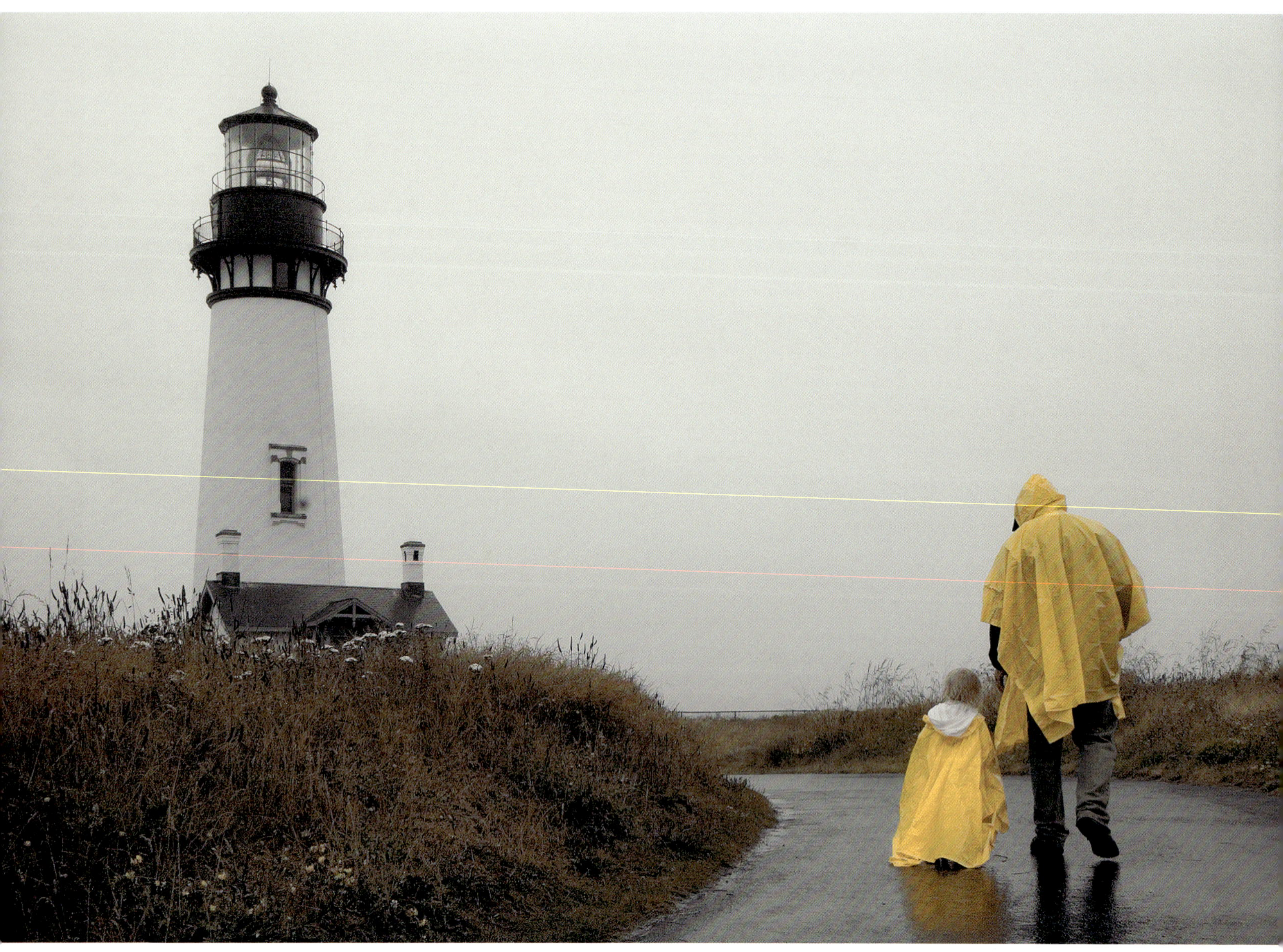

 Rainy day at Yaquina Head Lighthouse. *Photo by David Lorenz Winston.*

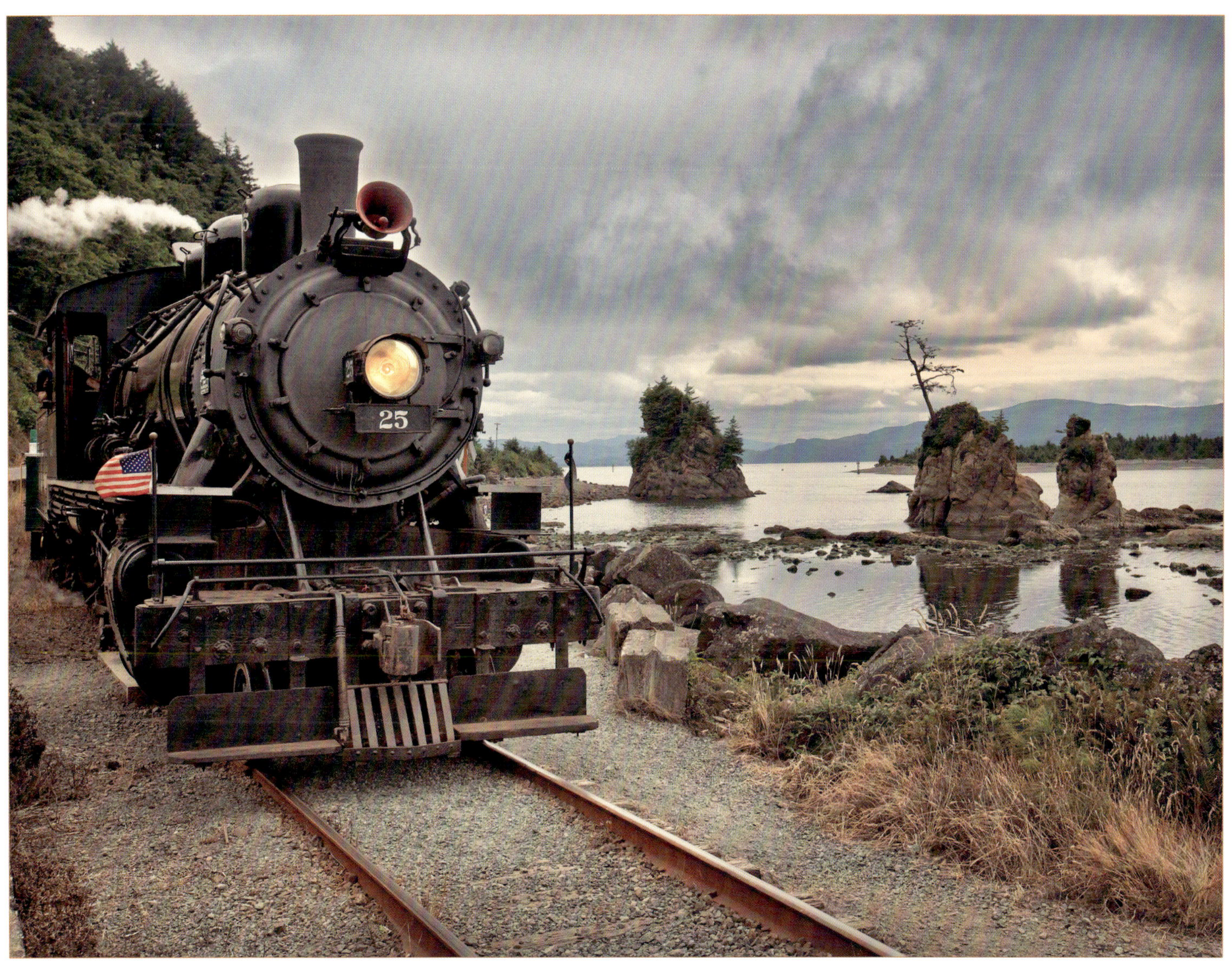

The Oregon Coast Scenic Railroad offers rides between Garibaldi and Rockaway Beach along Tillamook Bay. *Photo by Rudy Dierks.*

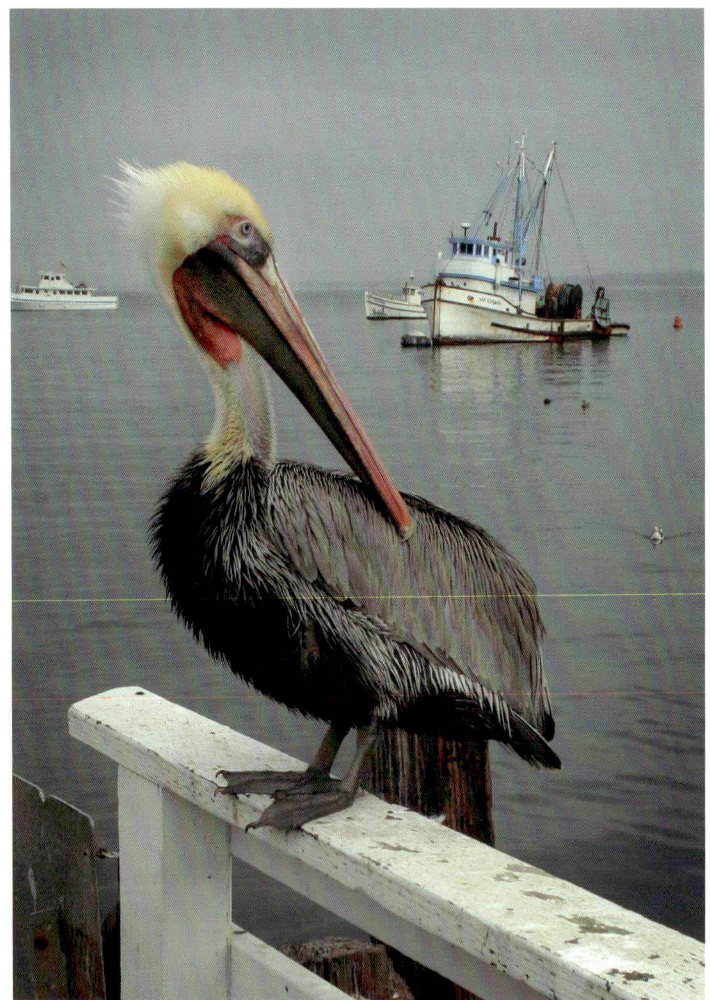

Pelican in the harbor. *Photo by John Kirk.*

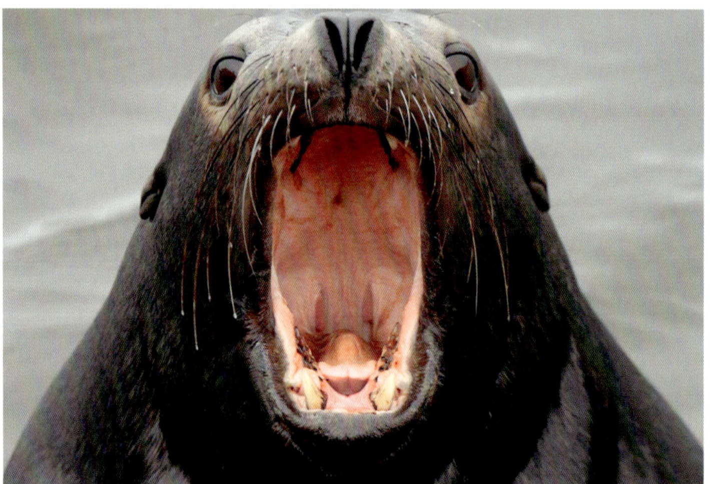

Barking California sea lion in Gold Beach. *Photo by Dan Elster.*

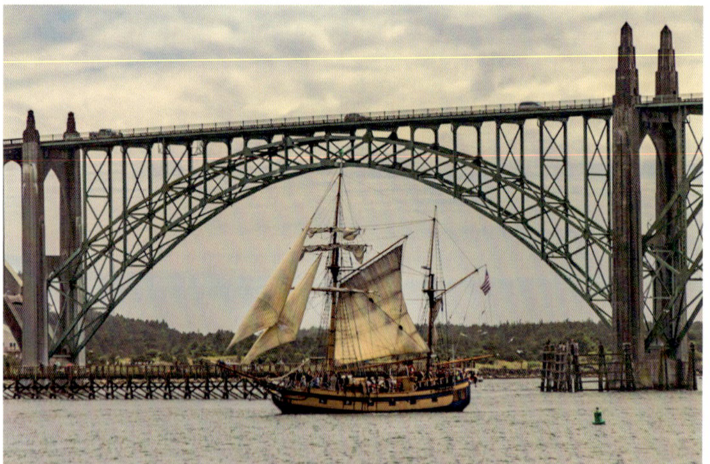

Tall ship at Yaquina Bay Bridge, Newport. *Photo by Vldn Taylor.*

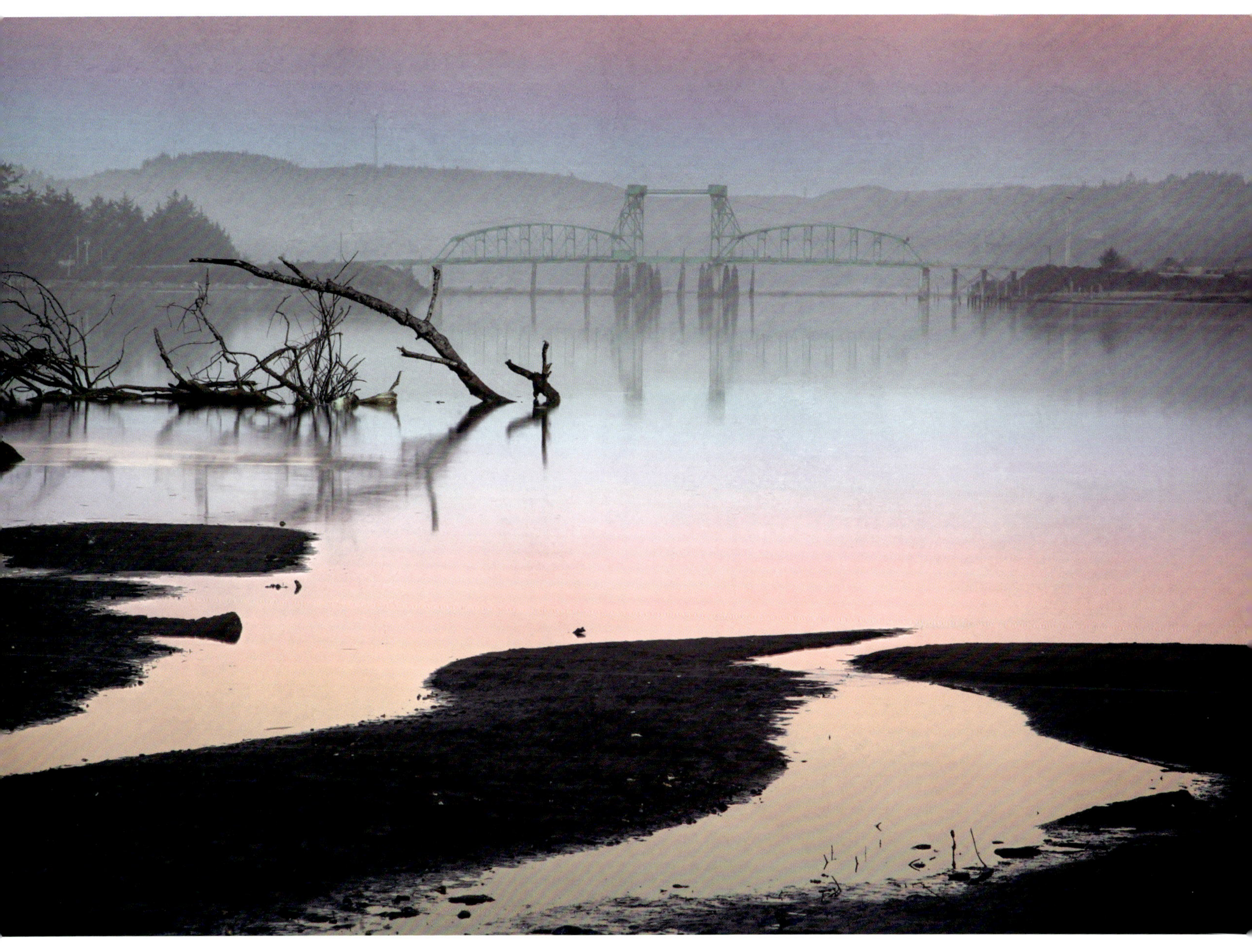

Bullards Bridge, Coquille River, opened in 1954. *Photo by John Kirk.* 167

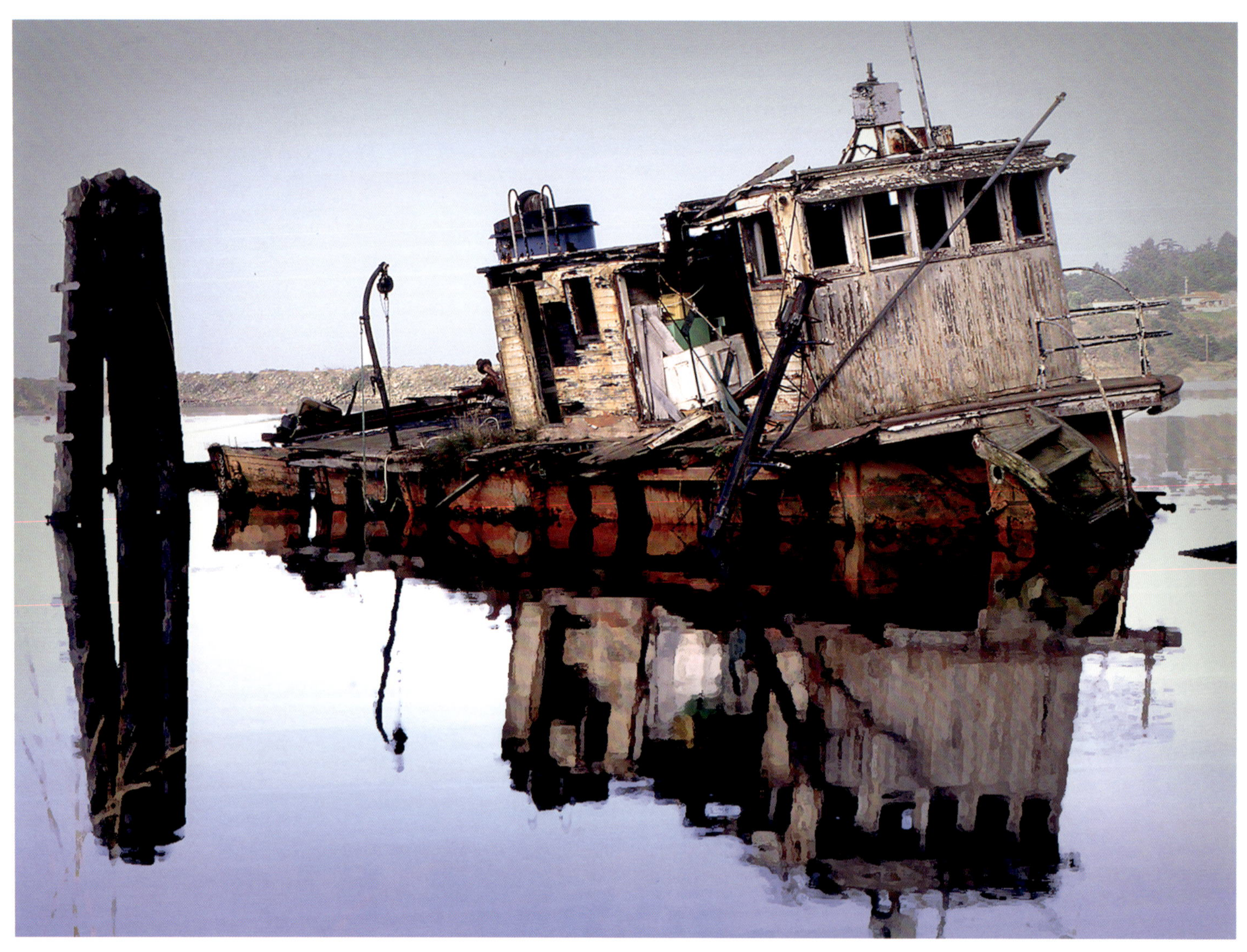

The *Mary D. Hume* was built in Gold Beach in 1881. The steamer also served as a whaling ship in Alaska and a tugboat. It sank in 1985 in the Rogue River, which empties into the Pacific Ocean. The *Mary D. Hume* is on the National Register of Historic Places. *Photo by John Kirk.*

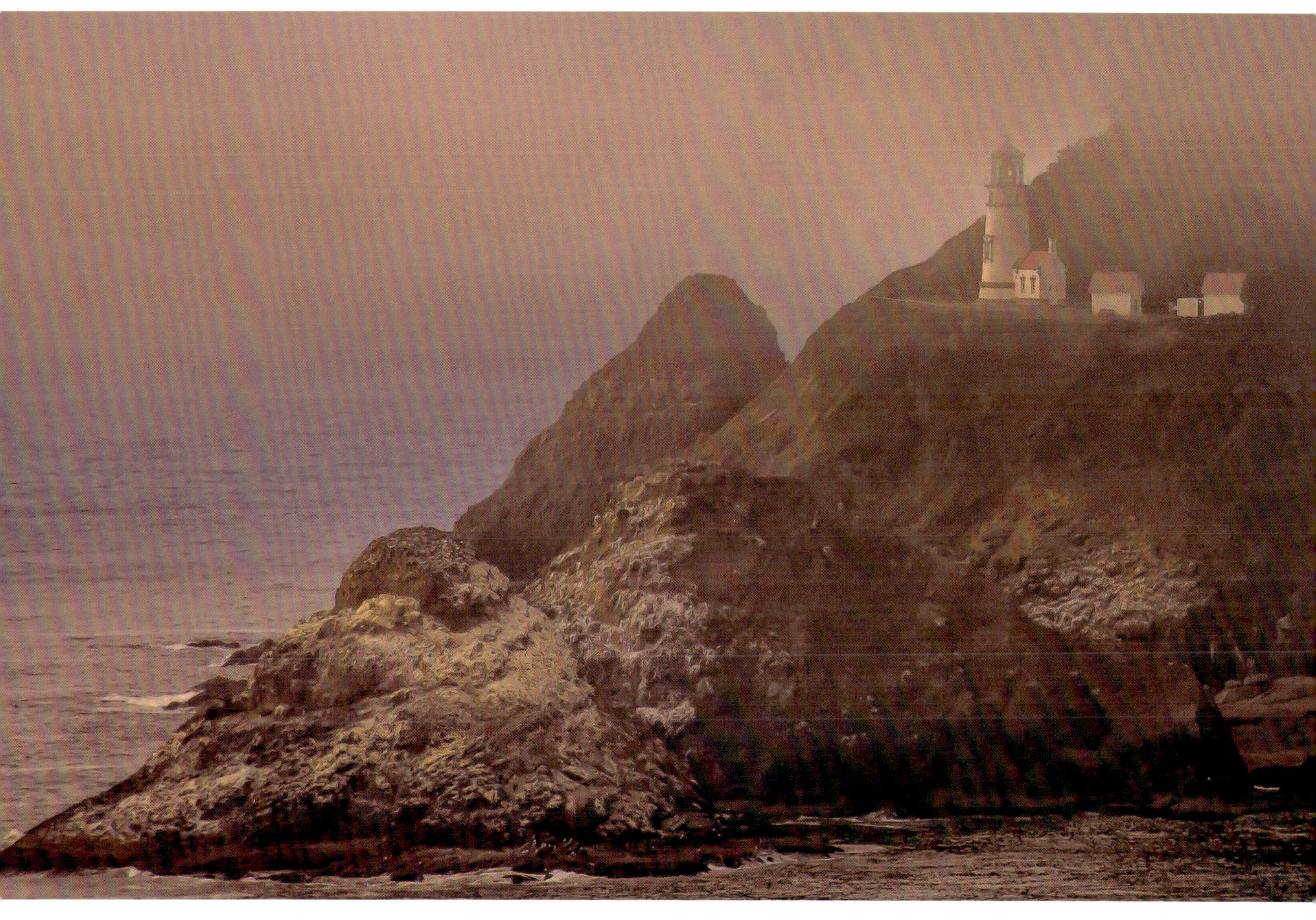

Heceta Head Lighthouse. The Oregon Parks and Recreation Department maintains the working lighthouse, and the light keeper's home is an interpretive center. The US Forest Service operates the six assistant lightkeepers' homes as a bed and breakfast. *Photo by Clem Paslack.*

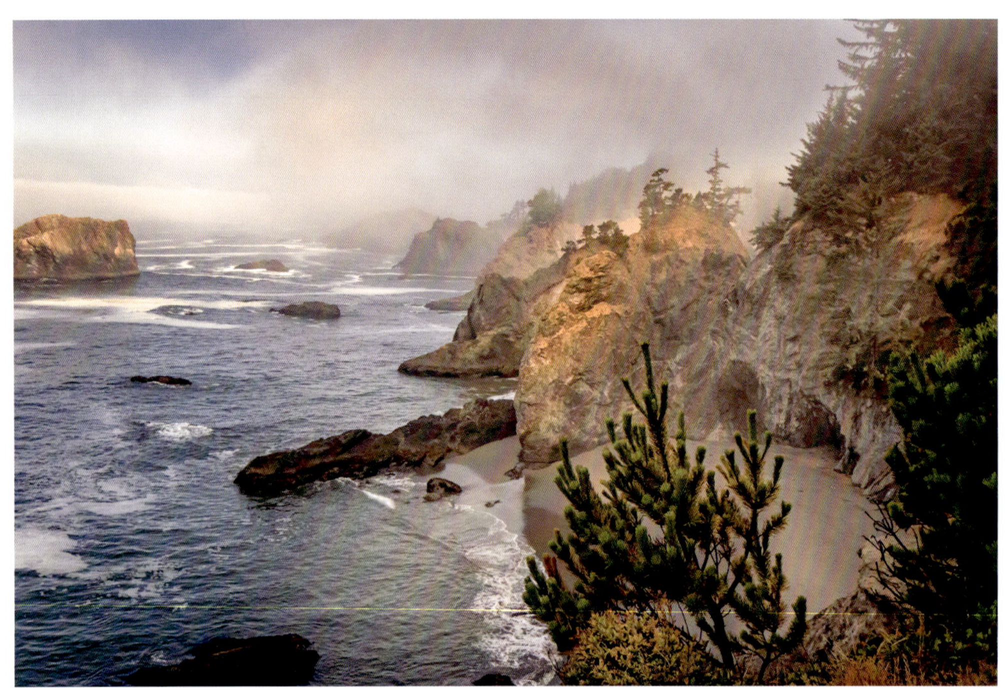

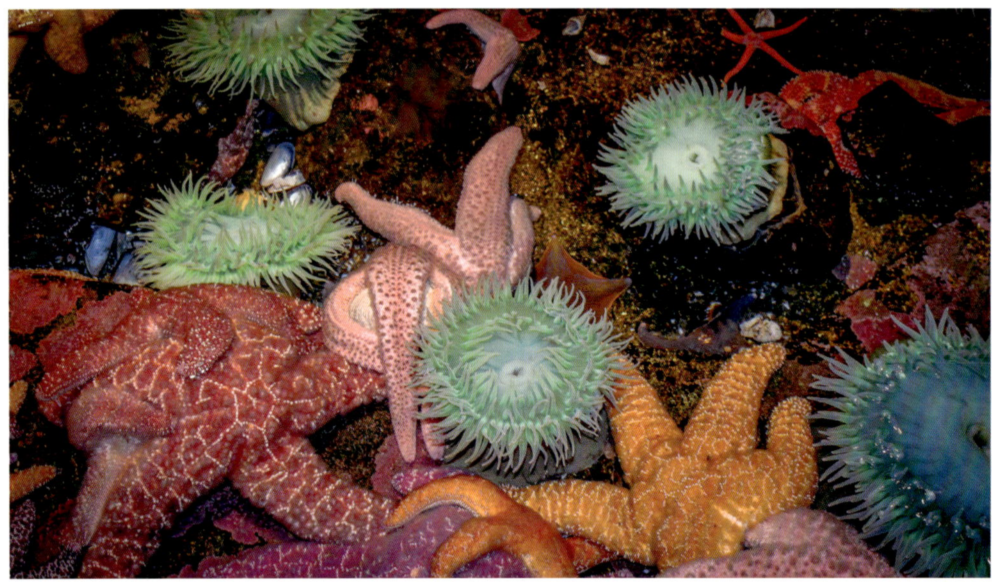

 Thunder Rock Cove, Brookings. *Photo by Ellen Ahern.* • Tidal pool life, Bandon, Oregon. *Photo by Ellen Ahern.*

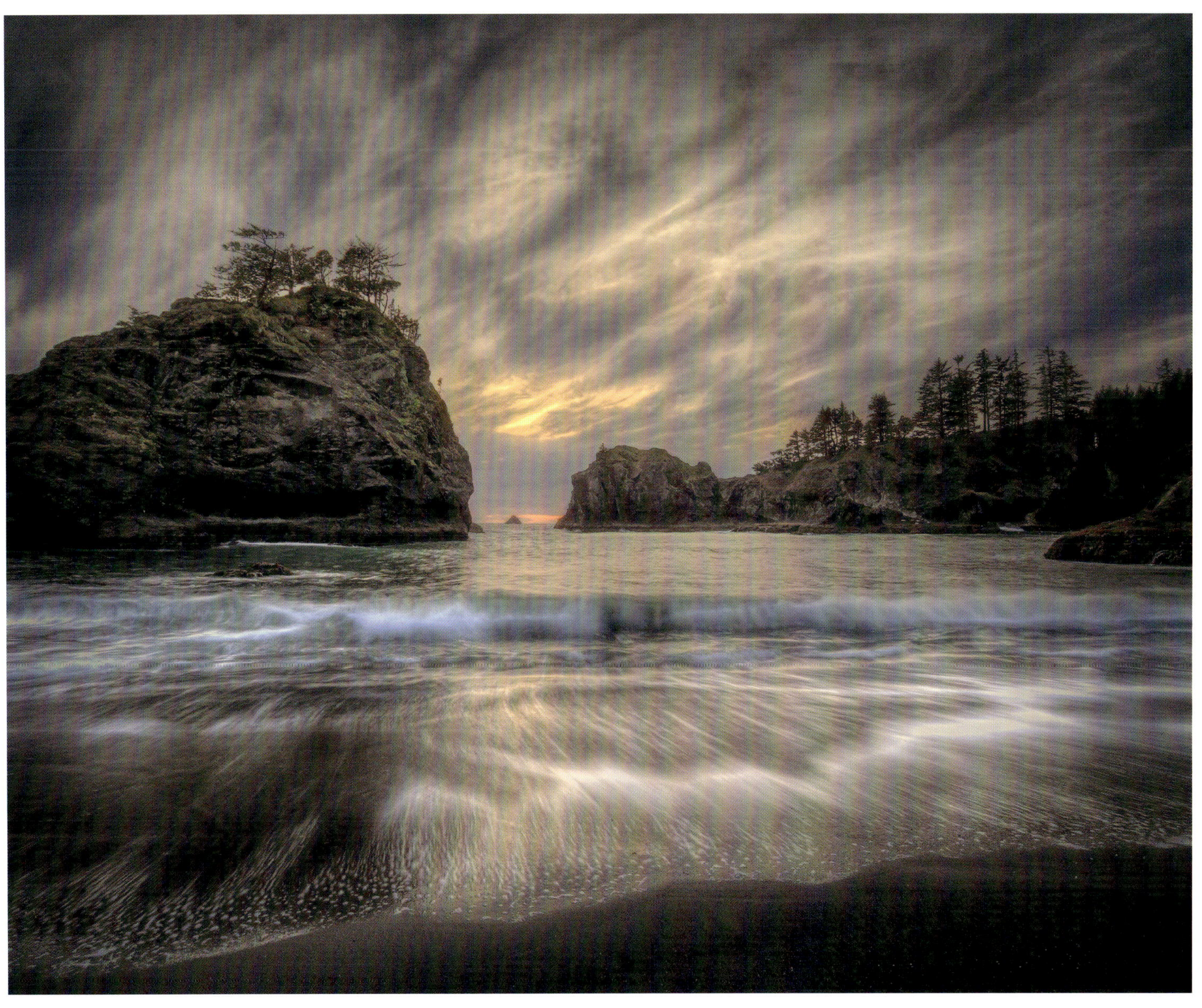

Secret Beach. *Photo by Rudy Dierks.* 171

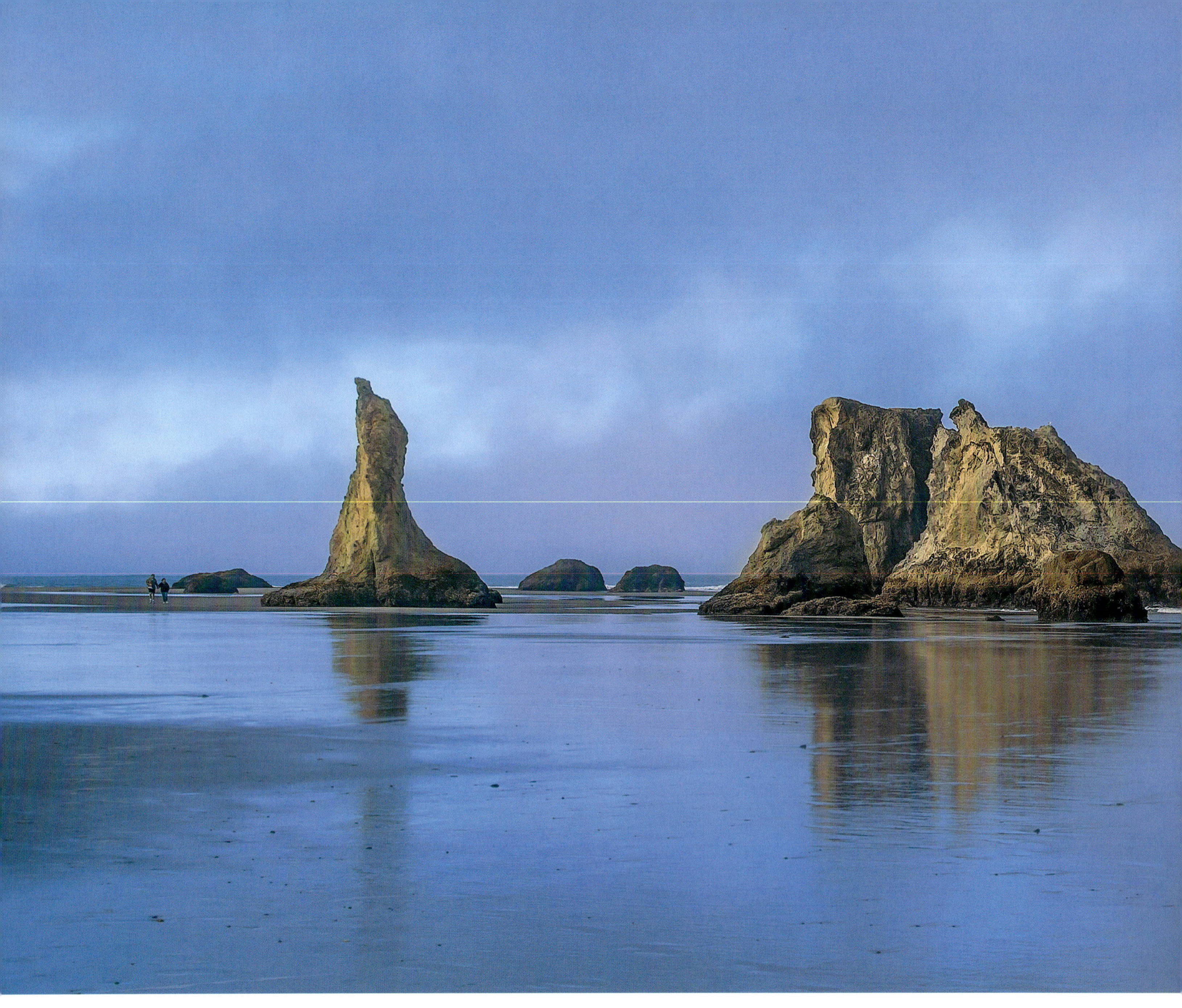

 Bandon at dawn. *Photo by John Christer Petersen.*

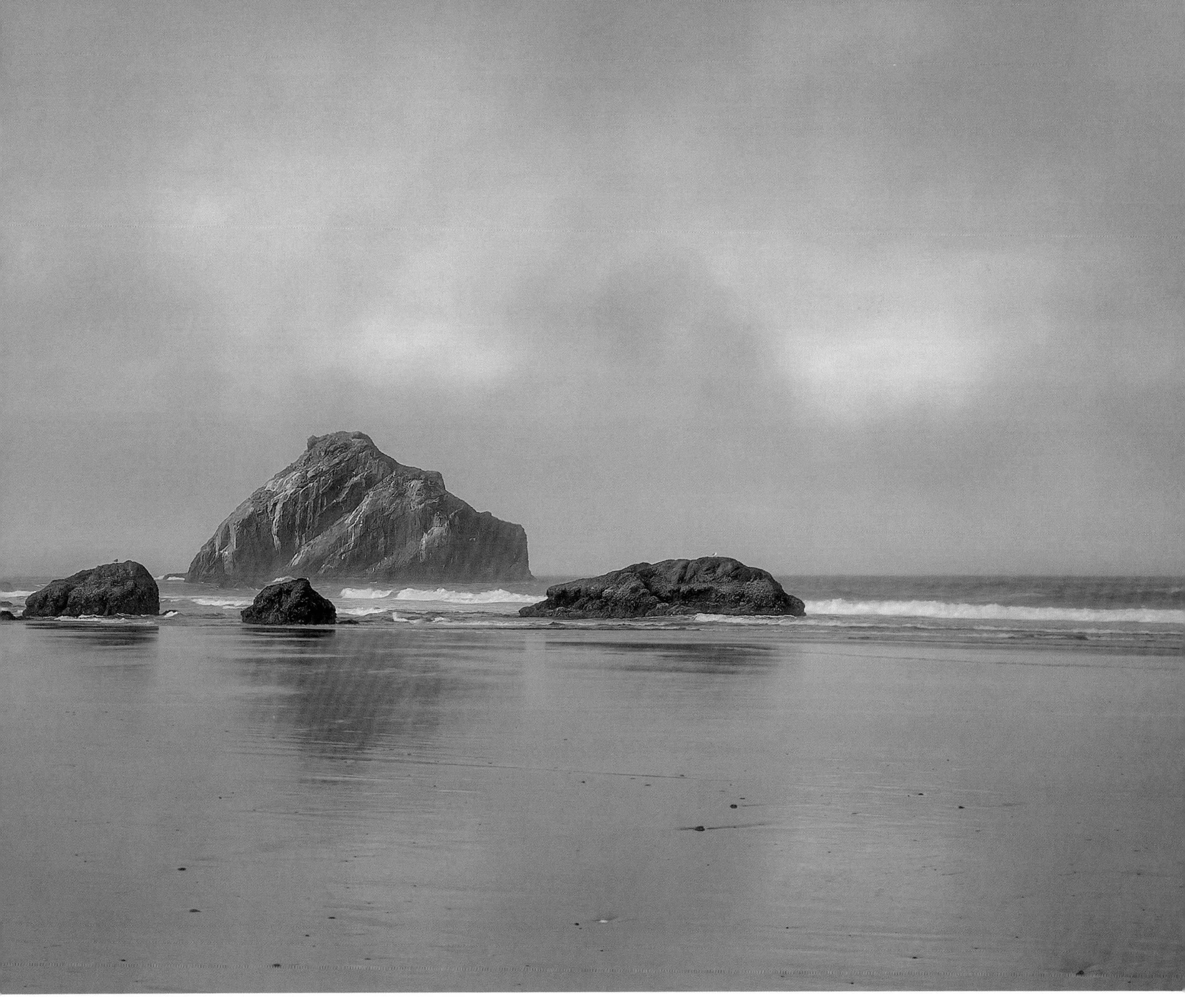

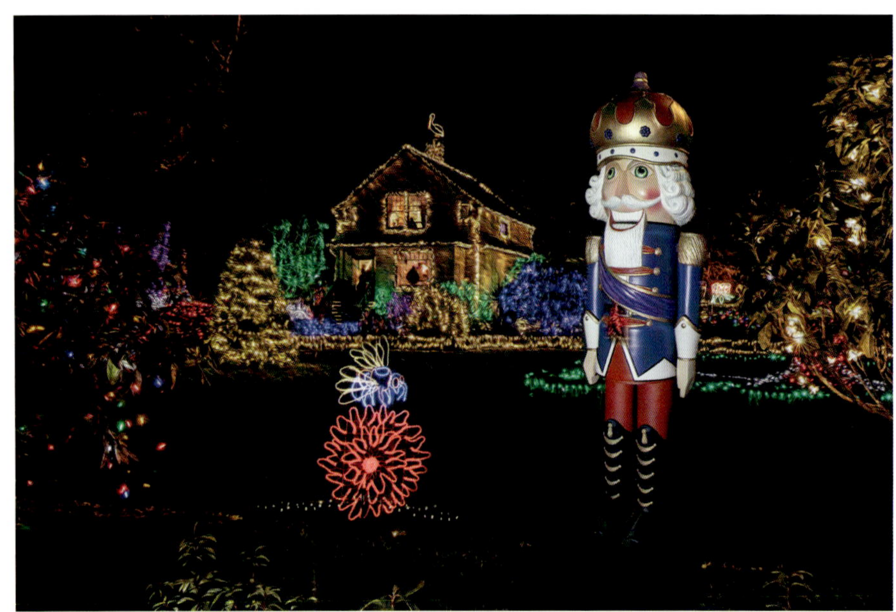

Holiday light display at Shore Acres. More than 325,000 LEDs adorn the grounds of Shore Acres between Thanksgiving Day and December 31. *Photo by Rudy Dierks.*

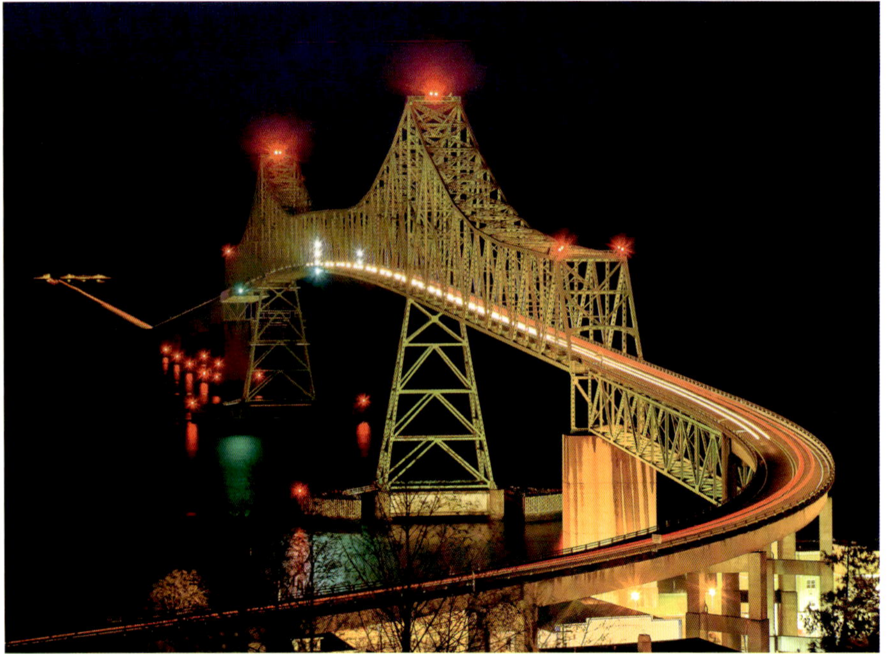

Astoria-Megler Bridge is the longest continuous truss bridge in North America. *Photo by Clem Paslack.*

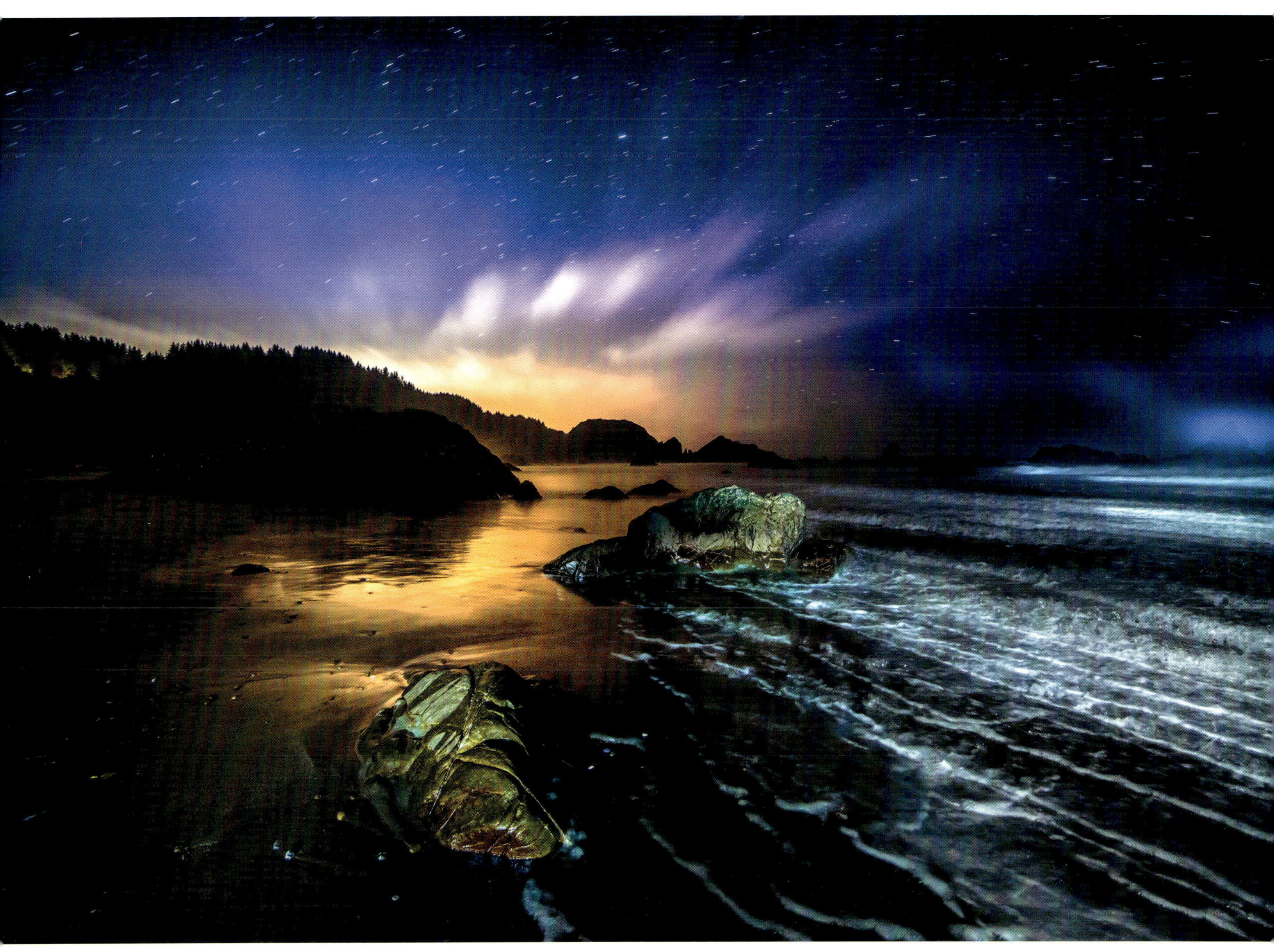

Coastline near Brookings. *Photo by Brandon Herring.* 175

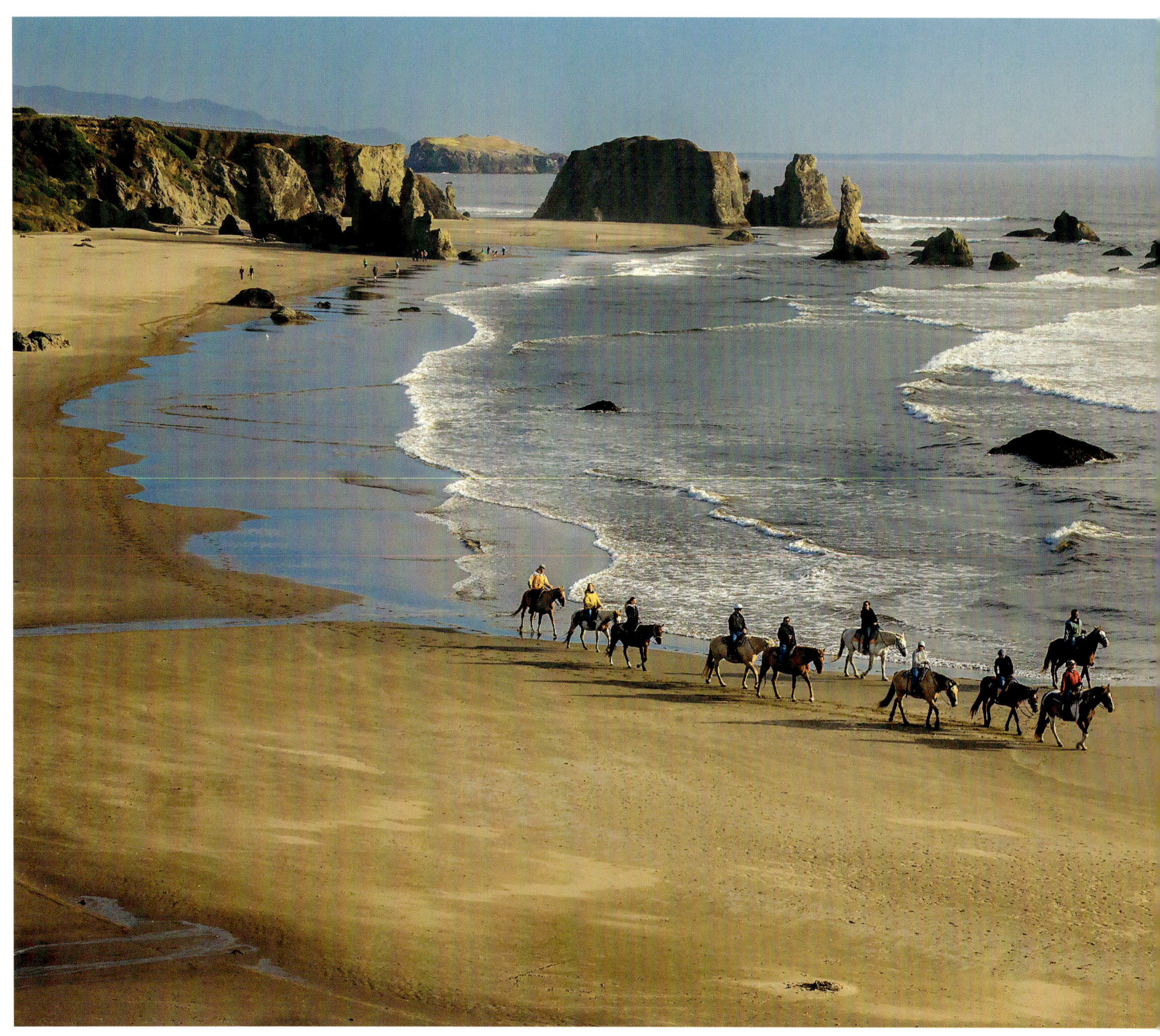

 Horseback riding at Bandon Beach. *Photo by Neal R. Thompson.*

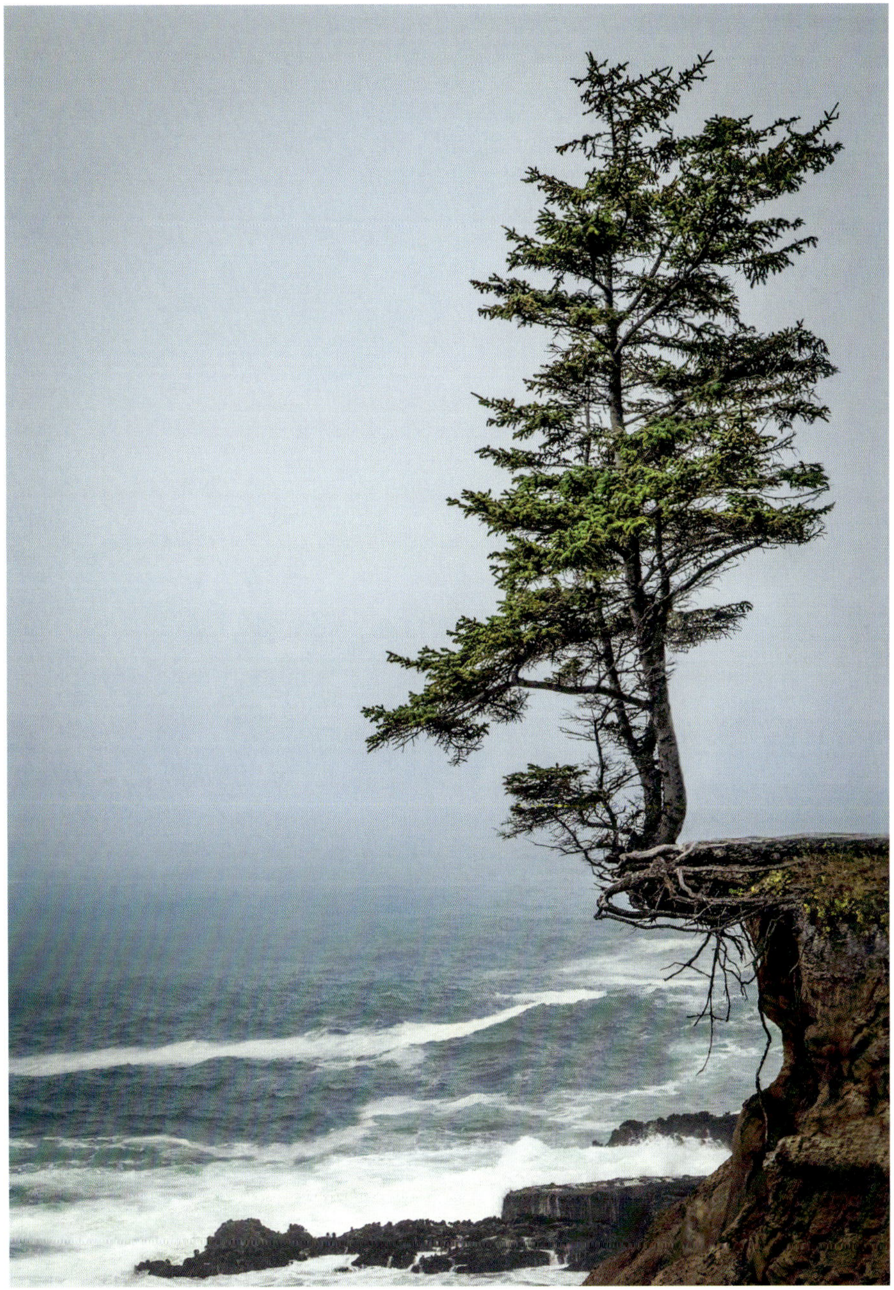

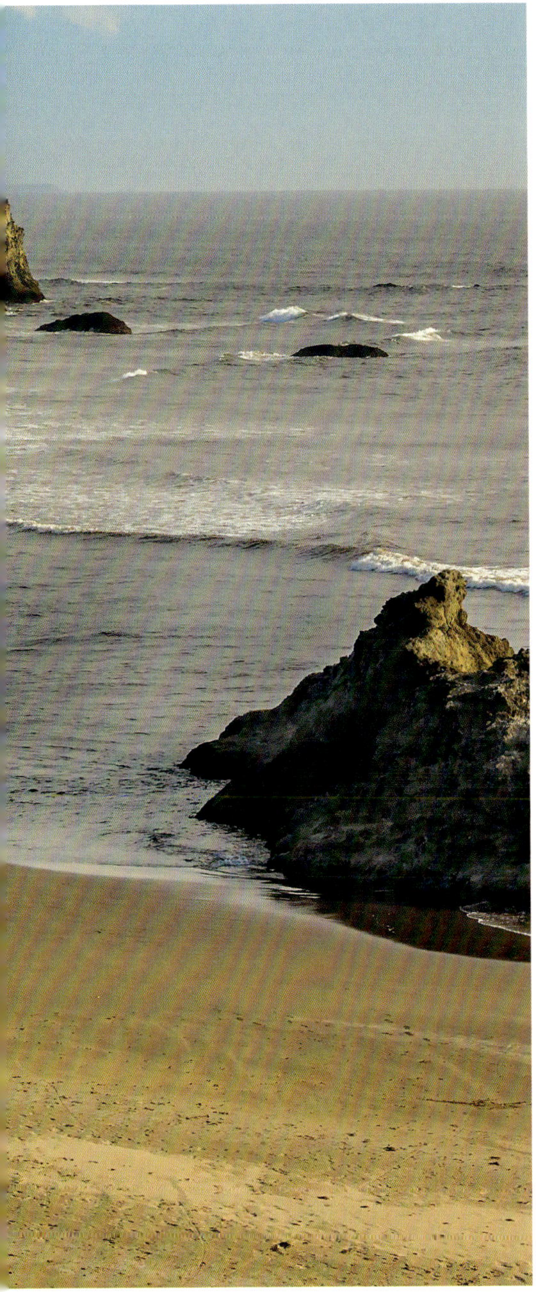

Perseverance at Shore Acres. *Photo by Sue Stendebach.*   177

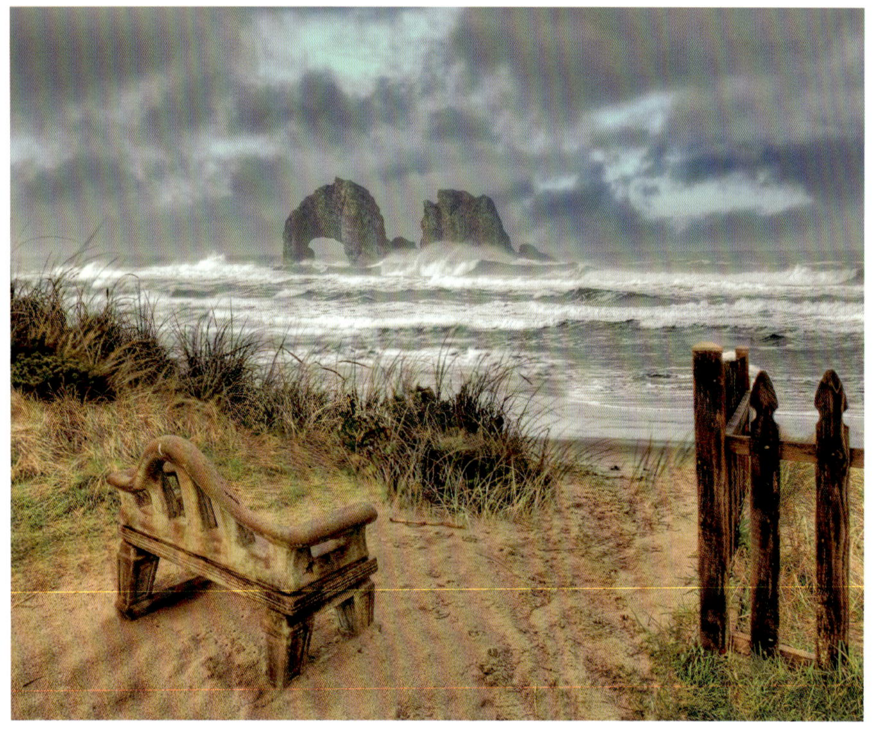

The Bench at Rockaway Beach. *Photo by Rudy Dierks.*

About three miles south of Yachats, Thor's Well appears to be a magical bottomless sinkhole in the ocean at high tide. However, it is actually a hole in the basalt rock, about 20 feet deep. *Photo by Earshel Hogan.*

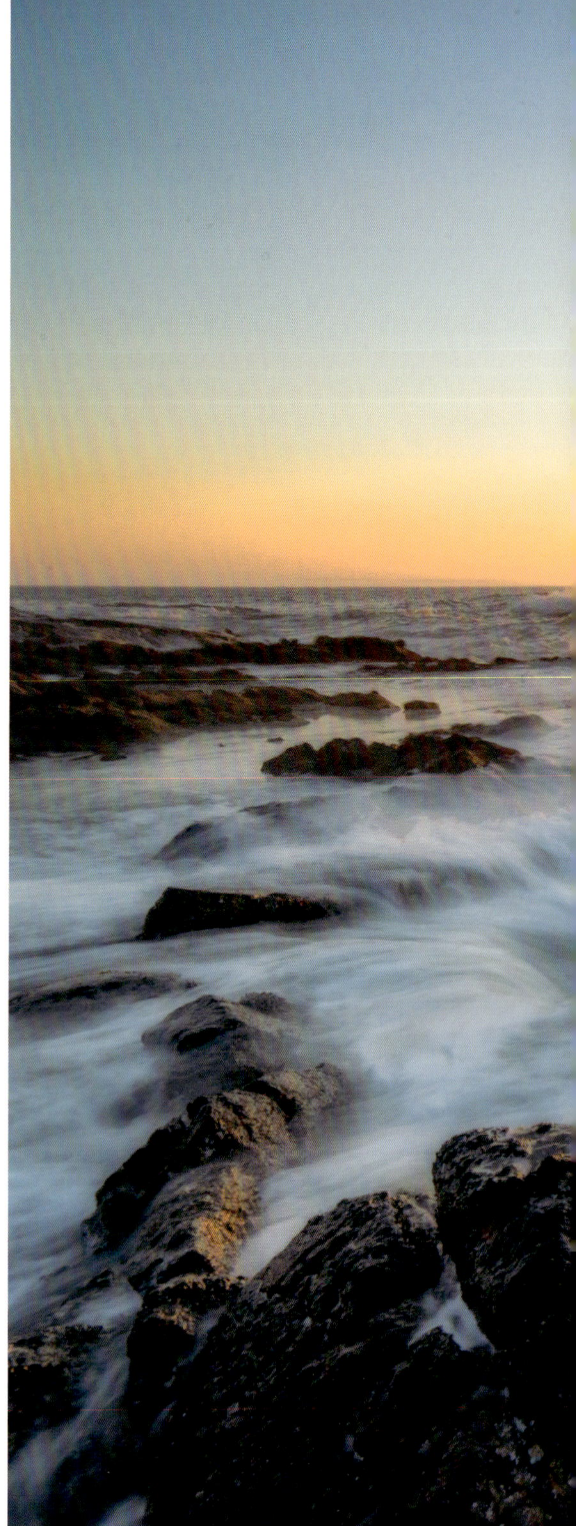

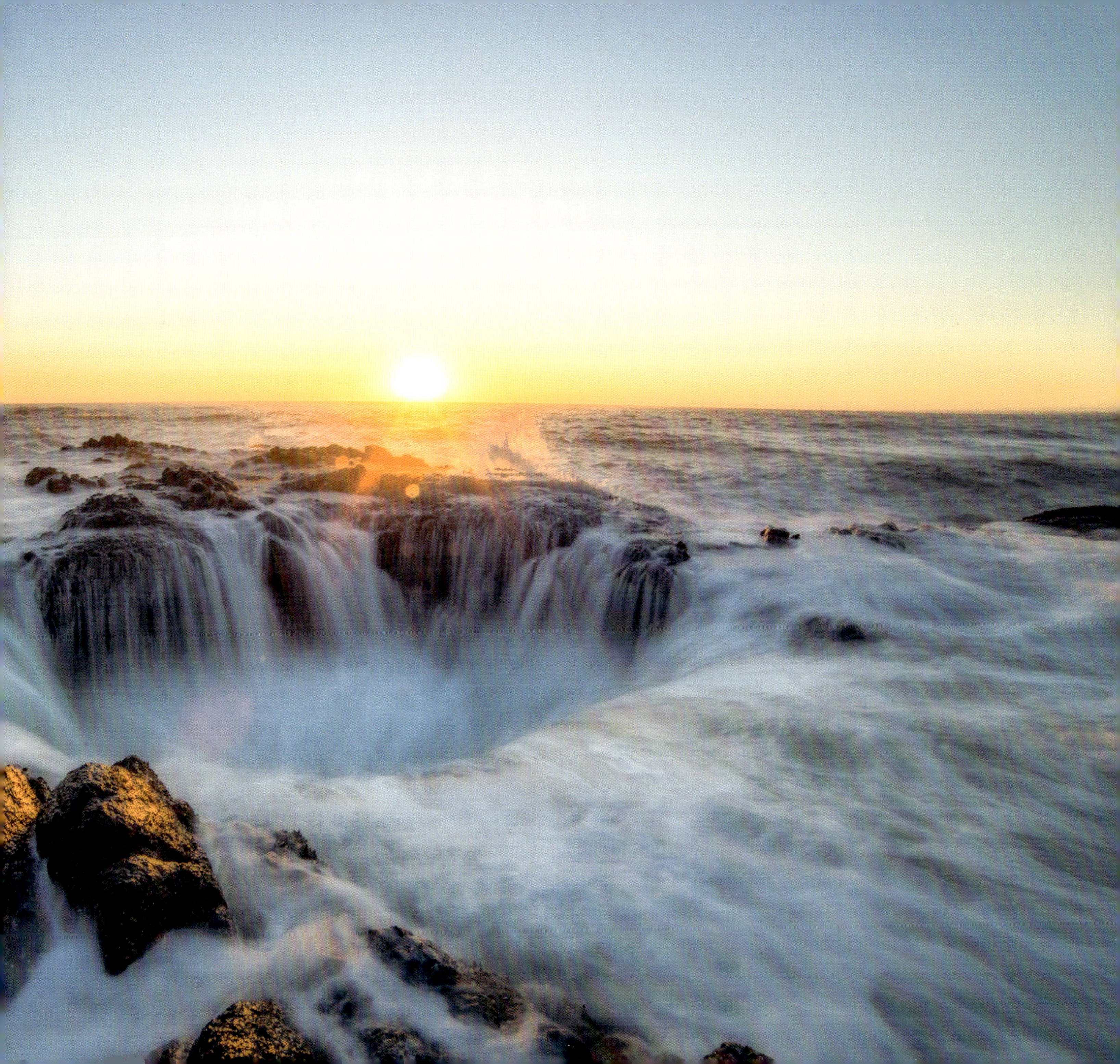

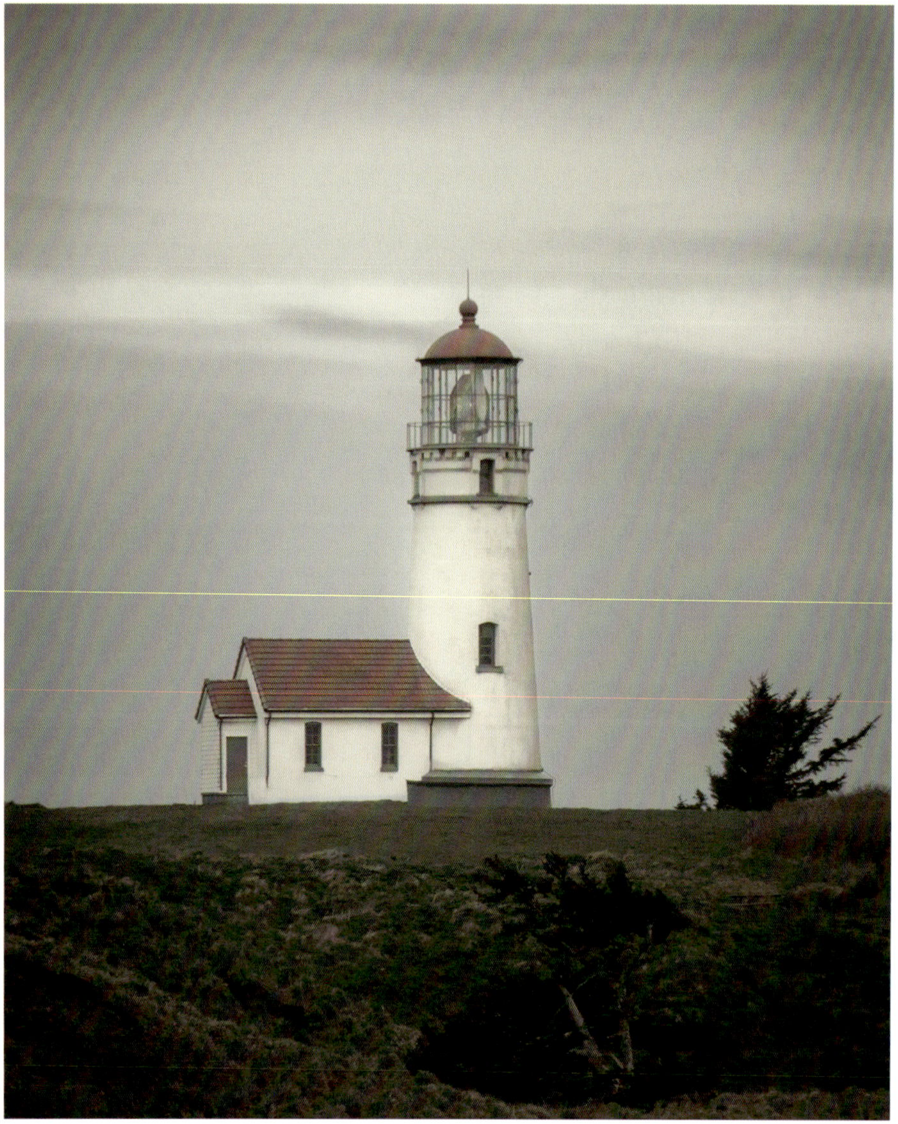

Cape Blanco Lighthouse was opened in 1870 in Port Orford. The most westerly light, it has the distinction of being the oldest continually operating Oregon light. The lighthouse has the highest focal plane above the sea (256 feet) and in 1903 hired Oregon's first woman keeper, Mabel E. Bretherton. *Photo by Geri H. Mathewson.*

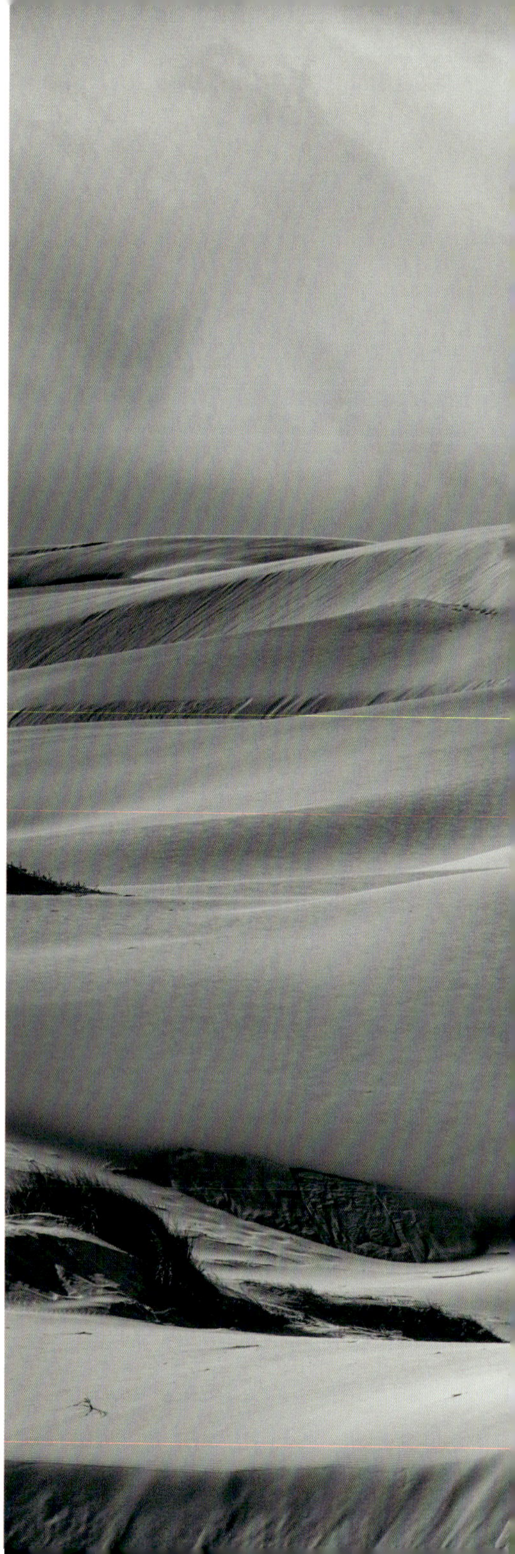

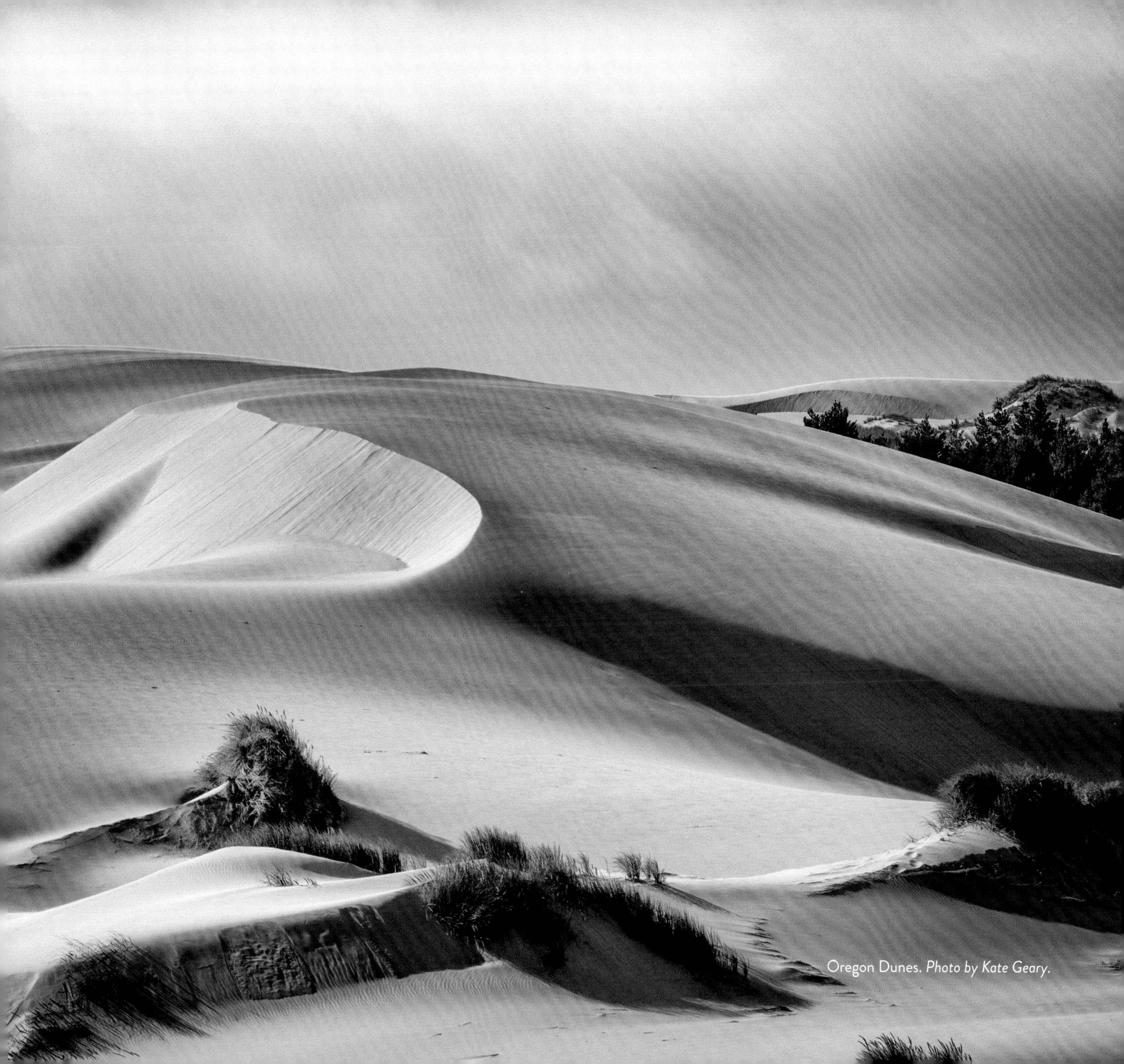

Oregon Dunes. *Photo by Kate Geary.*

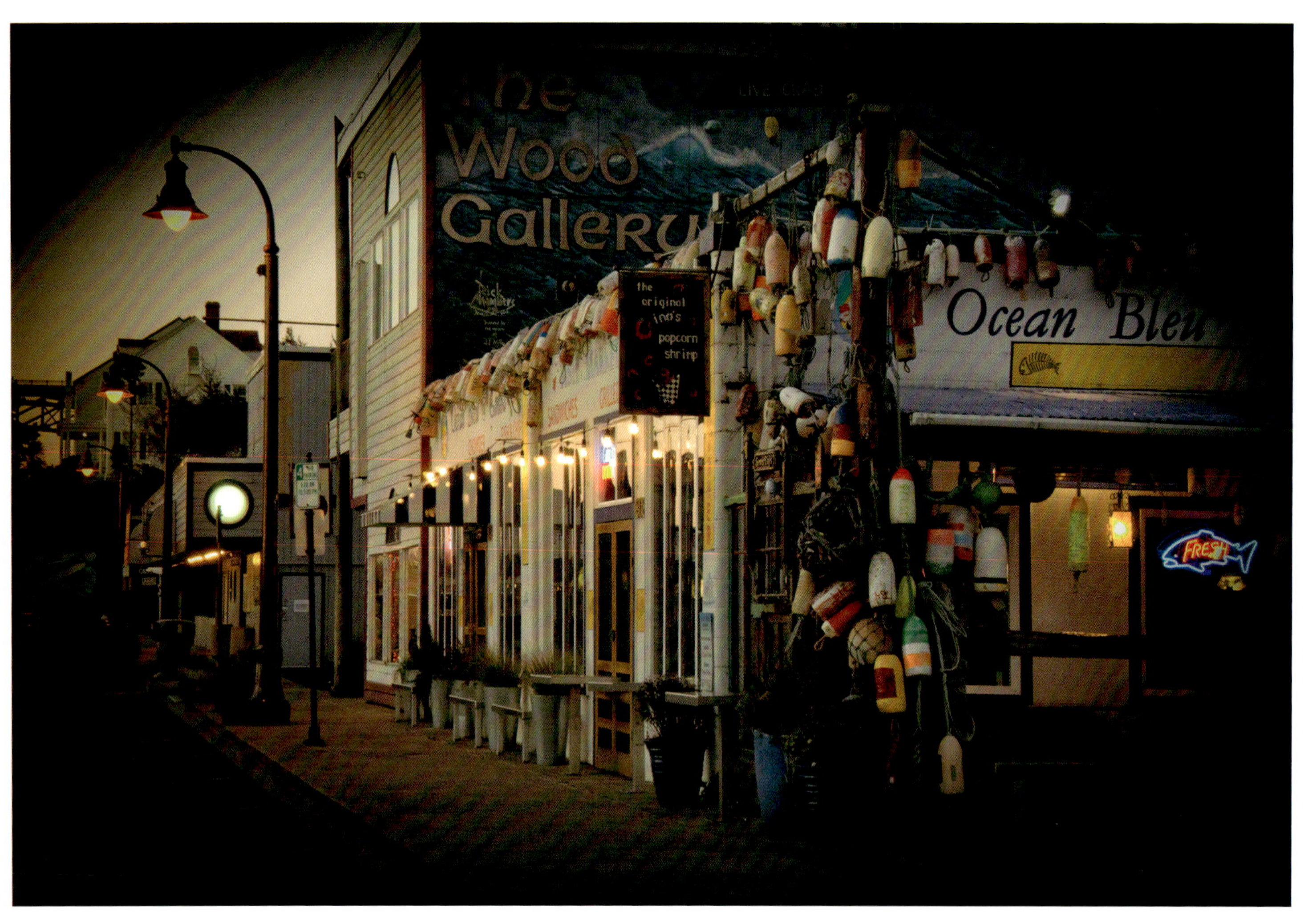

Newport at night. *Photo by Marilyn Dierks.*

(Opposite) Old Cannery Building, Astoria. *Photo by John Kirk.*

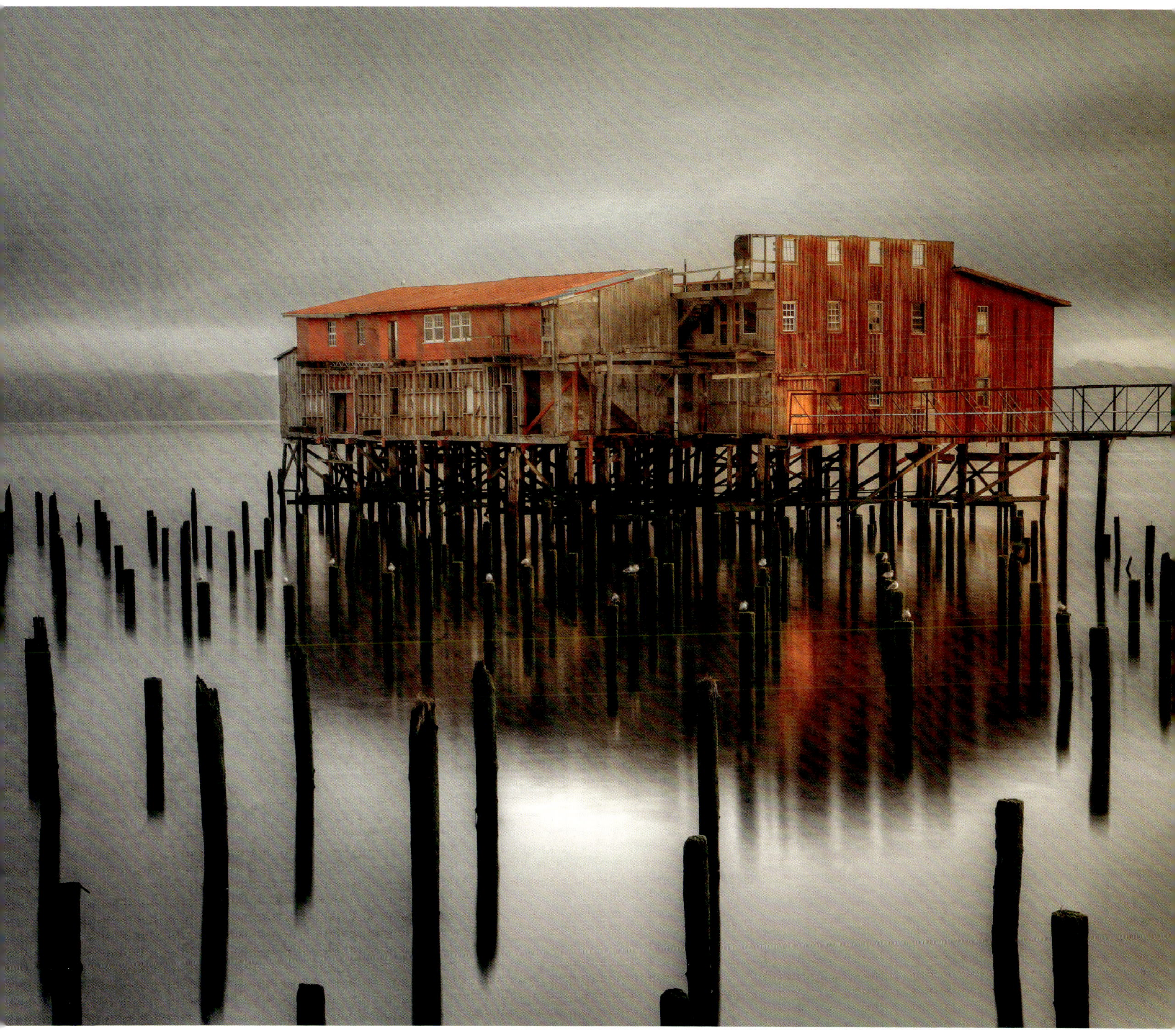

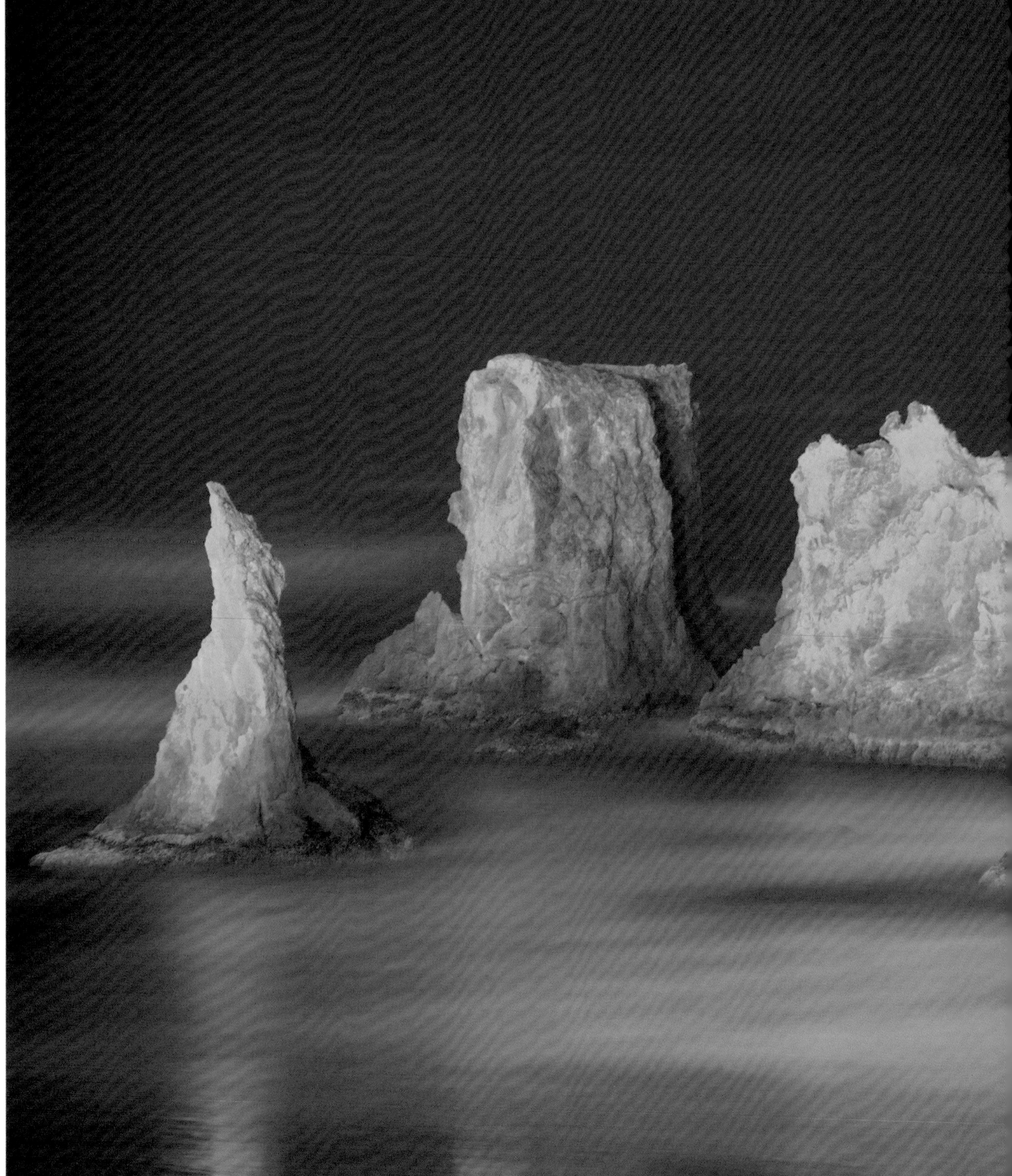

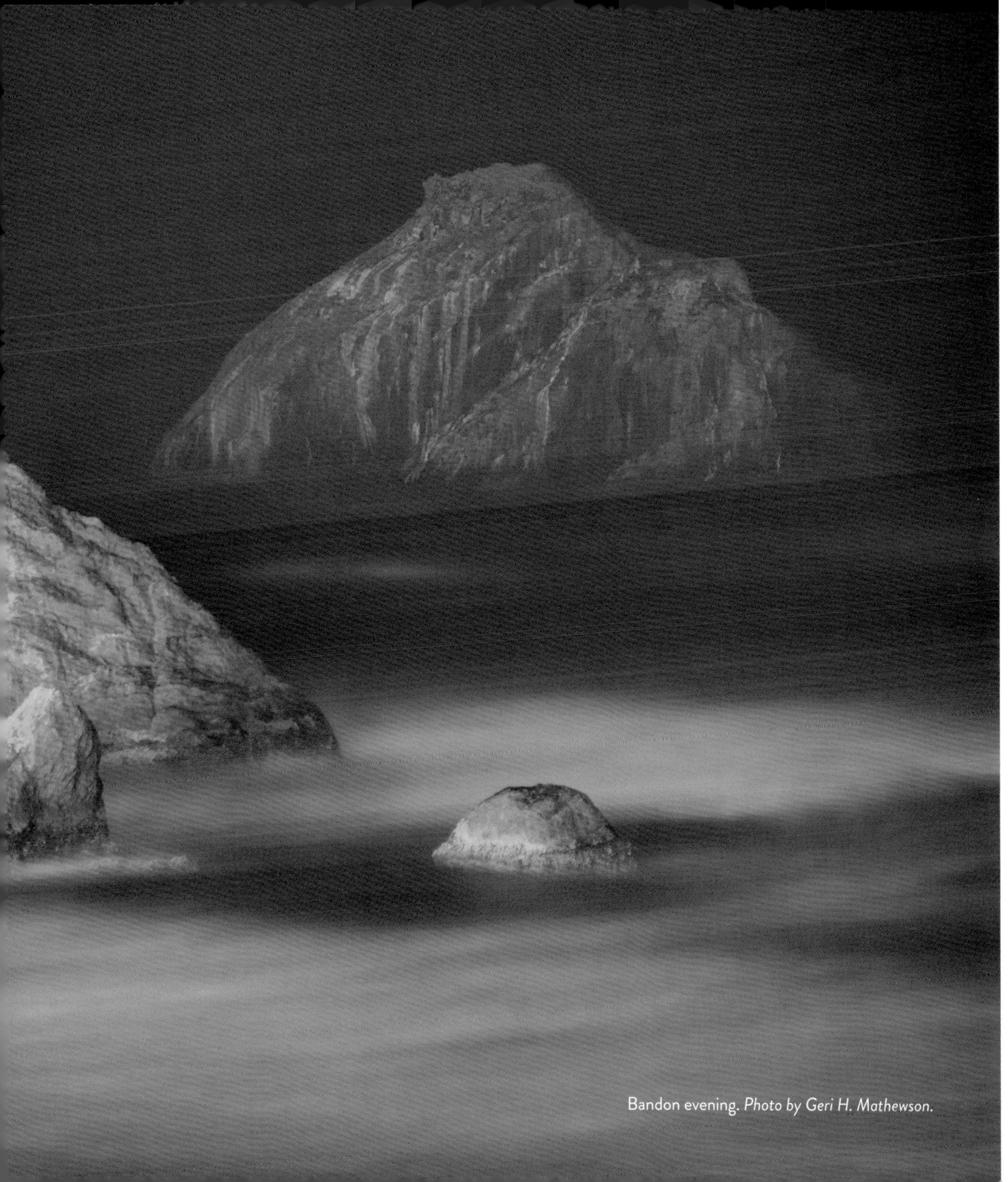

Bandon evening. *Photo by Geri H. Mathewson.*

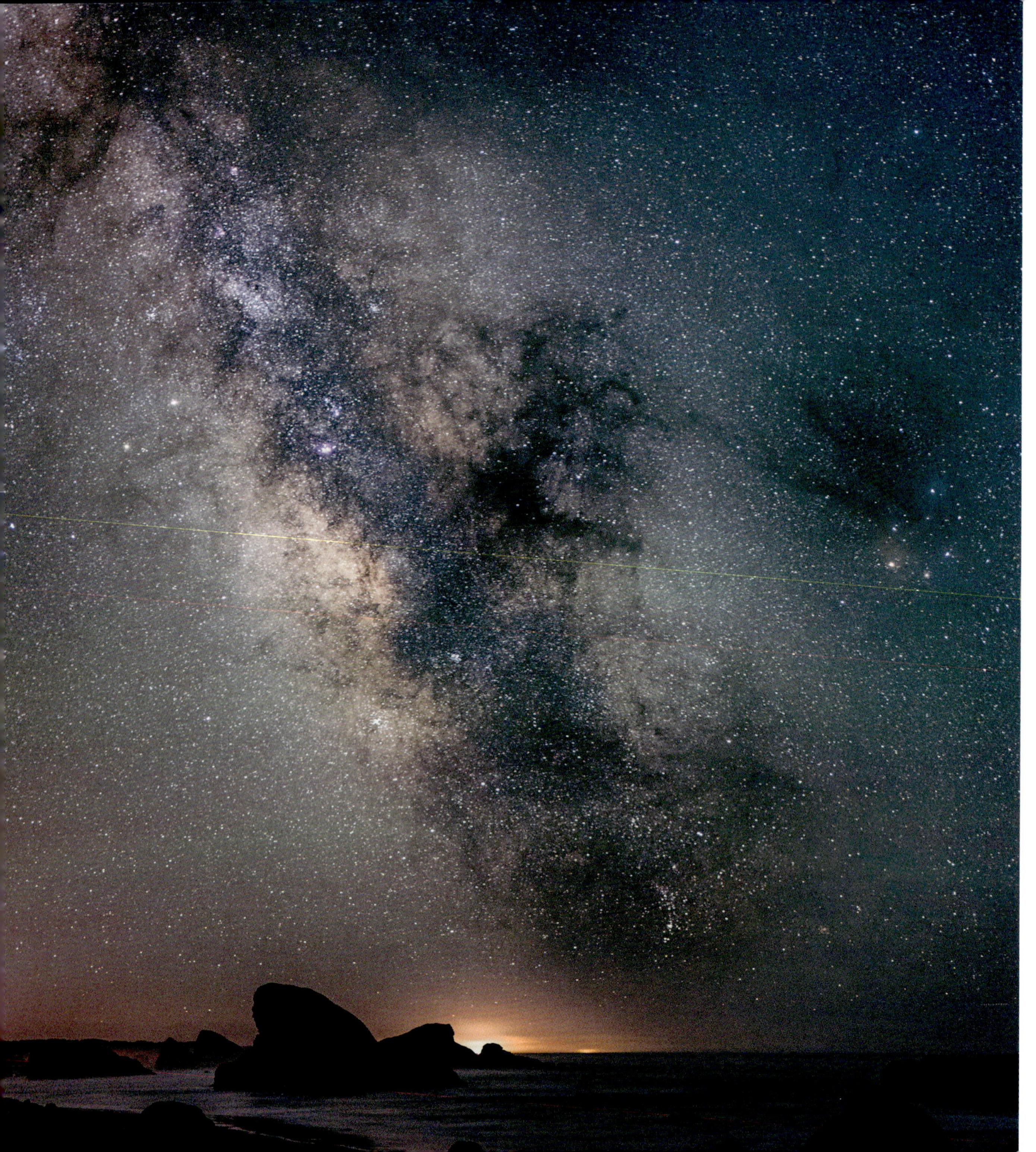

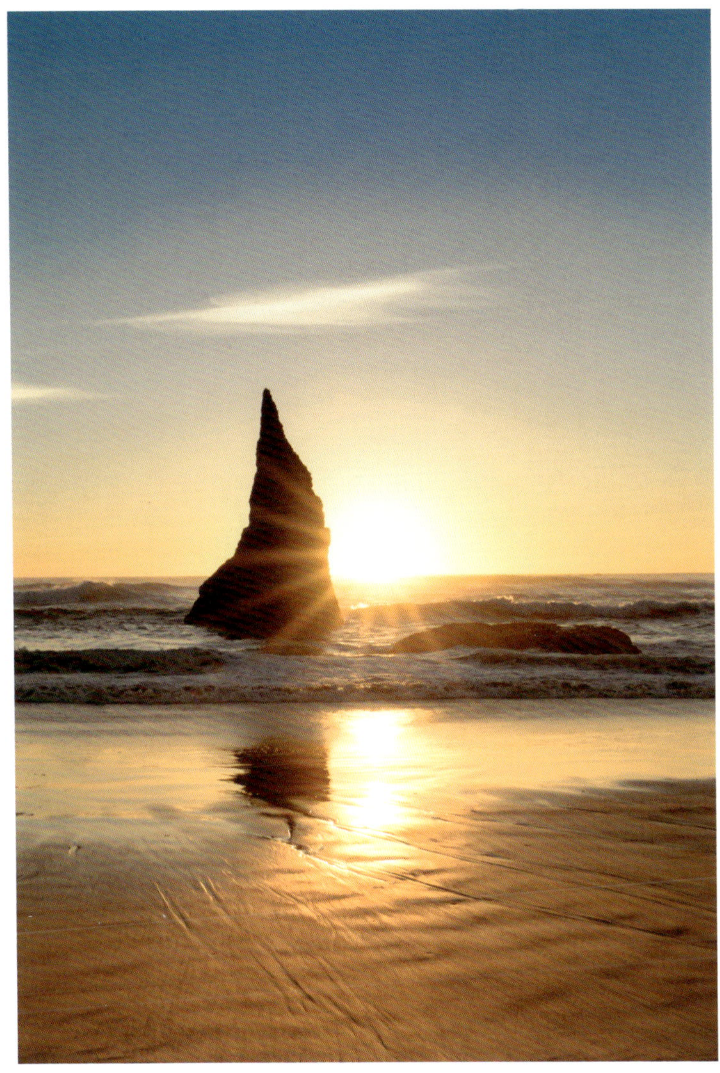

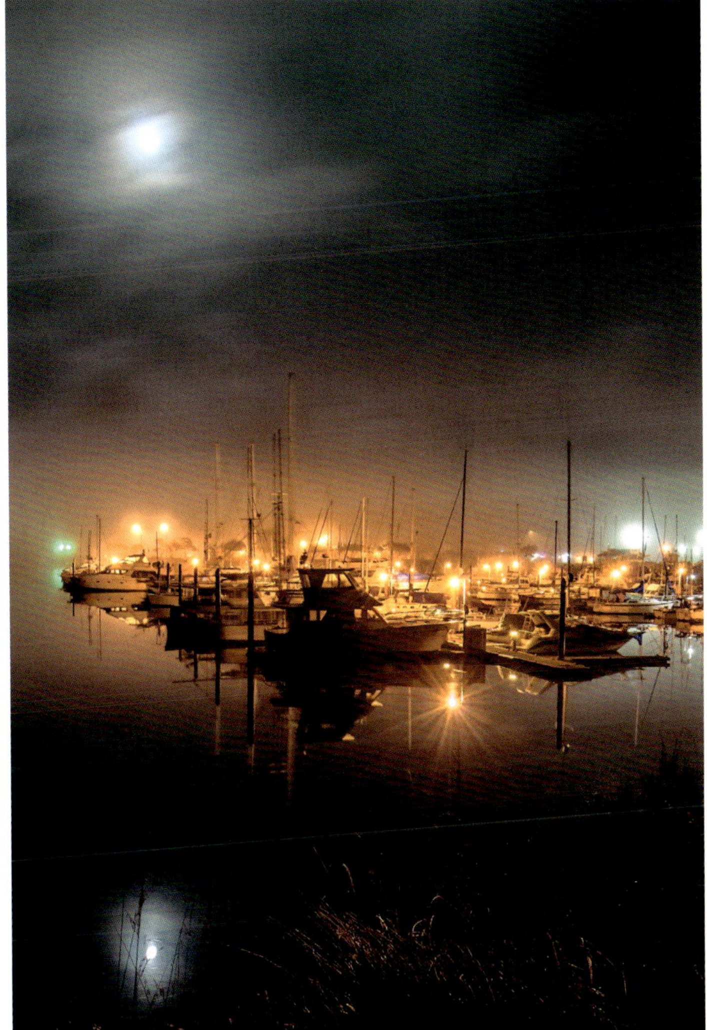

Wizard's Hat rock formation, Bandon Beach. *Photo by Barbara Tricarico.*

Charleston Harbor. *Photo by Sue Newman.*

(Opposite) Milky Way above Coquille River Lighthouse, Bandon.
Photo by Linda Rodgers.

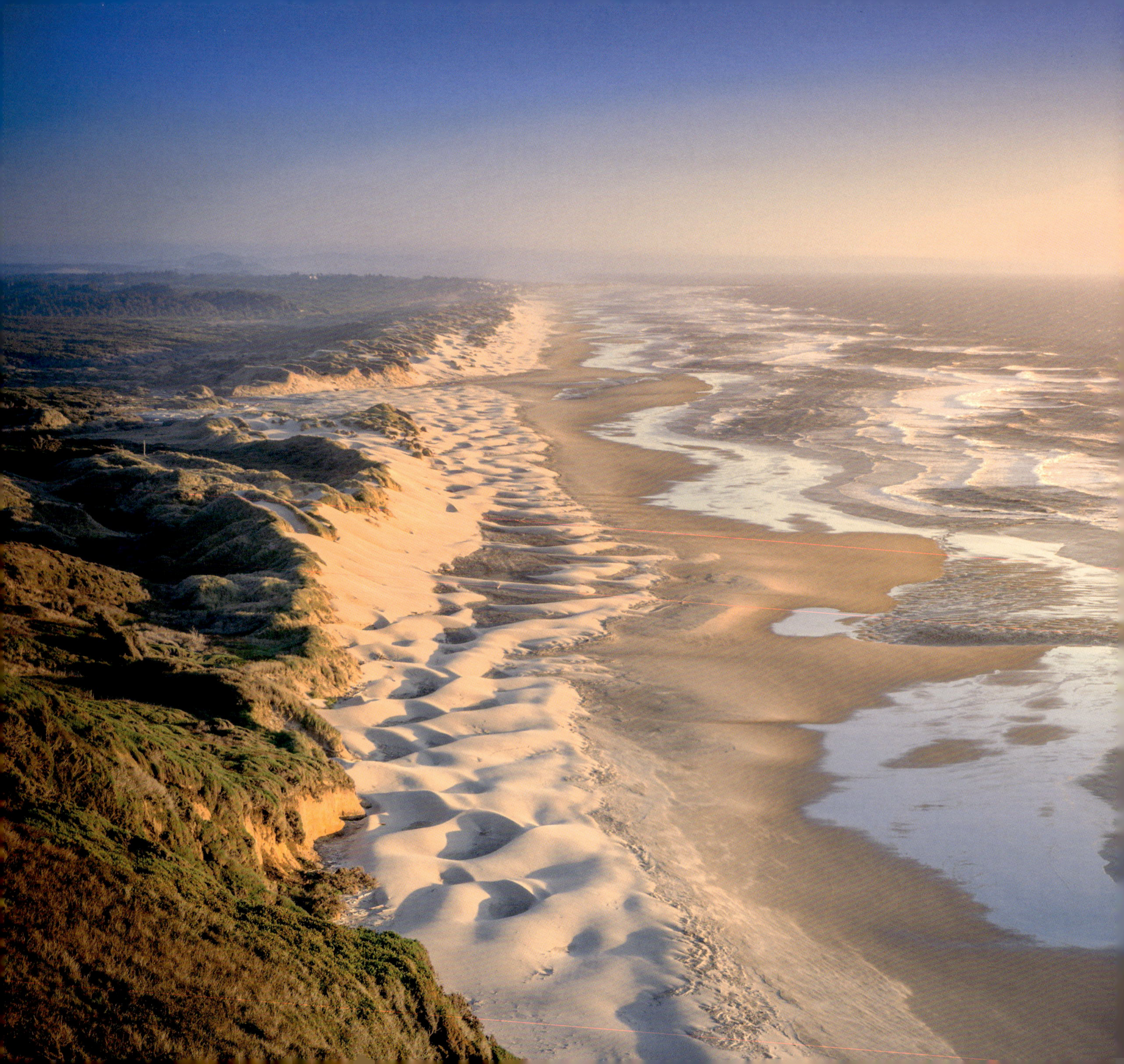

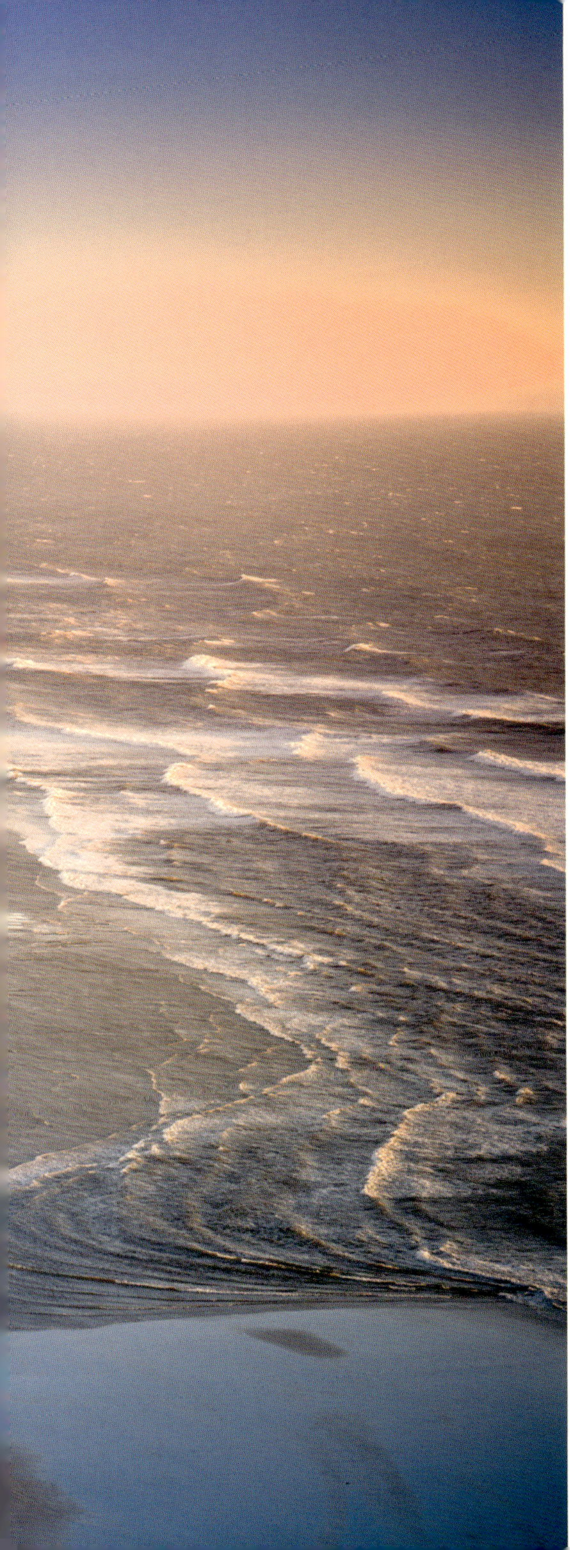

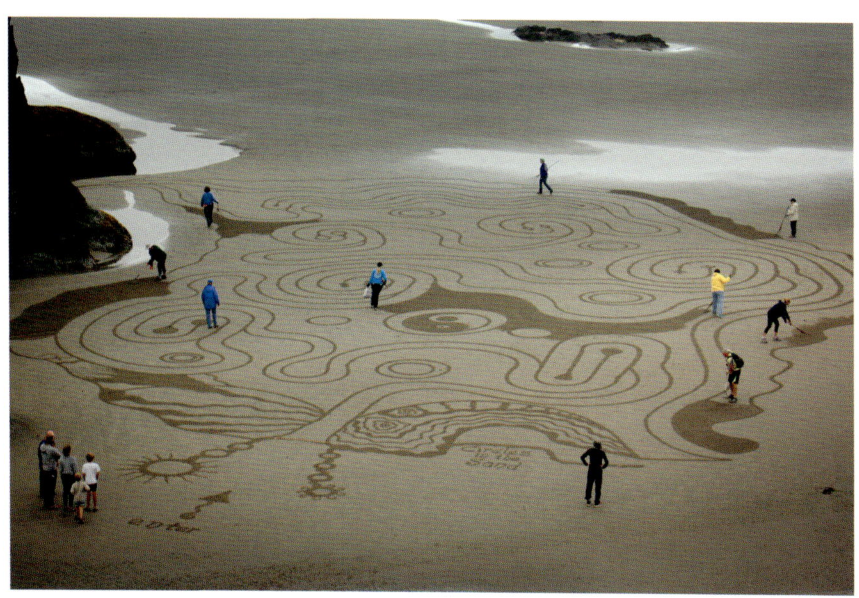

Highway 101 coastline north of Florence. *Photo by Brandon Herring.*

Circles in the sand, Bandon. Created and designed by Denny Dyke, this unique, albeit temporary, labyrinth art event draws hundreds of volunteers and visitors to the sand near Face Rock. *Photo by John Kirk.*

CREDITS

The following Oregon photographers contributed to this book.

Ellen Ahern

Sean Bagshaw

Julie Bonney

Randy Bryan

Jim Craven

Ken Deveney

Marilyn Dierks

Rudy Dierks

Dan Elster

Doug Farrell

Terry Fisher

Kate Geary

Nomeca Hartwell

Brandon Herring

Gary Hill

Charles Hillestad

Earshel Hogan

Howard Hunt

Alan Ingersoll

John Kirk

Richard Krieger

Judy Benson LaNier

Graham Lewis

Mason Marsh

Geri H. Mathewson

Cornelius Matteo

Vivian McAleavey

Atana Morell

Tysen Mueller

Jay Newman

Sue Newman

Bob Palermini

Clemens Paslack

John Christer Petersen

George F. Peterson

Linda Rodgers

Andrea Shapiro

Diana Standing

Alana Lynn Starkweather

Sue Stendebach

Hans Stroo

Andrew Studer

Vldn Taylor

Neal R. Thompson

Barbara Tricarico

Terry Tuttle

Nick Viani

Will Volpert

David Lorenz Winston

Matt Witt

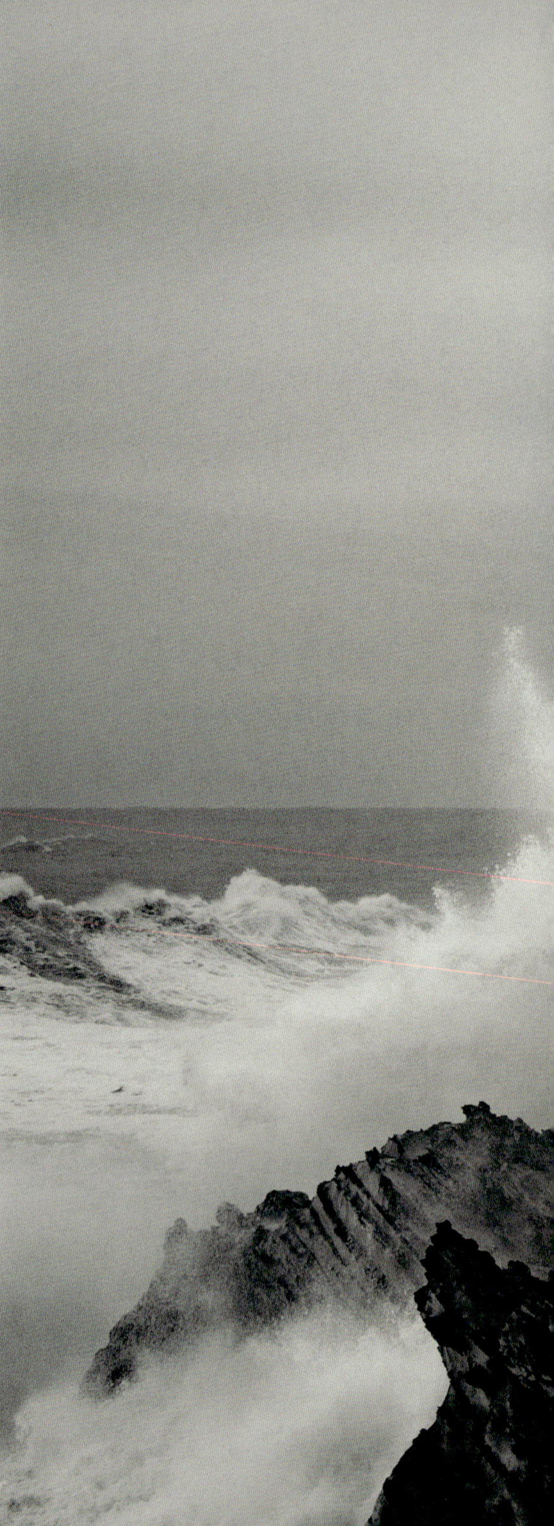

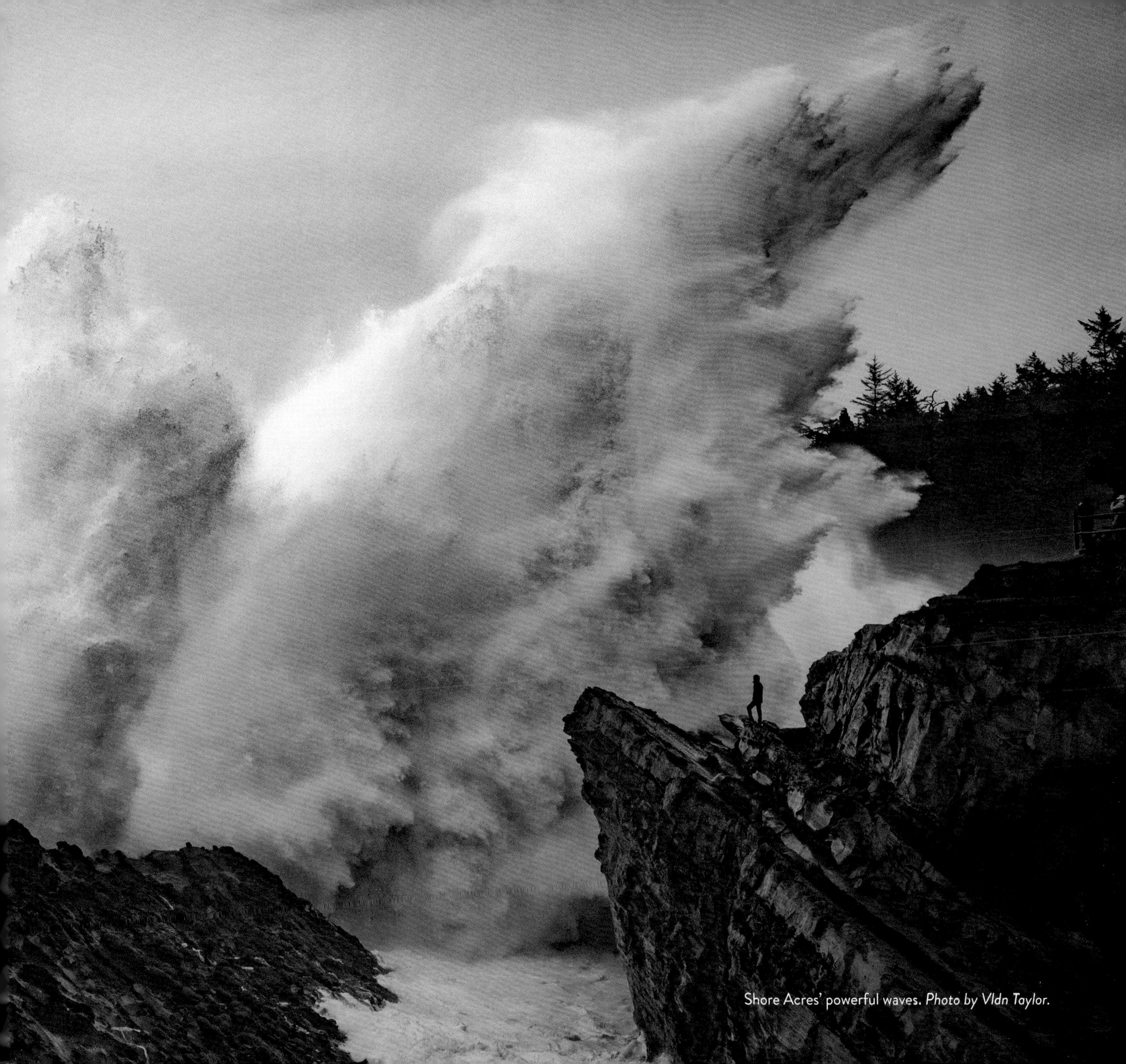

Shore Acres' powerful waves. Photo by Vldn Taylor.

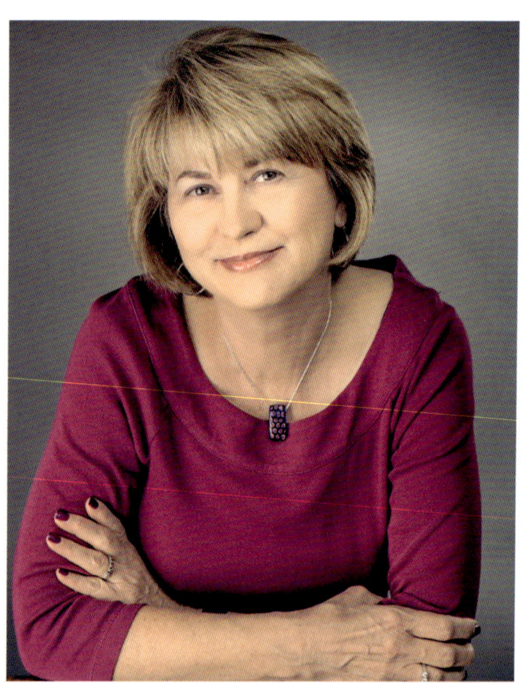

Barbara Tricarico has produced three coffee-table photography books by Schiffer Publishing: *Oregon*; *Ashland, Oregon*; and *Ashland, Oregon, Day Trips*, as well as coauthoring and photographing *Quilts of Virginia: 1607–1899*. She and her husband, Bill, moved to Ashland in 2010. Barbara is an active member of the Ashland Chamber of Commerce, is president of the Southern Oregon Photographic Association, and volunteers for the Ashland Food Project and the Oregon Shakespeare Festival. Barbara enjoys traveling and quilting. Follow her on Facebook at Barbara Tricarico Photography or visit her website, www.barbaratricarico.com.

Photo: Cornelius Matteo